THE DISSOCIATIVE MIND

THE DISSOCIATIVE MIND

Elizabeth F. Howell

Routledge
Taylor & Francis Group
New York London

Routledge
Taylor & Francis Group
270 Madison Avenue
New York, NY 10016

Routledge
Taylor & Francis Group
27 Church Road
Hove, East Sussex BN3 2FA

Routledge is an imprint of Taylor & Francis Group, an Informa business

Printed in the United States of America on acid-free paper
10 9 8 7 6 5 4 3 2

International Standard Book Number-13: 978-0-88163-495-2 (Softcover)
Library of Congress Card Number 2005048341

Earlier versions of chapters 10 and 11 appeared in Vol., 4 No. 3 and Vol. 3, No. 4 of *The Journal of Trauma and Dissociation* © Haworth Press.

Library of Congress Cataloging-in-Publication Data

Howell, Elizabeth F., 1946—
The dissociative mind / Elizabeth F. Howell
p. cm.
Includes bibliographical references and index.
ISBN 0-88163-495-6
1. Dissociation (Psychology). 2. Dissociative disorders. I. Title.
RC553.D5H69 2005
616.85'23—dc22 2005048341

Visit the Taylor & Francis Web site at
http://www.taylorandfrancis.com

and the Routledge Web site at
http://www.routledgementalhealth.com

CONTENTS

PREFACE

Dissociation pervades psychic life, and the capacity for it is built into our DNA. A variation on Harry Stack Sullivan's (1953) famous dictum that everyone is more simply human than otherwise might be that dissociation is far more common in humans than otherwise. Our ordinary language reveals an implicit conversance with a divided self. Such expressions as "falling apart," "coming unglued," and "being beside oneself" imply parts that are not cohesive. The common exhortation "Pull yourself together" implies parts that are segregated from each other. Various forms of dualism, Cartesian dualism (separation of mind from body), "Dr. Jekyll and Mr. Hyde," and even many gendered attributes imply a dissociation of one realm of experience from another.

Although dissociation theory has existed side by side with the doctrine of repression in the history of psychoanal[illegible] dissociation was, for many years, less focally examined, even largely dissociated. Although psychoanalysis traces its origins to the treatment of dissociation and trauma (Breuer and Freud 1893–1895), from the early 1900s until 15 or 20 years ago, the current dissociation field grew in a barren climate. Multiplicity and the dissociative structuring of the mind did not receive the attention they are beginning to draw today, and dissociative identity disorder, previously called multiple personality disorder, was thought to be extremely rare. In contrast, today the fields of psychoanalysis and traumatology are coming together. This is fitting because they complement each other.

Today, the mental health field is paying more and more attention to dissociation and dissociative experiences. In psychoanalysis, this is partially attributable to the growing appreciation of the relational model, in which multiplicity and dissociative processes are implicit. When we take into account the internalization of multiple aspects of attachment relationships, plus the likelihood of some relational trauma, it is clear that a construct of psychic structuring based on relationships must include dissociation. More broadly, the increased interest in dissociation stems from the recent public explosion of information concerning the widespread prevalence of psychological trauma. Following the Vietnam War, which prompted the formulation of the diagnostic term *posttraumatic stress disorder* (PTSD), not only the atrocities of war but other, more commonplace atrocities such as child sexual abuse suddenly became more thinkable. Traumatologists such as Brown (1991) and Herman (1992) noticed that trauma is not outside the realm of ordinary experience as it had been previously defined but exists within the realm of the ordinary especially for survivors of sexual and physical child abuse.

Trauma and Dissociation

Trauma is a confusing word. A common meaning of psychological trauma is of an objectively massive, threatening event, one that would be overwhelming to anyone. For instance, a condition for the diagnosis of PTSD in the *Diagnostic and Statistical Manual of Mental Disorders, Fourth Edition* (*DSM-IV;* 1994) is that the "person experienced, witnessed, or was confronted with an event or events that involved actual or threatened death or serious injury, or a threat to the physical integrity of self or others" (pp. 427–428). The "objective" meaning is often qualified, however, with the observation that not everyone who has been subjected to trauma develops posttraumatic stress. It appears that various kinds and severity of "traumatic" events affect people differently. More specifically, many believe that trauma refers to what is overwhelming to the individual.

A problem in this twofold way of thinking of *trauma* is that we often face the dilemma of using the same word to denote either meaning, with the result that the meaning stays fuzzy. When we focus on "objective" trauma, we often gloss more lightly over its effects on the individual mind. Yet from the traumatized person's perspective, trauma disrupts reflective functioning; indeed, it nearly wipes out the ability to think. As Herman (1992) said, "at the moment of trauma the victim is rendered helpless by overwhelming force" (p. 33). Thus, in this meaning, which refers to the individual, trauma is not just something upsetting or distressing, even if it is extremely so. Trauma refers to event(s) that could not be assimilated. If the traumatic event could not be taken in, it cannot be linked with other experience, and there is now a structural dissociation of experience, whether small or large (Van der Hart et al., 2004). In short, the result of trauma is dissociation.

For the reasons just described, I propose a simplified definition of trauma as the "event(s) that cause dissociation." Thinking of trauma this way, in terms of its effect, puts the focus on the splits and fissures in the psyche rather than solely on the external event. It might be argued that two apparent problems with this proposal are that (1) dissociation does not necessarily require trauma and that (2) dissociation is not always clearly discernable to others or to the self. However, (1) the larger definition of dissociation is not changed by this meaning of trauma. Moreover, (2) dissociated experience that does not intrude or appear to be otherwise evident can be occurring. A person can be functioning well and seemingly be resilient to trauma, only to break down when, for instance, her daughter reaches the age at which she was herself abused.

Trauma, Dissociation, and "Psychopathology"

The rising tide of trauma and dissociation studies has created a sea change in the way we think about psychopathology. Chronic trauma (according to the meaning I propose) that occurs early in life has profound effects on personality development and can lead to the development of dissociative identity disorder (DID), other dissociative disorders, personality disorders, psychotic thinking, and a host of symptoms such as anxiety, depression, eating disorders, and substance abuse. In my view, DID is simply an extreme version of the dissociative structure of the psyche that characterizes us all. Dissociation, in a general sense, refers to a rigid separation of parts of experience, including somatic experience, consciousness, affects, perception, identity, and memory. When there is a structural dissociation, each of the dissociated self-states has at least a rudimentary sense of "I" (Van der Hart et al., 2004). In my view, all of the environmentally based "psychopathology" or problems in living can be seen through this lens.

Few of us still use the word *neurosis*. Yet more and more problems in living are being understood as being trauma generated. Much of what used to be seen as neurosis can now be understood in terms of posttraumatic stress and dissociation. The concept of neurosis requires the operation of a punitive superego, enforcing repression of dangerous wishes. The kinds of psychic struggle we more often notice today, however, seem to be about keeping dissociated experience out of awareness. Moreover, the superego can be understood as a dissociated structure, serving just this purpose (Howell, 1997).

I agree with Bromberg's (1995) view that all of the personality "disorders" are dissociation based and that DID is the touchstone for understanding them. Herman (1992) and Van der Kolk (1996a) have contributed to the reconceptualization of personality disorders in terms of trauma and dissociation with their concepts of "complex PTSD" and "disorders of extreme stress not otherwise specified" (DESNOS). Both encompass a constellation of symptoms resulting from long-term psychological trauma. Among these are emotional dysregulation, amnesias, damage to identity and relationships, and the potential for revictimization. Another formulation of the effects on the personality of long-term trauma is that of "chronic relational trauma" (Howell and Blizard, accepted for publication), which like complex PTSD and DESNOS, is particularly applicable to borderline personality disorder (Howell, 2002).

Consistent with the sea change resulting from trauma and dissociation studies, our views of psychosis are modified. The hallmark of psychosis is not only poor reality-testing, but also the inability to distinguish the internal from the external. It is exactly this distinction that trauma disrupts.

Trauma, Dissociation, and Theory

Culturally engraved dissociative patterns are like the air we breathe: vital for life, a pervasive surround that is usually not examined. Common compartmentalizations of ways of thinking about our interpersonal relationships and the social world in which we live become part of what I call the "cultural unconscious," in contrast to Jung's collective unconscious. The cultural unconscious is often maintained by what Donnel Stern (1997) calls "dissociation in the weak sense," which pertains to maintenance of certain patterns of lack of awareness. Because these are common, we are used to them, and we don't think about them. However, the cultural unconscious also contains certain areas of awareness and anxiety that we deliberately avoid formulating, using "dissociation in the strong sense."

The patterns of unexamined contradictions in the cultural conscious and unconscious permit the execution of atrocities, which are then often denied or unexamined. For many of my patients, as well as patients of supervisees, who were massively abused in childhood, it is astounding that, often, nobody seemed to notice. How did the father, mother, grandparents, relatives in the extended family, family friends, and teachers not know? Often many people should have known if they had only been able to look and inquire. The story of a child's abuse can become a hidden theme in the extended family's drama. For instance, the abusing grandfather is wealthy, and the child's own parents are consequently loath to jeopardize their expected inheritance. Or it can simply be about personal and family harmony: the person who was abused wants recognition for what happened, but no one in the family wants to upset their illusion of harmony. They condemn one member of the family to exile to shield themselves from recognizing what they would rather not know. The failure to notice also extends to our larger culture, however. One of my patients, an incest survivor, once told me that her father, an eminent man, was close friends with another eminent man, a well-known mental health professional, who also happened to be one of my teachers. The father's friend knew of the incest and, according to her report, never uttered a word of disapproval. Not knowing does not stop with covert old boys' networks. Until recently, there has been a massive failure to notice child sexual abuse in churches, schools, and other institutions that serve children. Patterns of not knowing are endemic.

Thus, some people who have been especially traumatized carry the burden (in the form of dissociative problems in living) of experiences that others dissociatively fear. This makes the first group of people feel more shamed and everyone more isolated. The individual psyche as affected by the cultural unconscious thus becomes the subject of psychoanalysis.

Because until recently explicit attention to dissociation theory has been relatively sparse, this book covers two separate topics: (1) the relatively sequestered thinking of the dissociation "greats" and (2) how dissociative processes such as splitting, projective identification, and unconscious enactments, among others, contribute to our problems in living, as manifested in various conditions such as narcissism, psychopathy, and even gender patterns. Thus, we need to reformulate our psychological theory accordingly, which I attempt to offer in the following text.

ACKNOWLEDGMENTS

I express my appreciation to the people who generously gave of their time to read and comment on portions of this book: Philip Bromberg, Harvey Schwartz, Onno van der Hart, Marg Hainer, Melody Anderson, Anthony Ryle, Matthew Erdelyi, John O'Neil, Abby Stein, Donnel Stern, Ruth Blizard, Ellert Nijenhuis, Richard Chefetz, and May Benatar. I thank Philip Bromberg for his thoughtful and helpful commentary on several chapters and the sections on Sullivan and himself. Onno van der Hart read and commented extensively on the section on Janet, as well as on the section on his own work on the theory of the structural dissociation of the personality. He also provided me with many helpful resources on both. Harvey Schwartz painstakingly read the chapter on psychopathy and sent me many pages of notes and suggestions, including his wonderful phrase "outsiders to love," which I have gratefully used. Marg Hainer and Melody Anderson meticulously read and made extensive helpful commentary on several chapters. Anthony Ryle provided me with literature and thinking on the current work being done in cognitive analytic therapy (CAT) on dissociation, and he generously read and commented on the section on his own work. Matthew Erdelyi graciously offered his time to discuss an early version of chapter 9. John O'Neil made incisive and helpful comments on the section on Freud, Abby Stein helpfully commented on an early version of chapter 12, and Ellert Nijenhuis helpfully commented on the section on his own work. The suggestions and commentary of all these people have been invaluable in contributing to my thinking and my writing; their generous help greatly improved the manuscript. Of course, the responsibility for any errors rests with me.

I also thank the International Society for the Study of Dissociation (ISSD) for contributing to my understanding of dissociation. I have been a member of ISSD for many years and appreciate the atmosphere of scholarship, the dedication to improving extremely difficult clinical work, the courage to speak the truth about child abuse and its effects, and the friendliness that characterizes this organization and its members.

I thank my patients for what they have taught me. I am especially grateful to those who allowed me to present portions of their lives and their treatment in this book.

Finally, I am immensely grateful to my husband, Tony, for his multifaceted support, including his tireless reading and editing suggestions, coupled with his patience and tolerance of my unavailability for much of the period during which I wrote this book. I also thank my daughters, Eliza and Alicia, for much-needed help in library searching and computer and secretarial help.

I am grateful for the assistance of the staff at The Analytic Press during this project. Shari Buchwald, the production editor, was helpful and patient. Paul Stepansky, the managing director, provided expert guidance, suggestions for organization, and great care in the production of this book.

INTRODUCTION

> Full fathom five thy father lies;
> Of his bones are coral made;
> Those are pearls that were his eyes:
> Nothing of him that doth fade,
> But does suffer a sea-change
> Into something rich and strange.
> Sea-nymphs hourly ring his knell;
> Ding-dong.
> Hark! now I hear them—Ding-dong bell.
> —Shakespeare, *The Tempest*

Speaking of Freud's theory of the unconscious, Erich Fromm (1980) observed:

> This theory was radical because it attacked the last fortress of man's belief in his omnipotence and omniscience, the belief in his conscious thought as an ultimate datum of human experience. Galileo had deprived man of the illusion that the earth was the center of the world, Darwin of the illusion that he was created by God, but nobody had questioned that his conscious thinking was the last datum on which he could rely. Freud deprived man of his pride in his rationality . . . and discovered that . . . most of conscious thought is . . . a mere rationalization of thoughts and desires which we prefer not to be aware of [p. 134].

Freud's theories changed the world. Yet, following in the train of thought that greatness resides in the capacity to deprive humanity of narcissistic illusions, Freud might have dealt a much more decimating blow to human narcissism by formulating a model of the unconscious that included dissociated experiences and states. In *Studies on Hysteria,* Freud, along with Breuer (Breuer and Freud, 1893–1895), seemed to be headed toward formulating such a model. This "preanalytic" Freud, like his predecessor and contemporary, Janet, thought in terms of "dis-eases" of the dissociative mind. Had he not switched course–a switch that led to the development of the version of the unconscious with which most of us are so familiar, but which moved away from his earlier trauma theory–he might have developed a model of the unconscious that included dissociated states (Davies, 1996, 1998). As it happened, the version of the unconscious that Freud handed down to us did demolish our claim to reason, but it also left us with the comforting illusion that we possess knowledge of the basic content of the unconscious mind. This version of unconscious psychic determinism fostered another illusion, one of grandeur, for this version of the unconscious, filled with sexual and aggressive content, with agency and power, is grand. In contrast, a construct of the unconscious that includes dissociation is neither predetermined nor necessarily grand, because it offers us glimpses of different, far less familiar, sometimes frightening, versions of ourselves. These less familiar versions are often testimony to our utter helplessness at times of trauma.

Today, our concept of the unconscious is expanding, with dissociation taking at least an equal role to repression. Constructs of the unknown, hidden, but powerful directive and motivating forces within us and that *are us,* are being continually reformulated. Many of these new theoretical perspectives rest on dissociation as central. Bromberg (1998), among those in the forefront of the current writing about the "dissociative nature of the human mind" (p. 8), conceptualizes the unconscious in terms of dissociated self-states: "What we call the unconscious might usefully include the suspension or deterioration of linkages between self-states, preventing certain aspects of self–along with their respective constellations of affects, memories, values, and cognitive capacities–from achieving access to the personality within the same state of consciousness" (1993, p. 182). Davies (1996) also embraces the "presumption that the unconscious structure of mind is fundamentally dissociative rather than repressive in nature" (p. 564). Donnel Stern (1997) conceptualizes the unconscious and dissociation in terms of unformulated experience. Others (e.g., Lyons- Ruth, 1999; Zeddies, 2002) build on concepts of the procedural unconscious and of the relational impact of implicit memory.

The dissociative psyche is relationally structured. It is often said that with the robust advent of relational theories, psychoanalysis has been undergoing a sea change. The study of the dissociative mind radically furthers this change "into something rich and strange." The relational self and the dissociative mind are interlocking constructs. The self is thoroughly relationally embedded, from the inside going out, in terms of schemas of self in relation to others, and from the outside going in, in terms of the internalization of external relationships (Mitchell, 1993). We have learned who we are, and are not, from the words, affects, and gestures of early significant others and from the culture in which we live. When we take into account the inevitability of trauma, especially relational trauma, and the fact that dissociation is a common sequela of trauma, it is clear that a construct of psychic structure that emphasizes relationality must also encompass dissociation. Human beings are immensely variable (e.g., loving, empathic, cruel, ruthless) within, among, and between themselves. Human nature can be patterned into innumerable organizations in accordance with feelings, thoughts, and fantasies about significant others. In accordance with the demands of the attachment system, young human beings must find ways of staying in relationships with the significant others on whom they depend (Bowlby, 1969, 1984, 1988; Slavin and Kriegman, 1992); this means that psychic representations of these relationships may vary considerably. Dissociation is one way that the psyche modifies its own structure to accommodate interaction with a frightening, but needed, and usually loved, attachment figure.

The Ubiquity and Normalcy of Dissociation in a Relational Model of Self

Fairbairn, whose model of endopsychic structure elegantly articulated how the psyche can modify its own structure to accommodate a relationship with a painfully needed but abusive, rejecting, or too much unavailable other was the "first to formulate a true object-related (relational) nature of the self" (Grotstein and Rinsley, 2000, p. 4). He was also the first to formulate a theory of psychic structure that was both relational and dissociative. Fairbairn viewed libido as object seeking and people as innately object related. In his theory, impossibly frustrating and disappointing attachment figures are internalized and split in endopsychic structure. His model of schizoid personality structure can serve as a framework for understanding dissociative disorders, borderline personality disorder (Grotstein, 2000) and narcissism (Grotstein and Rinsley, 2000; Robbins, 2000; Sutherland, 2000). It can also serve, however, as a framework for understanding the problems of everyday life. Although Fairbairn (1952) worked with sexually abused children, and his understanding of their dilemmas influenced his thinking, he also felt that the schizoid dilemma was normative:

> Everybody without exception must be regarded as schizoid. . . . some measure of splitting of the ego is invariably present at the deepest mental level—or (to express the same thing in terms borrowed from Melanie Klein) the basic position in the psyche is invariably a schizoid position. This would not hold true, of course, in the case of a theoretically perfect person whose development had been optimum; it is difficult to imagine any person with an ego so unified and stable at its higher levels that in no circumstances whatever would any evidence of splitting come to the surface in recognizable form [pp. 7–8].

Pathological dissociation generally results from being psychically overwhelmed by trauma. Trauma is everywhere and highly prevalent. For instance, a 1995 National Comorbidity Study (Kessler et al., 1995, cited in Chu, 1995) estimates a lifetime exposure rate to severe traumatic events at 61% in men and 51% in women, along with a lifetime prevalence rate of PTSD of 7.8%, in the general U.S. population (p. 7). If trauma is defined as an "inescapably stressful event that overwhelms people's existing coping mechanisms" (Van der Kolk, 1996, p. 279) and that in its psychological sense overwhelms the integrity and continuity of the self because of its damage to the internalized links between self and other (Bromberg, 1998), then for a great many people there can be many small traumas (Bromberg, 1998; Frankel, 2002), generating many areas of sequestered, dissociated, and partially dissociated (Dell, 2001) experience. This is in addition to vulnerability to severe trauma. Survivors of complex trauma especially may develop a characterological structure around intrusion of partially or fully dissociated traumatic memories and defenses against such memories. Thus, it is often difficult to disentangle characterological issues from the effects of trauma.

Although dissociation may originally have been a way of staying in a relationship, what is most crucially at issue in dissociatively based psychopathology is the collapse of relationality—both interpersonal and intrapersonal (or interstate). Dissociation, as a state of being divided and as a chronic process, is ultimately a barrier to relationality, both within and between selves.

Because self-states exist in relation to significant others and to other parts of the self, they have different agendas. This divided agency, which results in the experience of being pulled in different directions (and, in cases of more extreme dissociation, of being taken over) is ultimately weakening and fatiguing. Another consequence is that because the dissociative system is one that seems to have worked, reliance on dissociation and the attachment of parts of the self to each other may at times be greater than reliance on or attachment to any real human being outside the system (Fairbairn, 1958). One severely dissociative patient explained to me that because her life had been so unbearably painful, dissociation was a "magic formula," the only thing she had ever had to rely on. It had always been there for her, and, at that time, she wasn't about to give it up. Although this is an extreme example, I believe that this patient's dilemma of an addictive proprietorship over her dissociative solutions is one she shares with most of us. The way we do this and how much we do it may differ, but I think we do it all the same.

Three Touchstones of the Dissociative Mind

I believe that dissociation perfuses everyday life, even though we may not always see it. There are three psychological processes that especially illuminate this more or less (depending on the person) crystalline structure of the psyche. Dreams, projective identification, and enactments, which are such staples of psychoanalytic work, can serve as touchstones, revealing the stress points and dissociative structure of the psyche.

Dreams vividly illustrate how parts of the self take on a character and a voice. They are often an internal theater in which these personifications declare their existence, starkly stating their perceptions, beliefs, fears, and desires. Dreams may express conflicts among self-states, and sometimes even roughly adumbrate dissociated behavior that was enacted on the outer stage of reality (Barrett, 1994, 1996; Brenner, 2001). An example of the expression of conflicts between dissociated self-states is the dream of a masochistic woman (whose aggressiveness was very much dissociated) about two women who looked very much alike. One was trying to strangle the other. The problems of the dissociated self are most apparent when self-states seek to dominate or annihilate each other, as in the dream just described, or when one self-state carries on as if no other parts of the self are relevant, analogously to overentitled "narcissism" of an individual with other people.

Dissociation creates confusion as to who is feeling what, and who is doing what to whom (Frawley-O'Dea, 1997), and this confusion creates a fertile field for the play of projective identification and enactments.

Projective identification is premised on dissociation and can be understood as the interpersonal language of dissociated self-states. Thinking in terms of projective identification and enactments is especially applicable to the effects of trauma, because to varying degrees and in different ways survivors have often been deprived of symbolic representations of what happened and of how they feel, and because of trauma-induced dissociation of self-states. As a result, the unconscious overwhelming experiences and feelings are often dealt with dissociatively, enactively, and by projective identification. The analyst's ability to identify and tolerate these feelings can provide some measure of experiential understanding of the patient's unconscious inner world; and this can then be communicated, given back to the patient (Bion, 1957; Ogden, 1986; Bromberg, 1998). This then helps the patient label, categorize, and accept experience. To me this is reminiscent of these lines in the Richard Fariña song, "Pack Up Your Sorrows," which was popularized by Judy Collins:

> Pack up your sorrows
> And give them all to me.
> You would lose them, I know how to use them,
> Give them all to me [Vanguard, 1999].

When this work with projective identification and enactments is carried on with various self-states, the analyst functions as a kind of relational bridge (Bromberg, 1998; Pizer, 1998), linking parts of the patient to each other through the shared interaction with the analyst. This relational connection of a given self-state to a significant other is often exactly what was foreclosed in childhood, or interrupted through some significant trauma.

Dissociated and switching self-states can be understood to underlie both projective identification and enactments. Traditionally, projective identification is understood as "disowned" affect, fantasy, or other unconscious and unwanted aspects of the self, which are projected into another person. According to Laplanche and Pontalis (1973), projective identification is defined as a "mechanism revealed in phantasies in which the subject inserts his self–in whole or in part–into the object in order to harm, possess or control it" (p. 356). Because interpersonal trauma damages self–other boundaries, when a person is not conversant with personal self-states the locus of feelings may be unknown, and aspects of the enacted relationship may be found in the other person in the current dyad. Inasmuch as projective identification is both an intrapsychic (or interstate) process and an interpersonal one, the dissociated affect may be located in other parts of the self as well as being found in other people, often simultaneously. In a more traditional view, this disowned, unconscious affect or fantasy stimulates unconscious aspects of feelings and fantasies in the other person; the enactment puts all of this into play (Maroda, 1998b). Another way of thinking about these phenomena, however, is in attachment-theory terms (Lyons-Ruth, 1999). Enactments may represent unconscious procedural relational knowledge of being with another person—a product of a two-person interaction (rather than a purely intrapsychic unconscious). These procedural ways of being with another may not have been (and may never be) verbally coded, even though they may influence behavior that includes words or the words that are used. They reflect implicit models of relationships, including interpersonal defensive maneuvers that respond to the attachment figures' own defenses and attachment systems. These "enactive procedural representations of how to do things with others" (p. 385), are internal working models of attachment, in Bowlby's sense. And, in Bromberg's (2001b) terms, "what Janet called a 'system or complex' is what I see as a dissociated self-state, or a self organized by its own dominant affect, its own view of social phenomena and human relationships, its own moral code, its own view of reality that is fiercely held as a truth" (p. 896). When these internal working models cannot be linked with one another—as, for example, when there are significant contradictions between implicit and explicit communications between caregiver and child that have not been examined—they can develop into segregated systems of attachment. We now have dissociated enactive procedural ways of knowing how to be with another. For example, one working model of relationships may be expressed in words, while another is played out procedurally (Lyons-Ruth, 1999). Understood this way, the interpersonal history clings to the concepts of enactment and projective identification.

Enactments reach back in time, replaying the emotional meaning of interpersonal events as they have been represented via various modalities, as well as replaying the twists of logic and intent that can occur in attempts to sustain attachment and safety. However, because this was a two-person process originally, so it always is. Interpersonally, there is always a perceiver, and as such, another actor, in enactments and projective identification. Once a dissociated self-state is expressed (in whatever way), it enters the interpersonal field as a way of being with another. Here this way of being with another meets another person who also has ways of being with another. In this way of thinking, projective identification and enactment are two sides of the same coin. For instance, in one clinical example, a therapist suddenly began to feel lovingly about a patient's sweet vulnerability, and the therapist's eyes momentarily fell on the patient's breasts. Awareness of these unfamiliar thoughts caused the therapist to internally recoil with shock, and suddenly a memory of Ferenczi's (1949) words about perpetrators' feelings of "tenderness" flashed across the therapist's mind. The therapist said nothing, and waited. After a while, the patient began to talk about her painful, shameful experiences of sexual abuse at her father's hands. The patient had been wearing on her skin, so to speak, and exhibiting in her posture, a procedural enactive representation of a particular kind of relationship, an unconscious, nonverbal anticipation of a particular kind of engagement with an other. Nonverbal cues say a lot. A common, but generally conscious, example might be how a woman with beautiful legs might sit in such a way as to communicate, "Look what beautiful legs I have!" And everyone does look and notice. Understood this way, projective identification does not have to be imbued with magic, but involves nonverbal communication of dissociated self-states—as well as, all too often, a dissociated "hearing" or "seeing" this message on the part of the other person.

The Dissociative Model of Mind

A model of the dissociative mind is potentially transformative of the way we conceptualize mental processes. Viewed through the lens of dissociation, many of our household-word concepts in psychoanalysis have a differently organized meaning. For instance, the structural model posits a tripartite unity of the ego, the id, and the superego, all in dynamic conflict. This model, which implies a unified, cohesive self, can appear differently: ego and superego are dissociated; that is, the connection between them is severed (Cameron and Rychlack, 1985; Howell, 1997), as are the conscious and unconscious (Putnam, 1997). The paradigm of the dissociative mind bridges the earlier apparent gap between neurosis and psychosis. Accordingly, even our concepts of sanity and insanity must undergo revision.

For most of the last century, until very recently, the topics of trauma and dissociation were not very important in mainstream psychoanalytic theory. Theorists, such as Janet, the Freud who believing in his seduction theory, a trauma theory, wrote "The Etiology of Hysteria" (in contrast to the Freud of 17 months later who denied his earlier seduction theory), Ferenczi, and Fairbairn, all of whom emphasized the dissociative mind and its link to trauma, have often been either relatively ignored or outrightly discredited. (In my view, an important reason has to do with cultural resistance to recognition of the prevalence of child abuse and, more generally, to facing evil in ourselves.) Janet, who developed a treatment for chronic and complex posttraumatic stress, with its accompanying dissociation, was well known and highly respected in the medical circles of his time. Like Sleeping Beauty in the fairy tale, the body of his work was largely forgotten for almost a century. Preceding the current resurgence, Janet's ideas influenced Jung's concepts and the work of Piaget, who was his student. Janet's ideas are, arguably, even found in Freud's work, among others (Ellenberger, 1970; Davies, 1996, 1998).

The work of Fairbairn, notable for his model of the self that was both relational and dissociative, was also relatively little known, until recently. Perhaps because he lived in Edinburgh, far from the psychoanalytic cultural center of London, he conducted his theoretical work in relative cultural isolation. Despite his by now strong influence on psychoanalysis, his earlier works were not published until 1994 (Scharff and Skolnick, 1998). Like Janet, he influenced other notable theorists, for example, Kernberg, and quite possibly Kohut (Sutherland, 2000).

Freud himself, together with Breuer, wrote of dissociative processes in *Studies on Hysteria* (Breuer and Freud, 1893–1895). Freud's (Breuer and Freud, 1893–1895) early trauma theory (the seduction theory), which included his view that psychoneuroses were the result of childhood sexual trauma, was presented in his 1896 paper, "The Aetiology of Hysteria." His immediate response to the chilly reception he felt he received following presentation of this paper was one of having been affronted, and "this after one has shown them the solution of a thousand-year-old problem the source of the Nile" (Gay, 1988, p. 93). Nonetheless, 17 months later, in 1897, he abandoned this model. The reasons Freud did this are controversial. They include Freud's own embeddedness in his culture and social milieu, and his complicated feelings about his parents, including his belief at one time that his father had sexually abused some of Freud's siblings, causing their neuroses (Masson, 1985, cited in Brothers, 1995). Other factors were his need to feel important and his patients' responses to his interventions, as well as the official theoretical reasons that were given (Ellenberger, 1970; Masson, 1984; Gay, 1988; Mitchell, 1988; Salyard, 1988; Pines, 1989; Kupersmid, 1993; Tabin, 1993; Davies and Frawley, 1994; Brothers, 1995; Freyd, 1996).

Ferenczi, following in Freud's 1896 footsteps, wrote eloquently about the traumatizing effect of childhood sexual abuse, and its often severely dissociative outcomes. He also suffered for writing about trauma, as Freud had felt he did. He was labeled by Freud and others in his inner circle as mentally ill on account of his refusal to recant his own trauma theory, which involved his belief that patients' recounting of childhood sexual trauma were generally basically true, and not in themselves fantasies (Masson, 1984; Aron and Harris, 1993; Rachman, 1997). Indeed, Ferenczi had linked the onset of the pernicious anemia that eventually killed him to his disillusionment with the man who had been his mentor for a quarter of a century—disillusionment based on his recognition that he must stand alone in honor of what he felt to be true, and face emotional abandonment by Freud for doing so (Aron and Harris, 1993; Rachman, 1997).

Evil

It is not surprising that, collectively, we have become more conscious of evil and dissociation at about the same time in current history. In many remarkable ways, the dissociative mind bears witness to a multitude of human contexts and relationships. And it is of paramount importance, especially today, in our current world culture(s), to note that the dissociative mind is a testament to the reality of evil. Evil has not been so easy to conceptualize as an external reality in the Freudian model because it was so easily construed as either id impulses that needed to be sublimated or controlled, or as expressions of unconscious guilt. Furthermore, the Freudian superego morality is basically relativistic and as such is meaningless in terms of any universal application (Kohlberg, 1971; Sagan, 1988; Howell, 1997a). However, when evil overwhelms us, it may become a part of us—until or unless we learn enough about it and our relationships to it. When we face this dilemma, we encounter a completely new realm of moral reality.

Three historical occurrences have raised our consciousness about how trauma and evil can massively puncture the psyche, creating black holes: the Nazi Holocaust, the World Trade Center disaster, and the relatively recent accumulating awareness of the extent and horrors of child abuse, especially child sexual abuse. The first two have been characterized by a collective awareness of evil as affecting its victims from the outside. With regard to child abuse, awareness of dependency on and attachment to the abuser (Fairbairn, 1952; Freyd, 1996; Blizard,

1997a, b; Howell, 1997b; Bromberg, 1998), clarifies how viable dissociation is as a means of endurance and survival, especially in the short run. Now that child abuse has become a focal issue on the public agenda, dissociation (which kept that knowledge, both private and public, in a separate category) is more accessible to our inquiries. Evil needs to be addressed both as a concept and as a reality, both in terms of how we think of evil, and as something that affects us from within and without.

I think Fairbairn's description of what normally remains in consciousness—the central ego and the ideal object, both of which have been laundered of the person's more problematic information and feelings about the attachment figure (the object)—is particularly apt. These laundered percepts and feelings have not been adequately linked, or have been unlinked in the course of trauma, and are not normally conscious. This is the schizoid condition, which Fairbairn saw as more or less normal. If we take this self-concept, dominated by the central ego and the ideal object, and see it as projected onto the world at large, then evil is simply incomprehensible. To deal with evil—as individuals, as dyads, and as a society—we need not only better models for understanding what it is, how it develops, and why and when it is enacted, but we also need better models of morality.

This is all about the sea change in psychoanalysis. And to go to the homonym, it is also about a "see" change—how we are like Miranda, the heroine of *The Tempest* (her name means "see"), who has a new vision. She sees "this brave new world/That has such people in't."

The chapters that follow give my perspectives on dissociation in everyday life as it can be conceptualized and worked with in treatment. Chapter 1, "Dissociation: A Model of the Psyche," gives a broad overview of the meanings of dissociation, the connection of dissociation to trauma, and its ubiquity. Various other topics, including neurophysiology, adaptive versus nonadaptive dissociation, and defensive dissociation, are discussed. This leads into chapter 2, "The Self in Context: Unity and Multiplicity," which covers the multiple self, context dependence, and the impact of trauma as it interferes with the linkage of states.

Chapter 3, "Pioneers of Psychodynamic Thinking About Dissociation," introduces the models of the dissociative mind developed by Janet, Freud, Ferenczi, and Fairbairn.

Chapter 4, "The Interpersonal and Relational Traditions," includes four models of the dissociative self developed by those in the interpersonalist and relational traditions: Sullivan, Bromberg, Stern, Davies, and Frawley-O'Dea.

Chapter 5, "Hybrid Models," includes four hybrid nonpsychoanalytic models of the dissociative mind: Ryle's multiple self states model; the theory of the structural dissociation of the personality, developed by Van der Hart, Nijenhuis, and Steele; Hilgard's neodissociation theory; and finally the general model of somatoform dissociation, to which many people have contributed.

The material reviewed in these three chapters can be gathered into four general ways of thinking about dissociation:

1. *Janetian dissociation.* Most of our theories of PTSD conform with, if they are not actually based on, Janet's ideas. This category includes Van der Hart et al.'s new theory of the structural dissociation of the personality (model 2), most theories of somatoform dissociation, and also Hilgard's neodissociation theory.
2. *A broad category of attachment-based, or relationally derived, dissociation.* Fairbairn's model is a prime exemplar of this category, as is disorganized attachment as described in current-day attachment theory. Under this category also comes Ryle's multiple self states model.
3. *Unformulated experience,* or *Sternian dissociationism.*
4. *Freudian repression,* which is a type of dissociationism.

It should be noted that the models covered in chapters 3 through 5 were chosen on the basis of their relevance to current thinking about dissociation. To be sure, theorists unmentioned in these chapters have made significant contributions to our understanding of the dissociated psyche–Jung, Winnicott, Klein, Khan, Herman, Pizer, Van der Kolk, Grotstein, Dell, Brenner, Harvey Schwartz, and Richard Schwartz among them. But owing to the scope of my presentation, and space limitations, I could not address their work.

Chapter 6, "Attachment Theory and Dissociation," addresses segregated models of attachment, disorganized attachment, mentalization, and the implications of Bowlby's concept of defensive exclusion for dissociation. It appears that disorganized attachment is highly related to early trauma and predisposes to experiencing events as overwhelming or traumatic (Fonagy, 2001; Blizard, 2003).

Chapter 7, "Attachment-Based Dissociation: A Different View of Splitting," addresses a particular organization of alternating dissociated self-states that occupy different relational positions, which may be based on discrete behavioral states, but develop on the axis of relational trauma. It addresses the hypothesized origins of phenomena that often come under the rubric of splitting, in different terms—those of dissociated states.

Chapter 8, "Projective Identification: Blind Foresight," addresses how the process of projective identification requires a multiple, dissociative self.

Chapter 9, "Concepts of Psychic Processes, Defense, and Personality Organization," covers important concepts such as repression, in contrast to dissociation, enactment, conversion hysteria versus somatoform dissociation, catharsis and abreaction versus integration, and the importance of interstate communication.

Chapter 10, "Narcissism: A Relational Aspect of Dissociation," addresses dissociation and certain aspects of pathological narcissism.

Chapter 11, "Good Girls, Sexy Bad Girls, and Warriors," discusses the creation and reproduction of gender in the context of trauma and dissociation.

Chapter 12, "The Dissociative Underpinnings of Psychopathy," addresses how the self-structure of psychopathy relies on dissociation. Dissociation works in several ways here, but a key one is as an aspect of Bowlby's concept of defensive exclusion, deactivation of the attachment system (Bowlby, 1973, 1980; Meloy, 1988). *Semantic dementia,* the term Cleckley (1941) used to describe the psychopathic process in his book, *The Mask of Sanity,* makes most sense in conjunction with dissociation. Although this chapter addresses the psychopath, psychopathy is also a process highly present in our culture. In this regard, collusion with psychopathy and dissociative, trauma-based "not seeing" are significant.

1

DISSOCIATION
A Model of the Psyche

September 11, 2001

My experience during the World Trade Center disaster of September 11, 2001, illustrates the initially protective role of dissociation in the moments of trauma, as well as its later consequences. I was on my way to work about 9:00 a.m. on the subway in New York City. People were talking about planes that had hit the World Trade Center, but I was focused on avoiding being late for a session with a patient, and pictured these as small planes, causing at most small fires. I thought to myself, "Small fires happen everyday." As I was on the subway and talked to more people and got more information, I decided I would get out and have a look at this fire, before proceeding on the subway under it (the next stop on the subway was the World Trade Center). When I exited, I saw the twin towers three short blocks away, burning rapidly, like matchsticks. They had already burned about a quarter of the way down. People were standing around staring, and appeared transfixed. I was transfixed too for a moment, and then I decided it was time to leave. But there was no way back by subway because the service had been stopped. Nor were there any cabs. It was too far to walk to my office, and I decided to walk home to Brooklyn. I made my way to the Brooklyn Bridge and walked across with a throng of others, many of whom had been in the towers and had escaped the fire. I talked with a man who had walked down 66 flights of stairs and believed that everyone had exited safely. At that moment, I believed that, too. Everyone was calm. No one was running. In short, people were in a state of shock en masse. I had an eerie moment of noticing what a beautiful, clear, crisp, near-autumn day it was, as a backdrop for the image of the towers rapidly burning, now more than halfway down. It was clear to me that they would collapse, and I began to worry about the impact of collapse on the stability of the bridge. Not knowing of the validity of this speculation in physics and not wanting to frighten others,

I walked faster alone, but like everyone else, I was calm. Now there was a huge black cloud of smoke and fumes and debris, billowing larger and larger and rapidly gaining on us. As I was exiting the bridge, I heard someone say that one tower had collapsed. (When someone asked me later if I saw the towers collapse, my answer was no, because I had been so absorbed, so intent on getting off the bridge.) As soon as I arrived home, there were calls from the superintendent to everyone to close their windows against the now arrived black cloud of soot and burned remains. I remained calm. It was a heartrendingly emotional time, but I thought that psychologically, *I* was fine. It was only a few days later that it hit me: I realized that I narrowly missed being caught in the conflagration. If I had stayed on the subway, the train would have either stopped at the World Trade Center, which was an underground maze, mostly leading into the towers, or in the tunnel, from which evacuation would have been, at best, a time-consuming process, with an exit close to the fires. I worried about all the people in the subway car, some with whom I had spoken, who had not left. I wondered what had happened to them, whether they survived. When I realized how imminent the danger had been, I couldn't stop telling anyone who would listen. To people who had no idea what had happened, this might have seemed a bit crazy. But many of the elements of trauma and dissociation are here—the calm narrowing of the focus of attention to only the most salient matters or helpful things, and the later realization of fear, concomitant with frightening, intrusive thoughts and hyperarousal. For persons who don't know or can't understand what the frightening event was, the subsequent agitated behavior might seem bizarre. Fortunately for me, I received enough understanding that my mild posttraumatic stress symptoms abated. However, people who are in chronic posttraumatic stress may be experienced by others as disordered or as behaving bizarrely, especially if the stressor is unknown, as is often the case.

PTSD Is Evidence of Dissociation

In posttraumatic stress a person may experience the intrusions of dissociated experiences, such as flashbacks, somatosensory experiences, or even obsessions, into consciousness, but may also vigilantly attempt to avoid any reminders of the trauma. These are the intrusion and avoidance aspects of PTSD. This was what happened to me in the World Trade Center disaster on September 11, 2001: my previous experience of terror was not accessible to me for a few days. Then, the memories began to intrude. Although I felt like Coleridge's Ancient Mariner (who had to wander from town to town, endlessly telling his story), I began to heal. This process assumes dissociation, because some experience had to be cordoned off from other experience (dissociated) to intrude (Van der Hart, Van Dijke, Van Son, and Steele, 2000). The intrusion aspects are the dissociated memories of the trauma, often intruding in response to "triggers" or reminders of the trauma. The hyperaroused behavior may appear senseless to an observer and even to the individual in question. The avoidance aspects of the PTSD refer to the efforts to avoid the dissociated material which could be triggered by a reminder of the trauma.

Trauma

Until fairly recently trauma was officially viewed as an "out of the ordinary" experience (*DSM-III* described trauma in these terms). But such a view is inconsistent with observable reality (Brown, 1991; Herman, 1992). In times of war, trauma is not rare. Neither has it been rare in times of relative national tranquility. Indeed, trauma has never been rare. Rates of child abuse, including physical and sexual abuse, are shockingly high. A recent national survey, conducted by telephone, of 2000 randomly selected youths, aged 10 to 16, found that almost one half of the boys and one third of the girls had been subjected to some form of violent victimization (Boney-McCoy and Finkelhor, 1996). In a large study in which 900 women were interviewed, Russell (1986) found that the rate of contact child sexual abuse of girls before age 18 was 38%, and the rate of incest was 16%. A recent study of 600 college men indicated that 18% reported contact sexual abuse before the age of 16 (Lisak, Hopper, and Song, 1996). Assuming that much of this trauma is not resolved and has dissociative sequelae, these rates might push expected normal personality structure into the realm of what one might call the "pathological normal"—that is, an area that is statistically normal but highly problematic, even pathological.

We now understand that trauma is ubiquitous. In the statistical sense, it is normal. And so is dissociation, which is often a sequela to trauma. It follows then that everyday functioning for most people is bound up in the effects of trauma and dissociation. Although significant trauma does affect the majority of us, there are also many less extreme traumas and dissociations of everyday life. And these affect us in ways that may be at first unexpected. Pollack (1995, 1998) contends that in our culture little boys frequently undergo a "normative developmental trauma" involving dissociation of affectively longing parts of the self and resulting in fears of isolation and feelings of deprivation. Indeed, many gender-related phenomena can be understood as posttraumatic adaptations, involving dissociation (Howell, 2002b).

Not Only Posttraumatic

Despite the prevalence of trauma-related dissociation, problematic dissociation does not proceed from trauma alone (Gold, 2000). It encompasses not only the "shattered self" of posttraumatic severed connections, but also more general failures of integration (Putnam, 1992, 1997). Poor psychological integration proceeds from family environments that are chaotic, abusive, neglectful, or all three; from attachment dilemmas, including disorganized attachment; and from severe interpersonal anxiety caused by interactions with caregivers and with a dissociogenic culture. Developmentally, lack of integration characterizes our beginnings (Siegel, 1999), and facilitative maturational environments enable disconnected sets of experiences to be linked (Putnam, 1997). In his important book, *Not Trauma Alone,* Gold (2000) amends the trauma–abuse model and emphasizes that individuals most likely to be characterized by severe dissociation have generally grown up in interpersonal environments that failed to provide the infant and child with requisite interpersonal resources to obtain full human status. He observes how remarkably consistent individual incidents of abuse often are with the family atmosphere in which they have occurred, and that atmospheres of neglect, deprivation, and rejection fail to nourish fundamental skills in living.

Fairbairn and Ferenczi (chapter 3) have articulated forms of dissociative adaptations to attachment dilemmas. Bowlby noted the importance of segregated internal working models, which modern attachment theorists such as Liotti, Lyons-Ruth, and Stern have observed is both phenotypic of dissociation and predictive of dissociative disorders. Interestingly, and counterintuitively, Lyons-Ruth (2003) has found that disorganized attachment is a better predictor of dissociation at age 19 than is trauma. The current attachment–theory emphasis on dissociated relational procedural enactments (chapter 6) intersects with current relational psychoanalytic models of Bromberg, Davies, and Stern (chapter 4).

Sullivan (1953) described the interpersonal genesis of dissociation. As a result of unbearable anxiety arising from interactions with caregivers, including extreme parental disapproval, certain kinds of experiences may become dissociated and part of "not-me." Selective inattention to anxiety-fraught areas of experience leads to experience remaining unformulated, and hence dissociated (Stern, 1997). Thus, dissociation refers to the unconscious avoidance of formulating certain aspects of experience into meaningful constructs (Stern, 1997). Finally, the culture itself may be dissociogenic and discontinuous, such that experiences of self are also marked by discontinuities (Gold, 2004a).

What Is Dissociation?

In a general sense, dissociation refers to the separation of mental and experiential contents that would normally be connected. The word *dissociation* is laden with multiple meanings and refers to many kinds of phenomena, processes, and conditions. Dissociation is both adaptive and maladaptive, both verb and noun, both cause and effect (Spiegel, 1990b; Tarnopolsky, 2003). Dissociation is often psychologically defensive, protecting against painful affects and memories, but it can also be an organismic and automatic response to immediate danger (Van der Hart, Nijenhuis, Steele, and Brown, 2004). Dissociation can be understood as taxonic or, alternatively, as existing on a continuum–describing all of us, varying in degrees (Putnam, 1997). It is both occurrent (in evidence or in process) and dispositional (a capability that can be tapped) (Braude, 1995). It refers to such psychical events as spacing out, psychic numbing, and even experiencing oneself as floating above one's body. Dissociation has been thought of in spatial metaphor, as acts of "keeping things apart" (Tarnopolsky, 2003) as well as "vertical splitting" (Kohut, 1971; Hilgard, 1977).

Thus, multiple views of the etiology and nature of dissociation exist. According to Putnam (1997), these views "converge around the idea that dissociation represents a failure of integration of ideas, information, affects, and experience" (p. 19). Yet, when dissociation is so many things, how do we understand it? All of these different meanings potentially create a conceptual confusion. A danger is that the word *dissociation* can be used so loosely that it begins to lose its meaning.

A significant divergence of opinion currently concerns whether dissociation is best understood in terms of a continuum model or a psychopathological taxon model. Both models are supported by the evidence. The first posits a continuum from adaptive, normative dissociation to the extremes of pathological dissociation. The taxon model addresses dissociation as classified by symptoms, exemplified by dissociative disorders.

The Health-to-Psychopathology Continuum

At the healthy end of this continuum are dissociative experiences that are normative, that enhance enjoyment and effectiveness in living, or both. Dissociation is not necessarily evidence of a history of trauma, or even of psychopathology. For example, hypnosis can result in one or more sets of experiences becoming inaccessible to ordinary consciousness. Many see dissociation as a capacity, which can be life-enhancing as well as defensive. A prime exemplar of such normative, life-enhancing dissociation is absorption, which appears to be normally distributed throughout the population (Putnam, 1997). Absorption, which is highly interrelated with hypnosis (Putnam, 1997; Maldonado and Spiegel, 1998), is the ability to be "carried away" in a narrowed, concentrated focus of attention, to become so immersed in a central experience that context loses its frame. It has been classified as dissociation because the intense focal concentration can result "in the exclusion (dissociation) of other contents from the phenomenal field and, often, the context in which it is experienced" (Butler, 2004, p. 4). Some examples of absorption are being engrossed in a book or movie, having a highly engaging fantasy while driving, contemplation, reverie, and "flow" (Csikszentmihalyi, 1990, cited in Butler, 2004, p. 7). Butler (2004) believes that normative, adaptive, and enhancing experiences of dissociation have been generally overlooked. She notes that flow

> shares many features with dissociative experience including intense, focused concentration, a merging of action and awareness (i.e., attention is completely absorbed in the present action that results in the loss of reflective self-consciousness and distorted time sense). The features that distinguish flow from other dissociative experiences are the sense of self-efficacy experienced with respect to the task at hand and the intrinsically rewarding nature of the experience [p. 8].

Similar to flow are meditative experiences and many positive trance experiences, which also involve loss of reflective self-consciousness.

Indeed, part of the process of yogic meditation involves a kind of surrender such that reflective self-consciousness is relinquished as it arises (Waelde, 2004).

A phenomenon commonly known as "highway hypnosis," in which the driver of an automobile travels a well-known route and arrives at the destination without remembering the drive, has often been cited as an example of dissociation. What happens here is that the driver, focally attending to other thoughts than the road, is able to perform the drive automatically. It is an example of automatic dual tasking. Highway hypnosis is one of the items in the Dissociative Experiences Scale (DES) and may also measure absorption (Putnam, 1997), but it is not one of the taxonic, or typological, items indicating dissociative pathology.[1] How likely we are to drive safely while under the influence of highway hypnosis may depend on our degree of absorption in our own thoughts.

Is dissociation phenomenologically the same in pleasant experiences of absorption as it is in trauma? And are the same processes involved? A key issue relevant to adaptive versus pathological dissociation is whether the dissociation is under voluntary control. Thus, in meditation and peak experiences, a person consciously decides to become absorbed or to allow absorption to occur, and the person can return to everyday modes of functioning without difficulty. Highway hypnosis would be extremely dangerous if the person could not return attention to the road when necessary. Furthermore, there is the question of whether dissociation promotes or impedes integration. For example, meditation, which is consciously controlled, tends to promote integration (Waelde, 2004), whereas involuntary dissociation impedes it.

The same ability, absorption, can be used to enhance experience or to avoid it; it can be used for pleasure (Butler, 2004) or for defense. Many highly dissociative patients report that they have found ways to voluntarily disappear from traumatic experiences: deliberately going into a state of trance or absorption, becoming lost in the wallpaper, or mentally going into a mousehole in the wall. Here we have an initially adaptive response to interpersonal violence or threat in which the ability to become absorbed or go into trance is a coping mechanism. The problem is that the outcome of continuously avoiding painful experience is that it cannot be integrated and will therefore intrude into experience or dominate it at times. In all forms of problematic dissociation, too much is involuntary. People with dissociative disorders and with PTSD often cannot control the intrusive experience. Often people with DID and BPD cannot control the switching between self-states. Unformulated experience is involuntarily enacted.

The Taxon

Taxon refers to type or classification. Hence, according to the taxonic perspective, dissociation is equated with severe dissociation. There are individuals whose dissociativity is so chronic and severe that they fit into a taxon or personality type. Despite the fact that dissociation has often been understood as highly interrelated with hypnosis, Putnam (1997) has found that the supposed dissociation–hypnotizability relationship does not hold for the general population (and that most DID patients are not "highly hypnotizable"), suggesting that the dissociation–hypnotizability relationship is nonlinear. However, high hypnotizability does seem to characterize a group of abuse victims who had an earlier onset of incest and many more perpetrators. He called this relatively small subgroup of subjects "double dissociators"; that is, they scored high on both dissociation and hypnotizability. This finding is consistent with a taxon rather than a continuum model of dissociation for this group of people.

Putnam's finding is also consistent with the age-related aspect of dissociative abilities: the ability to dissociate is greatest in childhood and gradually decreases with age, except for a period of increase in adolescence (Bernstein and Putnam, 1986, cited in Chu, 1998). High dissociative ability continues into adulthood only in situations of ongoing traumatic abuse (Kluft, 1984). Thus, people who encounter even extreme trauma in adulthood do not develop extreme, florid symptoms of DID (Chu, 1998) if they were not highly traumatized in childhood.

Structural Dissociation

One highly significant construct of pathological dissociation is Van der Hart et al.'s (2004) theory of the "structural dissociation of the personality." These authors believe that the word *dissociation* should denote structural dissociation, a division of experiential parts of the personality. Invoking Janet's postulation that "dissociation denotes an organized division of the personality," Van der Hart et al. (2004) note that this division involves inadequate integration among two or more systems of ideas and functions, each of which encompasses a "sense of self, no matter how rudimentary or vastly developed" (p. 907). They believe that "conceptual clarity regarding trauma-related dissociation is urgently needed. There is pervasive misunderstanding of the nature of dissociation. It precludes consensus as to which phenomena, symptoms, and disorders belong to the domain of trauma-related dissociation" (p. 906).

Van der Hart et al. (2004) believe that absorption, altered states, and experiences of depersonalization and derealization are such areas of conceptual unclarity because they do not necessarily involve structural dissociation. Although many people experience them under conditions of mild stress, depersonalization and derealization are often considered to be dissociative symptoms in the literature. Depersonalization, which involves a sense of strangeness with respect to the self, the body, or both, can be evoked by stress, illness, sleep deprivation, substance abuse, and sensory deprivation. In these instances, this sense of strangeness may reflect alterations in consciousness but does not necessarily imply structural dissociation. In contrast is "pathological depersonalization" (Steinberg, 1994), which involves a separation between observing and experiencing ego, as often occurs in child abuse, rape, combat, and motor vehicle accidents, and thus does qualify as structural dissociation.

This distinction between altered states and structural dissociation is a useful one. The concept lends itself to conceptualizing along a single continuum. Thus, PTSD caused by a tornado might involve a structural dissociation on a small scale. Events reminding the person of tornadoes might be triggering because a state of intense fear had been sequestered and never integrated. This might not seriously impede daily living, but the terror of the moment, normally unavailable to consciousness, might intrude at times. A war veteran with PTSD might have more significant structural dissociation, involving the sequestration of more and larger portions of experience. A person who was exposed to chronic or severe sexual abuse might be characterized by more massive dissociation of traumatic experiences, resulting in switching of self-states without the person's knowledge or volition. In this way, it is clear how DID is chronic PTSD. (The above progression is similar to Van der Hart et al.'s concept of primary, secondary, and tertiary structural dissociation.)

Van der Hart et al. (2004) note the importance of the intrusion of dissociative experiences (e.g., intrusion of thoughts or of sensory experiences): Intrusions imply a lack of integration of part(s) of the personality that remain fixated in traumatic events, thus a lack of integration of the personality" (p. 908). Consistent with Van der Hart et al.'s understanding of dissociative intrusions and negative dissociation is Dell's (2001) view of the phenomenology of dissociative disorders. On the basis of the testing of hundreds of patients with dissociative symptoms, Dell believes that the intrusions of dissociated self-states into ordinary consciousness are more characteristic of DID than is the more dramatic switching. Dell also distinguishes between full dissociation, characterized by amnesia, and partial dissociation, which includes such symptoms as flashbacks, hearing voices in the head, passive influence symptoms, and intrusions of dissociated experience.

Process and Effect

However, the divide between normal and pathological dissociation is unclear. Current research indicates that absorption is just as highly correlated with physical, sexual, and emotional abuse, as well as depersonalization, as are the taxonic criteria (the DES-T) themselves (Dalenberg, 2004). There may be several aspects of dissociative abilities, such as absorption and detachment, which are functionally interlinked and highly intercorrelated. These may be adaptive and enhancing, or they may become involuntarily used.

Another way of understanding these two different perspectives (of continuum and taxon) is as *process* (e.g., absorption), which may or may not have a structural effect, and *effect,* which is the structured outcome of a dissociative process. The concept of structural dissociation refers to an enduring organized division of the experiential contents of the self, and implies inadequate integration. Even though it may begin automatically, once structural dissociation occurs, its maintenance can be said to be "unconsciously" motivated. Examples are PTSD, DID, and unformulated experience, all of which avoid the psychic contents "held" by other parts of the self, including severe and overwhelming anxiety. Unformulated experience (Stern, 1997) qualifies as a form of structural dissociation because it is not under voluntary control and is subject to enactments.

Dissociation: A Salve to Trauma

Even though dissociation can arise from other sources as well, problematic or maladaptive dissociation is often a chronic, rigidified outcome of trauma. Initially, it is adaptive, protecting the traumatized person from unbearable pain and knowledge and preserving a sense of safety and control in dangerous and overwhelmingly stressful circumstances

(Putnam, 1997; Maldonado and Spiegel, 1998; Brenner, 2000) and thereby enhancing survival (Freyd, 1996). When the continuity of being is traumatically interrupted, when whatever has happened is too frightening to be assimilated, people may "trance out," develop "psychic numbness" (Lifton and Marcuson, 1990), go into "neutral gear" (Terr, 1994), or all of these. This dissociative ability appears to be an aspect of biological endowment, an organismic response to being overwhelmed (Levine, 1997). Livingstone (Freyd, 1996), the Scottish explorer, describes this experience well in his account of being attacked by a lion:

> Starting, and looking half round, I saw the lion in the act of springing upon me. I was upon a little height; he came at my shoulder as he sprang, and we both came to the ground below together. Growling horribly close to my ear, he shook me as a terrier dog does a rat. The shock produced a stupor similar to that which seems to be felt by a mouse after the first pounce of the cat. It caused a sense of dreaminess in which there was no sense of pain nor feeling or terror, though quite conscious of what was happening. It was like patients partially under the influence of chloroform describe, who see all the operation, but feel not the knife. This singular condition was not the result of any mental process. The shake annihilated fear, and left no sense of horror in looking round at the beast. This peculiar state is probably produced in all animals killed by the carnivora; and if so, is a merciful provision by our benevolent Creator for lessening the pain of death [p. 66].

In contrast to Livingstone's belief that this analgesia is a "merciful provision . . . for lessening the pain of death," it is more typically a state that is adaptive for survival in life-threatening situations (Freyd, 1996). For example, in many extreme situations, such as injuries in battle or in sports, in moments of emotional duress, even states of profound joy, people often unconsciously suppress the emotion. Even in less extreme situations, such as being in a hurry when we are intensely focused on something else, we may not notice the pain of a minor injury. As Livingstone describes so well, people may at the moment of trauma narrow the window of consciousness and calmly, perhaps even dreamily, adapt to the immediate situation confronting them. Dissociation allows one to separate oneself from the experience of the trauma (Van der Hart, 2000).

The value of the capacity for this kind of dissociation is inestimable. It can be lifesaving and preservative of sanity at the time of the trauma. However, if maintained for too long and not overcome, dissociation becomes maladaptive. For instance, separating oneself from the experience can lead to derealization and depersonalization. Dissociation often becomes increasingly maladaptive as unhealed trauma accumulates and the person's way of life becomes constrained to continuously avoid any reminders of it. However, this depends on context. For instance, a child who lives in a home in which she is continuously abused sexually, may best adapt to her situation by learning to chronically dissociate. This is despite the fact that once she steps into a more just and nurturing social environment, her formerly adaptive behavior becomes pathological.

Posttraumatic Dissociative Symptoms and Conditions

Often pathological dissociation is linked to trauma. For instance, 85% to 100% of those with DID have a history of childhood abuse (Putnam, 1989). After isolated, single traumas, such as a rape, people often have marked dissociative experiences and posttraumatic stress. For instance, one study (Koss and Burkhart, 1989), found that over 60% felt that they had not recovered in the first few months while four to six years after a sexual assault about a quarter of the victims felt that they had not yet recovered. The primary psychological task in such cases is recovery from one overwhelming acute stressor. However, when the trauma is repeated and occurs at an early age, the dissociative response may become automatic and achieve a secondary, functional autonomy, contributing to personality disorders and what Brenner (2001) calls a "dissociative character." Initially, each of the repeated traumatic incidents may result in a dissociative response. However, when a person is no longer in an abusive environment, the chronic dissociativity remains (Putnam, 1997). There is now a fear or a "phobia" (Janet, 1907; Van der Hart et al., 2000) of knowledge and affects contained by other parts of the self.

In psychological trauma, particularly at the hands of a person on whom one is dependent, dissociation allows a sequestering of the traumatic experience, allowing the traumatized individual to continue functioning in a double-bind relationship (Spiegel, 1986), without having to notice the inherent contradictions. For instance, a child who is subject to sexual abuse in the home may "forget" the night's events during the day and use all her resources to "be like" a "normal" person during the day. She hasn't repressed the abuse, for when it occurs again the next night, she can "remember" it again well, and she has a good idea of how she can or must deal with it.

Putnam (1997) has classified posttraumatic dissociative symptoms into sets of primary, secondary, and tertiary. Primary dissociative symptoms refer to the direct effects of dissociation on thought and behavior. Putnam follows Lowenstein in dividing the primary symptoms into two groups: (1) amnesias and memory symptoms and (2) process symptoms, such as depersonalization, derealization, trance states (dissociative), auditory hallucinations, switching, and altered personality states. Putnam also includes associated posttraumatic symptoms such as physiological avoidance, physiological reactivity, detachment, hyperarousal, and so on because of their common link through trauma and because they frequently occur together with dissociative symptoms. Then there are secondary responses to the primary dissociative and posttraumatic symptoms, which include affective and somatic symptoms as well as disturbances of self, such as the low self-esteem that often characterize trauma survivors. Finally, there are tertiary responses, such as self-destructive behaviors and substance abuse, which are understood as maladaptive ways of coping with the primary and secondary dissociative symptoms. This schematization is illustrative of the scope of dissociation in psychopathology as well as the extent to which it is intertwined in daily life.

Trauma and "States"

As Putnam (1992, 1997) observes, the word *state* comes from the Latin word *status,* meaning "state of being" or "condition." "States" characterize changes in the patterning of an individual's personality, behavior, and consciousness over time. They are contrasted to "traits," which are assumed to characterize constancy in individuals. Individual differences are measured in terms of "traits," a topic that has been a staple of psychological research. Mental states, or states of consciousness, are the building blocks of human behavior and consciousness.

Following Putnam (1997), although the effect of trauma on consciousness is complex, there are two particular ways in which it disrupts a person's sense of continuity: (1) by interrupting and retarding the linking of states in the course of development and (2) by creating new, highly discrete states. As for the first, trauma interferes with the associative pathways, according to which states would normally be linked. It limits the connections among states. For example, fear-conditioned states may be dissociated from other states. Or intense negative affect that cannot be integrated in a childhood dyad with attachment figures tends to increase the dissociation of self-states organized by these emotions (Lyons-Ruth, 1999). Trauma interrupts metacognitive, self-observing, self-reflective functions, which are to some degree independent of states, and which can facilitate the integration of states. This may also happen in an interpersonal, social way: Abusive families may evince and require different behavior in different circumstances, in public and in private, in day and in night. Posttrauma, narrative memory may not be connected with affective and state memory. However, as for the second way, trauma also contributes to the creation of specific altered states. Frightened, traumatized children may develop and rely on restitutive states of reality-altering fantasy (Putnam, 1997).

In sum, an important consequence of trauma may be a general increase in the number of discrete behavioral states (DBS), limiting the person's control over experience (Putnam, 1989, 1992, 1997). Putnam (1997) emphasizes that the DBS model implies that the identity fragmentation seen in DID and "other disorders associated with childhood trauma is less a 'shattering' of a previously intact identity, than a developmental failure of consolidation and integration of discrete states of consciousness" (p. 176). Although all young children have state-dependent aspects of self, childhood trauma can lead to a profound developmental failure to coherently bind these state-dependent aspects of self together.

Recent research emphasizes the role of state-dependent memory in the creation of segregated states of consciousness, especially in circumstances associated with strong emotions (Siegel, 1999). Some of the more dramatic illustrations of how mental states may be highly sequestered comes from patients with DID. For instance, a child state may emerge in which the patient does not know what a modern telephone looks like or what a computer is. Indeed, this phenomenon of the sequestration of certain self-states over long periods of time may find expression in certain fiction stories about time. For example, Washington Irving's Rip van Winkle fell asleep for 20 years during a walk in the Catskill Mountains. When he awoke the world about him was dramatically changed. He had set out as a subject of King George III, and emerged as a citizen of the United States. The story is actually explainable in terms of dissociative phenomena: A part of Rip van Winkle was asleep for 20 years while other parts of the self lived in chronological time, day by day. The part that had been asleep came out to find the world vastly different.

Somatoform Dissociation

According to *DSM-IV* (American Psychiatric Association, 1994), the "essential feature of Dissociative Disorders is a disruption of the normal integrative functions of *consciousness, memory, identity, and perception of the environment*" (p. 477, italics added). However, this is not a simple matter. If the traumatic experience has been too intensely overwhelming to be assimilated by ordinary consciousness, aspects of the experience may be encoded in somatosensory modalities, rather than becoming part of narrative experience.

Today our diagnostic system repeats the ages old Cartesian dualism, in the form of a mind–body controversy with respect to the "location" of dissociation. With the advent of *DSM-III* (APA, 1980) and the pursuit of a theoretical neutrality, the mind–body aspects of somatoform dissociation became, themselves, split apart, disassociated (Cardena and Nijenhuis, 2000).[2] Indeed, in *DSM-IV,* the cognitive and affective aspects of dissociation have been categorized as dissociative disorders, whereas those dissociative processes that are experienced as somatic, such as motor control and sensation, are classified as somatoform (Nijenhuis, 2000). As Nijenhuis has observed, according to the current *DSM,* the only dissociative disorder that even refers to bodily symptoms is depersonalization disorder, in which the person feels detached from or outside the body.

It is common to think of symptoms as compromise formations in which drive-related concerns are repressed but expressed motorically. However, to do so may obscure the real events that have become encoded in the "body memory." It may divert attention away from a more immediate historical source of the somatoform symptoms, which may be more directly expressive of real events, real violations, involving harm done to the body. Furthermore, the idea that these repressed wishes are located in *one unconscious* makes it difficult to see the fragmentation of experience and memory and to appreciate the many different loci of unconscious memory that are stored in the body memory.

Animal Defensive and Posttraumatic Biological States

Nijenhuis et al. (1998a) and Nijenhuis, Van der Hart, Kruger, and Steele (2004) have examined trauma from the perspective of animal responses to terror which may have counterparts in human response. They report the similarity between various animal states, including "total submission" and freezing/analgesic states, and human behavior following exposure to terror. The human animal may have a repertoire of discrete behavioral states that are adaptive to conditions of predation. For instance, bodily symptoms such as body stiffness, analgesia, and high muscle tension may all represent a human freezing response. Total submission involves anesthesia and low muscle tension. These animal defense states may underlie different dissociative parts of the personality.

Perry (1999) outlines how exposure to trauma alters neurodevelopmental processes via two primary responses of hypoarousal and hyperarousal. These responses become more pronounced with more severe, chronic, and early trauma. They are interactive, and most individuals suffering from this altered neurobiology use combinations of the two patterns. Hypoarousal, a pattern that Perry labels *dissociative,* involves dissociative symptoms such as fugue, numbing, fantasy, analgesia, derealization, depersonalization, catatonia, and fainting. Observed behaviors are robotic compliance, glazed expressions, and passivity. Heart rates go down. This defeat response, similar to "learned helplessness" (Seligman, 1975), is more characteristic of infants, young children, and females. It is adaptive to immobilization or inescapable pain. The other response pattern of hyperarousal involves "fight or flight" reactions. This begins as a neurophysiological alarm reaction and continues with elevated heart rate, vigilance, behavioral irritability, increased locomotion, and increased startle response. There is a tendency to overread cues as threatening, which can increase the probability of aggression.

Neurobiological Organizations Underlying Dissociated States

A complicated neurobiological organization and response system underlies these dissociated states. This process occurs through various pathways, including the altering of brain structures and the creation of neurobiological patterning in the brain. Repeated trauma leads to maladaptive gene expression, altering synaptic connections and resulting in neurological deficits and increasing vulnerability to trauma-based disorders (Stien and Kendall, 2004). Trauma overwhelms the autonomic nervous system with stress hormones, overactivating the amygdala, which is involved in immediate, automatic response. As a result, the hippocampus, which is more related to information processing, may be damaged and decrease in size (Van der Kolk, 1996b; Nijenhuis, Vanderlinden, and Spinhoven, 1998; B. D. Perry, 1999). A number of studies have found decreased hippocampal volume in adults with PTSD who have reported physical and sexual abuse (Nijenhuis, 2003). Ehling, Nijenhuis, and Kirkke (2003) found that patients with florid DID had 25-percent less hippocampal volume than controls, whereas patients with dissociative disorder not otherwise specified (DDNOS) had 13-percent less hippocampal volume, suggesting that hippocampal volume correlates with severity of dissociation. After successful integrative treatment, the DID patients recovered considerable hippocampal volume.

The neurological effects of trauma thus also contribute to decreased integration of states and decreased reflectiveness. Because linkage of states contributes to an awareness of context both within the self and within the world, and to the capacity for increased reflectiveness, people who have suffered more interruption of state linkage have more difficulty understanding their emotions, and tend to feel buffeted by circumstances. As a result, they tend to overrely on dissociation. Dissociation of self-states will be more numerous and severe.

B. D. Perry (1999) has described how induced behavioral states become traits. As a result of repeated activation of particular states, they become "use-dependent" and hardwired in the brain. For instance, terror involves activation of a certain patterning of brain stem, limbic system, midbrain, and cortex neurophysiology. "Because the neuronal systems alter themselves in a use-dependent way in response to patterns, repetitive neuronal activation, a state of terror will result in patterned, repetitive neuronal activation in this distributed and diverse set of brain systems—resulting in a set of memories" (p. 15). In PTSD the physiological hyperreactivity is a cue-evoked state memory, involving memories of a particular time and an alarm response. However, these memories are not necessarily conscious. As Van der Kolk (1996c) says, "the body keeps the score" (p. 214).

The brain is organized to promote survival and procreation. Thus, cues that herald danger to survival, such as the growl of the saber-toothed tiger, are most salient and need to be learned only once. This kind of information reaches the amygdala, which sends the message for action before the message reaches the cortex (Van der Kolk, 1996b; B. D. Perry, 1999). One outcome is that the state arousal may not result in the activation of the associated cognitive memories that would provide knowledge of why one is anxious or upset. B. D. Perry (1999) writes of a little boy he met in a residential treatment center who persistently refused to eat his hot dog unless it was cut up. There were frequent escalating confrontations with the staff around the issue of his problems with eating. Perry's inquiry revealed that the child had been forced to perform fellatio on his father and other men until he was removed from the abusive environment at age six. The oropharyngeal patterns of stimulation of eating—especially things like hot dogs—evoked state memories of the abuse, involving terror and confusion. Neither the child nor anyone else had any idea why this particular child was being so "difficult" until the matter was understood as "state and affect memories evoked by motor memories" (p. 26).

Dissociation in Neurosis, Psychosis, and Personality Disorders

Over the past two decades a number of theorists have argued that dissociation is an integral part of most psychopathology of nonorganic genesis. Those problems in living that used to be called neuroses may be largely dissociation based (Howell, 1997). Bromberg (2003c) views dissociation as underlying all personality disorders. As opposed to dissociative disorders themselves, in which the dissociation is focally identified as the problem, ego-syntonic dissociation underlies all personality disorders:

> Each "type" is a dynamically "on-alert" configuration of dissociated states of consciousness that regulates psychological survival in terms of its own concretized blend of characteristics. In each type, certain self-states hold the traumatic experiences and the multiplicity of raw affective responses to them, and others hold whichever ego resources (pathological and nonpathological) have proved effective in dealing with the original trauma and making sure the pain would never again be repeated (e.g., vigilance, acquiescence, paranoid suspiciousness, manipulativeness, deceptiveness, seductiveness, psychopathy, intimidation, guilt induction, self-sufficiency, insularity, withdrawal into fantasy, pseudomaturity, conformity, amnesia, depersonalization, out-of- body experiences, trance states, compulsivity, substance abuse).

Psychosis

As opposed to being distinct from the realms of experience we term *psychotic,* dissociation is often inseparably related to these. Primary process, which need not be considered a lesser form of thought (Lewis, 1981), often interlaces with dissociative conditions. Indeed, "dissociative thought disorder" (Lowenstein, 1991) can describe psychotic-like dissociative phenomena that are not indicative of schizophrenia. They can involve bizarre perceptions, such as flashbacks and other auditory and visual hallucinations that the experiencer does not believe to occur "outside the head." A trauma/dissociation model helps us to understand flashbacks as evoked capsules of dissociated and often implicit memory. Terr (1990) terms certain visual hallucinations *posttraumatic misperception* (p. 131). Although most of us do not experience hallucinations and flashbacks, we are likely to have dissociative psychotic moments when a cue or "trigger" evokes a state of mind contexted in state-dependent memory such that we misperceive or misinterpret in accordance with anticipatory fears.

Kluft (1987), Ross (1989), and Putnam (1997) have outlined how dissociative disturbances have often been misunderstood in terms of schizophrenia concepts. In a landmark study, Kluft (1987) found that patients with multiple personality disorder (now called dissociative identity disorder) endorsed 8 of the 11 Schneiderian (Schneider, 1959, cited in Kluft, 1987, p. 2) first-rank symptoms considered to be pathognomonic of schizophrenia. These symptoms were voices arguing, voices commenting on one's action, influences playing on the body, thought withdrawal, thought insertion, "made" impulses, "made" feelings, and "made" volitional acts. The hallucinated voices and the "made" actions are understood as the activities of an alter, rather than as indications of schizophrenia. Dell (accepted for publication) has incorporated these Schneiderian passive influence symptoms in his Multiaxial Inventory of Dissociation (MID) diagnostic questionnaire.

Dissociation Cross-Culturally

The human capacity for dissociation can manifest itself differently in accordance with the relational patterns, opportunities, and constraints of different cultures (Cardena, 2001). In many cultures, altered mental states, switching of mental states, "possession," and trance phenomena are considered desirable rather than pathological (Kirmayer, 1994). For example, shamanism involves a self-hypnotic trance state. Dissociative altered states can provide socially acceptable ways of expressing extremely intense feeling such as in *attaques de nervos* in Puerto Rico (Lewis-Fernandez, 1994) and of accessing highly unusual abilities, such as clairvoyance. In many cultures the dissociative abilities of mediums are highly valued, and certainly not considered pathological (Krippner, 1990). Throughout the world and throughout history, dissociative trances have been a part of many community religious ceremonies and have contributed to many personal, mystical religious experiences of rapture, ecstasy, agony, and transformation (James, 1902).

Various kinds of dissociative experiences have been well-known throughout history. For instance, records of the Society for Psychical Research, which in the late 19th century included members such as James, Janet, and even Freud as a corresponding member, indicate the spontaneous occurrences of trances, state-specific memory, and trance speaking without the use of hypnosis, during and before the 19th century (Alvarado, 2002). One particular kind of dissociative trance, possession trance, has also been well known throughout history. This includes both benign spirit possession and demon possession (Hilgard, 1977; Levine, 1997; Cardena, 2001). In many cultures, possession trance provides socially accepted ways for the powerless to exert some power and influence, and to get their needs met, often in otherwise almost intolerable socially oppressive circumstances (Ross, 1989). For example, it can be a highly efficacious, culturally accepted means of handling familial problems, such as difficult in-laws. Lewis-Fernandez (1994) describes such a case in India in which a powerless new bride was possessed by the spirit of a deceased relative. The spirit instructed the in-laws to treat the daughter-in-law with more respect and provide her with better care. Because the in-laws respected and feared the spirit, the possession syndrome also allowed the daughter-in-law greater control over her life.

Syndromes of Distress

Although none of the above are necessarily understood in terms of psychiatric illness, some culturally defined dissociation-based syndromes do cause impairment and distress and are recognized as pathological. For example, some indigenous disorders indicate cultural variations of learned dissociation. One such culture-bound syndrome is "amok," which often involves a sudden rampage ending in homicide and amnesia (Rhodes, 2003). Notable among these are certain dissociative reactions to startle stimuli, characterized by compulsive imitation of words and acts of others, called *latah* in Indonesian languages, *bah-tschi* in Thailand, *yaun* in Myanmar, *mali-mali* in the Phillippines, *miryachit* in Siberia, *imu* among the Ainu, and *Lapp panic* among the Sami (Somer, 2003, pp. 3, 12). However, even among those syndromes recognized as pathological, it is not always understood that these syndromes have their basis in dissociation.

Possession is listed in the World Health Organization's 1992 International Classification of Diseases (Krippner, 1990). Spirit possession—especially demon possession—may express important conflicts and cause sufficient distress to self and others to be considered pathological. For instance, one of Janet's famous cases, that of Achilles, involved demon possession linked to guilt about an extramarital affair. Janet induced the demon state to speak to him (Janet), and then to demonstrate his power by placing the patient (the host) under hypnosis, which Janet had been unable to do. With the host under hypnosis by the demon, Janet was able to discover the tormented man's guilty secret (Ellenberger, 1970). Ellenberger speculates that "instances of multiple personality may have existed long ago, but remained unnoticed" (p. 127).[3] In Western civilization, possession trances were common until they began to come under the medical domain and were considered symptoms of mental disease (Ross, 1989).

Somer (2004) documents the occurrence of trance possession in 16th-century Near Eastern Judaism, in which the phenomenology of these possession experiences is very similar to that of DID as currently understood. These possessions involved the *dybbuk*, a spirit of a departed one that clung to the possessed person. In his study of the records of exorcisms, he noted that the spirits, who were in these cases male, often entered and exited their victims' bodies through the vagina and the rectum, suggesting sexual intercourse. He concludes, "By allowing individuals to communicate about their forbidden secrets and inner conflicts through a 'non-me' agent, the dybbuk may have enabled ventilation and some processing of otherwise inexpressible traumatic and/or guilt-promoting experiences" (pp. 142–143).

Our Own Dissociogenic Culture

Referring to our own culture, Greaves (1980) wrote that fewer than 200 cases of multiple personality disorder had been reported in over 200 years of psychiatric literature. Perhaps many were misdiagnosed as schizophrenia, and then later as borderline (Howell, 2002). Of course since 1980, the numbers of people diagnosed with DID have vastly increased. Today, Hollywood is fascinated by DID (Butler and Palesh, 2004). In a fascinating review, Steve Gold (2004a) addresses *Fight Club*'s depiction of our own dissociogenic culture. The opening scene of this movie is a montage of scenes from airports and airplanes: "This is your life, ending one moment at a time. . . . If you wake up at different time, in a different place, could you wake up as a different person?" (Gold, 2004a, p. 21). Thus, the primary message of the movie is not that Tyler Durden, the main character, discovers that he has DID, but that the violence of contemporary culture has created a normative pathological dissociation.

Differentiating Multiplicity and Dissociation in Culture

In contrast to normal pathological dissociation, flexible multiplicity would be a desirable normative condition for the human mind. Differentiating multiplicity and dissociation, Colin Ross (1999) counterposes the more familiar bipolar continuum model, according to which the unified self represents the healthy pole, and a multiple, dissociated self represents the pathological end of the pole, with an alternate model that puts adaptive, flexible multiplicity at the healthy end of the pole, pathological pseudounity in the midrange of psychopathology, and DID, with its greater dissociation, but not greater multiplicity, at the extreme end of psychopathology. Similarly, Rivera (1996) suggests a continuum on which the robust multiplicity is at the healthy end of the continuum and the fragile self, which can be characterized by either pathological dissociation or pathological association is at the other end: "Defensive association pretends to simple unity to hide fragmentation, suppression, and complex humanity in all its contradictory manifestations. Defensive dissociation acknowledges the depth and complexity of the human condition through the interplay of a multitude of self-states, but denies it utterly at the same time through radical disconnection" (p. 34). Gold (2004b) interprets Rivera to mean that "'normal' people maintain a sense of integration and continuity . . . by systematically and routinely invoking processes that enable them to ignore the glaring gaps, inconsistencies, and lack of continuity in their experiences and behavior." Gold's own continuum puts this "normality" between an ideal mindfulness at the healthy end of the pole and fragmentation at the pathological end.

Two Myths: Cain and Osiris

Two great myths of civilization depict different prototypical psychological responses to the terror of brother murdering brother. These are the story of Cain and Abel, and the myth of Osiris. Cain and Abel were the children of Adam and Eve. Cain slew Abel, and hence, as his descendants, we inherit this identification. According to Genesis, Cain was cast out from the presence of God, and made to wander the earth. Ross (1989) observed that one solution to this dilemma is to push this sense of ourselves as murderous *down*—either into the id and the unconscious as Freud believed, or into Hell. In these nether regions, we are all renegades of civilization. This solution also appears to characterize a patriarchy that values a solitary independent self.

In contrast to the Cain and Abel story in the myth of Osiris, there is a very active, helpful sister. Whereas Abel simply died, Osiris is a survivor. In Egyptian mythology, Osiris, the god who symbolized the imperishability of life, was killed and cut up into many pieces by his brother, Set. His wife/sister, Isis, gathered together the scattered fragments of her husband, embalmed him, made him whole and resurrected him as king/god of the underworld. Later, his son, Horus, defeated Set, and Horus became king on earth. Here we find the themes of fragmentation, healing, and resurrection or transcendence into a new form.

In contrast to the legacy of Cain, the Osiris myth comes ready-made with a language of parts and an expected outcome of healing, connection, and continuity. Ross (1989) suggests that the Osiris complex as a metaphor of psychological dissociation may achieve prominence alongside the Oedipus complex as a model of repression. It gives us a language for understanding impediments to loving, authentic, satisfying life, and it helps us to understand these as outcomes of our early relationships with significant other people.

It is the Isis-like healing aspect of ourselves that allows us to recognize how we may often mistake the self-state, or particular organization of self-states that has provided the most security, for the "self." The Isis-like healing allows us to take a metaperspective on the self as an aggregation of self-states, and to understand that privileging the self- states that pursue security is not always necessary.

Rather than a unitary place, the unconscious might better be understood as containing rageful and murderous parts of ourselves, as well as parts that have all kinds of longings. Most of what we have understood as the unconscious is better described as the dissociative unconscious or, as Janet did, as multiple centers of consciousness. Bromberg (1998) argues that we are moving away from Freud's unitary conscious and unconscious, which are archeologically layered with respect to access to awareness, toward a "conception of mind as a non-linear, dialectical process of meaning construction . . . a view of the mind as a configuration of discontinuous, shifting states, with varying degrees of access to perception and cognition" (p. 225). As Davies (1996) observes, "we deal not with one unconscious, but with multiple levels of consciousness and unconsciousness—a multiply organized, associationally linked network of meaning attribution and understanding" (p. 562). The dissociative unconscious is not necessarily linked to forgetting over time (Bowers, 1994), but to contemporaneous, subjective realities that alternate as foreground and background.

2

THE SELF IN CONTEXT
Unity and Multiplicity

The "self" is plural, variegated, polyphonic, and multivoiced. We experience an illusion of unity as a result of the mind's capacity to fill in the blanks and to forge links.

Our intellectual heritage includes both unity and multiplicity. Often these two visions of the self seem to switch, like a Necker cube, as if one view repudiates the other. This is not necessary, however, for the self is characterized by a complex multiplicity of subunits and subselves, and is itself a part of larger systems (Erdelyi, 1994). The self can be a whole with reference to its constituent parts, and a part with reference to larger wholes.

From Multiplicity to Unity to Multiplicity Again

Psychoanalysis traces its origins to the study of dualism and multiplicity—in the observations of "double consciousness" of hysteria (Breuer and Freud, 1893–1895). Double consciousness implies dual centers of conscious and unconscious mental activity. But Freud soon abandoned belief in "double consciousness," adopting instead his construct of *the* (unitary) unconscious. However, the construct of subconscious subselves accommodates the same phenomena: lack of awareness of information held in another part of the self, and either dynamic clash or harmony between these subselves. Psychoanalysis, whose raison d'être depends so much on the existence of unconscious phenomena, may, according to Grotstein (1999a), "have suffered from Freud's failure to grasp the deeper significance of . . . dual consciousness or dual 'I'-ness, in which consciousness and unconsciousness, or ego and id (and superego) are each individual 'I's separately and compositely" (p. 36).

Some psychological writings at the beginning of the century, such as those of Janet, Jung, and James, emphasized dividedness of self-experience: Jung in his theories of complexes and archetypes, and

James (1890, 1902) in his interest in dissociation and altered states. However, with the rise of both behaviorism and psychoanalysis, the multiple self faded from public view (Hilgard, 1977; Kihlstrom, 1984). For most of the last century, psychoanalytic theory has tended to emphasize the "linear perspective on development and developmental arrests," as well as to assume that the infant "begins life with a whole, or integral, self, at least in potentiality" (Mitchell, 1993, p. 128). In psychology, traditions have tended to focus on traits (which are conceptualized as stable, enduring characteristics of the unitary individual, and which can differ among individuals) rather than on states (different organizations of the self within individuals) (Putnam, 1997).

In the late 20th century, Hilgard (1977, 1994) began to observe what he called the "hidden observer" in hypnosis demonstrations and experiments. The hidden observer is a hidden part of the self that appears to be aware of information that is unavailable to the hypnotized part. For instance, in a person who has been hypnotized to be anesthetized to pain, a dissociated, "hidden observer" may feel the pain, even though the normal consciousness is anesthetized. According to Watkins and Watkins (1997), most people have this capacity for inherent dividedness of the mind. Hilgard went on to develop the neodissociation model of the mind, which relies on multiple, parallel subsystems of information processing.

Due to a confluence of multiple trends, among which are the growth of relational theory, the resurgence of traumatology, and postmodernism, concepts of the multiple self have recently proliferated. Today we find an increasing emphasis on multiplicity and the plural psyche (Watkins, 1986; Bromberg, 1991, 1993, 1994, 1995, 1996a, b, 1998, 2000, 2001a, b, 2003a, b; Davies and Frawley, 1991, 1994; Slavin and Kreigman, 1992; Mitchell, 1993; Schwartz, 1994, 2000; Davies, 1996, 1998a, b, 2004; Flax, 1996; Harris, 1996; Stern, 1997; Pizer, 1998).

The Illusion of Unity of the Self

Research in cognitive psychology, neurophysiology, and child development indicates that the brain, the mind, and the self are normally multiple and that the idea of the unity of self is an illusion (Gazzaniga, 1985; Dennett, 1991; Erdelyi, 1994; Kirmayer, 1994; Siegel, 1999; Le Doux, 2002). We fill in the gaps of experience; we imagine ourselves in control of our hearts and minds when we are not.

Neurobiologists increasingly understand the brain as a modular system, with each module characterized by a high degree of autonomy (Lancaster, 1999). Le Doux (2002) compares the brain to a parallel computer that can perform various computations simultaneously. Like the parallel computer, the brain is organized into neural systems that to some degree function independently of one another. Le Doux marvels at "how fragile a patch job (the self) is" (p. 304). Gazzaniga (1985), who was Le Doux's mentor, also views consciousness as modularistic, and says that the notion of "linear unified conscious experience is dead wrong" (p. 4). Parallel and multitrack processing may help to explain dissociative experiences on a neurological level. With regard to parallel processing in the brain, Dennett (1991) remarks that the incomprehension and disbelief that many people exhibit about the existence of multiple personality may be due to a "simple arithmetical mistake: they have failed to notice that two or three or seventeen selves per body is really not more metaphysically extravagant than one self per body" (p. 419).

Norretranders (1998), who compares the brain to the computer, writes of the "user illusion" we have about the unity of consciousness. We have the illusion that what we see on the screen and what we have in consciousness represents everything that is potentially available even though it is only a minuscule fraction of the information processed. Putnam's (1997) DBS model outlines how, starting in infancy, behavior is organized as a set of discrete behavioral states, which become optimally linked over time. The ultimate seamless transitions between these states lead to the illusion that most of us have of a unitary self. Because trauma and neglect impede this linkage, and because trauma may create more unlinked states, some severely traumatized individuals, such as those with dissociative identity disorder, do not have this comforting illusion.

According to Siegel (1999), "studies in child development suggest, in fact, that the idea of a unitary, continuous 'self' is actually an illusion our minds attempt to create. . . . We have multiple and varied 'selves,' which are needed to carry out the many and diverse activities of our lives" (p. 231). Each of these selves has a state of mind or mental state as a building block. Siegel defines a state of mind as the "total pattern of activations in the brain at a particular moment in time" (p. 208). "These basic states of mind are clustered into specialized subselves, that have an enduring pattern of activity across time. . . . When a state of mind is repeatedly activated, it may become a 'self-state' or specialized self" (p. 231). These repeatedly activated self-states then gain a sense of continuity that creates the "experience of mind" (p. 231).

Postmodernism and Multiplicity

Postmodernism addresses the inseparability of context from what we "know," and thereby implies the inherent unavoidable multiplicity of the self. Postmodernism is characterized by the abandonment of the belief in positivism, the scientific faith of the Enlightenment, which itself replaced religious dogma as truth. According to positivism, "objective" knowledge is obtainable and scientific theory can adequately represent reality so as to render it accurately knowable. Postmodernism disputes the representation paradigm, including the idea that there is a single empirical pregiven world and that knowledge consists in mirroring or mapping it. Postmodernism, then, instead of asking what are the facts, asks how we construct our knowledge. Postmodernism argues that we cannot know the nature of reality for certain—we only have differing constructions of reality, which are themselves based on the context of the knower. More and more it has been demonstrated that scientific knowledge depends on context. For instance, in the 1920s Heisenberg articulated his uncertainty principle, according to which one cannot know the location and velocity of an electron simultaneously because the process of measurement affects what is to be measured. Thus, the result of an observation cannot be separated from the process. "Subject and object are inextricably linked" (Gergen, 1991, p. 89).

People actively construct their perceptions of the world, and they do so in accordance with personal context and culture (Gergen, 1991). Our understanding of the world is based on consensually agreed on social constructions. Postmodernism shifts the focus of analysis away from attempts to reveal "essences" and the assumed coherent internality to interpersonal and social contexts. Power relationships and language construct our subjectivities and our identities. Thus, postmodernism also involves the deconstruction of language and the elucidation of hidden contexts. Postmodernism is characterized by simultaneous pluralism, rather than serial pluralism (Rappoport, Baumgardner, and Boone, 1999). For instance, developmental theories have tended to describe a vertical, hierarchically organized transition through set developmental states. Postmodern developmental theory more often calls on concepts of "both/and." Hence, the postmodern emphasis on diversity, the plural self, and multiplicity.

Consistent with the emphasis on context rather than isolated objective facts, the therapist no longer functions as a monologic dispenser of "truth" to the patient, as was the ideal for Freud. In the postmodern approach to psychotherapy and psychoanalysis, meaning is mutually coconstructed by patient and therapist (Mitchell, 1993).

Social and Relational Contexts and Multiplicity

Much of memory is state-dependent. As contexts change, so do our views of ourselves and others. Contexts often provide cues for the evocation of "states." Certain memories are recalled more easily or evoked by certain states that are linked to specific contexts, such as when a person is in the same mental state as that in which the learning or the first event occurred.

The self is contextually and relationally embedded. Slavin and Kriegman (1992) have developed an evolutionary hypothesis according to which they believe that humans are likely to have evolved a psychic structure fostering multiplicity–in particular, an adaptive design that provides the capacity for shifting multiple versions of the self in relation to the social environment. Multiplicity, the encoding of our inner divisions "in the form of semicohesive 'alternate selves' . . . may serve as a crucial adaptive capacity or vehicle for knowing enough about the other." The capacity for multiplicity is adaptive to the "inherent inconsistencies, biases, and contradictions found in every parental environment" (Slavin, 1996, p. 623). As Mitchell (1993) notes, "if the self is always embedded in relational contexts, either actual or internal, then all important motives have appeared and taken on life and form in the presence and through the reactions of significant others" (p. 134).

The Dialogical Self and Polypsychism

The self-contained Cartesian mind is a single container that becomes filled with knowledge and is unresponsive to others. It is necessarily monological (Shotter, 1999). In contrast, the post-Cartesian self is dialogical and understood as constructed by context and by language. Bakhtin (1981) developed the idea that everything we say is relationally responsive. Language, he said,

> for the individual consciousness, is on the borderline between oneself and the other. The word in language is half someone else's. It becomes "one's own" only when the speaker populates it with his own intention. . . . Prior to the moment of appropriation, the word does not exist in a neutral and impersonal language . . . but rather it exists in other people's mouths, in other people's contexts, serving other people's intentions: it is from there that we must take the word and make it our own [pp. 293–294].

In addition, the style in which we speak is based on how we imagine the other person will receive what we say (Bakhtin, 1986). The *dialogical self,* a term used by Hermans, Kempen, and Van Loon (1992), in contrast to the notion of the individualistic self, "is based on the assumption that there are many 'I' positions that can be occupied by the same person. The dialogical self is conceived of as social . . . in the sense that other people occupy positions in the multivoiced self" (p. 29).

Implications of Internalized Object Relationships for Polypsychism

Several theorists' descriptions of the divided self—such as Freud's, Jung's, Klein's, and Winnicott's—have suggested polypsychism. But I think that Ogden's (1983) development of the implications of Fairbairn's endopsychic model, described in the previous chapter, has most decidedly set the stage for polypsychism as considered from the perspective of internalized object relationships.

Ogden (1986) observed that the idea of an internalized object must include the assumption of an internalized object relationship. In each of these internalized object relationships, both the self component and the object component have subjectivity. Once we take this step, the stage for polypsychism is set. Object relationships become the basic units, which can be linked to each other—with varying degrees of success, in a now, by definition, multiple self. There is an important difference between conceptualizing internalization as involving a single self internalizing an object (or objects), and conceptualizing a multiple self as internalizing relationships.

This conclusion has some similarity to Ryle's (2002) view (discussed in chapter 5) of internalized reciprocal role relationships. It is not a person or a quality that is internalized, but a role relationship. We all live out multiple role relationships, and these populate our experiences of ourselves.

From Segregated States to Coherent Linkages

As mentioned earlier, Putnam's (1997) DBS model deals with behavioral states, which were discrete in infancy and become linked over time, contributing to the later smooth transitions between states. Following Wolff (1987), Putnam describes how in infancy, various behavioral states, such as sleep and waking, eating and digestive elimination, are initially discrete, but in time become linked in sequences. There are orderly transitions, or "switches," which involve discontinuous jumps from one state to another, for example from fussiness to crying. Early on, these discrete "state/acts" are clearly biological states, involving such biological activity as eating and elimination. As states begin to succeed each other in orderly sequences, the transitions between them become regularly linked. As these linkages become more complex, the child gains the ability for self-modulation and recovery from disruptions.

The learning of state modulation is a highly social process. Sharing of states is an aspect of bonding. As children acquire control over their behavioral states with maturation, their different "selves" can be volitionally activated. Aiding in this is the development of what Putnam (1997) has called the "authorial self," appearing at about two to four years of age, which is independent of context or state and which can select and emphasize aspects of self. This capacity is clearly expressed in fantasy play, in which children pretend to be different selves, thereby unlinking sense of self from a given context.

The Effect of Trauma on Linking

Pizer (1998) sees the "universal structure of the human psyche" as like a "virtually infinite multiplicity of nuclei, or islands" (p. 72). Pizer observes that the problem is not the multiplicity, but that at times different parts, perspectives, or individuals proceed as if the other were not there: "At severe levels of shock and discrepancy . . . paradox becomes unbridgeable, and one deploys the default mechanism of dissociation. Here we recognize the essence of trauma: the disruption of the continuity of being (the 'illusion of being one self')" (pp. 141–142).

Dissociative identity disorder (DID) illustrates one extreme of trauma-interrupted linking and trauma-created multiple states. Dissociative identities often represent adaptations to certain contexts that contained so much terror and pain that they could not be linked. In severe dissociation, switches in identity state are often accompanied by somatic changes. Characteristic facial expressions can markedly change; physiological allergic reactivity can change; visual acuity can change; voice quality can change (Putnam, 1997); and even PET scans can demonstrate changes in the brain in different identity states (Nijenhuis, 2003).

Animal Identities

Even more markedly than human dissociative identities, animal identity states illustrate the powerful effect of unlinked structuring of self-identity according to context. Various circumstances can contribute to the adoption of an animal identity. As Goodwin and Attias (1999) note, the child may have been treated like an animal, or may have witnessed a beloved pet murdered in order to enforce their own silence, such that there is an identification through loss. The child may have been involved in sexual experiences with animals, leading to self-labeling as *bestial*. Animals may have been experienced as protectors, peers, or both in an environment where there was no protection and animals were among the only friends. While in animal identity states, people may feel like that animal and exhibit animal-like behaviors, such as running on all fours, scratching, growling, crawling, licking, or eating like an animal (Putnam, 1989; Goodwin and Attias, 1999). Also, animal calls heard inside the head (Goodwin and Attias, 1999), or visual flashbacks involving animal identities, may intrude into consciousness.

As Goodwin and Attias (1999) say, "these animal representations and internalizations provide a coherent set of metaphors for expressing unspeakable cruelty" (p. 262). They cogently observe that these images convey how the children perceived the "abuse as a violation at the level of a transgression of natural law, which calls into question not only their status as member of the family and as a 'good' member of the community, but also their status as a member of the human race" (p. 262).

My patient Janice experiences herself at times as a fish and as different kinds of snakes. She grew up on a coastal city where living fish were plentiful. At times she wakes up from sleep, unable to use her arms or legs, and feeling that she is wriggling like a fish. Perhaps the brutal way she was treated, often with her arms and legs pinned down, made her feel like a "beast of prey," and she understood this feeling in terms of something with which she was more familiar—as if she were one of the fish that were so much a part of her home environment. But the context of ruthless domination is built into her dyadic animal identity constructions: Sometimes she is afraid to go into the bathroom because she sees in there a big fish and a little fish. The little fish is no longer flapping around, but is now half-dead. At the times she had these experiences, she also felt half-dead, with no strength or energy. However, she also switches into snake identities. And snakes were not so plentiful where she grew up. Clearly, some of these represent identification with her abuser, specifically with the penis. Indeed, she has at times hallucinated her abuser as a six-foot-long snake in bed with her. She also has a cobra identity that she experiences as a protector. Sometimes in the sessions, when she switches to this identity, her face and chest puff up, almost as one would imagine a cobra. During the time of Janice's abuse when she was held as a household and sexual slave in a strange land far away from her home, there was no human being—other than another little girl at school, when she was allowed to go—to whom she could turn for empathetic understanding or help.

Most of our time in treatment is in my listening to her story; at times being on the other end of the phone line when she leaves a message about another flashback about a time in which she was treated in a subhuman fashion, and then left alone in unendurable pain, perhaps to die. She is not focally interested in the metaphorical meaning of her animal identities. She just wants the continual pain in the constant reminders of the flashbacks and other intrusions to go away. However, her animal identities are an important way of *telling*. In cases like this, words cannot completely convey the extremity of indescribable pain that Janice experienced. Only metaphors can approach this. But these metaphors also contain within them a truth about herself that is self-differentiating: In contrast to her captors, who were cold-blooded and reptilian, she is warm-blooded, despite everything that happened to her. Even though sometimes she feels that she is a reptile, she is not; her abusers were reptilian.

Of course, mythology is filled with tales of people being transformed into animals, which may depend on similar psychological processes. The witch, Circe, in *The Odyssey,* transforms unsuspecting men into pigs; Pinocchio is changed into a donkey; children are turned into toads or birds; and so on. These stories can be very frightening, but we, the readers, know that the story is a "pretend" one. Even Kafka's story of becoming a cockroach has an as-if, metaphorical intent, although, as Goodwin and Attias (1999) have so compellingly suggested, Kafka may have been close to experiencing himself as "as" rather than "as if." A person with dissociated animal identity states experiences the animal identity as singularly and strikingly real. No "as ifs" about it. These serial identities as animals have not been synthesized so that the metaphor "I was treated like an animal" could be fully comprehended and responded to.

The Healing Power of Narration and Listening

So how do mental states become linked? Mental states are linked to each other by links to other people, often by narration. Siegel (1999) notes that the sharing of a personal narrative with an intimate other fosters self-coherence. Breuer and Freud (1893–1895) found that Anna O got better when she "talked herself out," and she called that therapy the "talking cure." When a person's story is told to an accepting other, a link is made between the traumatic moment and the reality of the current relationship, rendering the traumatic event more "real."

But it is not only the narration. *Listening* is just as necessary for the creation of dialogical links. Parts of the self (self-states) need to be able to "hear" or be responsive to the affects of and wishes of other states. Bakhtin (1984) describes how Dostoyevsky's work can serve as a model for the vibrant, conflictual, but ultimately coherent multiple self. The characters of his multivoiced, "polyphonic novel" resonate with our own many different "I" positions. Even through their many moments of vehement discord, the characters authenticate the others' independent perspectives. Dostoyevsky's work is cohesive and vibrant because of the interaction and inviolable connection of the characters with each other.

As in Dostoyevsky's novels, the pivotal issue is not multiplicity versus unity, and not even the degree to which multiple parts are dissociated, but the degree to which a metaperspective can encompass conflict, and the degree to which an ultimate resolution of "negotiated" (Schwartz, 1994) harmony among variously contexted self-states can be achieved. Unity as a concept is differentiated from that of coherence and (ideal) harmony among constituent parts. What problematic dissociation does is to disrupt this ideally "harmonious functioning of the multiplicity that makes up human consciousness" (Rivera, 1996, p. 32). The self is characterized by a complex multiplicity of subunits and subselves (Erdelyi, 1994), and even the multiple parts themselves have parts, but the important issue is not how many parts there are, but how they hang together.

3

PIONEERS OF PSYCHODYNAMIC THINKING ABOUT DISSOCIATION
Janet, Freud, Ferenczi, and Fairbairn

> Man, all too proud, figures that he is the master of his movements, his words, his ideas and Himself. It is perhaps of ourselves that we have the least command. There are crowds of things which operate within ourselves without our will.
>
> —Pierre Janet

This chapter takes us into the psychodynamic thinking of the pioneers of dissociation theory: Janet, Freud, Ferenczi, and Fairbairn. Janet was the first to link dissociation with psychological trauma and to articulate a theory of subconscious psychic determinism. He developed a psychodynamic theory premised on multiple centers of consciousness. Although Freud's early writing reflects the influence of Janet, his own thinking focused on defense from the start. Freud was thinking in terms of dissociation, but he pursued different forms of dissociationism than Janet (Erdelyi, 1994). Four types of Freudian dissociationism are outlined: splitting of consciousness, splits between conscious and unconscious, splits between the ego and the superego, and splits within the ego itself.

Ferenczi, whose early work adopted Freudian premises, later broke with Freud. In his better known later work he presented a radically different view of the etiology and structure of the traumatized psyche, eloquently describing the fragmentation of the mind in response to trauma. As had the early Freud, Ferenczi (1949) became aware of the frequency of child abuse, and he wrote about the profoundly dissociative outcomes: "There is neither shock nor fright without some splitting of the personality" (p. 229). Especially in his now famous "Confusion of Tongues" paper, he cogently articulated how the experience of the relationship with the aggressor is internalized. Even though Ferenczi understood these psychic shocks to occur in relational contexts, his theory, like Janet's, was trauma based. In contrast, Fairbairn was the first to articulate the schism of the personality (the schizoid condition) as explicitly proceeding from problematic attachment relationships. In this way Fairbairn's work anticipates modern attachment theory, with its concepts of segregated internal working models and disorganized attachment.

Pierre Janet

We are all children of Salpetriere.
—Bessel van der Kolk

Janet (1859–1947) is the primary theorist on whose shoulders we stand when it comes to dissociation (Van der Hart and Friedman, 1989; Van der Kolk and Van der Hart, 1989). Janet was quite well known in his time, a sought-after clinician and an eminent scholar. His ideas about dissociation were fascinating to many of his contemporaries, such as William James and Morton Prince (Ellenberger, 1970; Kihlstrom, 1984). Janet has innumerable discoveries to his credit, and he wrote many famous case histories, as well as an extremely large number of publications on a variety of psychological topics. His published work is estimated to be at least 17,000 printed pages (Prevost, 1973, cited in Van der Hart and Friedman 1989). Despite this, his work has long been ignored. Indeed, his work has often been vehemently, if also at times, unobtrusively, discredited. Many texts introducing abnormal psychology do not mention Janet at all; if they do, it is often extremely brief or in a way that suggests Janet is not worth reading. Much of Janet's work has not been translated into English, and some has not even been reprinted. However, at present, Janet is becoming better known and more fairly credited. This is largely due to Ellenberger's (1970) reintroduction of his work, and to the recognition of what we now call posttraumatic stress–related and dissociative disorders. In the more recent past, many articles by Van der Hart, Van der Kolk, Nijenhuis, and Steele in particular, have presented and clarified the relevancy of Janet's concepts, and have developed the implications of these concepts.

It is rather astounding to consider how much Janet formulated and how much he understood in extremely sophisticated ways more than a century ago. Many of his concepts predate and anticipate current views of dissociative processes. Janet was the first to explain the link between trauma and dissociation and to use these concepts to explain the many symptoms included under the rubric of hysteria (Van der Kolk and Van der Hart, 1989; Nijenhuis and Van der Hart, 1999a). According to Van der Hart and Dorahy (accepted for publication), "of the many theorists of dissociation, Pierre Janet (1859–1947) unquestionably presented the most detailed and articulate account of the connection between division of the personality or consciousness (that is, dissociation) and hysteria." Hysteria was not one entity but included what we understand today as PTSD, somatoform dissociation, dissociative disorders, chronic and complex trauma disorders, borderline, and histrionic personality disorders (Lowenstein, 1990). Although convulsive hysterical attacks had been described by philosophers and doctors of ancient Greece, as well as in the Middle Ages, the Renaissance, and the 17th, 18th, and 19th centuries (Janet, 1907, p. 14), and although hysterical and dissociative reactions had been described in the 19th-century psychiatric literature (Van der Kolk and Van der Hart, 1989), Janet linked the occurrence of hysteria to previously unassimilated traumatic memories. He emphasized the various and complex ways in which dissociated memories of trauma could be expressed, such as in sensory perceptions, affect states, intrusive thoughts, and behavioral reenactments. In particular, Janet showed how traumatic memories are encoded in the body and how these traumatic memories consist of sensorimotor and affective components which have been labeled *positive somatoform dissociative symptoms* by Nijenhuis (1999) and Nijenhuis and Van der Hart (1999b).

Janet's work anticipated the current formulation of PTSD: He understood the biphasic nature of traumatic intrusion and numbing, now considered to be key aspects of PTSD (Nijenhuis and Van der Hart, 1999a). In particular, he noticed how the extreme agitation characterizing reenactments of trauma in patients alternates with emotional exhaustion, depression, and loss of will, as contemporary researchers and clinicians working with trauma have also found (Van der Kolk and Van der Hart, 1989). Janet also anticipated current knowledge about state-dependent learning, showing that traumatic information is often best retrieved when the person is in a state similar to the one in which the memory was encoded (Nijenhuis and Van der Hart, 1999a).

Janet introduced the term *subconscious* as well as many other concepts in current usage in psychoanalysis. For instance, his concept of "fixed ideas" underlay Jung's "complexes" (Janet, 1925; Ellenberger,

1970). Piaget, who was one of Janet's students, relied heavily on Janet's ideas about assimilation and accommodation. Bleuler's concept of schizophrenia owed much to Janet's concept of psychasthenia (Ellenberger, 1970, p. 406). Janet's theory of dissociation influenced Hilgard's (1977) neodissociation theory.

Many of Janet's concepts are implicit in current trauma and dissociation theory. Yet many of his rich insights and conceptual formulations are currently being explicitly applied to conceptualizations and theory regarding trauma, dissociation, and personality organization. For instance, Van der Hart et al. (2004) have integrated Janet's structural model with certain other theoretical systems, in their theory of the structural dissociation of the personality, a new theory that clarifies the meaning of the term *dissociation* and delimits the scope of the concept. Nijenhuis (1999, 2000) and Nijenhuis and Van der Hart (1999a, b) have articulated and further developed many of Janet's concepts about the inextricable interrelationship of mind and body, in discussions of what is currently labeled *somatoform dissociation*. Janet's writing contains a storehouse of useful and currently applicable formulations, which work very well when one is thinking about trauma. For instance, his concept of the retraction of the field of consciousness, written about extensively by Van der Hart, Nijenhuis, and their colleagues (2004), which refers to the narrowing or reduction of information that can be held in the mind at one time, applies to how the traumatized person becomes narrowly focused on only the most threatening cues during the trauma. This phenomenon, along with consequent storage of other information in other dissociated states of consciousness may have considerable bearing on how we understand identification with the aggressor (see chapter 7, on splitting).

Janet's writings about hysteria, trauma, and dissociation spanned more than half a century, and he continually expanded on his concepts regarding the impact of dissociation on mental illness during that time. However, the key premise of his theory on trauma and dissociation is that when people are terrified or overwhelmed by extreme emotion, they are unable to assimilate the experience into already existing mental frameworks, and are therefore unable to link the experience with the rest of personal history. Overwhelming terror or overwhelming "vehement emotion" interrupts the coherence of experience; as a result, the synthesizing functions of the psyche fail. This is still the key premise of trauma theory today.

Janet's conceptualizations regarding the workings of subconscious "systems of ideas and functions" can enable clinicians to understand a wide variety of psychological disturbances better. His understanding of the dynamic interrelationships among these different systems provides a long-neglected, but highly usable paradigm for a dynamic and psychoanalytic psychology that is premised on the recognition of multiple centers of consciousness.

Functional Losses and Intrusions: Mental Stigmata and Mental Accidents

Janet was "post-Cartesian" over a century ago, in his basic categorization of the symptoms of hysteria. Instead of a mind–body system of classification, he used a phenomenological one (Nijenhuis, 1999). He understood the symptoms of hysteria in terms of functional losses, such as anesthesia and amnesia, and in terms of acute, transient, distressing, and often intrusive symptoms, such as flashbacks, intrusive thoughts, or sudden bodily experiences. He called these *mental stigmata* and *mental accidents,* respectively. The mental stigmata are enduring functional losses to the usual personal consciousness and are understood as negative dissociation symptoms; mental accidents tend to be intrusive positive dissociative symptoms (Van der Hart and Friedman, 1989; Nijenhuis, 1999; Nijenhuis and Van der Hart, 1999a, b). What characterizes both sets of phenomena, the mental stigmata and the mental accidents, is that they belong to "dissociated systems not perceived or processed by personal consciousness" (Nijenhuis, 1999, p. 14). These dissociated "systems of ideas and functions of the personality" have not been synthesized among each other or integrated within existing mental frameworks. They can range in complexity from a memory, emotion, or simple bodily experience to a dissociative identity state (Nijenhuis, 1999). These dissociated systems are the reason for the gaps or losses in perception and function (the negative symptoms); they are also behind the painful intrusive states (the positive symptoms). The losses, which are notable by the absence of perception or function, are only apparent because these experiences are generally found to be available to another dissociative part of the personality; the intrusions are transient phenomena, in which "one dissociated part of the personality temporarily enter(s) the psychobiological domain of another part" (Van der Hart et al., 2004).

Van der Kolk and Van der Hart (1989), Van der Hart (2000), and Van der Hart et al. (2000) have observed that these alternating losses and intrusions, avoidant and intrusive symptoms, characterize PTSD.

In this way Janet's work anticipated current formulations of PTSD. By taking the current PTSD formulation back to Janet, Van der Hart (2000) and Van der Hart et al. (2000) conclude that the presence of PTSD implies the presence of dissociation.

Automatisms and Fixed Ideas

In his 1889 book, *Psychological Automatism,* Janet addressed the topic of automatisms, actions that are performed automatically, without a person's awareness or conscious volition. Here he introduced the idea of subconsciousness and subconscious psychic determinism. Unlike most previous and other contemporary theorists, who held that automatisms were performed mechanistically and without consciousness (Ellenberger, 1970; Van der Hart and Friedman, 1989), Janet asserted that psychological automatisms are not mindless. Janet believed that, although they do not belong to the usual personal consciousness, psychological automatisms operate below the level of consciousness, subconsciously.

Janet observed that normally people integrate complex information, including experiences, views, habits, and skills into current cognitive schemata. These automatic adaptations, or automatisms, are basically nonconscious actions, including simple reflexes as well as complex skills (Van der Kolk and Van der Hart, 1989). However, emotional arousal can prevent the integration of traumatic memories, and frightening or novel experiences may not be integrated into the existing cognitive schemata. As a result, memories of these experiences may become split off from ordinary awareness and voluntary control. Such memories are stored automatically and become subconscious. Thus, these subconscious phenomena, which are both biologically and psychologically encoded, become isolated from personal consciousness and will, where they can be triggered by emotions and ideas (Van der Hart and Friedman, 1989; Van der Kolk and Van der Hart, 1989, p. 1532).

Psychological automatisms can be complete or partial. Somnambulistic states are examples of the former; tics and anesthesia, in which only part of the experience is subconscious, are examples of the latter (Van der Hart and Friedman, 1989).

Automatisms, which are actions, are intimately connected with fixed ideas, which are volatile thoughts or images that have become subconscious, yet can powerfully organize symptoms. The cause of fixed ideas is usually a traumatic event that the mind could not assimilate. The frightening or overwhelming event is not lost to the mind, but remains active, subconsciously, as a fixed idea that becomes a subconscious center around which other aspects of psychological experience may cohere. As Janet (1907) said, "things happen as if an idea, a partial system of thoughts, emancipated itself, became independent and developed itself on its own account" (p. 42).

Fixed ideas, which are traumatic memories, or fragments of past experience that are irrelevant to the present, continue to intrude on and influence behavior, consciousness, moods, affects, and perceptions, causing automatic reactions to stress (Van der Kolk and Van der Hart, 1989). Janet (1925) emphasized that fixed ideas belong to a mental system that is not subject to conscious will.

> The power of such ideas depends upon their isolation. They grow, they install themselves in the field of thought like a parasite, and the subject cannot check their development by any effort on his part, because they are ignored, because they exist by themselves in a second field of thought detached from the first [p. 600].

Janet observed that fixed ideas are also interconnected and feed on the weakness and depression created by trauma and dissociation.

> The actual memory of the happening was constituted by a system of psychological and physiological phenomena, of images and movements, of a multiform character. This system, persistent in the mind, soon began to encroach. By association, it annexed a number of images and movements which had at first been independent of its influence. Thus enriched, prepotent in an environment of other thoughts that had been enfeebled by the general depression, it became able to realize itself automatically without passing through the intermediate states of ideation and suggestions, and thus gave rise to actions, dispositions, sufferings, and delusions, of various kinds [p. 597].

Somatoform Dissociation

Because Janet's view of the inseparability of mind and body is at variance with the current mode of conceptualizing mental disorders (e.g., *The Diagnostic and Statistical Manual of Mental Disorders*), it is worth emphasizing here. Janet's cases demonstrated the somatic storage of traumatic memories and how traumatic memories may involve a range of sensorimotor phenomena. He expounded on how in difficulties in vision, speech, paralyses, and motor agitation, the "subconscious and automatic motion is retained, whereas the voluntary motion is lost" (Janet, 1907, p. 206). He noticed that hysterical patients can produce disabling somatoform symptoms of nonorganic causation without conscious awareness, and demonstrated how this magnificently complex performance is a subconscious one, one of a second consciousness. For example, he showed how glove anesthesia and other similar anesthesias, as well as paralyses, are displays of a nonphysician's view of what would be the appropriate physical rendition of the nerve or muscle groups in question (Janet, 1907).

Janet's concept of fixed ideas included psychobiological states. His classification system for the symptoms of hysteria (mental stigmata and mental accidents), which involved functional losses and intrusions, embraced a psychobiological understanding of these events—of how trauma is encrypted in the body and in motor actions.

Memory

Janet saw memory as a creative act in which a person categorizes events and assimilates them into cognitive schemata. In ideal circumstances, the memory system works harmoniously, such that emotions, thoughts, and actions are assessed and integrated into a unitary consciousness that is under voluntary control (Van der Kolk and Van der Hart, 1989). However, the "vehement emotions" brought on by trauma prevent this assimilation, resulting in dissociation, which precludes this "sorting out" aspect of memory. As a result, traumatized persons are often amnestic for the trauma, and are unable to associate the memory of it with the rest of their lives (Janet, 1894).

Janet distinguished between narrative memory and traumatic memory. In fact, he regarded the term *traumatic memory* a misnomer, because traumatic memories are not memories at all. Rather, they are unconscious reenactments: "It is only for convenience that we speak of it as a 'traumatic memory.' The subject is often incapable of making with regard to the event the recital which we speak of as a memory" (Janet, 1894, p. 661). Over a century ago, he recognized that traumatized people are unable to tell their stories in words, as we conventionally understand memory, but are often compelled to reenact them, often remaining unaware of what their behavior is saying.

Anticipating current psychological knowledge of memory, Janet (1925) stated that memory "is an action: essentially, it *is the action of telling a story*" (p. 661). Not only is the subject often incapable of making the recital that we speak of as a memory, but "he remains confronted by a difficult situation in which he has not been able to play a satisfactory part, one to which his adaptation had been imperfect, so that he continues to make efforts at adaptation" (p. 668).

To illustrate his point, Janet contrasts a person with a traumatic memory to a sentinel outside a camp watching for the enemy. When the sentinel sees the enemy, he must act adaptively, either by hiding or fighting. After surviving, he must tell his commander in words what he saw. These words must tell a story that is independent of the particulars of what he experienced—that is, independent of the actual perceptions and experiences he had at the time, which could only be reproduced if he was in exactly the same situation again. The sentinel's linguistic narrative must organize the "recital of the event to others and to ourselves, and [put] this recital in its place as one of the chapters in our personal history" (p. 667). The narrative must also take into account many variables, such as the different contexts of his commander's life and his own. This sentinel composes a narrative, as opposed to the traumatized person who cannot put his story into words, but can only reenact it.

Irene. Unless traumatized persons can find a way to, or be helped to, make "that recital that is memory," integrating the aspects of experience that have been kept apart, such persons seem compelled to repeat their crises. Irene was 20 years old when she was brought to Janet at Salpetriere with many hysterical symptoms, including hallucinations, amnesia, somnambulistic crises, contractures, and disorders of sensation (Janet, 1907; Janet, 1925, pp. 657–658, 812–817; Van der Kolk and Van der Hart, 1991). The illness had begun two years before, right after her mother's death from tuberculosis. For the last two months of her mother's life, Irene, who had been passionately devoted to her mother, cared for her day and night, all the while working as a seamstress to provide for the family. She subsisted on very little sleep, frequently quarreling with her drunken father. Then her mother died. After Irene saw her mother's corpse fall off the bed, she tried to revive the corpse and even to administer water. Shortly thereafter, Irene became amnestic for her mother's death, refused to believe she had died, and attended the funeral only under pressure. In addition, she was no longer able to manage the household and began to behave strangely: She burst out laughing at the funeral and showed no signs of mourning. When Janet questioned her about these events, she told him that there was a perfectly good reason for her lack of mourning: She knew that her mother had not died, for she had not seen her mother die, and she would have seen this because she had been there day and night. She also insisted that there had been no funeral.

Janet noticed that all of Irene's symptoms, including her amnesia, hallucinations, and contractures had a particular order and focus to them. She had fits of somnambulism in which she reenacted the scene of her mother's death with apparent precision. When she was in the hospital, Janet noticed that when Irene was in a certain position looking at the bed, she would hallucinate and reenact scenes from the event, attempting to give someone water, to lift the body, and so on. These reenactments, of which she had no memory after they were concluded, were quite lengthy. Janet worked with her on recovering these memories. Although she was resistant and phobic about recovering these painful memories, she was ultimately able to put them into words. When she was able to achieve a narration that took only a few minutes, her symptoms disappeared.

Janet (1907) emphasized that Irene's amnesia–her inability to recall her mother's death–did not mean that the memory was lost. To the contrary, her somnambulistic crises, in which she reenacted the traumatic event, indicated that the memory was retained, albeit in a special form. He asked,

> Then where was the oblivion? The oblivion consisted only in this, that she could not recite in a waking state, with full consciousness of the other events of herself. . . . Somnambulism is not the destruction of an idea, but the dissociation of an idea, that has emancipated itself from the ensemble of consciousness, and that the ensemble of consciousness can neither recover nor control [p. 173].

Synthesis

Janet describes hysteria as a "malady of personal synthesis." His theory focuses on the overwhelming nature of trauma–in particular, on how trauma overwhelms the mind's capacity to synthesize. By *synthesis* he meant the ability to integrate multiple sensations, perceptions, and memories within one's own experience and personality. Janet (1907) believed that a "dissociation of consciousness" characterized all hysterical disturbances. Observing that several theorists, including Breuer and Freud in 1893, as well as himself in 1889, have noted the importance of dissociation in hysteria and in somnambulism, he seems at pains to emphasize the kind of damage and the extent of the damage wrought by dissociation.

> The point which seems to me to be the most delicate in this definition is to indicate to what depth this dissociation reaches. In reality we might say that dementias themselves are dissociations of thought and of the motor functions. We must remember that in hysteria the functions do not dissolve entirely, that they continue to subsist emancipated with their systematization.... *What is dissolved is personality, the system of grouping of different functions around the same personality*.... [Hysteria] is a malady of the personal synthesis [pp. 331–332, italics added].

Thus, the malady of the lack of synthesis goes to the heart of identity. The lack of synthesis results in the narrowing of the field of consciousness, which is the "reduction of the number of psychological phenomena that can be simultaneously united or integrated in one and the same personal consciousness" (Janet, 1907). When there are too many or too extreme incompatible and opposing ideas, the mind cannot contain them. Hence, it cannot engage in the "struggle that enables self-control and personal will" (p. 332). Dissociation occurs when the person is unable to integrate or synthesize the event, leading to the isolation of different regulating activities, which can range from seeing an image to a complex identity state. Part of this process is a lowering of the mental level, lowering the integrative capacity. In sum, "hysteria is a form of mental depression characterized by the retraction of the field of personal consciousness and a tendency to the dissociation and emancipation of the system of ideas and functions that constitute personality" (Janet, 1907, p. 332).

Narrowing of the Field of Consciousness and Deficiency in the Capacity for the Experience of Conflict

When only one or a few things can be held in the mind at once, it is difficult to make connections between them and to compare and contrast them. Dissociated parts of experience may appear one by one in consciousness. Janet (1907) observed that hysterics seem to see only one thing in the room: "Normal consciousness, as philosophers say, is always a fully illuminated point, surrounded by a strong penumbra. With the hysterical, the penumbra is wanting" (p. 298). Janet believed suggestibility derives from the preservation of automatism and the diminution of personal synthesis—in short, from dissociation. It depends on the absence of control. "But control is nothing but the struggle, the competition of the various psychological states united in the same consciousness. If it is wanting, it is because the mind is too narrow to contain several ideas opposing one another" (Janet, 1907, p. 307).

Thus, Janet also anticipated current relational psychoanalytic concepts about the importance of the ability to experience conflict. He underscores the importance of the ability to maintain conscious conflict and how deficiency in this ability is part of hysteria. It is clear, however, that he is also aware of the conflict between dissociated systems of functions and ideas. He wrote of how certain parts of the personality became phobic of painful memories and of other parts of the personality that held them—a statement that if translated into another theoretical system would be understood, perhaps somewhat less precisely, as referring to unconscious conflict. Janet's dissociation theory included subconscious motivation—motivation from sources not under voluntary control. This idea, however, was not the centerpiece of his theory, which was highly complex and broadly inclusive.

Janet (1907) emphasizes that too much posttraumatic dissociation can decrease a person's sense of will and cohesive integrity. As a result of too much dissociation and suggestibility, there is not enough of a sense of "I." What has become missing is the "faculty that enables the subject to realize this sensation, to connect it with his personality and to be able to say clearly, 'It is I who feels, it is I who hears'" (p. 172).

Resolution of the Trauma and Will

Janet (1925) observed that traumatized people often become attached to their trauma so intensely that they are seriously impeded in carrying out their lives. Traumatized, dissociative people tend to be stuck, to not be able to go on with their lives.

> They seem to have had the evolution of their lives checked; they are "attached" upon an obstacle which they cannot get beyond. The happening we describe as traumatic has brought about a

> situation to which the individual ought to react. Adaptation is requisite, an adaptation achieved by modifying the outer world and by modifying oneself. Now what characterizes these "attached" patients is that they have not succeeded in liquidating the difficult situation. Irene does not behave like a woman who has lost her mother [p. 660].

Janet (1925) observes that these patients "continue to make great efforts to react to the event, to assimilate the situation" (p. 662). Yet what they are doing is "continuing the action . . .which began when the thing happened; and they exhaust themselves in these everlasting recommencements" (p. 663). The reason for this persistence, Janet says, is that the action taken was ineffective. Effective action and resolution bring feelings of triumph and joy. The trauma has interrupted the possibility of a competent completion that would yield a sense of triumph, and this interruption contributes to a loss of will. People need to complete the action in a way that enables them to "repeat the recital that constitutes memory, to make that recital independent of the happening, and to settle it into its appropriate place in our life-history." He goes on to say, "If the close of the action is to be definitive we must demobilise, must disperse, the forces that participated in the action. It is this dispersal of the recuperated energies which produces the temporary excitation of joy . . . and all the feelings of triumph" (p. 666). The failure to act effectively in response to traumatic events is responsible for much of the abulia (lack of will to act and of the ability to focus attention) and depression in traumatized people. It is exactly this issue of confronting and effectively completing the action involved in the traumatic event toward which so many of today's trauma treatments are directed.

Traumatic Stress and Constitutional Vulnerability

Janet did propose, among many other things (among which traumatic stress was prominent), a biological predisposition to hysteria. The cumulative interactive toll of psychic trauma, physical illness or injury, as well as hereditary and constitutional predispositions could bring about a mental depression and physical exhaustion that constituted a weakness toward hysteria. As Van der Hart and Dorahy (accepted for publication) comment, "Janet acknowledged a role of constitutional vulnerability in illnesses of personal synthesis, but he regarded physical illness, exhaustion, and, especially, the vehement emotions inherent in traumatic experiences as being the primary causes of this integrative failure" (Janet, 1889, 1909, 1911). The untrue idea that Janet's theory rested entirely on a view of hereditary weakness has been consistently used against him, dismissively and unfairly, during the last century. Indeed, in 1895, in *Studies on Hysteria,* Breuer goes on at length about just this, saying that "Janet considers that the 'splitting of the personality' rests on an innate psychological *weakness* (*insuffisance psychologique*)" (p. 230), a view with which he then expresses disagreement, saying, "It is not the case that the splitting of consciousness occurs because the patients are weak-minded; they appear to be weak- minded because their mental activity is divided and only a part of its capacity is at the disposal of their conscious thought" (p. 231). The first part of the sentence subtly misstates Janet's view, and the rest of the sentence disagrees with this straw man using a reasoning that sounds very much like Janet's. Breuer has clearly read Janet carefully, and such a misreading is striking. He then states, "We are inclined to believe that Janet's views were mainly formed in the course of a detailed study of the feeble-minded hysterical patients who were to be found in hospital or institutions" (p. 232). Breuer seems at pains to emphasize his and Freud's view that "among hysterics may be found people of the clearest intellect, strongest will, greatest character and highest critical power" (p. 232). This particular dismissal of the value of Janet's work on the basis that he rested his theory on innate psychological weakness has been continuously regenerated over the last century as writers repeat as truth the lore that they themselves have read as truth. Interestingly, many other theorists have relied heavily on the concept of biological predisposition in their theories, without such unfair criticism.

Although he did not think that dissociation always followed on physical illness, Janet did believe that dissociation was an outcome of a traumatically stressed mind. Janet emphasized, as traumatologists do today, that the normal mind has a breaking point at which it is unable to cope with and integrate the traumatic experience and becomes divided.

Until recently, much of the importance of the opus of Janet's work has been eclipsed by the upsurge of Freudian psychoanalysis.

Janet and Freud

Freud and Janet were close contemporaries in age. Janet, who was born in 1859, was three years younger than Freud, who was born in

1856. It appears that Janet began to feel a competition and that his concepts were being usurped. According to Ellenberger (1970),

> although Freud had summarily acknowledged Janet's previous research in 1893 and 1895, he became increasingly critical of him. Janet's report on psychoanalysis at the London Congress in 1913, at which he claimed priority for the discovery of fixed ideas and cathartic therapy, was the signal for violent attacks against Janet by certain psychoanalysts [p. 408].

By 1914, Janet (1914/1915) published criticisms that were unambiguously accusatory of Freud, expressing the conviction that Freud took many of his ideas, renamed them, and called them his own. These criticisms are included in Janet's 1919 book, *Les Medications Psychologiques,* of which *Psychological Healing* (1925) is the English translation (Onno van der Hart, personal communication, 2004). Here Janet states that he introduced the term *subconscious,* after which Freud wrote of the *unconscious,* and that he wrote of *psychological analysis,* after which Freud developed *psychoanalysis.* Ellenberger (1970) adds that "Janet's 'function of reality' was transposed into psychoanalysis under the name 'reality principle'" (p. 539). Ellenberger concludes his discussion of this highly charged issue by saying, "Indeed, it is difficult to study the initial periods of Janet's psychological analysis and of Freud's psychoanalysis without coming to the conclusion, expressed by Regis and Hesnard, 'The methods and concepts of Freud were modeled after those of Janet, of whom he seems to have inspired himself constantly—until the paths of the two diverged'" (pp. 539–540). (For a lengthy statement by Janet on this topic, see Janet, 1925, pp. 600–656.) Although Janet's published work on dissociation (1889) preceded Freud's and Breuer's (1893–1895), Breuer's work with Bertha Pappenheim (Anna O) was in progress (1880–1882) (Breger, 2000).

Many of Janet's concepts have been assimilated into Freudian concepts, so that for the uninitiated, important differences may not be apparent. One of the most important of these is that of repression versus dissociation—or Freudian dissociationism versus Janetian dissociationism, as I see it—which is addressed in more detail in chapter 9, on concepts. The eclipse of the concept of Janetian dissociation obscured public awareness of multiple centers of consciousness—exactly what Janet was talking about in his discourses on automatisms, somatic hysterical troubles, lack of synthesis, narrowing of the field of consciousness, and so on.

Unlike Freud, Janet did not leave behind a movement, and he had no disciples, nor did he seek to accomplish either of these. Ellenberger (1970) compares the body of Janet's work to an ancient buried city: "Thus, Janet's work can be compared to a vast city buried beneath ashes, like Pompeii. The fate of any buried city is uncertain. It may remain buried forever. It may remain concealed while being plundered by marauders. But it may also perhaps be unearthed some day and brought back to life" (p. 409).

Indeed, Janet's work is now in the process of major excavation and revivification. In the final analysis, Janet's theory of trauma and dissociation may be much more applicable than Freud's theory of repression (at least as it has been handed down to us through official channels). (See Erdelyi's [1985, 1990, 1994, 2001] work on Sigmund [not Anna] Freud's view of repression.) Janet (1925) considered repression to be one of the many symptomatic outcomes of the retraction of the field of consciousness and of psychic exhaustion, rather than the general underlying cause of symptoms. I believe that he was correct to object that the concept of repression was inaccurately applied as an almost universal explanation of psychic phenomena.

There is an important difference in the two concepts when we think about defense. Freud emphasized defense, especially repression, which included unconscious will (or counterwill). Defense is active. Janet's view of dissociation encompassed both the active and the passive. Clearly, Janet indicated awareness of the active uses of dissociation in his writings. For instance, he spoke of the "phobia" of memory. But Janet also emphasized how the traumatized mind is overwhelmed and fragmented, characterized by both intrusions and losses. Perhaps Freud's approach was more appealing to those who eschewed helplessness. Freud's emphasis on defense appeals to concerns about power, competence, and self-esteem.

In contrast, Janet's theory prominently includes psychic fragmentation in the face of overwhelming circumstances. Freud was ultimately more concerned with the problems of men, the more powerful sex. Four of his five long case histories were of men, and he "recognized the castrate in himself" (Schafer, 1974). Most of Janet's patients (like Freud's) were women, but Janet wrote about women most frequently. Janet—who was emphatic, as was Freud and their teacher in common, Charcot (Breger, 2000), that male hysterics definitely existed—also wrote about patients of both sexes with other kinds of disorders. In short, if Freud constructed a vision of "Guilty Man," and Kohut of "Tragic Man," then Janet's was of "Traumatically Overwhelmed, Dissociative Woman."[1]

Freud

La theorie, c'est bon, mais ca n'empeche pas d'exister ("Theory is good, but it does not prevent things from existing"). So said Charcot when his student, Sigmund Freud, questioned him about whether his clinical innovations fit with existing theory. This response, reported by Freud in his obituary for Charcot (1893), became one of Freud's favorite and most often repeated quotations. Striking out with his own vision, Freud, the conquistador of the inner recesses of the mind, produced a massive body of work, a body of work that has been spellbinding, exciting, and satisfying to a great many people across several generations. As Breger (2000) says in the introduction to his biography, "[Freud] was a man . . . whose startling originality coexisted with a rigid adherence to dogma" (p. 4).

This section is not an exegesis of Freud's work, nor is it intended to capture the magnitude, depth, and breadth of Freud's thinking. In this section, I focus on the varieties of dissociationism in Freud's theories, which I call *Freudian dissociationism 1, 2, 3,* and *4*. Dissociationism 1 is the splitting of consciousness as described in the "Preliminary Communication" of *Studies on Hysteria* (1893); dissociationism 2 is repression, which can itself be understood as a form of dissociationism (Erdelyi, 1990, 1994, 2001; Van der Hart and Dorahy, accepted for publication); dissociationism 3 refers to the split between the ego and the superego; and dissociationism 4 is the splitting of ego. Freudian dissociationism 2, 3, and 4 differ from Janetian dissociationism primarily in the exclusive emphasis on defense.

Psychoanalysis Begins in the Study of Trauma and Dissociation

Freudian Dissociationism 1: Splitting of Consciousness. Psychoanalysis owes its beginning to dissociation. In his early years as a physician and psychologist, Freud credited his colleague and collaborator Breuer (1893–1895) for beginning psychoanalysis. The credit was given on the basis of Breuer's understanding of the dissociative symptoms of his famous patient, Anna O (Breger, 2000). Indeed, Anna O, whose real name was Bertha Pappenheim, had a severe dissociative disorder, most likely dissociative identity disorder (Ross, 1989). She clearly exhibited different identity states, which were amnestic for each other, including different spoken languages, such as English, French, and German. While she was ill, Bertha had complained to Breuer that she had "two selves, a real one, and an evil one" (Breuer and Freud, 1893–1895, p. 24). Thus, psychoanalysis can claim its origin in the treatment of dissociative disorders.

Right away, in the "Preliminary Communication," Breuer and Freud address the importance of dissociation in hysteria:

> The longer we have been occupied with these phenomena, the more we have become convinced that *the splitting of consciousness which is so striking in the well-known classical cases under the form of* "double conscience" [footnote: the French term "dual consciousness"] *is present to a rudimentary degree in every hysteria, and that a tendency to such a dissociation, and with it the emergence of abnormal states of consciousness (which we shall bring together under the term "hypnoid") is the basic phenomenon of this neurosis.* In these views we concur with Binet and the two Janets [p. 12].

Breuer and Freud link psychological trauma, dissociation, and hysteria, comparing the memory of the trauma to a "foreign body which long after its entry must continue to be regarded as an agent that is still at work" (p. 6), and they announce the cure they have found: remembrance and abreaction. The symptoms disappear when the memory and its affect can be discharged (abreacted), expressed in words, or both.

The hysterical reactions correspond to traumatic memories that could be healed neither by subsequent circumstances that connected the traumatic event with a more benign reality, nor by sufficient discharge (abreaction): "It may therefore be said that the ideas which have become pathological have persisted with such freshness and affective strength because they have been denied the normal wearing-away processes by means of abreaction and reproduction in states of uninhibited association" (Breuer and Freud, 1893–1895, p. 11).

Breuer and Freud describe two groups of conditions in which abreaction fails to occur. One has to do with the kind of memories, such as loss, unrelieved shame, or other situations the patient wished to forget, ". . . as in the case of the apparently irreparable loss of a loved person or because social circumstances made a reaction impossible or because it was a question of things which the patient wished to forget, and therefore intentionally repressed from his conscious thought and inhibited and suppressed" (p. 10). The other group is brought into existence, not by the kind of memories but by the psychological state in which the patient had the experiences in question, for example, fright or autohypnotic reverie and daydreaming. These abnormal states are cut off from normal consciousness. In either case, what occurs is a "splitting of consciousness." Breuer and Freud state, "The basis and the *sine qua non* of hysteria is the existence of hypnoid states" (p. 12). *Hypnoid states* was a term Breuer adopted from Charcot (Breger, 2000) and was his adaptation of the French expression for somnambulistic states (Van der Hart and Dorahy, accepted for publication). What these "hypnoid states" have in common with hypnosis is that they are characterized by intense ideation which is cut off from association with the rest of consciousness. Thus, hypnoid states and second consciousness represent dissociationism 1.

Breuer and Freud (1893–1895) note that the memories that emerge in hysterical attacks correspond to the precipitating causes of the illness and have been cut off from associational contact with the rest of consciousness. These memories relating to the trauma, which have not been abreacted or associatively linked with other thoughts, are "found to belong to the ideational content of hypnoid states of consciousness with restricted association" (p. 15). These ideas are, however, associated among themselves and form a "more or less highly organized rudiment of a second consciousness, *a condition seconde*" (p. 15). When the "strangulated affect" (p. 17) of the idea that could not be abreacted "can find its way out through speech" (p. 17), it can be associated with normal consciousness, and the symptom recedes. Breuer and Freud say that these new discoveries have yielded only the mechanism of hysterical symptoms, but not the etiology of hysteria.

The two different groups I have described form the basis for two very different theoretical approaches to dissociation that are offered in the "Preliminary Communication." In the first approach, the associative working-over fails to occur because the patients are "determined to forget the distressing experiences" (Breuer and Freud, 1893–1895, p. 11); in the second group, it fails to occur "because there is no extensive associative connection between the normal state of consciousness and the pathological ones in which the ideas made their appearance" (p. 11). Freud is describing how "one makes two"—that is, how two mental states (dissociation) result from the psychic defense of the unitary person. In contrast, Breuer is describing how one *becomes* more than one, or many. Breuer's understanding actually has more in common with Janet's views than with Freud's. As a result of the hypnoid state, a person becomes split.

In addition to the "Preliminary Communication" (Breuer and Freud, 1893–1895), *Studies on Hysteria* contains five case histories by the authors, and a theoretical section by each. In his theoretical section of

Studies on Hysteria, Breuer notes the pervasiveness of amnesia, the frequent alternation between the hypnoid and the normal states, and how restriction of the hysterical symptoms to the hypnoid state strengthens it by repetition and protects it from correction by the waking state. He refers to the two great pathogenic factors: being in love and sick-nursing (p. 219), the first characterized by a "rapt" state of mind, causing the "real environment to grow dim" and the second by the "quiet in which the subject is surrounded, his concentration on an object, his attention fixed on the patient's breathing—all this sets up precisely the conditions demanded by many hypnotic procedures and fills the twilight state produced in this way with the affect of anxiety" (p. 219). (Both of these could be understood in Janet's terms, as a retraction of the field of consciousness.)

Freudian Dissociationism 2: One Makes Two. Despite his earlier endorsement, in his theoretical section *of Studies on Hysteria,* Freud (1893–1895) states that he has never seen a case of hypnoid hysteria: They have all turned into defense hysteria. By this Freud means that the "second consciousness" observed has been brought about by active resistance to some upsetting idea, not by hypnoid states. Here the divide between dissociation 1 and dissociation 2 first occurs. Even though dissociation 1 predominates in the "Preliminary Communication," dissociation 2 is introduced with the topic of the "patient wished to forget," "intentionally repressed from his conscious thought and inhibited and suppressed." This is dissociation 2, even if motivating dissociation 1. Dissociation 1 is differentiated as "not by the kind of memories, but by the psychological state"—that is, as abnormal states cut off from normal consciousness. As John O'Neil (personal communication) comments, the "repression of contents of any kind, as opposed to mental states, becomes dissociation 2. Freud never really endorsed dissociation 1, and dissociation 2 was there from the beginning to upstage and replace it."

Freud's version of dissociationism has its genesis in psychic defense. In describing this kind of dissociation, he introduces the idea of the censor:

> [They are] all of a distressing nature, calculated to arouse the affects of shame, of self-reproach, and of psychical pain, and the feeling of being harmed; they were all of a kind that one would prefer not to have experienced, that one would rather forget. From all this there arose, as it were automatically, the thought

> of *defense.* It has indeed been generally admitted by psychologists that the acceptance of a new idea . . . is dependent on the nature and trend of the ideas already united in the ego . . . this process of censorship, to which the new arrival must submit. The patient's ego had been approached by an idea which proved to be incompatible, which provoked on the part of the ego a repelling force of which the purpose was defense against this incompatible idea. The defense was in fact successful. The idea in question was forced out of consciousness and out of memory [p. 269].

Carrying forward the idea of resistance and defense, Freud modifies his earlier statement made with Breuer in the "Preliminary Communication," in which they compare the memory of the trauma to a "foreign body," with a new view that the "pathogenic organization does not behave like a foreign body, but far more like an infiltrate. In this simile the resistance must be regarded as what is infiltrating" (p. 290). In other words, the former foreign body is now an aspect of the self. Thus, Freud is no longer thinking in terms of *condition seconde.* As Bromberg (1996a) tells us, "after *Studies on Hysteria,* Freud was for the most part, openly contemptuous about the possible usefulness of theorizing about dissociation, hypnoid states, or alterations in consciousness" (p. 227).

Splitting of consciousness was replaced by Freudian dissociationism 2, or "repression." Although Freud used the terms *repression* and *dissociation* interchangeably throughout his career, in his very early writings, he often used the term *repression* to describe phenomena whose psychic organization sounded like Janetian dissociation, such as "second psychical group" and *condition seconde.* As Davies (1996) observes, Freud first used the term *repression* to describe "psychic incompatibility and splitting," which were "more in keeping with Janet's descriptions of 'traumatic dissociation' than with his own later understanding of repression as a defensive manifestation within the (early) topographical model of unconscious, preconscious and conscious, and the (later) structural model of id, ego, and superego" (pp. 556–557). But until 1897, the content of the repressed consisted primarily of traumatic memories.

Freud (1896) claimed that he had found the etiology of hysteria (which he and Breuer had said in *Studies* that they had not), indeed, the *caput Nili* ("source of the Nile") of neuropathology (p. 203). (The discovery of the source of the Nile River was the most important discovery of the 19th century [Janet, 1925].) In this essay, he continued developing the links between trauma and hysteria, but here he explicitly refers to repression rather than to dissociation. He states that he has used Breuer's method of tracing the ideational precursors of the symptoms backward, through many linkages, and has discovered that in every one of 18 cases of hysteria, two of them corroborated, there were "one or more occurrences of premature sexual experience" (p. 203). This premature experience has been pushed out of awareness as an incompatible idea. Symptoms emerge when there is some reminder in the then current experience of the earlier sexual experience–for instance, an adolescent girl's experience of a boyfriend caressing her hand or her hearing an off-color remark. This reminder brings forth the conflict, which is expressed in the symptomatology: "Sexual experiences in childhood consisting in stimulation of the genitals, coituslike acts, and so on must therefore be recognized, in the last analysis, as being the traumas which lead to a hysterical reaction to events at puberty and the development of hysterical symptoms" (pp. 206–207). The outbreak of hysteria "can be traced to *psychical conflict* arising through an incompatible idea setting in action a defense on the part of the ego and calling up a demand for repression" (pp. 210–211). This thrusts the incompatible idea into the unconscious and the hysterical symptom arises in its place.

Freud is always at pains in this essay to emphasize the trauma. He makes a point of saying that stimulation of the genitals and coituslike acts in childhood must be understood as traumas; behaviors on the part of the hysteric that may seem extreme if one does not understand the cause no longer seem so once one does understand. Freud (1896) was clearly affected by the horror of what he had discovered, including the psychological effect on the child. He, not Ferenczi, wrote the following lines:

> For the idea of these infantile sexual scenes is very repellent to the feelings of a sexually normal individual; they include all the abuses known to debauched and impotent persons, among whom the buccal cavity and the rectum are misused for sexual purposes . . . on the one hand, the adult . . . who is armed with complete authority and the right to punish, and can exchange one role for the other to the uninhibited satisfaction of his moods, and on the other hand, the child, who in his helplessness is at the mercy of this arbitrary will, who is prematurely aroused to every kind of sensibility and exposed to every sort of disappointment, and whose performance of the sexual activities

> assigned to him is often interrupted by his imperfect control of his natural needs—all these grotesque and yet tragic consequences reveal themselves as stamped upon the later development of the individual and of his neurosis, in countless permanent effects which deserve to be traced in the greatest detail [pp. 214–225].

Despite the passion of his delivery and beliefs, Freud (1896) felt that his formulation was not accepted by his colleagues. Freud wrote to Fliess soon afterward that the "donkeys gave it an icy reception" and that his presentation was branded a "scientific fairy tale" by Krafft-Ebing, who chaired the meeting (p. 189). Several weeks later he complained to Fliess of isolation, and said, "The word has been given out to abandon me, and a void is forming around me" (Masson, 1984, p. 10). However, according to Ellenberger (1970), "This theory was seen by some, such as Krafft-Ebing, with benevolent skepticism, by others such as Lowenfeld with interest, but in the literature of that time no expression of hostility is to be found" (p. 490).

Whatever all the reasons may have been, his view of the child's dilemma soon changed significantly (Masson, 1986; Gay, 1988; Kupersmid, 1993; Tabin, 1993; Davies and Frawley, 1994; Brothers, 1995; Greenberg; 1998; Matari, 1998; Breger, 2000): Within a year and a half, Freud switched course and abandoned his "seduction theory." The formulation outlined in "The Etiology of Hysteria" was replaced by the theory of infantile sexuality, in which sexual and oedipal wishes, not sexual traumas, were repressed.

In the year and a half between his presentation of "Etiology of Hysteria" and his abandonment of the seduction theory, his father died and his self-analysis revealed dreams, memories, and fantasies that led him to his oedipal theory. In September 1897, he wrote to his friend Fliess, "I no longer believe in my Neurotica" (Gay, 1988, p. 88); by October 1897, he told Fliess that the oedipal relationship of the child to its parents was a "general event in early childhood" (p. 100). In the same month he also wrote to Fliess, "Another presentiment tells me . . . that I am about to discover the source of Morality" (Cameron and Rychlak, 1985, p. 74). But he also wrote to Fliess in 1896 and 1897 letters in which he "baldly asserted that his father had sexually abused several of his siblings and was responsible for their neuroses" (Masson, 1985, p. 231, quoted in Brothers, 1995, p. 8). Among the official reasons that Freud gave for changing course was that there simply could not be that many perpetrators, and that "in all cases, the *father,* not excluding my own, had to be accused of being perverse" (p. 8). However, he had already answered this objection himself quite vigorously in "The Etiology of Hysteria." Masson (1984), Kupersmid (1993), Brothers (1995), and Breger (2000) present evidence and reasoning that suggest that Freud's internal conflicts as opposed to the officially presented version of theoretical views led to his abandonment of the seduction theory.

Although Freud never denied that child sexual abuse does occur and is pathogenic, at this point in time, fantasy replaced reality for him as the universal route of pathogenesis. However, this substitution of fantasy for memory does not change the type of dissociation in operation. In both cases, the person repressing memories or wishes acts in unity, at least with respect to the material being repressed, and a structural dissociation is created. Part of experience, whether it is a memory or a wish, is no longer accessible. Conscious and unconscious are dissociated. Thus, one *makes* two but, in contrast to dissociationism 1, does not *become* two.

The traumatic roots in Freud's reconstruction of the myth of Oedipus. Even though his new theory seemed on the surface to move away from themes of child abuse, it was, in fact, embedded in these. In his formulation of his new oedipal theory, Freud focused only on the part of the story about the embattled tragic hero who marries his mother, and he "forgot" (in a way that could be understood as Bartettian reconstruction; see Erdelyi, 1985, 1990, 2001), the beginning framework of the Oedipus story, which had to do with sexual abuse and pederasty (Devereux, 1953; Fromm, 1980; Ross, 1982; Pines, 1989; Betcher and Pollack, 1993; Brothers, 1995). The reason for the curse, which was Oedipus's fate, was that prior to his ascension to the throne, his father, King Laius, had abducted and raped the teenage son of the king Polybus, the ruler of a neighboring kingdom. Polybus's retaliatory curse was the one we all know: Laius's own son would murder him and marry Laius's wife, his mother. To avoid the curse, Laius instructed that his infant son be abandoned to die with a stake pierced through his ankles (hence the name *Oedipus* meaning "swollen foot"). Oedipus was rescued and brought up as the son of a neighboring king. He left home to avoid the curse prophesied by the Delphic Oracle (Ross, 1982), but met his fate anyway when he quarreled with and slew another traveler, who, unbeknownst to him, was Laius, his real father. Thus, Freud's most famous myth was framed in themes of child abuse, both pederasty and infanticide; but he only focused on the tragic adult struggles that were the outcomes of these early circumstances—as if these meanings could be segregated from their earlier history.

Freudian Dissociationism 3: Split Between the Ego and the Superego. Whereas Freudian dissociationism 1 concerned the splitting of consciousness, and dissociationism 2 concerned the separation of repressed memories or wishes from the experiencing "I"—basically separating the unconscious from the conscious—the third type of dissociationism concerns the separation of the superego from the ego. Freud's discussion of the division of the ego in melancholia foreshadowed his later work on the splitting of the superego from the ego. In *Mourning and Melancholia* (1917) some of Freud's later ideas about the role of identification in superego formation are adumbrated. He notes that in contrast to normal mourning, in melancholia, the person berates himself or herself with a kind of shameless mercilessness. However, the castigation is usually not for the person's own qualities, but unconsciously for those of an intimate other, where there has been an attachment loss "owing to a real injury or disappointment concerned with the loved person." The melancholic has dealt with this loss by establishing an "identification of the ego with the abandoned object" (p. 249).

> Thus the shadow of the object fell upon the ego, so that the latter could henceforth be criticized by the special mental faculty like an object, like the forsaken object. In this way . . . the conflict between the ego and the loved person is transformed into a *cleavage between* the criticizing faculty of the ego and the ego as altered by the identification [p. 249, italics added].

As a result, "in spite of the conflict with the loved person, the love-relationship need not be given up" (1917, p. 249). As Freud later (1921) put it in *Group Psychology and the Analysis of the Ego,*

> these melancholias . . . *show us the ego divided, fallen apart into two pieces,* one of which rages against the second. This second piece is the one which has been altered by introjection and which contains the lost object. But the piece which behaves so cruelly is not unknown to us either. It comprises the conscience, a critical agency within the ego, which even in normal times takes up a critical attitude toward the ego, though never so relentlessly and so

> unjustifiably . . . some such agency develops in our ego which may cut itself off from the rest of the ego and come into conflict with it. We have called it the "ego ideal" [p. 52, italics added].

Thus, the "critical agency" (superego, ego ideal) which has been differentiated out of the ego, rages against the ego, which itself has been modified on account of identification. This has occurred, moreover, in order to preserve the "love relationship." In "The Ego and the Id," Freud (1923) develops these ideas about identification further. The child replaces the incestuous and parenticidal feelings that arose in response to the oedipal complex, with identification:

> The broad general outcome of the sexual phase dominated by the Oedipus complex may, therefore, be taken to be the forming of a precipitate in the ego, consisting of these two [the parents] identifications in some way united with each other. This modification of the ego retains its special position; it confronts the other contents of the ego as an ego ideal or super-ego [p. 34].

"The ego ideal is therefore the heir to the Oedipus complex, and this is also the expression of the most powerful impulses . . . of the id. By setting up this ego ideal, the ego has mastered the Oedipus complex and at the same time placed itself in subjection to the id" (p. 54). "Ego" and "superego" are dissociated (Cameron and Rychlack, 1985).

In the harsh superego, this dissociation is especially evident. The harsh superego may often describe more a relationship of dissociated parts of the personality (the "sadistic" superego and the "masochistic" ego), than mature morality. Castration threat, which Freud (1925) felt made the boy's superego superior to the girl's, is potentially traumatic. However, castration threat taken literally, as the terrifying threat of dismemberment and deprivation of masculinity, can be understood as more potentiating of dissociation than of mature morality. As Sagan (1988) says, "Thus is our morality, mankind's higher nature, born in the environment of the penitentiary" (p. 75). Kohut (1984) considers castration anxiety a pathological symptom of a disorder of the self, and states, "A boy who is exposed to the responses of psychologically healthy parents does not experience a significant degree of castration anxiety during the oedipal phase" (p. 14). As I suggested in an earlier paper (Howell, 1997a),

> a crucial distinction may hinge on whether the structure called "superego" arises from the child's need to control uncivilized impulses, which would be moral; or from the child's attempt to deal with traumatic impingement from an uncivilized world. Wishes, drives, and impulses are not necessarily problematic in themselves: It is the harsh punishment for them in this model that is problematic. Harsh superego, arising from the threat of castration linked to the oedipal conflict, may better describe how the child becomes self-punishing than how the child achieves mature morality. Uncivilized wishes can be forgotten (repressed) in an overall sense of the continuity of personal history (Ogden, 1986; Bromberg, 1996), whereas overwhelming terror seems more likely to lead to a segmentation of self-experience (dissociation) [p. 234].

In my view, the harsh superego can be understood as a dissociated structure.

Freudian Dissociationism 4: Splitting of the Ego. Toward the end of his life Freud developed a fourth kind of dissociationism: the splitting of the ego. In some ways, this is reminiscent of his first dissociationism, in that it explicitly addresses the difficulty in assimilating a traumatic reality. But this does not involve hypnoid states, nor does it concern memories or wishes that are inaccessible to the ego, but rather, a part of the ego itself that is split off. In his 1927 paper, "Fetishism," Freud describes a process of disavowal that is neither psychotic nor neurotic, but in between. This is exemplified by two men in analysis who each had failed to take notice of–had disavowed–his father's death. There was one current of thought that did not recognize the father's death, and another one that did: "The attitude which fitted in with the wish and the attitude which fitted in with reality existed side by side" (p. 156). This process of disavowal also characterizes fetishism: The fetish is a substitute for the woman's (the mother's) penis that the little boy once believed in and–for reasons familiar to us–does not want to give up" (pp. 152–153). The piece of reality that the boy did not want to give up has been disavowed by the ego in a way that is similar to the disavowal of castration by fetishists.

In "The Splitting of the Ego in the Process of Defense," Freud (1938) develops this idea of disavowal further, stating that it has to do with the boy's belief that the female has a penis, side by side with his knowledge that she does not. Freud writes,

> On the one hand, he rejects reality and refuses to accept any prohibition; on the other hand, in the same breath he recognizes the danger of reality. . . . It must be confessed that this is a very ingenious solution of the difficulty. Both of the parties to the dispute obtain their share: the instinct is allowed to retain its satisfaction and proper respect is shown to reality [p. 275].

Thus, there are two sets of contradictory views of reality that exist simultaneously, without any resolution of the contradiction and conflict between them. This develops in response to terrifying thoughts. In this paper, Freud seemed to be addressing again how psychic trauma can bring about structural dissociation, but he never finished this paper.

In my view, the specialness of Freud's thinking, in contrast to Janet's, does not derive from his emphasis on motivation, conflict, and active defense, for Janet also had a theory of motivation and conflict; nor does it derive from Freud's greater emphasis on normalcy, for Janet believed that every person has a breaking point. For me, the heart of the difference is that Freud—in addition to eschewing multiplicity—emphasized wishes and emotions.

Sándor Ferenczi: The Wise Baby

When I was in graduate school I learned that Ferenczi was notable for being the colleague of Freud's who foolishly thought that he could love patients into health. Therefore, he had nothing useful to say. Then, somewhat later, I read Peter Gay's biography of Freud (1988), where I learned that Ferenczi had been mentally ill, which compounded the earlier impression. When I finally did read Ferenczi's now famous paper, "Confusion of Tongues Between the Adult and the Child," I was amazed at the storehouse of clinical wisdom it contained. This paper, delivered in 1932, but published in English in 1949, along with Ferenczi's other late papers dating from 1928 to 1932 and the *Clinical Diary* (1988), contains a brilliant and passionately conceived theory of trauma and dissociation that will dramatically enrich the thinking of anyone who has not read it before.

Ferenczi (1873–1933) was the last of defecting or outcast Freudian disciples to leave the fold. He had been one of Freud's closest friends, a devout favorite son, disciple, and analysand, and had regularly gone on vacation to Italy with Freud. In his need to please Freud, he had even been one of the "palace guard," when called on to seal the excommunication of others, such as Jung and Rank (Breger, 2000, p. 341). However, Ferenczi began to deviate from Freud's approved psychoanalytic practices and beliefs. With respect to the latter, Ferenczi became aware of the frequency of "exogamous" (Ferenczi, 1949, p. 225) trauma, most notably childhood sexual abuse, in the histories of his patients; he chronicled the profoundly dissociative outcomes. Ferenczi worked with extremely difficult patients, who today would be diagnosed as borderline, narcissistic, severely dissociative, and psychotic (Rachman, 1993, 1997). Judith Dupont (1988) writes, "He believed that all patients who asked for help should receive it, and that it was up to the psychoanalyst to devise the most appropriate response. Thus, Ferenczi became the last resort for cases considered hopeless" (p. xix). Ferenczi developed a number of different treatment approaches and techniques to facilitate the healing of the deep psychical splits that he understood to be the outcome of trauma. In an attempt to cure him of his deviant analytical thinking and therapeutic practices, including his interest in trauma theory, Freud offered him the presidency of the International Psychoanalytical Association (Rachman, 1997), but Ferenczi declined, stating that his current pursuits having to do with his own personal development would not allow him to do the position justice (Dupont, 1988).

Aron and Harris (1993) emphasize that it was primarily Ferenczi's experiments with clinical technique rather than his belief in the frequency of childhood sexual trauma that angered and disturbed Freud. Some of these techniques were unorthodox (see Aron and Harris, 1993; Rachman, 1993, 1997); they were active, and he allowed physical contact and kissing with some patients. Ferenczi was attempting to create an atmosphere of maternal warmth (Rachman, 1997). In contrast to the rumors that Ferenczi had sexual contact with his patients, Rachman (1993) writes that from his 10 years of research into Ferenczi's clinical behavior, "as revealed in his own work and described by his analysands, his colleagues, his friends, and other researchers, I have concluded that *there is no evidence that he engaged in any direct sexual behavior with patients or encouraged any analytic candidate, supervisee, or colleague to do so*" (pp. 84–85). Ferenczi's differences in therapeutic approach are relevant to thinking about dissociation because it was by opening himself up to his patients, by truly listening to their experiences of him, that he learned about them and the dissociative structure of their psyches.

In his last visit to Freud, Ferenczi showed him the "Confusion in Tongues" speech, which he planned to deliver at the 1932 Congress. Freud was outraged and asked him not to deliver it. Freud misinterpreted it as a simple regression to his own earlier etiological views of the now discarded seduction hypothesis (Aron and Harris, 1993; Rachman, 1997). Ferenczi delivered the paper anyway, but the consequence was that vicious rumors were spread about him in the psychoanalytic circle. He was "diagnostically" slandered (Breger, 2000) by Freud and by Ernest Jones as being mentally demented, a view contradicted by various people close to Ferenczi at this time who reported that his mind was sound—even though he was physically weak because he was dying (Aron and Harris, 1993; Rachman, 1997; Breger, 2000). Furthermore, Jones prevented "Confusion of Tongues" from being published in English for 16 years after it was delivered.

"Confusion in Tongues" (1949) addresses two levels of damaging relational power and hypocrisy: one at the level of the relationship between child and parent and one at the level of the treatment relationship. Aron and Harris (1993) note a third (implicit) level: that Ferenczi's "Confusion in Tongues" was partially addressed to Freud.

The title of the paper—"Confusion in Tongues"—referred to how the common language of tenderness between the child and adult is distorted by the pathological adult, who mistakes the role play of the child for that of a sexually mature person. The child's desire to take the role of the other parent is merely fantasy, and actions based on a confusion as to the child's real intent results in the "real rape of girls who have hardly grown out of the age of infants, similar sexual acts of mature women with boys, and also enforced homosexual acts" (p. 227). Ferenczi then describes the traumatic shock accruing from the psychological dilemma of the child, who is paralyzed with anxiety, and is unable to express disgust and energetic refusal, as one might expect. The child's responses include severe psychical fragmentation, psychosis, and becoming an automaton.

Trauma and Dissociation

Anticipating current understanding of dissociative disorders, Ferenczi describes how psychic trauma splits the self. In "Confusion of Tongues," Ferenczi emphasized how "there is neither shock nor fright without some trace of splitting of the personality" (p. 229). He went on to say that as the shocks increase during a child's development, so do the splits, and soon "it becomes extremely difficult to maintain contact without confusion with all the fragments each of which behaves [as] a separate personality yet does not know of even the existence of others" (p. 229).

Ferenczi (1929) had unique conceptualizations of the various functions of split-off states. A particularly important one is that of the caretaker self. He described how one part of the psyche may become a caretaker for the rest. In situations of early, severe trauma, he envisioned a fragmented, damaged psyche as being like a "teratoma," a tumor that contains in it a foreign body, such as a tooth or hair: "The greater part of the personality becomes as it were, a teratoma, the task of adaptation to reality being shouldered by the fragment of personality which has been spared" (p. 124).

Ferenczi (1949) also wrote of the "wise baby" who "teaches wisdom to the entire family" (p. 229). This split-off part of the psyche, which does not experience the pain of the trauma, can be precociously helpful to the child. Aron and Harris (1993) observe that this formulation anticipated Winnicott's articulation of the "false self" as a dissociated protector of the "true self" which manages the impinging interpersonal situation through compliance. Ferenczi's (1949) thinking also anticipated Fairbairn in his understanding that abused children have taken the burden of badness of the aggressor into themselves to prevent it from achieving consciousness, so as to maintain the "situation of tenderness" (p. 228) with the abuser. Ferenczi also noticed, as did Fairbairn, that this internalized aspect of the traumatogenic relationship was deeply buried.

Psychosis

Ferenczi developed the theme of a caretaker self in different ways, pointing to the ways in which what we now think of as dissociative thought disorder and psychosis have so much in common. He felt that the traumatic shock of sexual abuse causes the child to become temporarily psychotic (Rachman, 1997). As he wrote in 1929, the "first reaction to a shock seems to be always a transitory psychosis, i.e., a turning away from reality." He went on to say, "It seems likely that a psychotic splitting off of a part of the personality occurs under the influence of shock. The dissociated part, however, lives on hidden, ceaselessly endeavoring to make itself felt, without finding any outlet except in neurotic symptoms" (p. 121). He wrote (1930) of the partial destruction of the psyche after a trauma or shock, which, as represented in dreams and fantasies, "shows the previously united personality in a secondarily narcissistic splitting, the 'dead,' 'murdered' part of the person—like a child—nursed, wrapped up in, by the parts which remained intact" (p. 226).

Ferenczi (1931) eloquently describes how an aspect of this process of self-splitting

> is the sudden change of the object-relation that has become intolerable, into narcissism. The man abandoned by all gods escapes completely from reality and creates for himself another world in which he, unimpeded by earthly gravity, can achieve everything he wants. Has he been unloved, even tormented, he now splits off from himself a part which in the form of a helpful, loving, often motherly, minder commiserates with the tormented remainder of the self, nurses him and decides for him; and all this is done with deepest wisdom and most penetrating intelligence. He is intelligence and kindness itself, so to speak a guardian angel. This angel sees the suffering or murdered child from the outside. . . . He wanders through the whole Universe seeking help, invents fantasies for the child that cannot be saved in any other way, etc. [p. 237].

In the 1949 paper, Ferenczi emphasizes the psychotic aspect of the "introjection" of the aggressor, that the aggressor

> disappears as part of external reality and becomes intra- as opposed to extra-psychic; the intrapsychic is then subjected, in a dream-like state as is the traumatic trance, to the primary process, i.e. according to the pleasure principle it can be modified or changed by the use of positive or negative hallucinations. In any case the attack as a rigid external reality ceases to exist and in the traumatic trance the child succeeds in maintaining the previous situation of tenderness [p. 228].

Identification with the Aggressor

Perhaps Ferenczi's most important contribution to the study of dissociation involves his description of what he called *identification with the aggressor* (1949). Identification with the aggressor is commonly referred to in trauma theory and is an extremely important concept, which can be difficult to understand. Use of the term often passes for explanation of why someone who was victimized by an aggressor may repeat the same behavior toward another, often in almost identical ways, or may be vulnerable to revictimization. Often it seems as if the aggressor has somehow "gotten inside" the former victim; the victim is, in this way, continually reenacting the aggression. What Ferenczi helps us to understand is how the psyche becomes split so that a part of the self takes on the behavior of the former aggressor. Ferenczi's meaning for this term is quite different from Anna Freud's later and more familiar use of the term.

Interestingly, Anna Freud was recording secretary at this conference at which "Confusion of Tongues" was presented. Her book, *The Ego and the Mechanisms of Defense* (1966), appeared four years after the conference. Rachman (1997) observes that, "since German was the mother tongue for Anna Freud and the Freudian circle, it is plausible that they were aware of Ferenczi's discovery. . . . The paper and its discoveries were not considered a part of mainstream psychoanalysis and therefore were not studied" (pp. 237–238).

Ferenczi's concept of identification with the aggressor is in contrast to Anna Freud's description of active identification with an authority or with the authority's aggression and power which often have a self-protective or agentic cast and which can presage superego formation. In contrast, Ferenczi (1949) is describing how the child is identifying with the aggressor's needs or wishes, rather than directly with the aggressor's role, even while his own mind is made numb and "dumb." He says,

> These children feel physically and morally helpless . . . , for the overpowering force and authority of the adult makes them dumb and can rob them of their senses. The same anxiety, however, if it reaches a certain maximum, compels them to subordinate themselves like automata to the will of the aggressor, to divine each one of his desires and to gratify these; completely oblivious of themselves they identify themselves with the aggressor. . . . The weak and undeveloped personality reacts to sudden unpleasure not by defense, but by anxiety-ridden identification and introjection of the menacing person or aggressor. . . . One part of their personalities, possibly the nucleus, got stuck in its development at a level where it was unable to use the alloplastic way of reaction but could only react in an autoplastic way by a kind of mimicry [p. 228].

Ferenczi (1949) also felt a need to modify and elaborate on his term *identification with the aggressor:* "Through the identification, or let us say introjection, let us call it introjection of the aggressor, he disappears as part of external reality and becomes intra- as opposed to extra-psychic" (p. 228).

Thus, the traumatic trance fosters the world of illusion and psychosis. In consciousness the relationship with the abuser is preserved as a "situation of tenderness."

W. R. D. Fairbairn

> Klein described splitting of the object; Freud, the splitting of the ego; and Fairbairn, the splitting of the self.
>
> –Arnold Modell

Fairbairn's endopsychic model is a potent depiction of the psychodynamics of the split self.[2] Ogden, Davies, Grotstein, Celani, and others have developed the implications of Fairbairn's model to show how all the constituent parts of the endopsychic situation can be understood as agentic and possessing a subjective sense of "I."

Ronald Fairbairn was the "first to formulate a true object-related (relational) nature of the self" (Grotstein and Rinsley, 2000). He was insistent that the "ego" does not need a reservoir of "id" energy to power it, but is itself a dynamic entity of both structure and energy. Ironically, the heart of his theory, premised on the view of the person as seeking interpersonal attachment and relatedness from the start, concerns how people in their attempts to manage attachments and affects resulting from their object-seeking nature, become internally split, which causes them to turn away from other people. His view of the split psyche presages concepts of segregated internal working models and dissociated relational enactments of modern attachment theory. He viewed the ego as a dynamic structure that is agentic and object-seeking of its own.

This section focuses on (1) the internalization of the bad object and the subsequent splitting of the object, which ensures self-blame rather than blame of the "frustrating" or abusive attachment figure; (2) the concept that endopsychic substructures, including internalized objects, are all autonomous agentic parts (although the idea that the internalized object could be dynamically agentic was a conclusion Fairbairn allowed, but did not develop); and (3) the usefulness of the concept of the central ego. The central ego is strong or weak in accordance with the power of the subsidiary egos and their objects.

Because he lived in Edinburgh, Fairbairn was physically isolated from his psychoanalytic peers. However, he was significantly influenced by the theories of Freud, Janet, and Klein. He used Klein's concepts of internal objects and the splitting of the object, as well as the term *schizoid.* Yet, the understanding he came to about internal objects was very different from hers. Whereas Klein saw the child as full of murderous and envious impulses, Fairbairn saw the child as initially innocent (Mitchell, 1981). Fairbairn's thinking was also influenced by Janet's writing, especially Janet's view of the causal role of dissociation in hysteria—that a deficiency of mental synthesis leads to a splitting of consciousness. However, Fairbairn did not pursue Janet's view of dissociation as the peritraumatic splitting off of parts of the psyche. Instead, the theory he developed emphasized the psychic structural consequences of problematic attachments.

Although Fairbairn initially tried to reconcile his own observations with Freud's theories, he was ultimately unable to do this, rejecting the view of the mind as hedonic and powered by impulse (id).[3] Even though Fairbairn relied on the concept of repression in his theory, he viewed it somewhat differently than did Freud; he ultimately placed more importance on splitting, the basis of psychic structure.

The Internalization of the Bad Object

Fairbairn's scheme of psychical division is that the psyche is originally whole. Internalization and splitting account for psychic structuring. In order to manage life with an intolerably frustrating attachment figure (or "object"), the child internalizes the "bad" aspects of the attachment figure. Fairbairn observes that the child cannot get away from or reject his bad objects. They powerfully force themselves on him, and he needs them. He illustrates (1943) with a patient's dream about a poisoned pudding:

> In the dream he was standing beside his mother with a bowl of chocolate pudding on a table before him. He was ravenously hungry; and he knew that the pudding contained deadly poison. He felt that, if he ate the pudding, he would die of poisoning and, if he did not eat the pudding, he would die of starvation. Here is the problem stated. What was the denouement? He ate the pudding. He incorporated the contents of the poisonous breast because his hunger was so great [p. 68].

This internalization of the bad object is the first of the psychic splits. The purpose of the internalization is to control the object, which in the world of real people and relationships is completely uncontrollable, because the child so desperately needs the object. The protective function of this defense is to "preserve the image of the mother as a safe person that the child can safely love" (Armstrong-Perlman, 2000, p. 226). By controlling the expression of his physical and emotional needs, this defense also protects the child against unbearable feelings of disappointment and against rejection from his mother. The problem is that in attempting to control his objects in this way, they retain their power–only now in the inner world. "In a word, he is 'possessed' by them, as if by evil spirits" (Fairbairn, 1943, p. 67).

This defense allows the child to see the mother as "good" by taking on the burden of badness within the self. The child's "ego is henceforth left at the mercy of a band of internal fifth columnists or persecutors" (p. 65). Fairbairn frequently observed this pattern of self-blame, along with holding the parents blameless, in the abused children he saw in treatment, and he noticed that it increased with the severity of the abuse. Immense grandiosity can come with this internalization of the bad object, for now there is the magical belief that events occurring outside oneself, over which one actually has no control, have occurred on account of one's badness. For example, after the World Trade Center disaster, more than one of my severely dissociative patients believed that she had in some way caused it, contributed to it, or to other disasters associated with it.

Fairbairn also described a "moral defense" that involves internalizing some good aspects of the parents, thus providing some internal goodness. Now the child can be morally and conditionally bad (and good) vis-à-vis these internalized good objects. As Fairbairn (1944), who liked to use religious metaphors, put it, it is "better to be a sinner in a world ruled by God, than a saint in a world ruled by the Devil. A sinner in a world ruled by God may be bad, but there is always a sense of security to be derived from the fact that the world around is good. . . . In any case, there is always hope of redemption" (pp. 66–67). The sinner in a world ruled by the Devil has no hope of redemption, and is also bad because the world around him is bad.

Attachment to Bad Objects

To varying degrees, the child must learn to inhibit the expression of both hatred and emotional longing. The expression of aggression toward rejecting attachment figures runs the risk of diminishing their love, thus making them less "good" in reality. However, failure to inhibit expression of need has potentially even more disastrous consequences. Expression of need to a person who is emotionally unavailable and unresponsive can be intensely shaming. The underbelly of this shame is an intense terror of psychic disintegration. As Fairbairn (1944) states,

> the experience is one of shame over needs which are disregarded or belittled. In virtue to these experiences of humiliation and shame, he feels reduced to a state of worthlessness, destitution, or beggardom. His sense of his own value is threatened and he feels bad in the sense of "inferior" . . . and intensity of need itself increases his sense of badness by contributing to it the quality of "demanding too much." At the same time his sense of badness is further complicated by the sense of utter impotence which he also experiences. At a still deeper level (or at an earlier stage) the child's experience is one of, so to speak, exploding ineffectively and being completely emptied of libido. It is thus an experience of disintegration and of imminent psychical death [p. 113].

This terror of psychic disintegration, so centrally related to the schizoid dilemma, contributes to the fierce attachment to the bad objects and to the maintenance of the closed system of internal objects.

In his depiction of the endopsychic situation involving the interdynamics of the libidinal ego and the antilibidinal ego, Fairbairn presents an astounding drama of submerged life, Captain Nemo fashion, of the passions in human life that, although submerged beneath ordinary consciousness, are structurally personified, in passionate conflict, but also operate in concert to keep themselves hidden from other people. All of the emotional action takes place internally. In contrast to the schizoid person's conscious experience of futility, the repressed suborganizations which are rarely expressed interpersonally are in constant, highly charged internal warfare.

The Endopsychic Situation

Fairbairn's (1944) dissociative psyche is elegant and precisely articulated. His final scheme of the endopsychic situation is as follows. Once the object is internalized, a second splitting occurs: Two parts of the internal object (the exciting object and the rejecting object) are split off from the main core of the object. The exciting object holds all the promises of gratification of tender yearnings and love, which the child so intensely desires. The rejecting object holds the child's memories and fears of rejection of his needs and feelings at the hands of his caretakers. These parts of the split-off, internalized bad object are repressed by the ego. Then these repressed objects carry with them into repression parts of the ego that have been attached to them, leaving the central core of the ego, which Fairbairn called the central ego, unrepressed, but capable of repression. In his final descriptions, Fairbairn (1963) named these parts of the ego the libidinal ego (attached to the exciting object) and the antilibidinal ego (earlier called the "internal saboteur," and attached to the rejecting, or antilibidinal, object).

As a result, the object and the ego are each split into three parts. The object is split into the ideal object (which is not repressed) and into the exciting object and the rejecting object (which are repressed). The original ego is also split into three parts: the central ego, which is conscious and not repressed, and the parts of the ego that have been attached to the exciting and rejecting object, the libidinal ego and the antilibidinal ego, respectively.

Because the antilibidinal ego is attached to the rejecting object, or antilibidinal object, it is aggressively rejecting of the exciting object and the libidinal ego. This rejection of the libidinal ego reinforces its repression by the central ego, thus perpetuating the endopsychic status quo.

Because the central ego has repressed the libidinal ego and the antilibidinal ego, intensified affects of longing and hatred are experienced by these subegos. The child uses a divide-and-conquer technique to aggressively subdue libidinal need. In this way, the child reduces the level of libidinal and aggressive affect that is outwardly expressed. The effect on the endopsychic situation is that

> the libidinal ego in its turn directs the excess of libido with which it becomes charged towards its associated object, the exciting object. On the other hand, the attack of the internal saboteur upon this object represents the persistence of the child's original resentment towards his mother as a temptress inciting the very need which she fails to satisfy and thus reducing him to bondage—just as, indeed, the attack of the internal saboteur upon the libidinal ego represents a persistence of the hatred

which the child comes to feel towards himself for the dependence dictated by his need [p. 115].

Internalized Objects as Agentic, Dynamic, Independent Centers of Initiative

Fairbairn's view of these endopsychic ego structures—the central ego, the libidinal ego, and the antilibidinal ego—was that they were dynamic agencies, each with a sense of "I," in passionate conflict with each other, but with the united purpose of maintaining safety for the child.

After admitting that even though he had treated internalized objects "simply as objects of ego structures and not as themselves dynamic" (p. 177), Fairbairn (1951) observed that,

> in the interests of consistency, however, I must draw the logical conclusion of my theory and acknowledge that, since internal objects are endopsychic structures, they must themselves, be in some measure dynamic; and it should be added that they must derive their dynamic quality from their cathexis by ego-structures [p. 177].

Although Fairbairn admitted the agency of objects by dint of logical consistency, he failed to account for how these objects obtain their agency. He recognized the logical necessity of giving an agentic status to the internalized objects that he saw as endopsychic structures. Because he recognized that parts of the ego are repressed along with parts of the object, Fairbairn was in essence recognizing that what is internalized is an object relationship. As Ogden (1983) brilliantly clarifies, "neither objects nor object representations are internalized, rather that which is internalized is an object relationship, consisting of a split-off part of the ego in relation to an object, which is itself, at least in part, a dynamic structure" (p. 98). Ogden (1983) observes that the internalized object is experienced as nonself because it is identified with a nonself (the external object): "In brief, internal objects are subdivisions of the ego that are heavily identified with an object representation while maintaining the capacities of the whole ego for thought, perception, feeling, etc." (p. 99).

Although he acknowledges the theoretical independence of the "objects," Fairbairn does not address the dynamic power of these parts in the personality system. Perhaps it was for fear of demonology, of which he had accused Klein, that he might be describing a multitude of objects flying around in the psyche (Ogden, 1983) or the dilemma of how a thought (object representation) can be an agent. Ogden follows Fairbairn's design to its natural conclusion and observes that these internal objects should be understood as "aspects of the ego identified with objects" (p. 104). As such, they can be tormenting, denigrating, needy, demanding, and so on.

As Ogden (1983) explains, the reason that the rejecting object refuses to change is that the rejecting object is itself a dynamic structure, one with a kind of subjectivity; and as a result, such a change in identity connotes annihilation. Ogden emphasizes the importance of the "unwillingness of the object to relinquish its tie to other aspects of the ego involved in internal object relationships" (p. 104). He describes how the self component and the object component (the ego suborganization identified with the object) each feel the wish of the other to annihilate them, causing each to retrench their own positions. The object component is under pressure from the self component to change into a good object. However, such a transformation would entail a loss of identity, equivalent to annihilation, and is hence strenuously resisted. At the same time, the self component needs the object component and experiences the prospect of the loss of the object (even though bad) as tantamount to annihilation. In addition, the object component needs the self component, and much of the taunting and humiliation is a way of attempting a bond with the self component. Bonds with an outside person, such as the therapist, greatly threaten this inner connectedness. In a case example of an overweight patient, Ogden (1983) describes how the internal object "experienced the ability of other aspects of the patient to engage in free association . . . as dangerous evidence of an enhanced capacity of those other aspects of the ego to engage in a more mature form of relatedness to therapist" (p. 107). This generated the fear that the self component would be less dependent of the object component. As a result,

> the object (suborganization of ego) then redoubled its efforts to subject the masochist self to sadistic torment in the form of guilt-inducing taunts about being overweight. There can be no mistaking that the nature of the ultimate threat made by the object component is that of abandoning the self component of the internal relationship. In the clinical sequence the threat of abandonment is projected onto the therapist [p. 107].

The hostile, dominating, sadomasochistic, and terror-ridden interrelationships of these parts is extremely reminiscent of DID and DDNOS. Fairbairn (1944) believed that hysteria is the prime illustration of the basic endopsychic structure and suggested that in order to appreciate psychic structure, we need to go "back to hysteria," where Freud started. Such a retracing of our theoretical steps takes us to an examination of the dissociative psyche.

Interestingly, in some of his earlier work, notably his 1931 paper, Fairbairn conceptualized an agentic part of the patient's psyche as based on an object identification. He discusses personified parts of his patient's psyche—the "mischievous boy," the "critic," the "little girl," and the "martyr"—that regularly appeared in dreams as well as in waking life. For this patient, the "personifications seem best interpreted as functioning structural units which . . . attained a certain independence within the total personality, and it seems reasonable to suppose that the mental processes which give rise to multiple personality only represent a more extreme form" (p. 219).

Grotstein (2000) observed that "Fairbairn saw that psychic structure is the personification of failed experiences with objects" (p. 177), and he characterized Fairbairn's substructures both as "alter egos" and as "six endopsychic characters in search of an author" (p. 174). Fairbairn, himself, spoke of his "endopsychic characters" as being in the "inner dress circle." Following Grotstein's analogy, Davies (1998) eloquently observes,

> In Fairbairn's schema it is more likely the characters who will propel the play's action by their endless search for peaceful coexistence and self-perpetuation. Indeed, they assure this coexistence and self-perpetuation by sacrificing aspects of their unique character in order to achieve a functional, dearly bought sense of internal order and integrity. The play itself, that action which we can witness at the outermost layers of experience, becomes a compromise that orchestrates and organizes a multiplicity of separate lives, distinct, but inextricably intertwined potentials, which may or may not see the light of day, depending on the bargains that have been struck among the players. This play, indeed, will tolerate no single author, for the play itself is nothing more than that on which its characters can agree; it is an action scripted by committee or by those renegades who choose to break from and undermine the agreed upon narrative [p. 64].

The Central Ego

One of Fairbairn's concepts that is especially useful in thinking about the treatment of dissociatively based psychic structure, is that of the central ego. The central ego is distinct from Freud's ego, and it is also distinct from Janet's concept of synthesis. The strength of the central ego can even be more important than the number and severity of internal splits. For instance, there are some patients with dissociative identity disorder (DID) whose problems in living are less severe than those with borderline personality disorder (BPD) because they have stronger central egos and are more capable of reflection.

Celani (2001) has observed that many present-day patients do not operate with these suborganizations repressed. They are dominated by libidinal or antilibidinal pursuits, searching for love or expressing their rage. Counterparts in reality have been found, often through projective identification, for the internal exciting object and the internal bad rejecting object. Because this feels so real, it is intensely meaningful to the patients, and they tend to go careening from domination by libidinal need to antilibidinal rage, and back and forth again and again. A problem is that they do not have enough central ego. As Celani says,

> the intense and undifferentiated emotionality of the subegos—one oversaturated with a desperate need for love, the other with enormous fear and anger—results in an adult with two sub personalities that are fanatic, single-dimensional, and lack knowledge of each other. . . . Many deeply split individuals operate as though they have little or no central ego, because the attenuated central ego cannot control the personality. Instead it is dominated by one or the other of the subegos who alternate as the conscious self while the central ego is pushed aside [pp. 401–402].

In my view, what Celani describes is "switching" between self-states. In conclusion, Fairbairn's model of the endopsychic situation, developed in these ways, is capable of depicting much of the intense, dynamic, dramatic interplay of self-states that we find in practice and in life.

Comments on the Dissociation Theories of Janet, Freud, Ferenczi, and Fairbairn

Even though each of these theorists—Janet, Freud, Ferenczi, and Fairbairn—reached his position by a different route, they are all describing a structural dissociation of the personality. Janet, who first conceptualized structural dissociation, understood it as posttraumatic. Freud also wrote of dissociation as proceeding from trauma, but he emphasized active, defensive dissociation. Ferenczi saw splitting of the psyche as a completely autoplastic response to psychological trauma: It was a splitting off. In contrast, Fairbairn's splitting was more of an attempt at mastery. The unfortunate result of this mastery was the constriction and relegation of emotional life to the inner world of the closed endopsychic system.

In the work of these four theorists, the understanding of dissociation was becoming more and more relationally based. Ferenczi's (1949) thinking anticipated Fairbairn's in his understanding that abused children have taken the burden of badness of the aggressor into themselves so as to enable the maintenance of the "previous situation of tenderness" (p. 228). However, Fairbairn was the first explicitly object-relational theorist. Fairbairn's description of how the child splits the psyche to accommodate problematic attachment relationships provides a theoretical basis for relational psychoanalytic theory. This leads us to the next section on interpersonalist theories of dissociation, starting with Sullivan. Sullivan had a very different approach to relationally based dissociation.

4

THE INTERPERSONAL AND RELATIONAL TRADITIONS
Sullivan, Bromberg, Davies and Frawley-O'Dea, and Stern

Harry Stack Sullivan developed an interpersonally based theory of anxiety, trauma, and dissociation. Bromberg, Davies and Frawley-O'Dea, and Stern, all theoretical descendants of Sullivan, have by different routes developed concepts of the dissociated, multiple self within the relational and interpersonalist tradition.

Sullivan's work is often contrasted to Freud's on the basis that he developed a two-person psychology, whereas Freud's was a one-person psychology. The more important contrast, however, may be with Janet, who developed a psychology of multiple centers of consciousness. Even though Sullivan thought in terms of dissociated systems, he thought of these as dissociated from one self-system. Like Freud, as well, Sullivan thought of one self developing through various epochs of life. These are two very different concepts: one self from which much is dissociated and multiple dissociated centers of consciousness. Yet Sullivan's theory had the seeds of a multiple, dissociative self theory. Bromberg, Davies and Frawley-O'Dea, and Stern, each in different ways, develop the implications of this gap in Sullivan's theory.

The concept of enactments is one of these implications. Davies and Frawley-O'Dea, who also draw on Janet and Ferenczi, describe the enactment of dissociated self-states in eight transference–countertransference positions. The connections between anxiety, trauma, and dissociation are a primary linking thread for Bromberg with Sullivan. Stern expands the implications of Sullivan's concept of selective inattention, which undergirds his own concept of unformulated experience. Stern also emphasizes that although for Sullivan the events preceding or evoking extreme anxiety are lost to consciousness, he understands these dissociative gaps not as being empty, but as being filled with—at times bursting with—unarticulated affects, expectations, and experience, which are then enacted.

Harry Stack Sullivan

Sullivan's interpersonal theory of human development was based on each person's history of interpersonal relationships with significant, real others. He saw the organization of the self as based on the internalization of the interactive patterns of these relationships, on characteristic patterns of avoiding or diminishing anxiety that have developed in the course of these relationships, and on the degree to which severe anxiety has prevented experience from being remembered, codified, elaborated, and linked with other experience. In short, Sullivan developed a model of the self in which dissociation was central. In Bromberg's (1998) view, Sullivan's (1953) theory of interpersonal analysis is essentially a "theory of the dissociative organization of self in response to trauma. . . . Sullivan restored to psychoanalytic thinking the centrality of the phenomenon of dissociation as the most basic capacity of the human mind to protect its own stability" (pp. 215–216).

Sullivan's thinking was greatly influenced by his interests in anthropology and field theory from social psychology, and by the theories of relativity and uncertainty from physics. As a result, he preferred to think in terms of processes and dynamisms rather than mechanisms. Although he had studied Freud and used his thinking in formulating his own, Sullivan rejected the "drive-structure" model (Greenberg and Mitchell, 1983), which he felt smacked of Newtonian physics and reified hypothetical structural entities. Instead, he developed a "relational/structure" model that emphasized how the "self is organized around relational configurations" and how "painful, anxiety-provoking aspects of early relations with significant others are unavoidably structured into the self" (Greenberg and Mitchell, 1983, p. 103). Sullivan emphasized that humans are brought up by other humans and continue to live in a communal existence with other humans. In the process of being brought up by humans, and as a result of experiencing anxiety and learning how to avoid it, dissociative gaps in consciousness inevitably form. The internalization of the processes belonging to the human relationships of upbringing, as it is organized by anxiety, is the basis of what constitutes the psyche. Hence, Sullivan's one-genus postulate: "We shall assume that everyone is much more simply human than otherwise" (p. 32).[1]

Anxiety and Dissociation

Sullivan's (1953) view of dissociation as central to the structure of the self derived, in large part, from his view of the contributing role of anxiety in the organization of human experience. Learning occurs on the basis of the anxiety gradient, which involves altering behavior in accordance with level of anxiety. Anxiety originally occurs by empathic induction from the mothering one; and in an ongoing sense, it "can be explained plausibly as the anticipated unfavorable appraisal of one's current activity by someone whose opinion is significant" (p. 112). The relief from anxiety yields interpersonal security.

Sullivan (1953) often compared the effect of severe anxiety to receiving a blow on the head. Its phenomenological effects are quite similar to the physiological ones that immediately follow severe head injury: The event(s) preceding, or evoking, the anxiety are lost to consciousness. "It tends to erase any possibility of elaborating the exact circumstances of its occurrence, and about the most the person can remember in retrospect, is a somewhat fenestrated account of the event in the immediate neighborhood" (p. 314). It creates a "sort of a hole" in that area of experience that was associated with the anxiety.

As Bromberg (1998) points out, to describe severe anxiety as a blow to the head is to describe trauma; and an anxiety/trauma theory of personality development is a theory that will be premised on acknowledgment of the importance of dissociative processes, as Sullivan's was. Sullivan (1956) felt that in our Western culture some degree of dissociation is inevitable, and that the necessary adjustment to it creates remarkable distortion in development. For example, he believed that all of us have dissociated integrative tendencies, including impulses for which our culture has allowed us little developmental channel, some of which are "choked off very early in our education to be socialized human beings. But they are not choked off utterly—it is probably impossible to do so. Like trees growing at the edge of the Grand Canyon, something happens, however, terribly distorted" (pp. 65–66).

There is another way in which anxiety is so central. Following from his readings of field theory and uncertainty theory, Sullivan viewed the individual as inseparable from the social matrix, both influenced by and influencing the interpersonal environment. Because the self-system has the purpose of protecting security and preventing anxiety, it can massively restrict consciousness of events in the world and in oneself. This can result in the dissociation of motives and tendencies that have not been approved by significant others, and hence are not part of what is acceptable to the self. Sullivan's concept of the "I," then, unlike Freud's, does not involve an agency that expresses and checks powerful drives emanating from within. Nor is his "I" a rational ego, struggling to tame the instincts, deal with the world, and accommodate the superego. Rather, Sullivan viewed the self as an organization of evasions and detours, constructed to avoid anxiety and preserve a feeling of interpersonal security. This self is often highly distorted, like the trees growing in the Grand Canyon: structured around the constraints, requirements, needs, anxieties, and forbidding gestures of significant others. This can be a fragile self, often avoiding massive anxiety and protected only by dissociation and those security operations that undergird it. The self is organized around dissociative gaps, such that when these gaps in self-experience are in some way prevented from being sufficiently obscured by security operations, extreme anxiety can follow.

Three Modes of Experience

Sullivan classified experience into three modes: the prototaxic, the parataxic, and the syntaxic. Prototaxic experience is the experience of momentary sensation, or simple sentience, that emerges in infancy. Later, in the parataxic mode, sentient experience becomes generalized and codified so that it can be used predictively. A great deal of experience occurs in this associationistic and private parataxic mode, and this contributes to how much remains unformulated and therefore dissociated (Stern, 1997). In contrast, the syntactic refers to experience that requires consensual validation, a consensus as to meaning that has been established with another. This experience that can be consensually shared with another has been, in a sense, interpersonally calibrated: It has been measured against the standard of other persons' understanding of shared meaning, and used accordingly. Syntaxis goes beyond egocentrism and involves the ability to see things as other people do (Bromberg, 1998, p. 42).

The Good-Me, the Bad-Me, and the Not-Me

Sullivan conceptualized the organization of the self around the requirements of anxiety in terms of three organizations of experience: the good-me, the bad-me, and the not-me. The good-me is the personification that organizes experiences involving satisfaction and tenderness and activities that have met with approval from the mothering one. It is the good-me that is invoked in general self-narratives, the "ordinary topic of discussion about 'I'" (p. 162). The bad-me is the personification of self that is associated with the increasing gradient of anxiety. Certain infant behaviors have been met with tenseness and forbidding gestures on the part of the mothering one. These gestures are anxiety-arousing to the infant and are part of the bad-me. It is important to note, however, both good-me and bad-me are "me." Both are accessible to consciousness, and can serve as guides to effective negotiation of reality, involving recognition of cause and effect.

In contrast, the not-me is out of consciousness and dissociated. It results from severe anxiety that, as indicated earlier, Sullivan (1953) understood to have an effect similar to a blow on the head, such that "these experiences are largely truncated. . . . What they are really about is not clearly known" (p. 314). The not-me is a gradually evolving primitive personification that is organized in the parataxic mode and sometimes in the prototaxic mode (Stern, 1997) of experience. It is "made up of poorly grasped aspects of living which will presently be regarded as 'dreadful,' and which still later will be differentiated into incidents which are attended by awe, horror, loathing, or dread" (Sullivan, 1953, p. 163). These experiences (1953) are marked by uncanny emotion and have been associated with intense forbidding gestures on the part of the mothering one and intense anxiety in the child.

> The not-me is literally the organization of experience with significant people that has been subjected to such intense anxiety, and anxiety so suddenly precipitated, that it was impossible for the then rudimentary person, to make any sense of, to develop any true grasp on, the particular circumstances that dictated this experience of intense anxiety [p. 314].

Thus, the not-me is dissociated, and anything evocative of not-me experience can be expected to arouse tremendous anxiety. In Sullivan's terms, it is the partition between the "me" and the "not-me" that *is* the dissociative organization of the psyche.

Selective Inattention and Dissociative Processes

Contrasting dissociation to the idea of just getting rid of some painful aspect of experience, perhaps of magically "flinging something of you into outer darkness where it reposes for years, quite peacefully," Sullivan (1953) emphasized that, when it works, dissociation works "by a continuous alertness or vigilance of awareness with certain supplementary processes which prevent one's ever discovering the usually quite clear evidences that part of one's living is done without any awareness" (p. 318).

Among the parataxic processes that avoid or minimize anxiety is selective inattention. This process, which maintains dissociation by controlling awareness of the events that impinge on us, "to a certain extent covers the world like a tent" (p. 304). In selective inattention one simply does not notice certain aspects of one's life. However, the inattention is *selective,* not random. There is a continuous vigilance to *not* notice something. The aspects of life that are selectively inattended must have been in some way attended or targeted as areas of danger (Sullivan, 1956):

> In other words, it is the way we avoid having to change as a result of the experience that we have had with others. And I stress it as the simplest and easiest way, because you see, it does not require the experience of anxiety, and the considerable discomposure which anxiety always implies [p. 56].

Sullivan observes that although this is similar to repression in its ultimate effects, it is distinct from repression in that there is no amnesia—the inattended item *can* be recalled if sufficient attention is brought to it; and it is not impulses that are inattended, but reminders of anything that would make one anxious.

Selective inattention is similar to the conscious tuning out of distractions in order to concentrate, but here the thing to be unconsciously concentrated on is the thing to be tuned out. One of the most "suave" (to use Sullivan's vernacular of the 1940s and 1950s) things about selective inattention, however, is the attitude with which serious life problems are overlooked: They are treated as irrelevant, unimportant. Often consciousness is shifted onto something seemingly higher and more important, with the result that the selectively inattended perceptions and thoughts lose their connection to other aspects of memory and personal meaning and are therefore less likely to be recalled (Sullivan, 1956).

Originally, the matters tuned out by selective inattention are not as inaccessible to consciousness as are dissociated processes, which are a functionally distinct part of the personality (Mullahy, 1970, p. 297).

However, the outcome of the dynamism of selective inattention can ultimately result in dissociation. It results in a kind of multiplication of inattended experiences, such that "processes in the pursuit of satisfaction" must be dissociated (Sullivan, 1956, p. 59). Sullivan (1956) felt that the "hierarchy of things that can happen about awareness of events begins with selective inattention and goes on to dissociation of events, with various degrees of awareness between, controlled largely by substitutive processes" (p. 63).

Substitutive behavior, which contributes to selective inattention, is designed to direct consciousness away from something else that arouses anxiety, thereby obscuring the dissociated. Hypochondriacal preoccupations are frequently observed examples of highly effective substitutive behavior. But any number of preoccupations and behaviors can serve a substitutive function. For example, Sullivan described how a much-picked-on puppy in his household took to diligently and compulsively digging holes whenever in the presence of the other dogs she was frightened of or when in the presence of unfamiliar humans. Sullivan (1956) felt that the "great wealth of substitutive processes in our culture" is evidence of serious dissociations (p. 63). The group of people most especially characterized by substitutive behaviors, however, are obsessionals. Yet here, too, as with selective inattention, the slide into more serious psychopathology is imperceptible. Sullivan felt that there is no clear demarcation between obsessional substitutive processes and episodes of schizophrenic living.

Dissociated Systems and Processes

What distinguishes dissociation is that it is not directly knowable by the individual in question: "The trick of dissociation is that one shall carry on within awareness, processes that make it practically impossible while one is awake to encounter uncanny emotion" (Sullivan, 1953, pp. 317–318). Sullivan was aware of what he considered the more unusual and/or dramatic manifestations of serious dissociative processes, such as multiple personalities and automatic writing. But what he wanted to emphasize was the everyday direct manifestations of dissociative processes.

Automatisms, which are observable to others but meaningless to the person performing them, exemplify the "everydayness" of dissociative processes. They can cut across various diagnostic conditions. One of Sullivan's examples of automatisms is interesting and perhaps speaks to aspects of experience to which he, as a gay psychiatrist, may have been especially sensitive. He observed that if one is a man who is walking down the street in a populated area of Manhattan, one might notice "quite a number of" other men at times looking at the fly of one's pants, then looking away, then looking up to meet one's gaze, seemingly to see if they have been noticed. If the other man who meets one's gaze shows embarrassment, then this is not an instance of dissociation at all, for he has been aware of his behavior. However, if this behavior is followed by numb and indifferent behavior, by complete unawareness of its occurrence, then it is dissociated. Dissociation involves behaviors singularly distinguished by the fact that their occurrence "is unknown, or at least meaningless to the person who shows them" (Sullivan, 1953, p. 322).

For Sullivan, major systems of motives become dissociated because they are antithetical or foreign to the self-system or concept of the self. Sullivan seems to have viewed dissociation both as a process in which tendencies unacceptable to the self are denied access to consciousness—that is, their development has been solely unconscious—and as a process in which they must be ejected from consciousness, which has some similarity to repression (Mullahy, 1970, p. 236).

Psychosis and Dissociation

Sullivan was considered a sort of clinical genius for the success he had and the care he took with schizophrenic patients (H. S. Perry, 1962). Unlike Freud, who thought that psychotic patients were incapable of object attachment, and therefore incapable of transference and meaningful communication with the therapist, Sullivan felt that his psychotic patients were communicating something by their behavior, even if not in words, or immediately intelligible groups of words. Sullivan felt that psychotic patients were capable of transference, but that they were distinguished from neurotics by the fact that all of their behavior was transference—that is, based on earlier patterns of behavior with significant others. He felt that here was very little "as if" in their view of the therapist (Thompson, 1967).

This view brings up interesting and puzzling questions regarding the role of trauma in the history of serious mental disorders, including those that Sullivan saw as schizophrenic. Today we know that one impact of trauma is the relegation of realms of thought that might otherwise encompass "as if" to the merely "is" or "are." Highly traumatized patients and those with severe personality disorders are especially plagued by this difficulty in grasping the subjunctive as a mode of thinking about self and other. One way of understanding this is in terms of the lack of intercontextualization of alternate perspectives and realities that can be simultaneously compared, because trauma can strip away the sense of context (Howell, 2002). Trauma makes it much more difficult for people to "stand in the spaces between realities without losing any of them" (Bromberg, 1998, p. 186).

Sullivan's understanding of the panic preceding a schizophrenic break was premised on a personality so precariously balanced between the self-system and dissociated systems, that the break meant the containing, structuring, dissociative barriers had failed. Even though Sullivan conceptualized the premorbid personality structure of schizophrenic patients as overburdened with dissociation of major motives, these patients were not usually diagnosed with dissociative disorders. However, these patients shared some interesting characteristics with today's dissociative patients: They were given to automatisms, to "made" thoughts and feelings, which are among the Schneiderian signs of schizophrenia that characterize those with dissociative disorders (Kluft, 1987). Like many highly dissociative patients, Sullivan's schizophrenics were highly subject to auditory hallucinations. And finally, as with dissociative disorders, the sense of the uncanny, of the awful and dreadful was too intensely and too often with them as a part of an ever enduring present moment. It should be noted that the way many people with acute PTSD and dissociative disorders survive prior to breakdown is by powerful selective inattention. When working with people who have these problems in living, when the dissociative barrier has failed, one can feel as if a lid covering and holding in utter terror has been lifted. One cannot avoid appreciating the power of dissociative processes.

Implications of the Interpersonal Theory

Sullivan's two-person psychology has often been contrasted to Freud's one-person psychology. Sullivan's concept of participant observation, of the therapist's inevitable part of the interpersonal field and influence on the processes observed, which derives from field theory, is consistent with his interpersonal approach to developmental theory. The most important contrast, however, may not be between Sullivan and

Freud, but between Sullivan and Janet. Although Sullivan seriously studied Freud and thought about his ideas, there is no indication that he studied Janet. Yet, for me, Sullivan and Janet represent the two systems of thinking about major issues in dissociation that are about as far apart as they can be. With respect to his theoretical works on trauma and dissociation, Janet's theory of multiple centers of consciousness can easily be extended to a theory of multiple self and multiple dissociated self-states as a condition of human life. Sullivan, on the other hand, even though he thought in terms of dissociated systems and did not discount the existence of multiple personality, conceptualized those dissociated systems as dissociated from *one* self-system. This makes the "dissociated" in many ways roughly parallel to the "unconscious" and functionally equivalent to it, even though Sullivan did not think in such terms.[2] Sullivan was well aware of the phenomenon of multiplicity, but he did not make this the basis of his model. Perhaps because Sullivan, as did Freud, thought in terms of one self developing through various stages or epochs of life, the realm of the dissociated becomes the dynamic blank space around the one developing self. These are highly divergent conceptions: one self from which much is dissociated and multiple selves that are not integrated or communicative with each other.

Other interpersonal theorists, such as Mitchell and Bromberg, have developed concepts of the multiple self, largely on the basis of Sullivan's interpersonal theory. Bromberg writes of not-me as including many dissociated parts, or self-states. Even though Sullivan thought in terms of "me–you" patterns and dissociated dynamisms, he did not make these extrapolations. For instance, contrast the theory of structural dissociation of the personality (Van der Hart et al., 2004) in which two or more selves alternate, with Sullivan's account of the self-system and dissociation. Contrast also with Kohut's (1971) and Hilgard's (1977, p. 80) metaphor of dissociation, as involving a vertical barrier, which they contrasted to repression (which is thought of as being deeper), as involving a horizontal barrier.

In Sullivan's model, much of dissociation is motivated by the person's intention to not know. In contrast, although Janet acknowledged defensive psychological intention—for instance, in phobias of parts of the self for each other—he also understood dissociation as a consequence of a psyche overwhelmed by stress. Yet, it would seem that Sullivan's not-me comes into being and grows because of being overwhelmed by anxiety. As Sullivan said, it is probably not a good idea to compare models very closely. However, it is hard not to do so.

Philip Bromberg

Bromberg's thinking about trauma and dissociation has had a profound influence on current psychoanalytic theory. He is in the forefront of relational thinking about dissociation and multiple self-states. He (1998) is the first among the new group of relational theorists who have been thinking about dissociation and multiple self-states to have articulated a model of multiple, dissociated self-states and to have starkly declared the "dissociative structure of the human mind" (p. 8). Bromberg has written many articles on trauma, dissociation, personality organization, and treatment, each one of them with a new focus and content. In 1998, he published the now well-known *Standing in the Spaces: Essays on Clinical Process, Trauma, and Dissociation,* which includes 19 of his pre-1997 articles.

The red thread that runs through Bromberg's recent work, especially that of the last two decades or so, is the centrality of dissociative processes in the human psyche. He has greatly extended Sullivan's views of how dissociation structures the personality. However, he emphasizes both multiplicity—that people tend to "feel like one self while being many"—and the indispensability of dissociation, which serves to protect our sense of illusory unity when the ravages of traumatic stress are overwhelming. He believes that mutative treatment and personality growth depend on engaging the patient's (and the analyst's) dissociated self-states in enactments in the analytic relationship, thereby enabling the unsayable to the said, with the result of personality growth and expansion.

Trauma and Dissociation

Often Bromberg illustrates his theoretical points with stories. One of his stories (2001a) concerns a panda:

> A panda walks into a bar, sits down on a stool, and orders a tossed salad and a beer. The bartender serves him, and the panda finishes his meal, pulls out a gun, and kills the man sitting on the stool next to him. He then gets up and starts to saunter out of the bar. The bartender, recovering from the shock of what he has just witnessed, shouts at the panda, "Hey, where do you think you are going? You can't just come in here, have a meal, shoot someone, and then casually leave!" The panda

> looks at him with self-righteous indignation and replies, "Hey, man, get off my back! It's no big deal. I'm just doing my thing. I'm a *panda,* for God's sake. Look it up!" And he walks out. The bartender, still in a state of shock, locates a dictionary, looks up *panda,* and, sure enough, it reads, "*panda,* a fur-bearing marsupial, indigenous to Asia. Typically, black and white. Eats shoots and leaves [pp. 385–386].

In telling the story of the panda, Bromberg illustrates the concrete state of mind. Black and white concreteness characterizes the traumatized, dissociative mind. Each self-state exists as an island of concreteness, without substantial connection to other self-states. How does this come about? In traumatic, extreme situations, when there is no hope of protection or relief, autonomic hyperarousal and affective flooding make it impossible for the mind to encode information in the usual way, into the verbal, symbolic registering of narrative memory. Instead, memory becomes registered in somatosensory modalities. Such extreme affect is disorganizing and undermining of the mind's ability to reflect on experience. But even worse is that such a subjectively terrifying experience "threatens to overwhelm sanity and psychological survival" (1998, p. 12).

How does this work? Dissociation is a human solution to the terror of dissolution of selfhood in the face of overwhelming trauma. Citing the work of Wolff (1987) and Putnam (1997), Bromberg (1994) observes that self-experience originates in relatively unlinked states, and that the "experience of being a unitary self is an acquired, developmentally adaptive illusion" (p. 260). This illusion of unity however, cannot be maintained under the press of psychological trauma, which is so cognitively and affectively overwhelming that information cannot be adequately symbolized, or schematized in a unitary fashion. Dissociation, then, preserves personal coherence, sense of continuity in time, and sense of sanity "by hypnoidally unlinking the incompatible states of consciousness and allowing access to them only as discontinuous and cognitively unrelated mental experiences." It works, *but the basic problem for the traumatized individual then becomes his own self-cure* (p. 260).

On Alert for Trauma

In his recent work, Bromberg (2003b) emphasizes how the dissociative personality structure is "on alert for trauma." What has happened is that the dissociative defense, which narrows the focus and complexity of attention, separating piece from piece of experience, has come to serve as a sort of early warning system, a fail-safe security system (p. 561). A part of the self is always on the lookout and in effect says, "Never again!" The traumatized person can't relax or have fun because so much energy has to go into this on-alert vigilance: "Thus, the continual readiness of the dissociative vigilance is what serves as the protection. It doesn't prevent a harmful event from occurring and, in fact, may often increase its likelihood. It prevents it from occurring unexpectedly" (Bromberg, 1996, p. 230). This vigilant intention to avoid current and future traumas that would feel like past ones results in a continual reenactment of these traumatic scenarios. This occurs because the traumatized mind has not been able to take in the meaning of the traumatic event. The unprocessed affective memory lives on continuously in a dissociated state and continues to reassert itself unrecognized by the person who has actually lived it under traumatic conditions. Thus, the dissociative cure continuously repeats itself in an effort to solve the environmental ills of long ago. Once we, as clinicians, begin to think this way it becomes clear that this state of affairs often leads to personality disorders.

Personality Disorders

One of Bromberg's insights involves his view that dissociation is the underlying condition of all personality disorders. Personality disorders are based on characterological structures organized as proactive, defensive responses to the potential repetition of childhood trauma. Conceptualizing personality disorders in this way allows defenses to be understood in terms of dissociative processes resulting from their traumatic etiology. Bromberg (1995) sees DID as providing a "touchstone" for understanding personality disorders:

> I have speculated . . . that the concept of personality "disorder" might usefully be defined as the characterological outcome of the inordinate use of dissociation, and that, independent of type (narcissistic, schizoid, borderline, paranoid, etc.), it constitutes a personality structure organized as a proactive, defensive response to the potential repetition of childhood trauma. If, early in life, the developmentally normal illusion of self-unity cannot safely be maintained when the psyche–soma is flooded

> by input that the child is unable to process symbolically, a configuration of "on-call" self-states is gradually constructed. . . . I am suggesting, in other words, that personality disorder represents ego-syntonic dissociation no matter what personality style it embodies. . . . A dissociative disorder proper (Dissociative Identity Disorder, Dissociative Amnesia, Dissociative Fugue, or Depersonalization Disorder) is from this vantage point a touchstone for understanding all other personality disorders even though, paradoxically, it is defined by symptomatology rather than by personality style [pp. 200–202].

Personality Growth in Treatment

Bromberg (1998) emphasizes the importance of the achievement of intrapsychic conflict. Personality growth in treatment entails an "interpersonal process of broadening a patient's perceptual range of reality within a relational field so that the transformation from dissociation to analyzable intrapsychic conflict is able to take place" (p. 8). The analyst functions as a relational bridge, consciously, and unconsciously, addressing different self-states of the patient. The fact that the analyst holds different aspects of the patient's self simultaneously in mind helps the patient to do the same. The safety and affective responsivity in the interpersonal relationship facilitates the bridging of dissociated self-states. Both analyst and patient now have "passports" to enter and leave different self-states. Thus, when dissociated self-states have incompatible goals and affects, this conflict can begin to be recognized. The increased recognition of differing and contrasting self-states increases the capacity for what Bromberg (1993) calls "health": the "ability to stand in the spaces between realities without losing any of them" (p. 186). This increase in the capacity for conflict is a gradual process that involves mutual responsivity to states of affective aliveness. But this does not happen in a technically predictable or producible way: It occurs through enactments. Because these dissociated affective memories have not been symbolized, they can only be enacted.

Enactments

The core of the mutative work occurs in enactments. The only way that the unsymbolized not-me states of mind can be communicated to the analyst and accepted by the patient is through enactment. They "must first become 'thinkable' while becoming linguistically communicable through enactment in the analytic relationship" (Bromberg, 1994, p. 252). For reasons that often have to do with shame, the analyst is unconsciously maintaining affective distance from the part of the patient that is screaming to be recognized. The internal pressure that the patient feels becomes expressed as an interpersonal one that puts pressure on the analyst. The patient is trying to force recognition into the analyst. This enactment will continue and increase until the analyst stops trying to manage the troublesome self-state by "understanding" it or interpreting it like a thing, and finds a way to welcome it into mutual space. Until this happens (Bromberg, 2000), the patient has been forced to hold on to

> unrecognized feelings as though they don't exist. And, indeed they do *not* exist because dissociated aspects of self will not be "real" unless they come to exist affectively in the mind of the "other." *If they are not personally real for the analyst, they are not personally real for the patient either* [p. 23].

Thus, dissociated, traumatic experience can only be symbolized in the context of this intersubjective affective recognition. In short, then, it is largely in enactments within the treatment that these unthought and uncommunicated islands of experience become thinkable, and therefore linkable, to the patient, by virtue of having impacted the analyst's mind.

Shame

The problem setting up the enactment is that the analyst, who is the source of the patient's shame feelings in the analytic relationship, has not been adequately attentive to the patient's feelings of shame. Thus, like Sullivan's depiction of the anxious mother who makes her baby cry and whose attempts at ministration only make the baby cry more because the mother is getting more and more anxious, the analyst is the source of the patient's shame and has to find a way with the patient to get out of the box of separate dissociative cocoons. "If the analyst does not respond with genuine concern to the patient's pain at that moment, the patient will almost always experience his or her own pain as toxic to the analyst (Bromberg, 2001a, p. 400).

However, the analyst is pulled repeatedly into the same enactment because of the difficulty in recognizing dissociated negative affect and shame. As a result, the same areas of trauma are reactivated and played out in the treatment. However, the analyst's own dissociated affect and shame is often what is getting in the way of accurate empathy: The analyst's own dissociated parts are resonating, but not communicating with the patient's.

Words and Feelings

> If one wished to read the contemporary psychoanalytic literature as a serialized Gothic romance, it is not hard to envision the restless ghost of Pierre Janet, banished from the castle by Sigmund Freud a century ago, returning for an overdue haunting of Freud's current descendants [Bromberg, 1995, p. 189].

Some of the words that Bromberg frequently uses include *abyss, spaces, strange, stranger, shock, surprise, safe* (as in *safe surprises*), *shadow, ghosts,* and *haunted.* Bromberg is keenly aware of the presence and power of the "uncanny," and its linkage, as Sullivan also detailed, with the realms of the dissociated. Dissociated experiences, often in horrifying and strange fragmented form, come back to haunt us until they are made a part of narrative memory, whether we are talking about trauma with a big *T* or a little one. Somehow, Bromberg's writings come close to the "abyss" of the readers' unprocessed experience, which his writing then helps to put into words. As was Sullivan's theory, Bromberg's theory is inclusive for all humans: All humans share in the common dilemma of dissociative response to trauma. The "shadow" of overwhelming trauma which requires a dissociative solution is an "inherent aspect of what to some degree shapes mental functioning in every human being" (1998, p. 12). Bromberg's (1993) overarching metaphor of health as "standing in the spaces between realities without losing any" (p. 186) captures an ideal, but also expresses his understanding of the potential of the human "I," in collaboration with other "I"s, to reach out to unwanted and often unrecognizable parts of the self, to not-me, and to bring these into the fold of common understanding.

Davies and Frawley-O'Dea's Model of the Dissociative Mind

Jody Davies and Mary Gail Frawley-O'Dea's book, *Treating the Adult Survivor of Childhood Sexual Abuse: A Psychoanalytic Perspective,* published in 1994, was a landmark contribution to both the psychoanalytic literature and the literature on trauma and dissociation. The book succeeded their 1991 groundbreaking article, "Dissociative Processes and Transference–Countertransference Paradigms in the Psychoanalytically Oriented Treatment of Adult Survivors of Child Sexual Abuse." In these works, the authors have successfully integrated the trauma literature with the psychoanalytic literature and brought dissociation concepts into the mainstream of psychoanalysis. In many ways, they have transformed trauma concepts into psychoanalytic paradigms.

Although they emphasize the importance of real sexual abuse that has occurred to real children and write about the impact of this trauma on psychic structure, they also stress that recovery of memories is, in itself, insufficient for psychological healing. Davies and Frawley (1994) go far beyond the trauma literature, which does not generally emphasize dissociation, per se, to emphasize the dissociative outcomes of trauma on personality structure; and they construct their model on this basis. They state their conviction that only an "approach that integrates what we have come to understand about the symbolization and encoding of traumatic memory within the framework of a relationally oriented psychoanalytic approach can provide an arena for working through such traumatic memories" (p. 45). They also state that dissociation is almost always a concomitant of sexual abuse in childhood.

At issue are not only *memories* of traumatic events and abusive experiences, but multiple, fragmented organizations of experience that have been dissociated from the stream of ongoing memory and need to be integrated with the rest of experience. They emphasize that "mutually exclusive systems of self- and object representations that have been formed in relationship to such traumatic moments" (pp. 45–46) need to be joined with the rest of experience.

Although Davies and Frawley (1994) see their model as a contemporary analog to Janet's work on dissociation, they have a very specific model of the dissociative psyche of the sexually abused survivor. At the center of their model is the recognition that the sexually abused child has had to split her experience of self into two parts: an external, daytime part and an internal, nighttime part that "nobody talks about." The adult patient, then, has two prominent parts: an adult, external persona, and one or more internal, child personae. (The child self may contain several different personae, such as the naughty, omnipotent child; the timid, good child; and the terrified victim of abuse.) The adult, external persona has managed to keep things together, go to work, and perform such tasks as bringing the patient to therapy. This external, adult self represents the "business as usual, the daytime self, the part that responds to the parent's denial of the traumatic abuse by imposing its own denial" (1994, p. 54). In contrast, the child, internal persona, experiences shame, rage, terror, experiences that have been cordoned off and made unavailable to the adult self. Because the abuse could not be spoken about, verbal links between the two dissociated aspects of self are lacking. The patient's "psychic world is organized around at least two different loci of experience, as it were, two entirely different and mutually exclusive systems of self- and object representations" (p. 55). They have different ego capacities that are reflective of essentially different sets of memories and life views. The therapist is undertaking the "treatment of two people: an adult who struggles to succeed, relate, gain acceptance, and ultimately to forget, and a child who, as treatment progresses, strives to remember and to find a voice with which to scream out her outrage at the world" (p. 67).

Davies and Frawley-O'Dea describe the internal psychodynamics between the adult persona and the child persona/e. They observe that the child and adult self each feel abandoned by the other. In particular, the child self feels that the adult self has sold out and betrayed her. Therefore, the child may undermine the adult's efforts to join the outside world and separate from her identity as a victim by self-injury, sending flashbacks or other painful intrusive reminders of her "true" identity. This, of course, incurs the adult self's wrath, making her more entrenched in viewing the child self as "bad" and responsible for her abuse. The authors observe that often when patients become more intimately aware of these internal dynamics, a third persona, an angry-adolescent protector self, emerges. This adolescent tends to be acting-out, self-abusive, and other-abusive: stealing, lying, and so on. It is this adolescent self's "job" to contain the child, and often by her own seeming "badness" to excuse the badness of the parents.

Like therapists who treat dissociative identity disorder, Davies and Frawley-O'Dea advocate addressing the parts, especially the internal child parts, directly. They understand that transference and countertransference are highly complex, involving multiple responses of various self-states of the patient and the therapist to each other. Once the clinician is clearly working with different parts of the patient, the transference–countertransference complications, stemming from the multiple and rapidly shifting changes in the patient's psychic organization, become evident. These are direct outcomes of dissociative phenomena, including shifts in the dominance of different states. In time, with the therapist's acceptance of and communication with each, the two ego states come to view each other with respect and understanding, even affection.

> For a long time, the subjective experience of each ego state is that she is a separate entity, having an autonomous cognitive, affective, and relational existence. Neither wants to relinquish her independence; both want to preserve the hard-won closeness they now enjoy. Psychically isolated for so long, each ego state cherishes having a trustworthy other around all the time. The therapist must respect the subjective experience of the patient(s), continuing to analyze both the transferences and countertransferences of each ego state to the clinician and to each other [Davies and Frawley-O'Dea, 1994, p. 155).

Davies and Frawley-O'Dea (1991) are among the first contemporary analysts to emphasize the desirablity of entering into the patient's dissociated experience, which can be a "royal road" to memory and experience that is otherwise unavailable: "Only by entering, rather than interpreting, the dissociated world of the abused child, can the analyst 'know,' through his own countertransferences, the overwhelming episodes of betrayal and distortion that first led to the fragmentation of experience" (p. 293).

Central to the thesis of Davies and Frawley-O'Dea's (1994) work is the absolute necessity of enactment within the treatment for therapy to be healing. The fact that enactment is necessary to knowing follows from the trauma model:

> It is only via the reactivation of such dissociated systems of self and object representations that the therapist working with the adult survivor can help the patient to integrate these otherwise inaccessible images that so influence his or her interpersonal experience of the world [p. 145].

Not only because the trauma could not be spoken of, but because of the nature of traumatic memory, which tends to be somatosensory and nonverbal, the nature of the transference–countertransference engagements are each time discovered anew through the enactment. These enactments enable the therapist to get to know her patient, including the child persona(e), because the therapist gets to "be" the patient in the many different role positions that are inevitably enacted (Frawley-O'Dea, personal communication). The authors state that the therapist must not only expect, but must enable the enactments, so that they can be played out, in play and in seriousness, in analytic space.

Transference–Countertransference Positions

The authors introduce four relational matrices for enactment, involving eight relational positions. These four matrices, with their corresponding positions, are (1) the "uninvolved nonabusing parent and the neglected child," (2) the "sadistic abuser and the helpless, impotently enraged victim," (3) the "omnipotent rescuer and the entitled child who demands to be rescued," and (4) the seducer and the seduced. More recently, Frawley-O'Dea (1999) has added a fifth matrix to the original four: the certain believer and the chronic doubter. The first of these matrices involving the unseeing parent and the unseen, neglected child, highlights the tremendous harm done to the child by the neglectful, nonabusing parent. Here a core issue of emotional abandonment emerges as either the patient or the therapist, and usually both, unwittingly replay the roles of the neglected child and the unseeing, neglectful parent. This relational matrix is usually the first one to emerge in treatment. The second matrix to emerge, the sadistic abuser and the helpless victim, is, like the first, also split off from consciousness in order to preserve a positive image of the relevant parent, in this case, the perpetrator. The reenactment of victim and perpetrator roles by both the patient and the therapist, and their enmeshment in this with each other, can be extremely painful and confusing. The therapist must negotiate a delicate balance between necessary confrontation and premature confrontation:

> To the extent that they ignore or minimize the patient's abusiveness, they recreate the unseeing, uninvolved parent and, ultimately, lessen the perceived safety of the analytic space. To the extent that they remain locked into a countertransference experience of victimization, they are likely to evoke intense feelings of toxicity and guilt in the patient [p. 174].

The third paradigm, of the omnipotent rescuer and the entitled child, is also a powerful one in which the child's intense wish to be rescued is reenacted. Of course, this dovetails with the therapist's role. Since there is frequently split-off entitlement, however, often no matter how much the therapist gives, it is never enough, repeating for the therapist, in her own role, the abused child's dilemma exactly. The last matrix, of the seducer and the seduced, also needs to be played out. The authors advocate that the therapist, like a good-enough parent, play within the patient's oedipal romance, delighting in romantic feelings while maintaining therapeutic boundaries. This can help the patient to nonconflictually accept herself as a sexual being.

Of course, these different matrices are often combined and can interact with each other, so that the diagrammatic simplicity of the foregoing often becomes immensely complicated. The action in treatment can shift instantaneously from matrix to matrix and from position to position. One moment the therapist may be a rescuer-helper to a needy, depleted, but thankful child; the next she is an abuser to a victimized child. One moment she may feel like a helpless victim to an entitled, enraged, abusive child; the next moment she may be an intelligent, powerful therapist, rescuing a helpless, little child; the next she is a helpless child needing to be understood by her patient. Davies and Frawley-O'Dea aptly observe that the affective intensity of these enactments can get under one's skin, and can be intensely disorganizing. But it is the only way to get to know the patient, and ultimately the only way to be helpful.

These matrices, as explicated by Davies and Frawley-O'Dea, have become keystones for practicing clinicians in the field of trauma work. They are frequently included in lecture material of presenters on the topic of trauma, frequently referenced, and have been included in the training materials for clinicians in courses sponsored by the International Society for the Study of Dissociation (ISSD). Their paradigm goes beyond the Carpman triangle, a staple of the trauma literature, which includes the positions of victim, abuser, and rescuer, each positioned at one of the heads of the triangle in a diagram. What is so important about the matrixes described by Davies and Frawley-O'Dea is that they envision the transference–countertransference enactments, with their myriad possible combinations and permutations. Here they have truly transformed trauma concepts into psychoanalytic paradigms.

Most of the patients under discussion in this book have some awareness of their different self-states; they do not experience amnesia for their alternative sets of experiences. Because of this, Davies and Frawley-O'Dea state that this highly dissociative personality organization that they so frequently find characteristic of survivors who have been sexually abused as children does not usually, in their experience, take the form of dissociative identity disorder (DID). Even though they do not emphasize this in the text, many of the patients they describe in the case examples would be classified as either dissociative disorder not otherwise specified (DDNOS) or borderline personality disorder (BPD), which can be considered to be dissociation based (Howell, 2002).

Both authors have expanded beyond the premises of their book in their subsequent thinking. Frawley-O'Dea has written a number of articles on dissociation and psychoanalysis, and supervision and sexual abuse. In addition to coauthoring a book on supervision, she has been the key psychologist involved in reporting on and analyzing the crisis of sexual abuse in the Catholic Church (Frawley-O'Dea, 2004a, b), and she has a forthcoming book on the topic. Jody Davies (1996) has continued to import Janet into contemporary psychoanalysis and to expand on Fairbairn's writings, noting how his work, which emphasizes the internalization of dissociated, interacting self–other constellations, "is a significant step forward in the articulation of a decidedly interpersonal theory of multiplicity" (p. 560). She challenges the exclusive emphasis on repression theory, suggesting that the "unconscious structure of mind is fundamentally dissociative rather than repressive in nature" (p. 564). Her metaphor of the kaleidoscope with its changing perspectives remains a very useful way of understanding changing self-states.

Donnel Stern's Model of Dissociation as Unformulated Experience

Stern's exposition of unformulated experience as dissociation has opened up new ways of understanding defense and the unconscious. Both broadening and refining the meaning of dissociation, Stern (1997) presents a view of dissociation as an active defensive process, a process involving the unconscious refusal to reflect on experience, the "unconscious decision not to interpret experience [but] to leave it in its unformulated state for defensive reasons" (p. 31). This model has the potential to reshape many of our major concepts in psychoanalysis, from problems in living, to transference–countertransference, to conceptualizing what is healing in psychoanalysis. "Unformulated experience" is not an add-on construct, as for example, "selective inattention" can be; it is one that can restructure the meaning of other constructs. The argument is encompassing: All that is dissociated is so because it is unformulated. "Unformulated experience" reverses the way we are accustomed to thinking of defense—of pushing unwanted ideas out of consciousness. Instead, Stern (1997) compares the formulation of experience to hauling up a rock from the bottom of the ocean:

> Usually we think of consciousness as the natural state of experience. We imagine that if we are unaware of something, we must have taken some action to be unaware. It is as if experience were a beach ball. It just naturally floats along the surface. If we want to keep it underwater, we have to push it down there and sit on it; and it takes work. We assume that action of exclusion of content from awareness requires effort. . . . But what if we reverse the terms and look at the appearance of experience in awareness, not as the state of affairs that occurs "naturally," "by itself," or without intervention, but as the effortful event in itself? What if things are the other way around? What if the natural tendency is for things to remain *outside* awareness? What if action and effort are required not to keep experience *out* of consciousness, but to bring it *in*? What if conscious experience is not so much like stifling the uproarious beach ball as it is like lifting a rock from the bottom and hauling it to the surface [pp. 85–86]?

This new model contrasts sharply with the idea of repression, which requires effort to get certain thoughts and impulses out of consciousness and to keep them out. According to the repression way of thinking, without a constant expenditure of energy, that beach ball pops up from underwater. "It is hard and tricky to force that ball down; we often lose our balance. And once we manage to find our balance, it is just as hard to keep that ball down there" (Stern, 1997, p. 85).

Formulation of experience is effortful and potentially risks the generation of anxiety and other painful affects. We unconsciously avoid formulating certain aspects of experience into meaningful constructs because doing so might yield knowledge that would generate intense anxiety, and also because it is difficult, requiring energy and focus.

Unformulated Experience Versus Repression

Stern (1997) contrasts his view of dissociation with Freud's view of repression, noting that the latter regarded the repressed contents as clear and discrete preformulated experience. The Freudian view of repression was based on the no-longer-accepted premise that perception is a sensory given. Thus, it becomes immediately and directly known to the person without further intermediary nonconscious decision making as to the form it will take. A new memory is added to the existing store of memories "as if it were an additional crate being stacked in a warehouse. . . . There is no place for the shadowy or unformed" (p. 53). The meaning of these stored perceptions and veridical experiences can be later defensively distorted, but this distortion is based on an initially fully formed veridical perception. Indeed, defenses may be so forceful that the "real" original meaning, the instinct that gives rise to the conscious idea, never does reach consciousness, but must remain in the unconscious. According to this view, all experience is permanently stored as fully formulated in the unconscious, but is largely inaccessible due to the distorting effects of drive and defense. It is also inaccessible because it's cast in a form that can't be cognized by consciousness—"thing presentations" of the primary process, not "word presentations," their "tamed" and diluted translation in conscious thought. "Despite appearances to the contrary, the fully formulated experience is hidden somehow in the form of what we can see, like the prince in the frog" (p. 54). Stern points out that according to this way of thinking, entry into consciousness requires a *loss* of information. In contrast, an unformulated thought, on entering consciousness, can become "more itself" (p. 45) and can *increase* the information available.

Harry Stack Sullivan and Selective Inattention

Rather than drawing on Freud's theory of repression, Stern turns to Sullivan's theoretical work in developing his own thinking about unformulated experience. He extends Sullivan's (1940) statement that "much of that which is ordinarily said to be *repressed* is merely unformulated" (Sullivan, 1940, p. 185, quoted in Stern, 1997, p. 56) by exploring one of Sullivan's key concepts, selective inattention, which addresses how a person may, in a motivated way, simply not attend to information that is threatening or frightening to know about. The end result is very much like that of repression: The person is unaware of the threatening information. However, the posited mechanism is quite different. It is not that something is pushed down out of awareness. Rather, the topic is just avoided. Sullivan believed that selectively inattended material often becomes dissociated and then lost. The self-system, which has the purpose of avoiding anxiety, is structured around these dissociated gaps. Endorsing Sullivan's emphasis on the need for interpersonal communication and self-reflection to lessen these dissociated, unformulated gaps, Stern observes that these areas of experience that could not be communicated or thought about remain unformulated and parataxic, the mode of experience that Sullivan described as nonrationally associationistic. Parataxic experiences have occurred together in a certain pattern, suggestive of certain meanings that have simply been accepted as implied, without further thought. Stern (1997) states that unformulated experience "is screened out prior to its articulation; it remains undeveloped, prototaxic (rarely) or parataxic (usually) in form" (p. 60). This experience is excluded from the self-system and deprived of its potential linkage to other areas of experience. It "can never be elaborated" (p. 60). Selective inattention, then, maintains dissociation because the selectively inattended experiences never reach consciousness.

From "Familiar Chaos" to "Unbidden Perception"

Stern comes from the constructivist position that all experience is interpretation. He views unformulated experience as a kind of "familiar chaos." Familiar chaos is unformulated experience that is forced to remain unformulated for defensive reasons. A great deal of what is unformulated, though, is that way for other than defensive reasons. This involves ways of thinking, feeling, acting, and reacting that feel like our own because they are familiar. They occur in familiar "grooves." However, this familiar chaos lacks the clarity and differentiation that examination and formulation of the experience would yield. Stern (1997) states, "Defensively motivated unformulated experience, then, or 'familiar chaos,' is the way the dynamic unconscious looks in a constructivist, dissociation-based model. Familiar chaos is to dissociation what repressed content is to repression" (p. 87). Stern observes that Sullivan seemed to assume that parataxic experience could be formulated in only one way—that there was a point-to-point correspondence between parataxic experience and the language that could potentially spell it out. According to this view, if we sufficiently attended to our unformulated experience, we should be able to formulate it. However, Stern observes, we must do more than this. Moving beyond Sullivan, Stern observes that unformulated experience is not only a source of defense, but also a source of creativity. We must allow the unformulated to organize itself. We cannot predict what form this uncreated experience will take. Emphasizing the constitutive function of language, Stern (1997) says, "Verbal-reflective meaning is never preordained, and therefore it is always ambiguous prior to its creation in each moment" (p. 30). Out of familiar chaos come unbidden perceptions. We do not construct any particular interpretation of our experience. Every new formulation occurs unbidden. This requires allowing the imagination free play. Otherwise, we would simply be translating the unformulated into prespecified concepts; if we simply translated one language into another, there would be no surprise, and no creativity. Formulating experience is an act of creation, not one of refinding something previously clear, but hidden. Drawing on Finagrette's view that consciousness is the exercise of the skill of "spelling out," Stern uses the term *spelling out* to describe interpretation in reflective consciousness. Consciousness requires that we "spell out" our experience.

Dissociation in the Strong Sense and Dissociation in the Weak Sense

Stern differentiates what he calls "dissociation in the strong sense" from "dissociation in the weak sense." However, this differentiation comes with the proviso that the strong and the weak types do not always occur in isolation: Much of unformulated experience is the result of the combination of the strong and the weak forms. Dissociation in the strong sense is an active defensive process. It is the unconscious refusal to verbally articulate experience that has some kind of nonlinguistic structure, such as can occur in highly charged transference–countertransference enactments (Stern, 1997, 2003). The strong sense of dissociation pertains to disavowed intentions "or in those instances of dissociated memories that are actually recovered in specific form at some later point" (Stern, 1997, p. 114). In the strong sense, the formulation of a meaning, or range of meanings, is defensively avoided. This is the kind of story that *must* not be told.

In contrast, dissociation in the weak sense is the kind of story that is *prevented* from being told, because other stories are more dominant, or because the story is implicit, but obscured by other formulations. In contrast to the strong sense, which derives from selective inattention, the weak sense derives from selective attention. The weak sense is passive and indirect. It is a product of "narrative rigidity" (Stern, 1997,

2003), which involves being so caught up in one story line that one does not see others. In this kind of dissociation, one simply does not see any number of things that might otherwise be understood differently—for example, meanings that might be glaringly obvious to someone outside the social system that supports them, but not to someone whose life is contexted by that social system. Being bound to one particular storyline such that one's narrative is rigid, does not imply the need to avoid formulating *particular* other kinds of possibilities. Rather, it involves being stuck in one self-limiting, self-reinforcing set of possibilities.

Encompassing both the strong and the weak sense, Stern (1997) says that the basic defensive process is the "prevention of interpretation in reflective awareness" (p. 87). We refuse to allow

> prereflective experience to attain the full-bodied reflective meaning it might have if we left it alone and simply observed the results of our capacity to create it. Dissociation is an intervention designed, in advance of the fact, to avoid the possibility that a full-bodied meaning will occur. . . . Dissociation is the deletion of imagination [p. 99].

Transference–Countertransference Enactment

In some of his more recent publications (2003, 2004) Stern has developed a model of enactment based on unformulated experience, coming to the same formal or logical position regarding the forms of interpersonal expression and defensive functions of enactments that Bromberg (1998, 2003a) holds. However, Stern (2004) has arrived at it by a different route; actually, he has been writing about enactment all along, without always using the term. He begins by reminding us that there was no concept of enactment available to Sullivan. He notes that Sullivan believed that selectively inattended material that became dissociated was then simply lost. "'Not-me' is unsymbolized experience banished from the self; and in that exiled state, while it threatens to break through when circumstances are right (or rather, wrong), it does not compete with self-experience for conscious representation" (Stern, pp. 218–219). As a result, Sullivan saw the self as structured around these blank spaces created by dissociation. Stern emphasizes that for Sullivan, this dissociated material that became "not-me" did not express itself in reflective awareness. However, Stern observes that what was not available to Sullivan is that this dissociated experience, which is unformulated because it has never been attended, must then be enacted. Thus, for Stern, dissociated states lead to enactments, and enactments are expressions of dissociated states.

Stern (2004) brings our attention to the absence of conscious experience of conflict in enactment. He describes enactment in interpersonal and constructivist terms. Because the interpersonal field is largely determinative of what is experienced by the persons in it, the ensuing enactments are interpersonal coconstructions. This means that both parties, not just the patient, are fully engaged dissociatively in any enactment.

> Enactment is the limitation of both participants' experience to one pole of what *would otherwise be* a conflict; in enactment it is precisely the point that we and the patient are each trapped within a single perception of the other. We cannot perceive anew; each of us is "singleminded." We cannot experience a way of understanding the interaction that would conflict with the perception that traps us. Taken together, the patient's and the analyst's explicit experiences comprise a conflict, but this is a fragmented conflict located across the divide of the minds, not contained within one. *Internal* conflict can be absent, and that absence of conflict, when it is clinically salient, appears as enactment [p. 220].

Stern (2004) contrasts his view of dissociative enactment as unformulated experience with the concept of splitting. He observes that in splitting, as it is generally understood (although this is not the model that he himself endorses), the different parts of segregated experience are assumed to be formulated, but unconscious. In this way, splitting is similar to repression. Whereas in dissociation (and dissociative enactment), there is the absence of a sense of conflict, in splitting the enactment "is the disavowal, by each participant, of the internal conflicts between their respective, dissociated self-states. Both parts of the conflict continue to exist in each person's mind; but they are kept apart; they may sometimes be experienced alternatively, but never simultaneously" (p. 221).

Conclusion

Stern's articulation of how unformulated experience influences personal problems in living and is a constraining aspect of human relationships, is in the Freudian and Sullivanian traditions. These emphasize psychic defense, as opposed to the Janetian tradition, which emphasizes more (than does unformulated experience), how dissociation is an automatic response to overwhelming reality, and in which there is an inability (rather than a refusal) to reflect on experience. Ultimately, this may be a "pretheoretic" distinction (Erdelyi, 2001). How can we say at what specific point the defensive functioning of the human organism, as organism, gives way to, or is superceded by, the defensive functions that belong to consciousness?

Comments on Sullivan, Bromberg, Davies and Frawley-O'Dea, and Stern

Sullivan understood the self to be organized around dissociative gaps that were reflective of unmanageable anxiety, arising in the course of early significant interpersonal relationships. Anxiety and "dreadful" experiences were relegated to the not-me, and the partition between "me" and "not-me" is *the* basic dissociation organization of the psyche. Bromberg, Davies and Frawley-O'Dea, and Stern have independently developed concepts of dissociated self-states as revealed and healed in transference–countertransference enactments.

The interpersonal focus is significant for dissociation theory because once we understand relationships to be internalized, the stage is set for a multiple self. Extreme anxiety, abuse, and interpersonal neglect in these relationships are dissociogenic. Ryle continues the relational tradition with his multiple self states model based on dissociated reciprocal role relationships. Although Ryle is not formally a psychoanalyst, his thinking, including his emphasis on enactments, has much in common with relational psychoanalysis. His clinical approach, which involves helping the patient to formulate un–thought-through meanings of early important role relationships, is in many ways consistent with Stern's. Ryle's multiple self states theory, premised on dissociated enactive processes, leads off the next section on nonpsychoanalytic hybrid perspectives.

5

HYBRID MODELS
Ryle's Multiple Self States Model; Van der Hart, Nijenhuis, and Steele's Theory of The Structural Dissociation of the Personality; Hilgard's Neodissociation Theory; and Somatoform Dissociation

Ryle's multiple self states model is a hybrid one, par excellence. It is influenced by object relations theories, cognitive theories, Bowlby's attachment theory and modern attachment theory, and the works of Vygotsky and Bakhtin. Ryle understands the self in terms of relationship or dialogue with internalized figures and voices. He calls his model a semiotic object relations model. Despite the multiple genetic strands, what emerges is one cohesive theory of which the basic units are enduring patterns of interactions based on early role relationships with significant others.

Hilgard's neodissociation theory is also a hybrid theory in that although it formally emerged in the context of the author's hypnosis experiments, he had preexisting knowledge of theories of divided consciousness and he was familiar with psychoanalysis. What he added to these areas was psychological knowledge of information processing and brain function. Hilgard states his debt to Janet in the development of his model. His neodissociation theory brought back recognition of the omnipresence of dissociation in mental functioning. Hilgard hypothesized multiple cognitive systems or structures that interact with each other, but that are also relatively independent. This model of how attention, thought, and behavior can become autonomous and isolated is similar to Janet's model of the dissociated psyche.

The theory of the structural dissociation of the personality, proposed by Van der Hart, Nijenhuis, Steele, and colleagues, is another hybrid theory. Based on the thinking of Janet, this theory incorporates other trauma theories, theories of animal defense, and psychobiological states. This is a cohesive theory, which is clearly articulated, and which addresses the central issue of how we understand dissociation. Although the theory of the structural dissociation of the personality includes somatoform dissociation within its own terms, somatoform dissociation is also treated separately in this section because it is also a hybrid model unto itself with many contributing sources. Somatoform dissociation is always enacted in one way or another. In this way, it shares much in common with current relational psychoanalytic theory. And current psychoanalytic theory is more and more including somatoform dissociation and relational enactive procedures.

Ryle's Cognitive Analytic Therapy and the Multiple Self States Model

For more than 15 years, Ryle has been writing prolifically about multiple self states and dissociation. Although his books on cognitive analytic therapy (CAT) have been widely available, most of his papers have been published in British medical, psychological, and academic journals. CAT emphasizes the embeddedness of the individual in the social matrix and the importance of the internalization of reciprocal role relationships in the development of the personality. The developmental theory of cognitive analytic therapy has itself been an evolving process, influenced at different times by many different sources, including object relations theories; cognitive theory, especially Kelly's personal construct theory; Bowlby's evolutionary attachment theory; current-day attachment and infant development theories, as well as Vygotskian theory; and Bakhtin's model of the dialogic self. Despite the multiple genetic strands, what emerges is one cohesive theory of which the basic units are enduring patterns of interactions based on early role relationships with significant others. These internalized reciprocal role procedures (RRPs) structure and limit how we think and behave as well as what we continue to expect from others and ourselves. They operate internally, between self and self, as well as interpersonally, between self and others.

Cartesian Monadism Versus the Dialogic Self

The great majority of our psychological theories assume monadic mental processes. For instance, both schema theory and psychoanalytic theory assume a monopsychism. Even Sullivan, whose interpersonal theory emphasized the self's dependence on the responses of others and included description of me–you patterns, still conceptualized this self in monadic terms. In contrast, in Ryle's cognitive analytic therapy model, processes of the self are understood in terms of relationships or dialogue with internalized figures or voices. As Ryle and Kerr (2002) say, the "'I' is more a federation than a single nation" (pp. 35–36).

Ryle (1997) calls his model a *semiotic object relations model.* Following Vygotsky, he emphasizes that before formal language is acquired, babies and children learn meanings and intentions conveyed by gesture, voice tone, mimicry, movement, and so on:

> Our first learning occurs through interaction with others; internalized in the form of mediating signs, this interaction provides the basis of that internal dialogue which constitutes thought. That the essential basis for mediated thought is learned in a social context means that those aspects of thought concerned with concepts of self and other are learned from others who provide both our first experiences, and to a considerable extent, provide the means we have of making sense of them [p. 19].[1]

Ryle (Ryle and Kerr, 2002) emphasizes that affects, behaviors, and cognitions are not isolated and that "learning and becoming a person occur essentially within the context of relationships with others. . . . We do not store representations to which we then spread a mayonnaise of meaning, representations are imbued with meanings acquired in the course of our activity in an intersubjective universe" (p. 40).

Ryle also draws on Bakhtin's concept of the dialogic self, which posits that the self is constituted by interpersonal dialogues and emphasizes how dependent the self is on others for consciousness and thought. As Bakhtin said, "I am conscious of myself and become myself only while revealing myself to another . . . a person has no sovereign territory; he is wholly and always on the boundary; looking inside himself, he looks into the eyes of another or with the eyes of another" (Bakhtin, 1986, quoted in Ryle and Kerr, 2002, pp. 36–37). The Cartesian "I think, therefore I am" becomes replaced in the CAT dialogic model with "We interact, and therefore I become" (p. 59).

Reciprocal Role Procedures, States, and Self States

The basic unit of description in CAT is the reciprocal role procedure (RRP), a relational unit involving generalized procedural memories. According to CAT, reciprocal role procedures are acquired and linked in sequences in the course of development. These procedures not only incorporate, but seek and predict responses from the other. This dependence on the responses of others continues to characterize the self throughout life. As a result of interactions with significant others in childhood, these procedures come to embody particular meanings and feelings, which may not be understood or formulated in any formal or verbal sense.

Unlike the static images or representations of self and object, described in the more well-known currents of psychoanalytic theory and object relations theories, the reciprocal role procedures described by CAT are enacted. Relational processes, rather than objects or object relationships, are internalized. Here Ryle is in agreement with current writers and workers in the attachment theory and infant development field, such as Sander (2002), D. N. Stern (1985, 2004), Lyons-Ruth (1999, 2001a, b), and others in the Boston Process of Change Study Group, who write of the internalization of implicit relational procedural enactments.

In particular, Ryle's model of reciprocal role patterns is similar to Lyons-Ruth's (1999, 2001a) view that dissociation can result from disconnections among systems of dyadic, procedural enactments—especially in families with hostile or helpless relational patterns. Both Ryle and Lyons-Ruth present a two-person model of cognition, affect, and behavior. Both models are based on procedural learning of dyadic roles. When dissociated, these two-person self states provide templates for rigid reenactments of old experience.

Ryle (1997b) understands a state as a "state of being," or mental state, as a distinct, contrasted aspect of being, feeling, and behaving. Examples of states are victim state, bully state, rage state, revengeful state, dismissive contemptuous state, powerful caretaker state. Although states are generally experienced in terms of particular emotion and mood, similar emotions or moods may characterize more than one state. The state represents one pole of a reciprocal role pattern and is understood in relation to its reciprocal. States tend to be identified with roles, which are defined as "combining memory, affect and action organized in relation to the search for, or the experience of, reciprocation" (p. 27). Thus the role, like the state, is identified in relation to its reciprocal.

Dissociation and the Multiple Self States Model

Although healthy development relies on the internalization of positive reciprocal role interactions, neglectful and abusive environments make an integrated, adaptive, flexible sense of identity much more difficult.

When a person grows up internalizing dysfunctional role relationships, this fosters pathological dissociation in several ways. A child who is neglected, abused, or both is likely to lack adequate assistance in naming experiences and in linking them together in the context of interpersonal experience. Furthermore, trauma can bring about the dissociation of aspects of overwhelming experience, fragmenting the self. Finally, in a neglectful, dysfunctional family environment, there is inadequate repair of the fragmented self.

The multiple self states model (MSSM) reformulates problems and disturbances in living along a continuum of degree of dissociation between self states, which include the role and its reciprocating role in interaction. Whereas healthy identity development is more characterized by coherent, integrated configurations of RRPs, less fortuitous development is characterized by dissociated and contradictory self states which dominate interpersonal interactions and self-experiences. These partially and wholly dissociated self states alternate and exert pressure on others to respond with the expected reciprocation, thereby perpetuating the same unhappy attitudes and distressing situations. Along the continuum, there is an increasing lack of integrity within the system of self states. This spectrum of dissociation extends from normalcy (or optimum development) through severe personality disorder, such as BPD, with an endpoint of DID.

Much of psychopathology, when conceptualized in terms of the relative integration of reciprocal role repertoires, comes under the realm of the dissociated and partially dissociated. Thus, Ryle understands personality disorder and much of psychosis in terms of dissociated and partially dissociated self states. Ryle has focused in particular on borderline personality disorder, which he sees as characterized by a narrow range of roles—some with extreme affects, and partially dissociated self states. What he means by partially dissociated is that "between these states there may be impaired memory but complete amnesia is rare, and some capacity for self-observation across all, or nearly all states is present" (Golynkina and Ryle, 1997, pp. 430–431). In BPD there is an alternating dominance of a constricted range of reciprocal role patterns.

In people diagnosed with BPD, confusing state switches occur too often. Understood in reciprocal role terms, these changes may involve response shifts and role reversals within the same self state as well as self state shifts. With reference to the first, responses may shift in relation to one reciprocal role, for example, shifting from striving to resisting in relation to demanding. Or there may be a role reversal between, for example, striving and demanding. In the self state switch, an example would be shifting from striving in relation to demanding to another self state entirely, such as involving anger in response to threat. (Golynkina and Ryle, 1997).

A recent pilot study by Ryle and his colleagues (Bennett, Pollock, and Ryle, 2005) investigated characteristic features of common borderline states, using his States Description Procedure. All of the 12 participants identified with the Victim and Bully states, supporting both the probability of a background of abuse in BPD and the concept of the reciprocal role procedures. Thus the participants identified with both poles of the abusing–abused pattern. This is confirmatory of my own view of BPD as a dissociation-based disorder which is an outcome of trauma (Howell, 2002).

Defense

As Sullivan did, Ryle has a distaste for positing "deep," unconscious motives, especially in the absence of confirming evidence other than the analyst's theory. He is especially sensitive to the potentially destructive consequences of attributing unconscious motivation to the patient, to which the patient may not be privy, and which can be experienced as blaming. Like Sullivan, also, Ryle is appreciative of the extreme dependence of the self on confirming responses from others.

He prefers pragmatic and parsimonious views of "defense." For instance, he sees splitting as simply a form of contrasting, polarized reciprocal role patterns, and projective identification as a form of procedural enactments, in which the two parties have become engaged, fueled by a special need of one or both parties for a particular kind of confirmation from the other. This is most evident where dissociated RRPs are concerned. The internalization of self–other procedures implies the corresponding ability to elicit reciprocation from others. The more narrow the reciprocal role patterns, the greater will be the need for confirmation of self from others within these limited role repertoires. Consequently, the other person in interaction is more likely to feel pressured (see chapter 5, on projective identification).

Levels of Deficit and Damage

The multiple self states model describes three levels of deficit and damage in personality development. The person who has grown up with neglect, abuse, or both is likely to show problems in three primary areas. The first level concerns the reciprocal role relationships themselves, including their enhancing or restrictive qualities for well-being. For the survivor, this involves the negative and restrictive RRPs that the person has internalized. Examples are "contemptuous–contemptible" and "abusing–abused." Such RRPs (Pollock, 2001) have been internalized because the survivor's "experiences of the perpetrator's actions which have induced or forced the survivor to experience certain roles, states of mind and emotions. Living in an abusive, rejecting or neglectful family environment, therefore, colours the range, flexibility and scope of the repertoire of RRPs acquired by the survivor" (p. 61).

The second level involves higher order metaprocedures that link the level 1 procedures and organize smooth transitions between them. Thus, a combination of many different RRPs involving different people and different relationships can be executed simultaneously. For example, by means of level 2 functions, a child at breakfast may combine (a) silent obedience to an irritable father, (b) nurturance for a depressed mother, and (c) cheerful mutuality with a sister (Pollock, 2001). In contrast, deficits in this level cause segregation of RRPs into a number of distinct, segregated self states that are dissociated or partially dissociated from each other. Level 3 concerns consciousness itself, including the capacity for self-reflection and reality testing. Frequent shifting between self states evokes confusion about reality and interferes with the capacity for self-reflection.

Problems in living occur because of the self-reinforcing nature of these reciprocal role procedures which are dysfunctional. Clearly, dissociation is a very important source of this continuing dysfunction.

Case Example. Barry grew up with an exceptionally depriving and neglectful father and was able to identify two primary RRPs in therapy: depriving–deprived and neglectful–neglected. Barry's daily existence was colored with feelings of deprivation. He frequently found himself in continuous internal dialogues that centered on these RRPs. Whenever he wanted something, there would be an internal voice that would say, "You can't have it." Ironically, without Barry being aware of it, a generational pattern had been asserting itself with Barry's son, who was putting himself through graduate school mostly on loans, just as Barry had had to do in college. Somehow Barry's son was able to communicate to his father how deprived and neglected he felt. This led to Barry's making a decision to sell his boat in order to provide substantial help to his son. Barry's decision ended up being transformative, not only of his relationship with his son but also for himself. He found that he had stepped outside the constraining bounds of the depriving–deprived, neglecting–neglected RRPs to discover a whole world of possible ways of feeling and relating that he had not known existed. Although in many ways he had been quite nurturing and confirming to his son and had made a strong effort to treat his children differently and better than his parents had treated him, he realized that he had not been aware of how, in other important ways, he was enacting the same RRPs with his son that had been formed in his relationship with his own father. With this experience he had of stepping outside these two constraining dominant RRPs of his life, he realized that his continual experience of being deprived had important sources beyond the reality constraints of finances. He found that *he* did not feel deprived anymore. The deprived–depriving RRP had in many ways dominated his consciousness and foreclosed other ways of experiencing himself in relationships with important others.

Barry's psychic life was characterized by restricted RRPs and dissociative shifts between them: from states of deprived to depriving, from neglected to neglecting, and from these self states entirely to others, involving "unconsciously" (or in an un–thought-through, unformulated way) idealizing his father for being depriving. This understanding of state shifts helps to explain enactment, which, as a concept, is such a staple of relational psychoanalysis. Here the issue is not so much repression in a dynamic unconscious, but dissociation as unformulated experience (Stern, 1997).

Treatment

The theory contains the language of treatment. The therapeutic process rests on the description and revision of reciprocal role procedures, especially in identifying dominant dysfunctional RRPs. Dominant RRPs, including self states and the shifts between them, are the focus of the identified problems of the patient and are the basis of understanding the transference and the countertransference. Especially with reference to transference–countertransference, the therapist needs to think reciprocally.

The emphasis here is on description, rather than formal interpretation on the part of the therapist. Of course, interpretation cannot be entirely avoided inasmuch as all understanding is interpretative (Stern, 1997), but the emphasis is on a description that is ultimately agreeable to both parties. Because the meanings and implications of these early role relationships, especially the problematic ones, have not been formulated, that becomes the task of treatment. This is similar to Stern's (1997) view of unformulated experience. Ryle's treatment approach involves not only the use of words, but also other linguistic modalities such as diagrams, to help to formulate with the patient the dominant interactive paradigms of the patient's life. Therapy is conceived to be a collaborative and noncollusive enterprise, involving a relationship of emotional mutuality.

Ryle has also spearheaded, conceptualized, and participated in many descriptive and measurement devices that help patients and clinicians conceptualize and visualize the particular problems and personality structures under discussion. Among these are the previously described MSSM, the Procedural Sequence Object Relations Model (PSORM), the States Description Procedure (SDP), the Self-States Description Diagram (SSDD), the Procedural Sequence Model (the PSM), and the Personality Structure Questionnaire (PSQ). Most of these can be used psychometrically, enabling Ryle's hypotheses to be tested empirically.

Ryle's work has much to offer the fields of dissociation and psychoanalysis. Ryle's voice is independent, and his theory is synthetic. His model of RRPs affords clear, logically consistent and user-friendly concepts for understanding dissociation.

Theory of the Structural Dissociation of the Personality

The theory of structural dissociation of the personality was formulated and introduced into the literature by Van der Hart, Nijenhuis, Steele, and colleagues (Nijenhuis and Van der Hart, 1999a, b; Van der Hart et al., 2000; Steele, Van der Hart, and Nijenhuis, 2001; Van der Hart et al., 2004). It is a new, conceptually clear theory of dissociation, which synthesizes certain classical and contemporary theories of trauma and dissociation. The primary focus is that "dissociation" denotes a structural dividedness of the personality. It is a "lack of integration among psychobiological systems that constitute personality" (Van der Hart et al., 2004, p. 906). The theory "postulates a common, psychobiological pathway for all trauma-related disorders. Trauma-related dissociation is maintained by integrative deficits and phobic avoidance" (p. 906).

Although its basic premise is simple, the entire theory of structural dissociation is a complex but cohesive synthesis. Although the contributory sources of the theory are divergent, they all have one thing in common: an emphasis on structural dividedness. Van der Hart et al. (2004) observe that this clear limitation of scope sets their theory apart from other theories of dissociation, which encompass related but nondissociative phenomena.

In the development of this theory, Van der Hart, Nijenhuis, Steele, and their colleagues have incorporated not only Janet's discoveries, but some of the concepts of Charles Myers, a World War I physician and psychologist and student of Janet's, as well as Putnam's discrete behavioral systems (DBS) model; Van der Hart's delineation of primary, secondary, and tertiary dissociation; Nijenhuis's concepts of animal defense systems; and other theories of emotional and behavioral operating systems.

According to the theory of structural dissociation, the most basic structural division of the personality is between what is referred to as the "emotional part of the personality" (EP) and the "apparently normal part of the personality" (ANP). (The original terminology, proposed by Myers, is discussed shortly.) Together, the EPs and the ANPs constitute one personality that has not been sufficiently integrated.

At its base, the theory endorses Putnam's discrete behavioral systems (DBS) model of the personality, which emphasizes, as described in chapter 2, that, rather than starting out as a unity, the human personality must become integrated over time. Psychological trauma and neglect impede the process of integration. Deficits in integration are antecedently related to the existence of dissociated parts of the personality.

Next, the theory includes the actions of psychobiological action systems, which are innate, self-organizing behavioral systems. They include both (1) action systems devoted to carrying on daily life, such as those concerning reproduction, child rearing, attachment, sociability, exploration, and play, and (2) defensive action systems and subsystems, which are devoted to the survival of the individual in conditions of threat. These latter defensive action systems include hypervigilance, fight, flight, freeze, and total submission. The freeze state is accompanied by analgesia; the total submission state is accompanied by anesthesia. Related to defense is a subsystem of recuperation, in which pain perception is reinstated and wound care begins (Nijenhuis, Vanderlinden, and Spinhoven, 1998c; Nijenhuis, 1999; Nijenhuis et al., 2004; Van der Hart et al., 2004).

Under the impact of trauma, especially chronic trauma, these two types of psychobiological action systems—the ones devoted to daily life and the ones devoted to defense—become segregated and divided against each other (Van der Hart et al., 2004):

> The essential and primary form of trauma-related dissociation of the personality is a lack of integration between parts of the personality that are mediated by daily life action systems and defensive action systems as a result of threat to bodily integrity and threat to life. The action tendencies involved in these two sets of action systems tend to inhibit each other once they are strongly evoked, hence are not easily integrated in circumstances of major threat, particularly chronic threat [p. 909].

Van der Hart et al. (2004) have noted the remarkable correspondences between these two sets of psychobiological action systems, relating to daily life and defense, with the parts of the personality identified by Myers: the emotional personality (EP), devoted to defense, and the apparently normal personality (ANP), devoted to actions of daily functioning. Myers treated acutely traumatized combat soldiers in World War I. He introduced the term *shell shock,* although he later regretted that choice of words (Van der Hart, personal communication), which now comes under the rubric of PTSD. Building on Janet's initial observation that dissociation denotes an organized division of the personality, characterized by insufficient integration of systems of functions, Myers developed a conceptualization of what happened to the personality in trauma. Although Myers's basic terminology of EP and ANP has been retained in this theory for the sake of clarity and historical accuracy, it does not literally denote a "personality," but a part of the self. It refers to one personality that has not been sufficiently integrated. The descriptive words in the new theory have been changed to reflect this meaning. Thus, according to the theory of structural dissociation, the emotional part of the personality (EP) remains rooted in the trauma, often reenacting it, and focused on a narrow range of cues that were relevant to the trauma. The apparently normal part of the personality (ANP) is devoted to daily living, which is interfered with by the traumatic memories of the EP.

According to Myers (1940, cited in Van der Hart et al., 2000), the EP, which is stuck in the trauma, becomes segregated from the more constricted ANP as a result of trauma. This process enables the person to avoid the affect and information held by the EP. Importantly, ANP is only apparently normal; the appearance of normality is belied by the periodic intrusions of the EP. The dissociated emotional part of the personality (EP) intrudes in nightmares, dreams, somnambulisms, intrusive thoughts, flashbacks, and somatoform symptoms. In addition to the intrusion of the EP into the ANP, the EP and the ANP often alternate:

> Gradually or suddenly an "apparently normal" personality usually returns–normal save for the act of all memory of events directly connected with the shock, normal save for the manifestation of other (somatic) hysteric disorders indicative of mental dissociation. Now and again there occur alternations of the "emotional" and the "apparently normal" personalities. . . . On its return, the "apparently normal" personality may recall, as in a dream, the distressing experiences revived during the temporary intrusion of the "emotional" personality. The "emotional" personality may also return during sleep, the "functional" disorders of mutism, paralysis, contracture, etc., being then usually in abeyance. On waking, however, the "apparently normal" personality may have no recollection of the dream state and will at once resume his mutism, paralysis, etc. [Myers, pp. 66–67, quoted by Van der Hart et al., 2000, p. 40].

The Emotional Part of the Personality (EP)

Van der Hart et al. (2000) give examples of the sudden emergence of the EP in dissociative hysterical attacks from the psychiatric annals of World War I. One young soldier had frequent episodes in which he would suddenly fall to the ground and then reenact a forgotten scene from the trenches: In the effort to repel the enemy, he would begin to work the machine gun and shout to his comrades. These dramatic reenactments would then give way to contorted spasmodic motions, which would then subside, followed by sleep (McDougall, 1926, cited in Van der Hart et al., 2000, p. 49). In another example of a dissociative attack (of an EP), a young captain

> exhibit[ed] a purposive motor delirium like that of a man suffering with terrifying hallucinations; thus he sat up in bed muttering continuously, moving his head and body from side to side,

> stretching out first one hand and then the other as if pushing away some hateful object, alternating his movement by that of passing his hand across the forehead. There appeared to be a perseveration of the gestures of horror. . . . It was ascertained that . . . [a] piece of exploded shell had knocked off the head of a brother officer while he was talking to him, scattering blood and brains over his face [Mott, 1919, pp. 166–167, quoted in Van der Hart et al., 2000, p. 50].

Another young soldier was often subject to a spasm that gave the facial appearance of rage. Although he had no understanding of this symptom and no memory of its origins, under hypnosis he "relived a forgotten scene: he oversaw, while lying hidden in the enemy's territory, several enemy soldiers maltreating one of his comrades; he was overcome with rage, and at that moment he received a bullet-wound and lost consciousness" (Simmel, 1919, quoted by McDougall, 1926, pp. 300–301, quoted by Van der Hart et al., 2000, p. 46). This soldier's tic ceased when the memory was recalled and the dissociation was overcome.

The Apparently Normal Part of the Personality

Both the ANP and the EP are dissociative parts of the personality. Even though the ANP may often appear to have a larger scope and greater functionality, once there is an EP, the ANP can only be a part of the personality. It is not correct to say that the EP is dissociated from the ANP as if the ANP is unaffected except for this intrusive trouble-maker, the EP. Their alternations are manifestations of the dividedness of dissociation (Van der Hart et al., 2004).

The ANP is vigilantly avoidant. The topics of trauma may be passively avoided or actively suppressed. In either case, over time the avoidance may become automatic. Because of the vigilance and contraction required by such avoidance, this aspect of the self, which is only apparently normal, does indeed differ substantially from the premorbid presentation. This is clearly evident in the stories of the survivors of sudden, extreme, acute trauma, such as the Holocaust, rape, war, and so on.

Untreated severe trauma can lead to chronic severe characterological hopelessness. Krystal (1995) describes the results of a 30-year follow-up on the lives of Holocaust survivors. He found that problems of "chronic depression, masochistic life patterns, chronic anxiety, and psychosomatic disease continue" (p. 77). His attempts to engage aging survivors in psychotherapy were for the most part unsuccessful: "Unable to grieve effectively, most survivors become severely depressed, become ill, and die early. While they are alive, they live in constant pain" (p. 97). One could characterize the tragic outcome as being due to a chronic unrelenting ANP. Here, topics of trauma are often actively suppressed or passively avoided (the common advice, "Try not to think about it"). In either case, the avoidance may over time become automatic; such an automaticity can fill a lifetime: "Apparent normality can evolve into a detached lifestyle that relies on avoidance of intimacy and emotion" (Nijenhuis and Van der Hart, 1999a, p. 43).

Primary, Secondary, and Tertiary Structural Dissociation

Primary structural dissociation involves one EP and one ANP. Examples of primary structural dissociation are simple PTSD, simple dissociative amnesia, and simple somatoform disorders, such as conversion disorders, as described in *DSM-IV*. In these cases, ANP tends to be detached and numb, characterized by partial or complete amnesia of the trauma, whereas EP is usually limited in scope, but is hypermnestic, reexperiencing the trauma (Van der Hart et al., 2004).

Secondary structural dissociation involves one ANP and more than one EP. Examples of secondary structural dissociation are complex PTSD, complex forms of acute stress disorder, complex dissociative amnesia, complex somatoform disorders, some forms of trauma-related personality disorders, such as borderline personality disorder, and dissociative disorder not otherwise specified (DDNOS). Secondary structural dissociation is characterized by dividedness of two or more defensive subsystems. For example, there may be different EPs that are devoted to flight, fight, freeze, total submission, and so on (Van der Hart et al., 2004). Gail, a patient of mine, does not have a personality disorder, but she describes herself as a "changed person." She survived a horrific car accident that killed several others, and in which she was the driver. Someone not knowing her history might see her as a relatively normal, but somewhat anxious and stiff person (ANP). It would not occur to this observer that only a year before, Gail had been a different person: fun-loving, spontaneous, flexible, and untroubled by frightening nightmares and constant anxiety. Fortunately, Gail has been willing to pay attention to her EPs; she has been able to put the processes of integration in motion; and she has been able to heal.

In tertiary structural dissociation there are two or more ANPs as well as two or more EPs. This is descriptive of dissociative identity disorder (DID), which is often comorbid with complex PTSD and some personality disorders. Thus, there may be different ANPs who perform aspects of daily living, such as work in the workplace, child rearing, and playing (Van der Hart et al., 2004). Often DID is associated with disorganized attachment style, which occurs early in life, often following abuse and neglect. In disorganized attachment there is an alternation between different systems of attachment (Liotti, 1999; Blizard, 2003).

Janice, a patient of mine, who as a child was frequently raped and used as a prostitute by her caretakers, at times wakes up from sleep with her arms and legs flailing, as if fighting someone off. She has no control over this activity, which is the intrusion of an emotional part of her personality (EP) while it is occurring. When she initially presented for treatment, Janice had florid PTSD and DID. She was almost totally amnestic for any memories of the causes of her symptoms. In treatment she has been recapturing and piecing together memories of her early adolescence by means of flashbacks and somatic reenactments. Sometimes these relived traumatic experiences take hours, or even days to unwind–like an unstoppable film, from beginning to end. She has been, in effect, spellbound to watch and participate in, again, the horrors that have already happened. However, unwelcome as they have been, many of these memories have now become narrative memories. These lengthy flashbacks can be understood as the intrusions of different EPs. Like many of the victims of child sexual abuse, Janice did not initially remember these events as narrative memory. Rather, they came upon her in the form of horrifyingly painful flashbacks, dissociated visual imagery, and somatic, motor reenactments.

In many such cases, the intrusions are "hallucinatory, solitary, and involuntary experiences (that) consist of visual images, sensations and motor acts that engross the entire perceptual field. They are characterized by a sense of timelessness and immutability" (Nijenhuis and Van der Hart, 1999a, p. 42).

Here it is useful to return to Myer's (1940) thinking, with his goal of treatment:

> The treatment to be recommended . . . consists in restoring the "emotional" personality deprived of its pathological, distracted, uncontrolled character, and in effecting its union with the "apparently normal" personality hitherto ignorant of the emotional experiences in question. When this re-integration has

> taken place, it becomes immediately obvious that the "apparently normal" personality differed widely in physical appearance and behaviour, as well as mentally, from the completely normal personality thus at last obtained [pp. 68–69].

ANP and EP

EP generally corresponds to the intrusive positive symptoms, such as acute reexperiencing of the trauma; ANP generally corresponds to negative symptoms of loss and inhibition, such as amnesia, anesthesia, paralysis, blindness, mutism, and so on. However, negative symptoms are also related to the subsystems of animal defense, such as freezing, analgesia, and anesthesia, and thus may also be present in EP.

ANP may normally appear undisturbed, but be constricted and have significant losses—for example, the memory of the trauma. Yet, when traumatic memories are triggered, it may be inactivated, to be succeeded by an EP. ANP avoids the information and affect held by EP and is likely to be partially or totally amnestic for the trauma. As a result, ANP becomes phobic for EP and everything contained in it, including the memory of the trauma, cognitions, emotions, as well as sensory memories encoded in the body (Van der Hart et al., 2004).

PTSD

The theory of structural dissociation encompasses PTSD and the entire range of posttraumatic disturbances. Van der Hart et al. (2004) are emphatic in showing how this construct demonstrates the dissociative nature of PTSD. They point out that intrusion is a key diagnostic feature of PTSD in *DSM-IV,* which has often not been understood as dissociative. Furthermore, "Intrusions imply a lack of integration of the part(s) of the personality that remain fixated in traumatic events, thus a lack of integration of the personality. Positive dissociative symptoms, including intrusions, are common in trauma-related disorders" (p. 908). Earlier, in 2000, Van der Hart et al. emphasized that

> all phenomena that are manifestations of trauma re-experiences (reactivated traumatic memories), such as flashbacks, should be seen as positive dissociative symptoms. To the extent that this theoretical position can be accepted by students of

> trauma, they cannot but consider the re-experiencing phenomena in PTSD, such as "recurrent and intrusive recollections of the event, including images, thoughts, and perceptions" (APA, 1994, p. 428) as positive dissociative phenomena. The same is true of acute stress disorder (ASD) [p. 51].

The various manifestations of EP and ANP are also illustrative of somatoform dissociation, which will be discussed in the following section. EP stores the traumatic memories and intrudes into the consciousness of ANP in sensorimotor ways, such as with vivid visual hallucinations, occasional auditory hallucinations, tics, contractures, and sudden frozen immobility, or sudden motor activity, such as waking from sleep to fight off an attacker. Likewise, the ANP, with its sensorimotor losses, such as mutism, paralysis, blindness, deafness, and sensory anesthesia, also represents somatoform dissociation

Ernest Hilgard's Neodissociation Theory

Ferenczi and Hilgard, the first a clinician and the second an experimental psychologist, had something important in common: The most important things that they learned in their work resulted from their openness to the experiences and input of other people, either their patients or their students and experimental subjects. The origin of Hilgard's neodissociation theory—the phenomenon of the "hidden observer"—emerged quite spontaneously. This experimentally revealed phenomenon is highly illustrative of dissociated structures and processes (Hilgard, 1977, 1994).

One day Hilgard (1994) was demonstrating hypnotic deafness to his undergraduate class. His subject was a blind student who was known for his hypnotic talent. Hilgard and his volunteer subject proceeded to demonstrate some rather amazing feats of hypnotically induced deafness, such as the subject's lack of reaction to the sound of wooden blocks loudly banging close to his head. One of the students in the class asked if some part of the subject might know what was going on, because his hearing was normally functional. Hilgard then asked the hypnotized subject to raise the index finger of his right hand if the answer was yes that there was a part of him that was hearing and processing the information. The subject's index finger rose, and the subject immediately said, "Please restore my hearing so that you can tell me what you did. I felt my finger rise in a way that was not a spontaneous twitch, so you must have done something to make it rise" (p. 35). This spontaneous demonstration then gave rise to many other experiments involving the hidden observer, indicating in different ways the presence of an intelligent information source that was functioning as an aspect of the person, but of which the hypnotized subject was not aware. Hilgard reports that about half of highly hypnotizable subjects appear to have a hidden observer. This phenomenon coincides with a person's tendency to double attention, as exemplified by experiencing the self in a double way—both as the young child and as an observer of the child, during hypnotic regression to childhood. About 40% of highly hypnotizable subjects do this, whereas others will simply become the child.

Now a bit of background: Hilgard already knew that some of the information outside the hypnotized subject's awareness could be recovered by automatic writing. He remembered William James's experiment with automatic writing in which James pricked the anesthetic hand, and the hand wrote, "Don't you prick me anymore," even though the subject was consciously unaware of the pricking (1977, p. 199). Although Hilgard had been interested in the topic of divided consciousness as early as his dissertation research, his focal interest in dissociation came via hypnosis. In addition to the undeniable and stark evidence of dissociation as revealed in hypnosis experiments, he began to notice that other phenomena as well, such as automatic behaviors and dissociative disorders, required a theoretical integration. As a result, Hilgard, who was also able to compare concepts in psychoanalysis and dissociation theory, endeavored to "reformulate the theory in contemporary terms, using what psychologists have since learned about information processing, divided attention, and brain function" (pp. 12–13).

Hilgard noted that around the turn of the last century, William James, Morton Prince, and Boris Sidis, among others, were highly receptive to Janet's views of dissociation and developed their own as well. At that time, the "concept of dissociation was apparently so familiar that it had become anonymous; that is, it was no longer identified as any one person's term" (Hilgard, 1977, p. 5). Hilgard describes several reasons that after a brief period of great popularity during the first decades of the century, the concept of dissociation became less well-known. One had to do with the growth of behaviorism, according to which concepts of consciousness—and much more so, of subconsciousness—were eschewed. Another reason was the rapid growth in the popularity of psychoanalysis, which absorbed and/or offered alternative conceptions to those of dissociation theory. Another development that may have contributed to the decline of the popularity of dissociation theory was the noninterference theory, promulgated by some academic dissociation theorists, which held that there was a complete independence between dissociated parts of the mind. It was correctly attacked by other scientists, and this theory of noninterference then became a refutation of dissociation theory itself (Hilgard, 1977). As a result, "dissociation theory went out of favor without effective criticism" (Hilgard, p. 12).

Hilgard was one of the first of modern psychologists to observe that the idea of a unified consciousness is an illusion. He pointed out that our attention is constantly shifting and divided. Furthermore, dissociation is endemic because often attention and planning take place outside awareness. The model of parallel processing is in his view the best explanation of these phenomena, and it is the one that is best confirmed by experimental evidence.

His formal neodissociation theory requires three assumptions in addition to recognition that dissociation exists. The first assumption is that there are subordinate cognitive systems, each with its own unity, persistence, and autonomy of function. Although these systems interact, they may at times become isolated from each other. This helps to explain shifts in consciousness and even apparent lapses in awareness, such as occurs in what has been called "highway hypnosis," which is a form of automatic functioning. The second assumption is that there is a hierarchical control that manages the interaction between the substructures and ensures that consciousness proceeds in some orderly fashion so that thoughts and behavior do not all go on at once. And finally, his third assumption is of an "executive ego," an overarching monitoring and controlling structure. This central control structure plans, monitors, and manages the other functions. Thus, Hilgard is hypothesizing multiple cognitive systems or structures, which may interact with each other, but which are also relatively independent in that they each have their own inputs and outputs. Whereas Janet viewed the reflex as the basic unit of mind and behavior, Hilgard proposes various subsystems that are distinguishable from the larger control and monitoring functions. These subsystems are highly numerous and may be latent or actuated. Each activated subsystem has its own internal executive monitoring system, which is distinguishable from the overarching executive monitoring system. Thus, Hilgard's subsystems bear a high resemblance to Janet's automatisms, and his model of how attention, thought, and behavior can become autonomous and isolated is also similar to Janet's explanation. Hilgard was highly pleased that Donald Hebb, who promulgated the concept and the phrase that "neurons that fire together, wire together," found his neodissociation theory neurologically feasible.

The "hidden observer" was a striking illustration of the dissociative nature of the mind, and Hilgard's neodissociation theory was a cognitive theory that brought back recognition of the omnipresence of dissociation in mental functioning. The hidden observer is an illustration of a dissociated consciousness with an amnestic barrier, much as exists in dissociative identity disorder. Although the hidden observer generally does not function as an encapsulated part of the personality, it can; and many therapists have found an analogue of the hidden observer in their patients, often called the "internal self-helper" (Beahrs, 1982). The hidden observer phenomenon makes clear that "subconscious" cognitive processes can be going on underneath the surface that are not always evident, and that they can be made conscious.

Somatoform Dissociation

Somatoform dissociation refers to dissociative symptoms that are experienced somatically and to the failure to integrate these somatic aspects of experience. Somatoform dissociation "denotes phenomena that are manifestations of a lack of integration of somatoform experiences, reactions, and functions" (Nijenhuis, 2000, p. 9). The area of somatoform dissociation covers a large range of topics. This section alone will cover such various and diverse aspects of somatoform dissociation as classification according to the *DSM,* the somatic storage of traumatic memories, state-dependent somatic dissociative reactions, how animal defense states may underlie dissociative states, and the impact of forced physical immobilization.

Although somatoform and "psychoform" dissociative symptoms are strongly correlated (Nijenhuis, 2000), there are important conceptual differences. If somatoform dissociation is excluded from the category of dissociation by our concepts and measurement instruments, such that only psychoform (Nijenhuis et al., 2004) dissociation is noticed and measured, we are likely to get an inadequate and misleading understanding of the scope of dissociation. We may come to erroneous conclusions and miss the importance of physical abuse and physical threat in the development of dissociative symptoms. An example of such an error is the conclusion reached by a recent study (in which only psychoform instrumentation was used) that although dissociation is a response to sexual abuse, it is less strongly associated with physical abuse (Carlson et al., 1998, cited in Nijenhuis et al., 2004).

It is important to remember that prior to integration, traumatic memories are exhibited and experienced as somatoform experiences. As a result, it would be expected that somatoform symptoms would be part and parcel of traumatic reexperiences (Van der Hart et al., 2000). Janet's cases demonstrated the somatic storage of traumatic memories and how traumatic memories may involve a range of sensorimotor phenomena. Indeed, Janet's concept of traumatic fixation, or *idées fixes,* included psychobiological states, extending far beyond a simple fixed idea or obsession (Van der Hart et al., 2000). Following Janet, Van der Kolk, Nijenhuis, Van der Hart, Hopenwasser, Terr, Goodwin, and Attias, among others, have been highly instrumental in clarifying the significance and forms of bodily dissociation.

Somatoform dissociation is highly associated with reported trauma, especially physical and sexual abuse among psychiatric patients (Nijenhuis, 2000). More recently, Nijenhuis et al. (2004) have found that somatoform dissociation was best predicted by interpersonal bodily threat and threat to life. This is a very important finding, indicating the potential dissociogenic power of physical abuse. Nijenhuis et al. (1998a) found that somatoform dissociation is associated with post-traumatic stress symptoms, and that 94% of patients with dissociative disorder were correctly classified by somatoform dissociation symptom clusters: those of freezing, analgesia, total submission, and urogenital pain. The study also suggests that these events of recurrent interpersonal threat to the body are likely to evoke defensive psychobiological systems, which then manifest as somatoform dissociation. In support of this are recent neuroimaging studies (Nijenhuis et al., 1999; Reinders et al., 2003, cited in Nijenhuis et al., 2004) that illustrate how emotional parts of the personality, but not the apparently normal parts of the personality, of DID patients who were listening to trauma scripts "had more cerebral blood flow in the insula and parietal operculum, and less flow in medial prefrontal, parietal and occipital cortex" (Nijenhuis et al., 2004, p. 679). They also experienced more somatoform symptoms such as analgesia, anesthesia, and motor inhibitions, and had increases of heart rate and blood pressure. "In summary, somatoform dissociation was a potent predictor of reported cumulative traumatisation. Among a wide range of trauma types, somatoform dissociation was associated most strongly with recurrent bodily threat from a person, intense pain, and emotional neglect that started early in life" (Nijenhuis et al., 2004, p. 685).

Some somatic memory includes state-dependent dissociative reactions, which will emerge when the person enters the mental state in which the trauma was originally salient. Such somatoform, psychophysiological memory (Hopenwasser, 1998) exemplifies how "hysterics suffer mainly from reminiscences" (Breuer and Freud, 1893–1895, p. 7). For instance, localized, but otherwise inexplicable body pain may be a reactivation of a traumatic memory, often located in the part of the body that was hurt during the trauma. Pelvic pain may indicate a triggering of dissociated memories of sexual abuse, back pain, physical abuse, and so on. Other examples are state-dependent allergic reactions, skin reactions, and motor reactions. Nijenhuis and Van der Hart (1999b) describe a patient who would develop reddening and notching on both wrists on recalling being tied up, and another patient who developed spontaneous bleeding of a facial scar on recalling its origin. My patient Janice has reported several times gasping for breath, with her throat filled with mucus following a flashback of being strangled. She often feels like fluid is coming out of her vagina and rectum when it is not. Perhaps because she was forced to spend long hours without shoes in an unheated basement during freezing winters in order to do laundry, she is anesthetic to sensation in her feet. Now at times she unexpectedly loses sensation in her feet, and this often causes her to fall. At times her visual perception has become reversed, so that she sees the angle of a stairway in reverse and cannot find a place to put her foot down. These sudden sensory losses and rearrangements have caused her many physical injuries. In addition, there are times during which the positive symptoms intrude, when with no additional injury, she suffers extreme, immobilizing back pain. She has identified the location on her back as where she was severely beaten at age 12. There are times when her face swells up in a way that has no medical explanation: This is the side of her face that was brutally hit. Often her physicians have not understood, and have written her off as "hysterical" in the pejorative sense of the word. At times she experiences her body as that of a snake, and she frequently hallucinates snakes in her bed. In almost all of these instances, the somatic reaction was inseparable from the traumatic memory. In treatment, different aspects of body memory have been pieced together, and spontaneous memories have occurred. These are almost unbearable for her to remember. As Janice says, "it's like people have taken little pieces of your body and planted things like snakes and dirt there instead. How do you put back the pieces they took away, and take away the nasty things they put there?"

Terr's (1990) reports of her work with children demonstrate this principle of somatic nonverbal memories quite powerfully. In one vignette, she describes the behavior of a five-year-old patient who would draw age-inappropriate pictures of anatomically correct naked people. This child had intensely inappropriate fears of projectile objects. As a toddler, she had screamed while being diapered—an odd behavior, since most children this age allow themselves to be diapered without protest. She was inordinately protective of her upper abdomen, and as a younger child she had often pointed to this area. Then, when she was five years old, photographs surfaced that showed her as a child of 18 months being pinned down on the diaper table by a man's hard, erect penis, *exactly in the location of her upper abdomen.*

Terr (1990), calling this kind of event "psychophysiologic reenactment" (p. 271), notes that often the part that was injured or hurt during the trauma manifests or "recalls" the pain. In her book, *Too Scared to Cry,* Terr (1990) tells the story of a group of children from a rural town, Chowchilla, who were kidnapped on their school bus and imprisoned in an underground "hole," a truck buried beneath several hundred pounds of dirt. After their rescue and return home, she followed these children for symptoms of PTSD. Four of the Chowchilla children later developed bladder problems, including urinary incontinence, urinary withholding, and urgency to go to the bathroom, with no physiological disease. She states that these bladder problems "mimicked the children's original urinary dilemmas in the vans" (p. 271).

To foreshadow the next section, what probably saved these children from dying in the underground hole in which they had been left, was the emergence of a different kind of potential disaster than that posed by their captors. The roof of the underground hole in which they were imprisoned began to cave in. This emergency forced some of the children to "come to," with the result that they dug their way out and escaped. If it had not been for this event, these children might have perished in the hole because hypothetically they would have remained emotionally stuck in the freeze or total submission responses.

Animal Defense States Underlying Dissociative Parts of the Personality

The study of dissociation and posttraumatic disorders has brought to light another way in which human experience is structured by the body, and can become dissociated in terms of this underlying structure.

Nijenhuis and his colleagues have pointed to animal defense states as underlying some forms of human somatoform dissociation. They have examined trauma from the perspective of animal responses to terror, which may have counterparts in human response. Proposing a phylogenetic parallel, they have noticed the striking similarities between animal and human responses to threat—in particular, the similarities between the responses typical of dissociative patients and animal defensive and recuperative states.

They note that the human animal may have a repertoire of discrete behavioral states that are adaptive to conditions of predation. Among these are freezing and total submission, as well as fight or flight. In many species, freezing, rather than fight or flight, is the dominant response after an encounter with a predator. Freezing increases the chances of survival by eliminating the motion cues that allow the predator to detect the animal and that activate the predator's strike response (Nijenhuis et al., 1998a, c). It may also create the impression that the prey is dead, and therefore less desirable meat (Scaer, 2001).

Although freezing is characterized by stilled movement, it involves increased rapid heartbeat, rapid breathing, high muscle tone, high blood pressure, and analgesia. Although motor actions are inhibited during the moments of freeze, the organism is ready to explode into the actions of fight or flight. Freezing involves activation of the sympathetic nervous system and appears to be mediated by the loss of the ventral vagal parasympathetic brake on the sympathetic nervous system (Van der Hart et al., 2004). Another defensive response to predation is "total submission." This involves a different kind of physiological activation—that of the parasympathetic nervous system, in which the organism "plays possum." Here, heart rate drops, including at times, syncope (fainting); there is low heart rate variability, loss of muscle tone, emotional and bodily anesthesia, eye aversion from threat cues, and defocusing. This appears to be mediated by the dorsal vagal branch of the parasympathetic nervous system (Van der Hart et al., 2004). Total submission involves body paralysis, or at least low muscle tension, and can also involve being out of the body (Ellert Nijenhuis, personal communication, 2004).

Nijenhuis and his colleagues currently distinguish between EP sympathetic (EPs), which engages in fight, flight, or freeze; and EP parasympathetic (EPp), which totally submits. The proposed model of differentiated EP parasympathetic and sympathetic, is quite promising, for if the model would hold, we would be able to understand very inconsistent research data in PTSD studies. For example, cortisol would go up for EPs, down for EPp, and remain unaltered from baseline for ANP. This would also help us to understand why re-experiencing trauma (EPs) is associated with very different patterns of neural activity in PTSD and DID, compared to being detached (ANP or EPp) [Nijenhuis, personal communication, 2003].

Forced Immobility

One precursor of dissociative response that is extremely important is forced, helpless immobility. The helpless immobility of situations of terror appears to be prominently linked to the development of PTSD. Van der Hart et al. (2000) write of the high incidence of shell shock among World War I, as opposed to World War II, veterans. World War I was characterized by fighting in the trenches, where the solders were simultaneously immobilized and terrified for long stretches of time. They faced continuous threat to life without hope of being able to move out of harm's way, with extreme loss of internal locus of control. The authors note the very high rate of PTSD in balloonists who were immobilized and easy targets in the line of fire. For these men, unlike those in other branches of the armed services, psychic casualties were much greater than the physical wounds. In contrast, pilots, who were more in control of their actions and more mobile, had much lower rates of mental breakdown. Van der Hart et al. (2004) note that emerging data indicates that certain negative somatoform symptoms, such as anesthesia, analgesia, and motor inhibitions, best predict trauma. They hypothesize that the "high rate of somatoform dissociative symptoms in World War I combat soldiers was, at least in part, due to forced immobility in the face of threat to bodily integrity, thereby evoking chronic animal defensive states, in particular, freezing, with concomitant somatoform manifestations" (Van der Hart et al., 2000, p. 53).

Scaer (2001), who has examined thousands of motor vehicle accident patients, observes the high incidence of whiplash syndrome, an incidence that greatly exceeds the likelihood of purely organic causation. He observes that whiplash patients, in contrast to racecar drivers and football players who are frequently subject to impacts of much greater force and velocity, were relatively helpless and immobilized at the time of the accident. Scaer suggests that many of these patients entered a freeze state and dissociated the states of frightening experience at the moment of the accident. He views "whiplash syndrome" as a prototype for somatoform dissociation and PTSD, as a "model of traumatization with long-standing and at times permanent neurophysiological and neurochemical changes in the brain that are experience-based rather than injury-based" (p. 33). Scaer is in agreement with Peter Levine's (1997) conclusion that posttraumatic responses are "fundamentally, incomplete physiological responses suspended in fear" (p. 34).[2]

Comments on the Multiple Self States Model, The Theory of the Structural Dissociation of the Personality, Neodissociation Theory, and Somatoform Dissociation

Somatoform dissociation takes us back to Janet. The mind–body inseparability of dissociative phenomena was one of Janet's key tenets. Psychoanalytic theory has generally emphasized active psychic defense. However, Janet's work, Van der Hart et al.'s work, Ryle's work, and that of somatoform dissociation suggest that this is not always so. This relationship between active and passive dissociation is an aspect of theory that should be further formulated. Psychoanalysis could broaden its horizons by including passive, automatic dissociation of the psyche.

6

ATTACHMENT THEORY AND DISSOCIATION

Although they use different words and concepts, some of the strands (Stern, 1985; Fonagy et al., 1995; Lyons-Ruth, 1999, 2001a, b; Fonagy, 2001) of present-day attachment theory describe dissociation quite well, both in the language of segregated, disconnected internal working models and in that of disorganized attachment. Bowlby's proposal that under extremely difficult attachment conditions, multiple, segregated working models could develop has proved to be an extremely fruitful way of thinking about human cognitive and emotional development, especially with regard to dissociation. Given the striking functional similarity between the concept of incompatible and segregated working models and that of dissociated self-states, it seems probable that these two different languages are describing much the same phenomena. Indeed, inasmuch as internal working models involve an expectation of a particular kind of relationship, involving self-experience and sense of the other, along with organizing feelings about these, one could say that internal working models are self-states. A dissociated self-state is defined by Bromberg (2001b) as "what Janet called a 'system or complex' . . . or a self organized by its own dominant affect, its own view of social phenomena and human relationships, its own moral code, its own view of reality that is fiercely held as a truth" (p. 896).

The Attachment Paradigm

Prior to Bowlby's work, theories of attachment in psychoanalytic and Hullian learning theory assumed that the infant's attachment to specific caregivers was a result of association with the gratification of more basic instincts. Attachment behavior was understood to be a secondary drive, an outcome of the satisfaction of primary drives, such as hunger.

However, this view was problematic: If attachment were secondary, young children would not be expected to become anxious on separation from their primary caregivers, as long as their more basic needs were met (Hesse and Main, 1999). Indeed, a growing number of clinicians in the 1930s and 1940s, such as Spitz, Burlingham, and Anna Freud, as well as Bowlby himself (Bowlby, 1988), were noticing not only that young children became anxious on separation, but that institutionalization or lengthy separations from their caregivers could have severe psychological consequences. Furthermore, ethological studies, such as Lorenz's work with goslings, indicated that animal attachment does not have to be tied to feeding. Bowlby was proposing that attachment was just as important as feeding and mating. In short, he was proposing a new instinct theory (Bretherton, 1992), a theory of an evolutionary origin and biological basis for attachment behavior.

Bowlby (1969) presented ethological and observational evidence that infant primates, including humans, are hardwired for attachment in the service of survival. Originally, Bowlby postulated that proximity to the mother provided protection against predators. Since this increased the chances of survival, the goal of the attachment system appears to be proximity to the attachment figure. However, more recent attachment theorists also consider this in terms of the infant's reduced anxiety and enhanced feeling of security (Fonagy, 2001). Lyons-Ruth (2001a) views the attachment system as analogous to the immune system: just as the biological immune system modulates physical disease, the attachment system modulates psychological fear and distress. This emphasis on reduction of fearful arousal is a large departure from libidinal and aggressive drives as motivational systems. Instead, attachment theory "regrounds clinical theory in the developmental dynamics of fear" (Lyons-Ruth, 2001a, p. 40).

Attachment is intrinsic to emotional security, and the need for it pertains to us throughout the life cycle. As Bowlby (1984) put it, "all of us, from the cradle to the grave, are happiest when life is organized as a series of excursions, long or short, from the secure base provided by our attachment figures" (p. 11).

Bowlby came to understand attachment, often indicated by such infant behaviors as clinging, crying, and following, as a behavioral system. A behavioral system is a motivational system that is not secondarily derivative of more primary drives. The attachment system is not the only behavioral system, but is one among others such as those that control mating, feeding, exploration, and parenting (Bretherton, 1992). Behavioral systems may operate together, often activating or inhibiting each other. For example, the attachment system and the fear system work in tandem, and fear often activates the attachment system, such that the "attachment figure is the developing individual's primary solution to experiences of fear" (Hesse and Main, 1999). The exploratory system is also linked to the attachment system, since the attachment figure is the infant's secure base. The infant's exploratory behavior is inhibited in the absence of the attachment figure.

Patterns of Attachment

Initially, three patterns of attachment were delineated based on the behavior of one-year-olds in the Strange Situation, a standardized procedure devised by Mary Ainsworth that evaluated infants' reactions to separation from their mothers. These included secure attachment and two insecure attachment styles: anxious avoidant and anxious resistant attachment. Most infants were securely attached. Insecure attachment styles were understood to be internally consistent patterns, linked with unavailability or insensitivity on the part of the caregiver but not maltreatment and gross insensitivity (Lyons-Ruth, 2001a, b). A fourth, later-described category, disorganized attachment (D-attachment) (Main and Solomon, 1986), is associated with maltreatment or gross insensitivity on the part of the caretaker. When the child faces the dilemma of both seeking safety from and fearing the caretaker, her attachment strategies are likely to become disorganized. As a consequence, multiple, segregated, incompatible working models of attachment may develop (Blizard, 2003).

Although Bowlby thought that adult psychopathology would follow from insecure attachment, recent research has yielded mixed results for this general hypothesis. "In contrast to Bowlby's prediction, the secure, avoidant, and resistant classifications tend not to be strongly related to later measures of maladaptation" (Fonagy, 2001, p. 30). In contrast, disorganized attachment (D-attachment) has been linked to adult psychopathology in a number of studies, including aggression, personality disorders, and dissociative disorders (Ogawa et al., 1997; Carlson, 1998; Lyons-Ruth, 2001a).

Even though Bowlby used the language of repression to describe some aspects of defensive exclusion, it appears that, at least in the more extreme cases, dissociation, rather than repression, is the organizing principle (Blizard, 2003). With reference to insecure attachment, Bowlby (1980) described the psychological defenses against disorganization under the broad category of "defensive exclusion." These defenses were of two types, deactivation and disconnection. Deactivation, which he likened to repression, involved the exclusion of all affect and thought that "might activate attachment behaviour and feeling" (p. 70), and resulted in a state of emotional detachment. This included both cognition, such as lack of recall, and actual behavior, such as shifting one's gaze. In disconnection, attachment is maintained, but painful information inconsistent with the attachment is "disconnected" from awareness. The child maintains a favorable view of the caregiver in consciousness while knowledge of less favorable treatment by the parent (neglectful, rejecting, and so on) is excluded from the information system pertaining to the first view. Deactivation tends to characterize avoidant attachment, whereas disconnection has been thought to be more typical of ambivalent attachment. In the service of defensive exclusion, segregated, relatively incompatible systems of multiple representations of self and other can develop.

Internal Working Models

Bowlby's first revolutionary insight was his evolutionary point of view. As his thinking evolved, it became less behavioral and more concerned with mental processing. Probably the most important concept in Bowlby's attachment theory is that of internal working models (IWMs), which involve mental representations of the self and the attachment figure, and concern the infant's expectation of the availability of the attachment figure. Bowlby observed that people have multiple internal working models (1973), that internal working models can generalize from past experience, and that working models can conflict with each other, as well as operate defensively (Bowlby, 1980). Internal working models organize the child's cognitions, affects, and expectations about attachment relationships. They are "superordinate structures that combine numerous schemas 'of being with' (and which) regulate the child's behavior with the attachment figure" (Fonagy et al., 1995, p. 235).

These segregated internal working models can also be organized in a way that can be understood in terms of a "split." One set of working models, a set accessible to awareness, represents the parent in idealized terms and the rejected child as "bad." The other set represents the disappointing aspects of the parents which the child has experienced but has excluded from awareness (Bretherton, 1992).

Disorganized Attachment

Although Bowlby suggested that defensive exclusion would characterize insecure attachment, more recent research has revealed that this degree of segregation of systems is more characteristic of D-attachment (Main and Morgan, 1996). The perspective has increasingly been accepted that in contrast to secure attachment, in which internal working models are coherent and integrated, in disorganized attachment, they are more likely to be segregated, multiple, and incoherent. Thus, the "disorganized attachment behavior . . . may be related to multiple and dissociated mental structures that control the child's actions. These structures may be related to incoherent, simultaneous representations of the self and the attachment figure" (Liotti, 1995, p. 348).

Disorganized attachment behavior is now viewed as representing malfunction of the attachment relational system (Lyons-Ruth, 2001a). D-attachment is predicted by maltreatment and neglect (Carlson, 1998; Blizard, 2003). This may reflect the failure of the attachment system to function as a buffer against extreme fearful arousal (Lyons-Ruth, 2001a) in attachment situations involving stringent double-binds; that is, if the attachment figure arouses fear, the attachment system is aroused, leaving the fearsome attachment figure as the solution to the fear.

However, about 15% of the infants with D-attachment have come from low-risk families and do not appear to have been abused or neglected. Hesse and Main (1999) had earlier hypothesized that frightening or frightened (FR) parental behavior could lead to D-attachment in the absence of overt maltreatment. Lyons-Ruth and her colleagues (Lyons-Ruth, 2001a) suggested that rather than any one particular behavior, grossly insensitive parenting, including contradictory caregiving strategies and the parents' inability to regulate the infant's fearful arousal, would lead to D-attachment style. In the course of a 19-year longitudinal study, Lyons-Ruth and her colleagues (Lyons-Ruth, 2001a) found that mothers of disorganized infants exhibited conflicting affective cues—for example, a mother's laughing at her baby's distress while picking up the baby at the same time. Thus, the infants' disorganized behavior mirrored their mothers' mixed signals. Importantly, failure to coherently respond to the infant's attachment bids means failure to regulate the infant's fearful arousal.

Liotti (1992, 1995, 1999) has proposed that D-attachment is predisposing to dissociative disorders, and a longitudinal, prospective study (Ogawa et al., 1997) has shown that D-attachment and dissociated disorders are significantly related. Indeed, disorganized infants exhibit trancelike and disconnected behaviors. On videotape, they appear to simultaneously approach and withdraw, or to do both in quick succession (Jacovitz, 2000; Lyons-Ruth, 2003).

In a comprehensive review of the literature on disorganized attachment, Blizard (2003) observes that developments in attachment theory, psychodynamic thought, and clinical observation of child abuse survivors, together with findings from longitudinal child development studies, indicate two things: (1) the importance of dissociative processes in disorganized attachment and (2) that D-attachment predisposes to later vulnerability to pathological dissociation. The first includes the findings that many of the behaviors exhibited by D-attached infants are phenotypic of dissociation (Main and Morgan, 1996). As Blizard notes, "dissociative processes observed in both children and adults with D-attachment include trance-like states, disconnected behavioral responses . . . and lapses in discourse related to unresolved trauma or loss" (p. 31). The second issue, concerning how D-attachment predisposes to later vulnerability, includes Liotti's (1992) observation that D-attachment may constitute the prototype for dissociation of ego states.

If the parent cannot be used as a secure base, then fearful affects will be inadequately regulated. Indeed, Hesse and Main (1999) emphasize that frightening parental figures put their offspring in an irresolvable and disorganizing paradox in which

> impulses to approach the parent as the infant's "haven of safety" will inevitably conflict with impulses to flee from the parent as a source of alarm. Here, we argue that conditions of this kind place the infant in a situation involving *fright without solution,* resulting in a collapse of behavioral and attentional strategies [p. 484, italics added].

Fright without a solution describes the prototypical dilemma of the child who develops D-attachment. Insisting on the importance of the real interpersonal environment, as opposed to an exclusionary emphasis on fantasies, Bowlby once stood up at a psychoanalytic meeting and insisted to the audience, "But, there *is* such a thing as a *bad* mother" (Mitchell, 2000, p. 84). This outcry is echoed by some of Hesse and Main's (1999) descriptions of some of the mothers of disorganized infants. Offering none of the metasignals of play, some of these mothers would spontaneously enter into predatory, animal-like behavior—

growling, hissing, baring their teeth, stalking their infants on all fours, in one case mock-mauling the baby, with fingers extended like claws.

Both trauma and disorganized attachment are associated with the inhibition of carefree play and decreased reflectiveness and ability to symbolize and use metaphor. Like trauma, disorganized attachment is associated with the overproduction of cortisol, which can damage the hypothalamus, leading to emotional dysregulation (Fonagy, 2001). Thus, attachment clearly affects the mental processes that underlie personality organization and psychopathology.

The Adult Attachment Interview (AAI) and Intergenerational Transmission of Attachment Style

The extremely frightening mothers described by Hesse and Main were not consciously intending to harm their children. They probably had not integrated in their own minds how their babies would register their actions. Quite likely, they were transmitting unresolved trauma from their own histories. Indeed, Main and Hesse have proposed that frightening and frightened parental behavior is the means by which parental unresolved trauma contributes to D-attachment. Hesse and Main (1999) documented a correspondence between the attachment styles of the infant and those of the mothers. Secure, autonomous parents tended to have secure babies; dismissing parents, avoidant babies; and preoccupied parents, anxious, resistant ones. In addition, behavior of parents classified as Unresolved/Disorganized corresponded to that of disorganized infants. They coded the parents' attachment styles by use of the Adult Attachment Interview (AAI), an interview developed by Main and her colleagues in which respondents are asked to recall and evaluate the effects on current functioning of their own early attachment experiences, including separations from attachment figures. Coherence and collaborativeness of discourse, rather than life history, per se, were key criteria for coding these interviews. Coherence and collaborativeness were scored in accordance with the four maxims proposed by the linguistic philosopher, Grice, regarding coherent and collaborative discourse: quality (be truthful and give evidence for your statements), quantity (be succinct and complete), relation (be relevant), and manner (be clear and orderly) (Main, 1995, p. 438). They found that the parent's ability to have coherent and collaborative discourse while describing life events and early attachment experiences was predictive of her infant's attachment style. The fact that coherence of narrativity on the AAI is associated with secure/autonomous attachment of the parent and predicts secure attachment of the infant (Hesse and Main, 1999; Fonagy, 2001) suggests a source of intergenerational transmission.

Main's development of the AAI provided an extremely important new way of connecting the dots within the related themes of trauma, internal working models, disorganized attachment, and coherence of narrativity. Although specifically measuring attachment style, the AAI presented a model of coherence. This instrument seems to score unresolved trauma: "Discontinuities in the way a person tells his story reflect breaks in the holding environment in childhood" (Holmes, 1995, p. 35). Unresolved trauma leads to dissociated mental structures, whether we call them self-states or internal working models.

Organizations of Attachment Behaviors

Another route of transmission of D-attachment concerns the organization of attachment behaviors. Lyons-Ruth (2001a) found that disorganized infants could be put into two groups that she categorized behaviorally as "D-Approach and D-Avoid Resist" (p. 42), corresponding respectively to their mothers' two groups of behavioral profiles of helpless or hostile. Disorganized children of helpless mothers approached them, whereas disorganized children of hostile mothers avoided them. (Interestingly, both of these parental groups had been exposed to trauma or unresolved loss, but in different ways. The helpless mothers tended to have been subjected to sexual abuse or unresolved parental loss, whereas the hostile mothers had been subjected to, or had witnessed, physical violence in the home.)

As they grew older, and especially by the time they reached school age, these disorganized infants reorganized their attachment behaviors such that they began to control their mothers and other people in particular ways. These controlling behaviors were grouped into an oversolicitous "caregiving" style and a hostile, punitive style. Like their mothers, they become "hostile or helpless." Because of the failure to regulate fear arousal and because in both the hostile pattern and the helpless pattern dominance and submission are not balanced, "these models are also likely to be imbued with more traumatic affects, may be particularly susceptible to dissociation of either the hostile or helpless component" (p. 44). Lyons-Ruth (2001a) concludes that the

> developmental transition from disorganized behaviors to controlling forms of attachment behaviors over the preschool period supports the notion that one "grows into" a borderline or narcissistic stance through a complex series of alternative developmental acquisitions. . . . The child in a disorganized attachment relationship appears to use emerging developmental capacities to construct increasingly polarized coercive or role-reversed "false-self" relations with the parent [p. 45].

What are the mental processes that underlie and mediate the personality disorders or dissociative disorders arising from D-attachment? The ability to think about and describe personal experience in a coherent way and to empathically think about what others are thinking about fosters the child's emotional development. And the lack of the opportunity for narration of self-experience with important figures is detrimental to the development of integrating capabilities. Thus, a parent's unresolved trauma would be expected to affect coherence and collaborativeness of discourse. Liotti (1995) has observed that, not surprisingly, the parents of dissociative patients are more likely to have experienced a major loss either immediately preceding the birth or in the first few years thereafter.

Mentalization

Disorganized attachment interferes with the ability to mentalize, to think about what others are thinking about—an ability that develops from the child's experience of finding his or her mental state represented in the caregiver's mind (Fonagy, 2001). "The psychological self develops through perception of oneself in another person's mind as thinking and feeling. Parents who cannot reflect with understanding on their child's inner experience and respond accordingly deprive the child of a core psychological structure that he or she needs to build a viable sense of self" (pp. 167–168). Mentalization then enhances emotional regulatory functions as well as capacities to symbolize.

According to Fonagy et al. (1995), the child needs to find her mind in the mind of the parent or caregiver. When the view of the self as reflected by the caregiver is intolerable, and when the caregiver is unable to help the child process overwhelming and painful experiences, as may be in situations of abuse, trauma, and severe neglect, then the child may lose interest in trying to find the self in the caregiver's mind.

The child may turn away from the mentalizing caregiver in order to protect against being overwhelmed by the hostile or indifferent intentions in the caregiver's mind. This disruption in the attachment connection then leads to a diminution of self-reflectiveness, for one's own mind cannot be found in the mind of the other in a nontraumatic way. Because the means of finding the self has been disrupted, traumatic representations of self and others cannot be linked with safe ones, and inconsistent and segregated attachment models of relationships develop.

An additional feature of Fonagy and his colleagues' model of mentalization is of utmost importance: It has provided the scaffolding for the articulation of a groundbreaking new model of internalization. The traditional psychoanalytic concept of internalization assumes that the child internalizes the image of the caregiver. By the process of internalizing a caretaker who is capable of emotional containment, the child acquires a self-containing self-structure. Fonagy et al.'s (1995) model proposes that the child internalizes the caregiver's image of the intentional infant. This internalization constitutes the core of the child's mentalizing self:

> If the caregiver's reflective capacity enables her to accurately picture the infant's intentional stance, the infant has the opportunity to "find himself in the other" as a mentalizing individual. If the caregiver's capacity is lacking in this regard, the version of itself that the infant encounters is an individual conceived of as thinking in terms of physical reality rather than mental states [p. 257].

Segregated Systems of Attachment and Negative Affects

Whereas Fonagy's thrust with respect to the effect of trauma on mentalization as described above is that it stunts the development of metacognitive processes, Lyons-Ruth's (1999, 2001b) work emphasizes segregated internal working models themselves. These working models represent unconscious procedural knowledge of being with another person which reflect implicit models of relationships, including interpersonal defensive maneuvers that respond to the attachment figures' own defenses and attachment systems. When these internal working models cannot be linked with one another, as for example when different relationship patterns between parent and child are highly contradictory and this contradiction has not been examined or resolved, these patterns can develop into segregated systems of attachment. These can be understood as dissociated self-states.

Like Fonagy, Lyons-Ruth (1999) emphasizes that the collaborative dialogue is "getting into another's mind and taking it into account in constructing and regulating interactions" (p. 583). This dependence on the partner's participation makes implicit relational knowing especially vulnerable to lack of integration of implicit meaning systems. Especially when collaborative relationships within which to articulate relational understanding are unavailable, conflicting internal working models of procedural enactments will remain unintegrated. Situations in which only one person's subjectivity is recognized make the integration of negative affects particularly difficult. If the child's negative affects are excluded from further discourse, there will be greater difficulty integrating conflicting internal working models. "If many of the patient's goals have been overridden and excluded from further interaction, negative affects related to the frustration of those goals will remain unresolved while caregiver negative affects toward the pursuit of those goals will also be represented" (p. 607). This bears heavily on how we understand "splitting" and dissociated self-states in accordance with intense conflicting affects—a topic taken up in more detail in chapter 7.

Protest, Despair, and Detachment

Now looking backward from the perspective of current theory in the dissociation field, it is possible to recast some of Bowlby's early work on attachment. In his descriptions of children who have been separated from their mothers, Bowlby (1973) outlined the stages of reactions to separation—protest, despair, and then detachment. The initial response to the realization of the separation is protest, anger, crying, and searching for the parent. Next comes despair, in which the child cries less, appears sad, withdraws, and moves less, but is still preoccupied with the mother and is vigilant for her return. In the final phase of detachment, the child appears to lose interest in the mother's return, no longer spurns the attention of others, and is superficially more sociable. Generally, this undesirable state of affairs is remedied on the mother's return. The child tends to be detached at first, then ambivalent, angry, hostile, and rejecting, but demanding of the mother's presence. However, Bowlby observes that in cases of very long or repeated separations, the detachment can operate indefinitely.

Bowlby states that protest raises issues of separation anxiety; despair raises issues of grief and mourning; and detachment raises issues of defense. If detachment, as Bowlby describes it, is viewed as a defense, then what is excluded from consciousness? In my view, what is kept out of consciousness is the experience of the terrified, lost, abandoned child. This experience is sequestered from the rest of consciousness in the phase of detachment. This development is consistent with the Structural Theory of the Dissociation of the Personality developed by Van der Hart et al. (2004).

During trauma the EP is the experiential state, but afterward, if the trauma is not resolved, the EP is dissociatively sequestered, and the ANP takes over. The ANP superficially appears to be the same as the original personality, but is actually more constricted and vulnerable than the original personality. Perhaps the period of reunion after prolonged separation that Bowlby describes could be viewed in terms of the reemergence and resolution of the EP. Indeed, the first chapter of Bowlby's 1980 book, *Loss* (the last in the series), is titled "The Trauma of Loss" (p. 7).

Enactive Interaction in the Psychotherapy Dyad

The implications of the interface of attachment theory and dissociation theory are extensive for psychoanalysis and psychotherapy. As Lyons-Ruth (2001b) observes, attachment research provides general support for the concept of internalized objects in its concept of internalized ways of being with others. When these internalized ways of being with others are highly segregated and incompatible, they can be understood as dissociated self-states. Although he uses a different language, Liotti (1995) joins relational psychoanalysts such as Bromberg and Davies as well as clinicians in the dissociative disorder field in his attention to the patient's different internal working models, all of which need to be discerned and addressed. As Blizard (2003) writes, "thus, it may be more helpful for treatment purposes to identify the internal working model of each self-state, and try to discern what relationship it is based on, rather than to characterize the person as a whole as having a particular attachment paradigm" (p. 39).

Implicit relational knowing emphasizes the process of communication rather than only the verbal content of communication. In many ways, the most important aspects of therapeutic action take place in the realm of implicit relational knowledge. This is reflected in the current emphasis on enactments and projective identification as essential ways for the therapist to learn what the patient needs to communicate, and often as the only form of communication possible. In a recent paper (1999) that emphasizes the learning from a clinical case, Davies describes how she spontaneously provided a blanket for a patient who was shivering in a flashback. Her act was the beginning of many enactments of varying intensity and difficulty, in which she functioned both as a secure base and a relational bridge to the different self-states of her patient. Not the least important in her capacity to provide these was her access to her own shifting self-states, often having to do with her own sense of self as a humiliated child, which resonated with her patient's. This kind of empathy can only be enacted rather than planned, and it has much in common with the matching described in the infant development and attachment literature. As Davies says,

> our new psychoanalytic milieu has ceased to value verbal insight and understanding above all else. Though we continue to rely on such processes, we have finally come to understand and accept the ineluctably interactive nature of psychoanalytic work. We seek a level of emotional resonance and empathic attunement that will facilitate the emergence of intense, deeply moving affect states and interpersonal fantasies. . . . This is . . . a way of being with the patient and with oneself that brings into enhanced focus those aspects of unconscious or unformulated experience (see Stern, 1983) which could not otherwise be psychically represented and elaborated [pp. 202–203].

Another way of describing her work in this case is through relational procedural enactments. Although Davies does not use the words of attachment theory, what she says bears much the same message.

Clearly, D-attachment, trauma, and dissociation are inextricably interrelated concepts. Unlike the effects of disorganized attachment, however, the effects of trauma and dissociation are not limited to infancy, but can occur throughout the life cycle. In this sense, dissociation is the overriding and more general concept. On the other hand, the meaning of psychological trauma, whenever it occurs, refers back to issues of attachment. The meaning of psychological trauma is largely nested in attachment. As Laub and Auerhahn (1993) have stated, the "essential experience of trauma [is] an unraveling of the relationship between self and nurturing other, the very fabric of psychic life" (p. 287). When the links of holding context are removed by relational trauma, the resulting schisms in the human psyche are often ways of organizing attachment.

7

ATTACHMENT-BASED DISSOCIATION
A Different View of Splitting

At the end of the last chapter, we began to differentiate between Janetian-type dissociation (which includes PTSD) and attachment-based dissociation. In Janetian-type dissociation, the sequestration of experience is not necessarily in response to traumatic attachment or organized in terms of affect relating to the attachment figure: It can result from nonrelational traumatic events, such as isolated stranger rapes and earthquakes. I propose that splitting rests more heavily on attachment-based dissociation. As such, the etiological core of what we call splitting involves an enactment of relational positions derivative of traumatic attachment and dominant–submissive relationships in which intersubjective space has collapsed. In this process, a particular organization of alternating dissociated victim-identified and abuser-identified states develops on the axis of relational trauma. This organization of experience is characteristic of borderline personality disorder (Howell, 2002).

In the relational trauma route, the child's experience of an abusive caregiver is likely to be contextually fractionated, and, at least in part, procedurally encoded. This means that the sense of self, including affect, view of the self, view of and anticipation of the other, as well as contextual features, will be contained in the procedural enactments that are relevant to the particular situation. Often these experiences are framed in terms of abuser–victim roles, in variations of what has been termed *identification with the aggressor* (Ferenczi, 1949; Frankel, 2002; Howell, 2002a). But they also illustrate the dissociogenic power of psychological trauma and severe neglect.

I am in agreement with Lyons-Ruth that attachment-based dissociation, or splitting, can be an outgrowth of disorganized attachment. As we have seen, the development of D-attachment may reflect interpersonal events in the infant's life that were emotionally and psychologically overwhelming (although they might not be overwhelming or traumatic to an older child or adult), demanding the development of multiple, segregated, and incompatible working models.

Like *dissociation, splitting* has many meanings. Although it may be understood as a form of dissociation, often it is not understood this way, for the two words have different historical paths that connote different ways of thinking about psychic development and psychic derailment. *Dissociation* starts with Janet, who used the word *disaggregation* to describe a posttraumatically and potentially multiply split psyche. *Splitting* is most often associated with Klein, Kernberg, and others such as Masterson, who followed a Mahlerian timetable of child development. Freud (1927, 1938) was the first to refer to splitting as a defensive process, but the concept of splitting was substantially expanded especially by Fairbairn (1944, 1952, 1958) and Klein (1946).

Today, *splitting* usually denotes a psychic defense that divides the experiential world and the people in it into good and bad. Splitting, as opposed to dissociation, has a more limited meaning that emphasizes the contradictory aspects of experience, and the oscillation between halves—that is, between rageful feelings and demeanor and idealizing passivity and helplessness. Splitting is understood as the primary defense of borderline personality organization, which includes borderline personality disorder, narcissistic personality disorder, and "low-level" personality disorders and addictions (Kernberg, 1975). For Kernberg, it is an outcome, among other things, of too much preoedipal aggression. Masterson (1976) specifically links splitting to disruptions in the rapprochement subphase of separation-individuation.

Although the concept of splitting is clinically helpful in delineating and understanding psychodynamics, it appears to be misplaced in a developmental chronology (D. N. Stern, 1985). Stern criticized Kernberg's developmental concept of splitting, asking first how, according to the Mahlerian timetable and the Kleinian view, as elaborated by Kernberg, "can one postulate a 'good self' and a 'bad self' before there is a 'self'" (p. 251)? Observing that "good" and "bad" imply intentions, standards, even morality, he states, "Good and bad as encountered in the splitting of borderline patients requires a level of symbolization beyond the infants' capacity" (p. 252).

How, then, do we understand the pervasive clinical phenomena associated with splitting? Although clinically we use the word to describe certain kinds of identifiable behaviors and thought processes, the concept relies on developmental paradigms that now appear untenable.

Are there alternative explanations for the origins of the many common phenomena that come under the rubric of splitting?

I am in agreement with Kernberg that splitting is a dissociative process. However, the concept does not require an underpinning in aggressive and libidinal drives. Rather, what we call "splitting" involves a reenactment of posttraumatic dominant–submissive relational patterns. In this process, a particular organization of alternating dissociated helpless/victim and abusive/rageful self-states develops on the axis of relational trauma. These self-states reflect the impact of relational trauma on defenses, on neurological hardwiring, and on arousal systems. They may have developmental underpinnings in attachment style and biological states. In the process that is often termed *identification with the aggressor,* these self-states, which reenact and embody the relational positions of the victim and the aggressor, become partially or entirely dissociated. Their oscillation appears to be a continual reenactment of the traumatic violation of the relational boundary. This view suggests changes in how projective identification and the other defenses related to the model of splitting are understood.

In describing the development of this configuration of oscillating and layered self-states, which I see as splitting, I will refer to some specific literature on identification with the aggressor. Some of this literature emphasizes the importance of implicit, or procedural, memory in this process. Then I will discuss the impact of trauma on the linkage of mental states and on attachment.

Traumatic Violation of Relational Boundaries, Dissociation, and Identification with the Aggressor

How does it happen that an internalized object becomes an agentic structure, a part of the self that at times can even take executive control? Present-day attachment theory can give us new ways of thinking about the process of identification with the aggressor, which may rely on processes of somatoform dissociation, and enactive, procedural, relational knowing.

What is ordinarily thought of as identification with the aggressor may rely to a large extent on procedural imitation. Traumatic experiences are often encoded in procedural repertoires and somatosensory modalities rather than in declarative memory (Terr, 1994; Van der Kolk, 1996; Courtois, 1999). Under normal circumstances, procedural and declarative memory systems may be dissociated (Lyons-Ruth, 1999). For instance, *knowing how* to ride a bicycle is not the same as *knowing that* one can ride it. In traumatic memory, the declarative is likely to have been more or less knocked out, leaving intact only the procedural repertoires (Erdelyi, 1994).

Lyons-Ruth (1999) has described implicit relational knowing, the unconscious relational knowledge of how to be with another person. These "enactive procedural representations of how to do things with others" (p. 385) are internal working models of attachment in Bowlby's sense. These models can develop into segregated systems of attachment: in other words, dissociated, enactive, procedural ways of knowing how to be with another. Inasmuch as internal working models involve an expectation of a particular kind of relationship involving the person, the other, and a dominant affect, one may say that internal working models are self-states.

Mutuality and interdependence in a relationship, including mirroring and validating of the other's experience, affect, and perspective, allows the child to articulate her own perspective as well as to learn the roles of both persons in a connected fashion. In contrast, in traumatic procedural learning and in dominant–submissive relationships, there is no opportunity for interchange of perspectives, no modification of the aggressor's behavior in response to the victim's plea for understanding, and the roles of victim and aggressor cannot be linked. Hence, they remain rigid and dissociated. There ensues a very constricted internal working model of the aggressor controlling the victim, and a similarly constricted model of the victim complying with the aggressor (Blizard, personal communication, 2003).

Janet described how constriction of the field of consciousness often characterizes traumatic situations. In chaotic, neglectful, or abusive familial environments, the child may focus intently on the abuser's postures, motions, facial expressions, words, and feelings, for these are the most immediately relevant to personal welfare. As a result of being intensely attached to the aggressor (often much more intensely than if there had been no abuse), the child's mimicking of the aggressor's behavior becomes a form of enactive, procedural learning. All other stimuli and aspects of self-experience, such as proprioceptive cues or awareness of any affect other than fear, may be irrelevant. Although the child learns the roles of both abuser and victim procedurally, this learning is adaptively focused on the *abuser's* behavior and experience.

Over a half century ago, Emch (1944) described this sort of traumatic procedural knowing as an aspect of imitation, which she called "identification-knowing." She proposed that for some traumatized people, imitation is a behavioral memory that captures essential knowledge about significant others. She noted that this kind of identification-knowing takes place very early and is remarkably faithful to the original, "expressing itself in motor ways whose patterns of mimicry soon become astonishingly faithful to the life, and are frequently as keen an exposition and economical a representation as the most caustic of caricatures" (p. 14).

Striking examples of such identification-knowing in more recent literature can be found in the study of gender identity disorder in boys. In a series of fascinating papers, Coates and her colleagues (Coates, Friedman, and Wolfe, 1991) and Coates and Moore (1995, 1997) have described the posttraumatic identifications of the boys who compulsively reenacted "being the mother" with such behaviors as putting on makeup and dressing up in jewelry: As opposed to believing that they were girls, as would be more the case with a transgendered child, they simply did not like being boys. They did not behave like girls, but rather adopted a stereotyped cartoon of girl behavior. The authors felt that this "false-self personification" (Coates and Moore, 1997) was a defensive response to the mother's emotional unavailability.

In such personification, this child, who had experienced psychological trauma, has described the experience of having his own sense of identity traumatically replaced by that of the aggressor. The authors called this the "experience of being taken over from the outside" (Coates and Moore, 1997, p. 301).

The phrase "being taken over from the outside" describes so well the assault on the self by trauma. In the extreme, this has been called "soul murder" (Shengold, 1989). In his book, *Soul Murder,* Shengold reminds us of a scene in Orwell's *1984,* in which O'Brien, who is Winston Smith's boss, torturer, and brainwasher, says to Winston, "You will be hollow. We will squeeze you empty, and then we shall fill you with ourselves."

This creation of an inner emptiness and lack of cohesiveness is an important difference between identifications that are the products of secure attachments and those that are products of traumatic ones. Nontraumatic identifications add to the person's already coherent identity (Bonomi, 2002). In contrast, trauma-related identifications detract from a person's identity because, for reasons that we will explore, the aggressor's goals and behaviors appear to have replaced the child's own agency and initiative.

In his famous paper, "The Confusion of Tongues Between Adults and the Child," Ferenczi (1949) discussed in depth how the child's identity and integrity of self are diminished in the process of identification with the aggressor while, at the same time, the aggressor's behaviors and ways of understanding the world are replicated. In his discussion of the effects of child sexual abuse in this paper, Ferenczi coined the term *identification with the aggressor.* He wrote,

> These children feel physically and morally helpless . . . for the overpowering force and authority of the adult makes them dumb and can rob them of their senses. The same anxiety, however, if it reaches a certain maximum, compels them to subordinate themselves like automata to the will of the aggressor, to divine each one of his desires and to gratify these; completely oblivious of themselves they identify themselves with the aggressor. . . . The weak and undeveloped personality reacts to sudden unpleasure not by defense, but by anxiety-ridden identification and introjection of the menacing person or aggressor. . . . One part of their personalities, possibly the nucleus, got stuck in its development at a level where it was unable to use the alloplastic way of reaction but could only react in an autoplastic way by a kind of mimicry [p. 228].

But this comes about in an anxiety-ridden way. Ferenczi is describing how the child is responding to the aggressor's needs or wishes by knowing his mind (Frankel, 2002) rather than specifically with the aggressor's role and position of power–behavior with a very differently motivated self-protective purpose from that which Anna Freud three years later labeled *identification with the aggressor* (Rachman, 1997).

How then does it happen that the aggressor's behaviors seem to be reenacted? The child orients around the aggressor from the victim position, yet as a result of trauma procedurally learns the aggressor position. As a consequence of peritraumatic dissociation, the child's agency and initiative have not been adequately synthesized among various self-states, and aggression has been dissociated. It is not that a part of the aggressor's identity has literally become part of the child, but that the child mimics out of intense attachment and dissociates out of sheer terror. Thus, rageful self-states are likely to be dissociated from more situationally adaptive ones.

The term *identification with the aggressor,* here used in Ferenczi's sense, is not identification in the positive sense of adding to the qualities that a person already possesses, such as behaviors, affect, ways of thinking, and so on. It is not a question of how the object becomes part of the self, but of how the object overtakes the self. This latter kind of identification (Ferenczi's identification with the aggressor) occurs as a result of trauma. Ferenczi states that as a result of the "introjection of the aggressor, he disappears as part of external reality and becomes intra- as opposed to extra-psychic; . . . The attack as a rigid external reality ceases to exist and in the traumatic trance the child succeeds in maintaining the previous situation of tenderness [p. 228].

The child maintains and protects the situation of tenderness by keeping it apart from the memories of the abusive situation. This formulation is very similar to Kernberg's view of the motivation for splitting: to protect the good from being overwhelmed by the bad. The traumatic trance engenders an illusory view of reality in which the abuser is registered as "good." This illusion is relied on to maintain the "situation of tenderness." Although the terror-filled part of the relationship is not in ordinary consciousness, it motivates action and views of others quite powerfully. Although many such individuals may consciously abhor abusive behavior and may have developed the lack of its expression as a personal ideal, this often ends up as an illusory ideal.

There are now at least two highly incompatible self-states involving the child's relationship to the caregiver. And there are at least two dominant internal relational positions: victim and abuser.

Even though I have outlined two self-states, the situation is generally more complicated in real life. My patient Jessica, a very intelligent and thoughtful woman in her 30s, grew up with a mother who seemed to take pleasure in undermining her self-esteem and in different ways often treated her as a commodity for her own use. Not only did she frighten Jessica with implicit threats of abandonment and exploit Jessica's love, but she also exploited her for labor, requiring excessive housework. She also turned a blind eye when a rich uncle took advantage of Jessica sexually. Despite her exploitative attitude toward Jessica, her mother regarded herself as the pinnacle of propriety. And she did most of the things a mother is supposed to do, including supplying meals, transportation, doctor visits, meeting with Jessica's teachers, and so on. For many years, even into her adulthood, Jessica's opinion of her mother matched her mother's view of herself: Jessica idealized her. Yet, in other mental states, isolated from this one, she was afraid of her mother. And in still others, she hated her.

Now, in treatment with me, Jessica tells me of how she frequently cannot stand up for herself with others, and sometimes submits to the wishes of others entirely (victim state). She readily agreed to my conditions for treatment—perhaps too readily. Sometimes her demeanor with me has been eager to please and idealizing. At times, a childlike, needy, almost mute state, has emerged. At other times, her treatment of me has been encapsulated in a view of me as an object for her use (an "overtakenness by the aggressor" state). At these times she has not understood, for instance, that if she does not show up for an appointment, my time has still been spent. She has at times been outraged that if she is upset, I may not always call her back. Yet, at other times, she is fleeing me, and wants to keep me as if "on ice" and does not want to have to bother to come to sessions: I should just be there for her. Many times she has been so put out with me that she has threatened to leave treatment, and she once did leave treatment. Sometimes her entitlement has been breathtaking: for instance, stating that she should not have to pay the bill if she did not like the services. I even complied—not because I was afraid she would leave, but because there was something about her demeanor that made me feel I had to appease her (my victim-identified state). While in the moment, she has maintained such views aggressively. At most other times, she has been able to see how aggressive and exploitative (and like her mother) she has been, without even meaning to be so. Jessica had different aggressor-identified states, self-states, and different forms of victim-identified states (mute, fleeing, idealizing), but her presentations conformed to this basic pattern.

In sum, both victim states and dominating and rageful self-states, which often embody rage, contempt, and omnipotence, may arise as procedural, imitative, dyadic enactments. These are procedural ways of being with another that reflect implicit models of relationships. They arise from the confluence of trauma and attachment, and may be understood as internal working models in Bowlby's sense. Such working models lie at the root of some of the narcissistic, unilateral, and entitled behavior that are aspects of splitting.

Generally the extreme cases, such as Ferenczi's, have been linked with descriptions of trauma. However, trauma and its effects can be unequivocally normative. It is a matter of two things: (1) overwhelming psychological interactions and events may occur more frequently than generally recognized, and (2) an interpersonal context may include many events, which in themselves may be what Breuer and Freud (1893–1895) called "partial traumas," but which together become cumulative. In a recent paper on Ferenczi's concept of identification with the aggressor, Frankel (2002) writes,

> But habitual identification with the aggressor also frequently occurs in people who have not suffered severe trauma, which

> raises the possibility that certain events not generally considered to constitute trauma are often experienced as traumatic. Following Ferenczi, I suggest that emotional abandonment or isolation, and being subject to a greater power, are such events. In addition, identification with the aggressor is a tactic typical of people in a weak position; as such, it plays an important role in social interaction in general [p. 101].

Frankel (2002) makes the important point that identification with the aggressor characterizes any number of relational solutions that derive from power inequities. This means that trauma has actually had an important shaping influence in the lives of many people who would not overtly appear to have been traumatized. Following Ferenczi, Frankel believes that someone's power over us, even if it is benign, may be traumatogenic. Because of our inherently social nature and the power of the attachment system, not only threats of abandonment but also fears of abandonment and the breaches in empathic contact that breed them are potentially traumatic.

This kind of identification with the aggressor is not a consciously manipulative attempt to appease the aggressor. Frankel observes that any interpersonal situation in which there is a power difference is a potential setting for identification with the aggressor, because open negotiation of goals between participants may be precluded. According to Frankel (2002),

> in identification with the aggressor, the parameters that define one's experiential world have not been negotiated between the participants in an interpersonal relationship; rather they have been directly imported from the mind of the threatening other person. . . . Identification means trying to feel something that someone else feels—essentially getting into *his* head, molding one's own experience into *his* [p. 106].

The role of dissociation here is an interesting and complex one. Frankel (2002) elaborates on Ferenczi's concept by pointing out that one thing dissociation does, in this situation, is to clear the way for "identification with the aggressor by emptying the mind of spontaneous emotional reactions so that we can feel what we must" (p. 110). He stresses that dissociation and identification work together. The process of identification with the aggressor informs us not only about what we must feel, but also about what we must dissociate.

Taken together, dissociation and identification with the aggressor operate in a very reality-oriented way to avoid and anticipate real world danger—the danger posed by the possibility of thought, and therefore exhibited behavior, that would be threatening to the "aggressor." To a larger degree than we may often generally like to admit, the child all too easily disappears as a *self*. Frankel observes that chronic identification with the aggressor can result in two particular things. One is that one does not know one's own mind, for the aggressor's beliefs have supplanted one's own. The other result is that a person may end up trying to control others emotionally, using a kind of "gentle fascism," trying to "manage the emotional agenda rather than being vulnerable to it" (p. 116).

All of the above pertains to how the object becomes part of the self. However, in a traumatic circumstance, aspects of personal experience that are not relevant to the danger at hand are also lost to the self-state that dealt with the trauma. A person who has identified with the aggressor ends up having been overtaken by the point of view and needs of the attachment figure or abuser, to the point of losing spontaneity, *joie de vivre,* and reflectiveness.

Trauma, States, and Affective Splitting

Recall Putnam's discrete behavioral states, or DBS, model according to which states are the building blocks of human behavior and consciousness (Putnam, 1992, 1997), as described in chapters 1 and 2. Although the effect of trauma on consciousness is complex, it disrupts a person's sense of continuity in two ways: by interrupting and retarding the linking of states in the course of development and by creating new discrete states. The neurological effects of trauma also contribute to decreased integration of states and decreased reflectiveness. Because linkage of states contributes to an awareness of context both within the self and within the world, and to the capacity for increased reflectiveness, people who have suffered more interruption of state linkage have more difficulty understanding their emotions and tend to feel buffeted by circumstances. As a result, they tend to rely on dissociation, and dissociation of self-states will be more frequent and severe.

Human beings, adults as well as children, categorize experience in terms of opposites, high and low, good and bad, nice and mean, positive and negative, and so on. This is simply an aspect of the categorizing mind and is not at all specific to psychopathology. Young children categorize their behavior and experience of self and other evaluatively in terms of good and bad, mean and nice. According to Fischer and Ayoub (1994), "affective splitting"—the development of children's "skills" in structuring experience and achieving goals—depends on various strands of experience based on context. Thus, the mind is naturally fractionated; experience is divided as part of the process of thinking. In the course of development the child constructs progressively more complicated control systems or skills which are a product both of the individual and the situation. Emotions "are adaptive reactions arising from the control systems: People evaluate how a situation relates to their goals and concerns, and they react emotionally based on that evaluation. . . . These emotional reactions bias or constrain activity to certain action tendencies or scripts for the particular emotion" (p. 151). These scripts and skills develop in increasingly complex ways, which are adaptive to each person's interpersonal world. "Because of the pervasiveness of fractionation, people often do not even recognize elements that go together in the world. When we encounter a task that is complex or confusing for us, we simplify it by dropping out components or splitting it into separate tasks" (p. 154). Thus, affective splitting occurs in normal development; but abusive and neglectful early interpersonal environments do not facilitate, and will expectably impede, the integration of these separate, contextually segregated strands of meaningful experience (Fischer and Ayoub, 1994; Putnam, 1997).

Possible Biological Substrates of Victim and Aggressor States

Certain victim-identified and aggressor-identified self-states may have biological underpinnings in discrete behavior states that are analogous to animal states, such as those involving fight, flight, freeze, and total submission, all of which are adaptive to conditions of predation (as described in the section on Van der Hart et al.'s theory of structural dissociation of the personality, and in the section on somatoform dissociation, in chapter 5).

The hypoarousal of the state of total submission is in contrast to the hyperarousal of the freeze state. Nijenhuis et al.'s description of total submission may be similar to the hypoarousal "dissociative" states that Bruce Perry has observed in children. Perry outlines how exposure to trauma alters neurodevelopmental processes via two primary responses of hypoarousal and hyperarousal. The hypoarousal state includes such dissociative symptoms as fugue, numbing, analgesia, derealization, depersonalization, catatonia, and fainting. This is a defeat response, similar to "learned helplessness," which is adaptive to immobilization or inescapable pain. In contrast, hyperarousal involves fight or flight reactions, which involves vigilance, behavioral irritability, increased locomotion, and a tendency to interpret cues as threatening.

If the child is a dependent of the aggressor, the passive hypoarousal state, such as going limp, may be the most adaptive alternative for survival, especially if one is young, weaker, or overpowered (Perry, 2000).

Van der Hart et al. (2000) have observed that prolonged forced immobilization may result in loss of locus of control, especially physical control involved in the ability to move in the face of threat. They hypothesize that this forced immobility evokes "chronic animal defensive states, in particular, freezing, with concomitant somatoform manifestations" (p. 53). Thus, an immobilized and frightened child may well enter a freeze state. However, more is going on than simply being in a freeze state. Because memory is processed differently in this state, a procedural reenactment of the behavior of an abusive attachment figure may appear as a dissociated part in this child's inner world. This is not conventional identification; this is "overtakenness" by the aggressor.

Traumatic Attachment

Children spontaneously imitate the mannerisms, postures, speech, and other behaviors of those around them, particularly adults. In addition to imitating adults who are warm and attentive to them (Bandura and Huston, 1961), children also imitate those they perceive as powerful (Bandura, Ross, and Ross, 1963). Unconscious imitation is ubiquitous. For instance, at times, analysands may unconsciously imitate the mannerisms of their analysts. Procedural learning relies in part on imitation. In traumatic attachment, the abuser's behaviors have an extremely high salience, and the child's attention is fixed on the abuser. Although the attachment system is only one among various motivational systems, it is superordinate when aroused, and it is activated by threat (Bowlby, 1969, 1984), including psychological threat. Thus, psychological trauma can increase the arousal of the attachment system. In this way, the intensity of procedural identification-knowing–the enactive replication of the abuser's behaviors–may increase as well.

Attachment is also an impetus to imitation. In a recent article by Van der Hart and his colleagues (2000), there is a striking description of a soldier's somatic manifestation of traumatic loss of an attachment figure, indicating the power of attachment-driven mimicking. Referring to fixations in trauma, the authors discuss "traumatic imitation which Rivers (1920) referred to as *mimesis:* i.e. 'the motor or effector side of the process whereby one animal or person influences another unwittingly'" (p. 47). They give an example of a wounded soldier who had a posttraumatic twitch in his jaw that must have mimicked the agonized gasping for breath that he witnessed on the face of a dying officer to whom he was very attached. Evidently, the traumatic moment impelled the soldier to seek the comfort of attachment, intensifying procedural identification-knowing.

In a way that may seem paradoxical, psychological trauma can increase attachment to the abuser, demonstrating a pattern of traumatic attachment often called *traumatic bonding* (Dutton and Painter, 1981), and at times labeled *masochistic* or *Stockholm syndrome,* in which the victim seems increasingly compelled to seek greater bonding to the abuser as the abuse increases (Howell, 1997b). Yet this bondage, through attachment and trauma, involves intimate, procedural identification-knowing of the abuser's behaviors and psyche.

Let us bring together all these factors. There is the freeze state, with its concomitant loss of locus of control, and the hypnoid narrowing of attention to only the most relevant stimulus, which in this case is the abuser, with the concomitant lack of attention to other aspects of self-experience. There is the unconscious process of "getting inside the abuser's head" as an aspect of enactive procedural knowing, with the concomitant fragmentation of much of self-experience. Finally, there is the overriding activation of the attachment system, because of the imminent danger and the unmodulated fear, often seemingly paradoxically, driving the person *toward* the abuser. Taking all these factors together, how could a severely traumatized person *not* identify with the aggressor?

It is important to remember that this reenacted identification involves dissociated affect. Even though the behavior and affect may seem as if transported from one person into another, the identifying person's own rage is expressed, not that of the original aggressor.

Play, Symbolization, Metaphor

Trauma is associated with the inhibition of play, decreased reflectiveness, and decreased ability to use metaphor. Trauma remands the imaginative and can mire its victims in the literal (Bromberg, 1993, 1995;

Meares, 1995). Symbolic play represents different roles and identities and links them. Pretend play also links play with mental experience, thus helping to differentiate fantasy and reality (Fonagy, 2001). Often traumatized persons and those in whom trauma has contributed to the organization of personality into a disorder may misinterpret their own symbols for what they signify. For example, one highly shame-based (and not wealthy) patient dreamt that he had too many suits. Attempting to honor the wisdom of his unconscious and to be a good patient by paying attention to his dreams, he threw out almost all of his suits before we had a chance to discuss in the session the meaning of suits in terms of self-image, multiple self-presentations, representations, and dissociation, among other things. However, this behavior may have represented more than the tendency to be concrete: The road to Hell is paved with the best of conscious intentions. A somewhat diabolical, or at the very least untrusting, self-state may have orchestrated such apparent concrete compliance with the purpose of demonstrating to the patient that therapy would only bankrupt him. Another patient, in a desperate, angry, and devaluing frame of mind, insisted that her therapist, whom she deemed at that moment inadequately knowledgeable about her problems and therefore unable to help her, find a clairvoyant for her. This patient was unable at that moment to take an "as-if" attitude and say something like, "I feel so distraught, as if I know nothing about myself, and I need someone to tell me." Often this reversion to the concrete interpretation from the symbolic can appear to be psychotic. Here flashbacks may contain fantasy-interwoven symbolizations along with a dissociated memory of a traumatic event. For example, one patient who was brutally raped, kept experiencing blood in her eyes. The blood may have symbolized the brutality of the event, the fact that she bled in other places, and that she saw the blood in horror. Another example is of a severely dissociative patient who momentarily believed right after September 11, 2001, that the Statue of Liberty had been beheaded and that the head was in the passenger seat of her car talking to her (Shusta-Hochberg, 2003).

One reason that people are concrete (when they are) is that the state of mind in which something has been symbolized—an affect, feeling, perception, idea—lacks access to another state of mind that could provide context for the symbol and that could give it the quality of "as if" that metaphor has. The patient who wanted her therapist to get her a clairvoyant was a bit like the people who listened to the fictional radio broadcast "The War of the Worlds" and thought it was real. She lacked connection to another mental state that could contextualize her experience and frame it as an experience of self rather than as an immediate need. When people are concrete, they lack the benefit of associative context with other states of mind (Bromberg, 1993, 1994). This prevents them from being fully able to reflect on their experience. A version of this happens in the reenactment involving overtakenness or identification with the aggressor in the way that has been developed in this chapter. The self-state(s) manifesting such overtakenness operate too much as solipsistic wholes, unlinked to other states.

Lack of Contextual Integration and Splitting

The fact that unlinked and switching self-states are decontextualized impedes a person's capacity to experience the self as the center of personal initiative. Although identification with the aggressor or overtakenness begins as an automatic, organismic process, it becomes with repeated activation and use a defensive one: It becomes a dissociative defense. This involves at least two dissociated enacted relational parts: the part of the victim and the part of the aggressor. The vicissitudes and interactions of these dissociated self-states constitute the core of splitting. Neither the object representation nor the self-representation is split, but certain roles with respect to the abuser–victim interaction are reenacted.

Not only does the disconnection defend against tremendous anxiety and terror, but integration may require tremendous painful mourning, which can be overwhelming to undertake all at once. Continual activation of these states contributes to the greater impermeability of intrapsychic, interstate boundaries. In the long run, this highly motivated defense is a cure that poisons a person's life and relationships. As Bromberg (1994) observes, the "basic problem for a traumatized individual becomes his own self-cure" (p. 538).

Let us bring together Stern's (1985) observation about the problems with the assumed chronology of splitting in infancy with Frankel's views on the outcomes of identification with the aggressor—that those who have identified with the aggressor tend to employ a "gentle fascism," trying to control others emotionally—and with Lyons-Ruth's perspective on D-attachment. Lyons-Ruth's proposal that potentially one "grows into" a borderline or narcissistic stance through a complex series of alternative developmental acquisitions is a remarkable one, especially given the view of Kernberg (1975) and others that splitting underlies personality disorders. Although Lyons-Ruth has categorized the school-age children who were disorganized infants as "hostile" or "helpless" (see chapter 3), these terms also characterize relational positions vis-à-vis the aggressor. We can also link Lyons-Ruth's discussion of the helpless and hostile aspects of disorganized attachment and her suggestion that the formerly disorganized children may become borderline or narcissistic as adults, with Bromberg's view that dissociation underlies all personality disorders.

A Case of DID

For my patient Michelle, as for most people, there are more than two contradictory self-states. Michelle lives out her life in quite a few different organizations of existence. Some of them know about each other and communicate with each other, and some of them do not. There is one part of her, John—who experiences himself as a five-year-old boy—who often comes to sessions, explaining with the greatest of tact why Michelle couldn't come herself. John is the peacemaker and the unifier. Part of John's job is to build trusting relationships wherever possible. John came into being when Michelle was very young, and both he and Michelle agree that John did something that Michelle could not do on her own: John bonded with the good in caregivers, even when they were being abusive (idealizing aspect of the victim role). John seemed to be untroubled by the terrors that beset Michelle as she tried to figure out her difficult young life, and seemed always to find a way to feel hope and manage other people. For instance, when Michelle's grandmother locked her in a crawlspace under the house—a dark, cold, filthy place inhabited by scary spiders—and told her to wait until she returned, Michelle was terrified and could not think (freezing victim state). In part, she was emotionally paralyzed because she was being treated so cruelly. John was not so downhearted and figured out a way to escape. He led Michelle outside, where they hid in a tree until nighttime, when it was safe to return.

As both John and Michelle will say, John represents a part of a split in her personality. John, along with another, older male part of Michelle, named Jerry, does most of the negotiating and interacting on the interface with the social world. John and Jerry have told me much of Michelle's history, including some parts of it that she herself does not know. Even though he experiences himself as young, John is not vacuous or shallow, but amazingly intelligent, emotionally attuned, and cued in to me. He understands both my feelings—how I might be upset if, for example, nobody could come at all to a session—and he understands Michelle's feelings (she is too scared to come). So, he figured out a solution: He came instead. He is not troubled by emotions of shame, or embarrassment, or fury—although of course, other parts of Michelle are.

There are other parts of Michelle that are more aggressive and harder to get along with. One, in particular, named Jeffrey, can be extremely hostile and rageful (aggressor state). On rare occasions he has come out in sessions, but most of the time he expresses himself by giving Michelle excruciating headaches and by frightening her with very scary thoughts of people being killed. He expresses his rage more against Michelle than against anyone else.

Creating or allowing John to come into existence was very ingenious and very hopeful on Michelle's part. However, in other ways her extremely dissociative personality structure has left her defenseless. For instance, when she was raped, she could not even imagine taking steps that in reality would protect her against further aggression, in the form of pursuing prosecution. She threw out all the evidence with the thought that now her rapist would be appeased and that that would insure her safety (victim state).

Conclusion

This dissociation of the masochistic victim and the rageful aggressor self-states, recast in attachment theory terms as "helpless" and "hostile" and understood in terms of identification with the aggressor, may constitute much of what we see as splitting. These oscillating masochistic victim and rageful aggressor self-states represent different relational positions derivative of trauma: the position of the victim and the position of the abuser.

This dissociative structuring of the self in response to traumatic attachment repeats the cycle of abuse. The abuser or chronically and grossly insensitive caretaker did not recognize the sovereign separateness of the child. As a result, the person's inner psychic structure has dissociated self-states that do not recognize the feelings in other parts. They may oscillate side by side so to speak, as in BPD and DID, or they may be layered in ways that describe other disorders typified by more stable configurations, but the dissociative nature of splitting remains clear.

8

PROJECTIVE IDENTIFICATION
Blind Foresight

The concept of projective identification is by now a staple of psychoanalytic work. The manifestations of this process can be stunning and powerful. Yet, the descriptions of how it works have often been murky, confusing, and contradictory. The thesis of this chapter is that the process we call projective identification can be best understood as the interpersonal language of dissociated self-states.

I take my title from Sullivan's pragmatic view of the concept of projection, which he boiled down to "foresight": "To begin with, we project in all interpersonal relations. We attempt to foresee action; we foresee it as the activity of embodied others, and that in itself, is projection" (Sullivan, 1953, p. 359). Sullivan qualified his statement with the observation that we tend to project the wrong thing, usually something negative. Even though Sullivan did not favor use of the term *projection,* he was prescient in his insistence on the concept of foresight with respect to projection, and its application to projective identification. The blind foresight or anticipation of relational processes that have been dissociated is, I believe, implicit in the concept of projective identification. In this section, I will expand Sullivan's view with respect to foresight; projective identification will be described in terms of a multiple-self model of dissociated parts.

Projective identification has been an extremely useful concept in clinical work. However, it has also become a concept used widely and loosely to describe all kinds of processes: interpersonal as well as intrapsychic, adaptive processes of normal development as well as processes of psychopathological defense. Although the concept was originally introduced by Melanie Klein as a strictly intrapsychic process, today many also view projective identification as a form of communication and as an interpersonal and an intersubjective process. If we are on the receiving end, it is a source of information about the other person and potentially about ourselves.

The meaning of the term has radically changed over time, as it has been variously understood, elaborated, and reappraised by different writers. Like a game of Memory, the concept has kept pace with the times, undergoing transformation upon transformation, until the final resulting usage and meanings bear little resemblance to the first entry. Melanie Klein was herself somewhat doubtful about the value of the concept because of its vulnerability to misuse (Spillius, 1988, p. 81).

In this chapter, I will describe some different meanings of the term with the purpose of presenting a conceptual shift, an alternative way of thinking about these processes that we call projective identification. I intend to show how the process, as it is generally conceptualized, requires a model of a dissociated, multiple self. I am in agreement with Ryle (1994) that projective identification can best be understood in terms of reciprocal role relationships. I am drawing again on models of enactive procedural learning (Lyons-Ruth, 1999, 2001b) or internal working models of attachment (Seligman, 1999), as well as other nonverbal, right-brain processes (Schore, 2003) to describe an interpersonal and intrapsychic process that we often call projective identification. In certain ramifications of these models, projective identification and enactment are two sides of the same coin.

In a general sense, the term *projective identification* has been used to refer to a person's unconscious attempts to disown experience by "putting it into" another person. A disowned affect, fantasy, or other unconscious and unwanted aspect of the self is projected—in the Latin root, "thrown forward"—into another person. Through identification with the other into whom the disowned aspect has been projected, however, a feeling of control over and contact with the other person is created and maintained. According to Laplanche and Pontalis (1973), projective identification is a "mechanism revealed in phantasies in which the subject inserts his self—in whole or in part—into the object in order to harm, possess or control it" (p. 356).

Projective identification was initially conceptualized by Melanie Klein, in her paper "Notes on Some Schizoid Mechanisms" (1946), as a purely intrapsychic and unidirectional activity, involving fantasy about body parts and excretory processes, and about expelling the bad parts of the self into the mother or the breast. Bion (1957, 1959) enlarged the concept of projective identification to include interactions in the transference–countertransference as well as interactions of the infant with the mother. Whereas Klein's formulation emphasized the infant's fantasy and had little to do with the actual mother,

Bion's concept very much involved the real mother and what the patient as infant needed from her. In addition, Bion explicitly addressed the effect of projective identification on the other person, the therapist. In "Attacks on Linking" (1959), Bion wrote of projective identification as an ideally transformative communication in which the role of the therapist or mother is to receive and keep the projection long enough to transform its contents so that it can be given back to the patient in a modified tolerable form. Bion stays with Klein's grounding of projective identification in physical experience in his descriptions of how the patient demands to be understood. He writes of how when the patient felt Bion's "refusal to accept parts of his personality . . . he strove to force them into me with increased desperation and violence" (1959, p. 96).

Several decades later, Ogden (1986) elaborated the concept of projective identification, emphasizing the importance of the therapist's or the mother's ability to tolerate the projected feelings. He emphasized the process by which the infant disowns and the mother metabolizes, and then feeds back, the information/affect to her baby in more metabolizable form. With each new assimilation, the baby's expectations and way of experiencing perceptions changed–the baby felt more nourished. Thus, when the projective identification cycle repeats again, it has a somewhat different content and meaning.

In its interpersonal application, projective identification is often used to describe a form of induction of disowned affect in the other person. The direction of projective identification is usually described as being from the baby to the mother or from the patient to the therapist, with the latter party receiving the effect of the projections. More recently, there has been increased emphasis on a joint process that works both ways, on mutual projective identification (Stern, 1997; Bromberg, 1998; Maroda, 1998). It has also been recently observed that the process often dramatically affects the less powerful member of a dyad. For instance, the direction of projective identification may go from the parent into the child, or from the therapist into the patient, rather than the other way around (Knapp, 1989; Seligman, 1999; Silverman and Lieberman, 1999). As Silverman and Lieberman (1999) describe it, projective identification revolves around acceptance of, or enactment by, the other person of certain attributions of the projector. Certainly emotional dependence, involving childhood or psychological immaturity, is highly relevant to a person's vulnerability to projective identificatory processes. An important consequence is often that the less powerful person on the receiving end of the projective identification may be seriously destabilized, as is frequently observed in family systems (Knapp, 1989).

Clinicians are becoming increasingly open about feeling destabilized by projective identificatory processes in treatment (Frawley-O'Dea, 1999; Bromberg, 2003a) If this process affects treating clinicians so profoundly, how must it affect children and patients who have been subjected to it without being helped to understand what is happening between the parties?

Problems with the Concept

All meanings of projective identification described here are important ways of describing forms of unconscious activity and defense, often involving interaction between two people. But there are problems with the concept.

Some people who prefer exactness, who are uncomfortable with vague metaphors, or both, feel uncomfortable with, even stymied by, the term. After all, how do impulses, affects, or split-off parts of the self get "put into" one person by another person? Grotstein (1999b) offers an important clarification by pointing out that it is not possible to literally put a part of oneself into another person. What happens in projective identification, he says, is that the projector puts a split-off part of the self into the *image* or *representation* of the object.[1]

Projection and Projective Identification

Many authors distinguish between projection and projective identification. In general, projection is thought to involve a greater sense of separateness on the part of the projector, whereas projective identification often implies that the recipient has been affected. Baker (1997) observes that projection is "onto" the object in a way that does not change the object, whereas projective identification is "into" the object, resulting in experience of the object being changed. Projective identification is often characterized by boundary violations and unclarity about personal and interpersonal boundaries. Perhaps the latter contributes to the strangely "intimate" feel of projective identificatory processes.

Kernberg (1975) differentiates projection from projective identification on the basis that projection is a more mature and more impersonal defense, related to repression, whereas projective identification is more primitive, often characteristic of borderline personality organization, and is related to splitting. Whereas projection succeeds as a defense that rids the unacceptable material from consciousness, in projective identification, according to Kernberg, the projected material is kept close at hand in the "identification" part of the process. The projector must have a sense of control over the object of projection.

In contrast to Kernberg, Spillius (1988), a Kleinian writer, believes that projective identification does not need to be differentiated from projection as an operative defense. The two are really identical in her view. According to Spillius, Klein added depth to Freud's concept of projection, by emphasizing that

> one cannot project impulses without projecting a part of the ego, which involves splitting, and further, that impulses do not just vanish when projected; they go into an object, and they distort perception of the object. Unconsciously, if not consciously the individual retains some sort of contact with the projected aspects of himself [p. 82].

I agree. Even if we take some of the best examples of projection, such as racism or sexism, the idea that the projector is not dependent on the recipient, in a very intense way, is illusory. Often, it is vital for the projector's self-esteem to be in this form of relationship, even when the relationship is unstated. For example, the projector's superiority may be dependent on the assumed inferiority of the object. The recipients of these projections generally feel the impact of the negative attributions quite powerfully. The illusoriness of the idea of simple projection may be well illustrated by Toni Morrison's (1992) compelling description of "American Africanism" in the United States, involving the intense, unstated meaning of whiteness and blackness in American culture and literature, or the "denotative and connotative blackness that African peoples have come to signify" (p. 6). In short, "Africanism" is the "vehicle by which the American self knows itself as not enslaved, but free; not repulsive, but desirable; not helpless, but licensed and powerful; not history-less, but historical; not damned, but innocent; not a blind accident of evolution, but a progressive fulfillment of destiny" (1992, p. 52).[2]

As Knapp (1989) and Silverman and Lieberman (1999) suggest, perhaps the potency of the process of projective identification often depends on the relative power and personal resources of those projected "onto" or "into." The potency of projective identification may also depend on the willingness and ability of the recipient to either contain (more ideally) or exploit (less ideally) the intolerable feelings of the projectors. An example of the latter might be a self-defeating attribution of anger or contempt into the recipient by someone who feels powerless and needy of attachment. A collusive exploitation would be a feel-good superiority of the recipient in relation to the projector.

The Problem of the Unified Self

Projective identification seems to describe something important that occurs within and between people, but it is very hard to specify how it works. There are intertwined conceptual and logical problems with the concept. Even though the original language of projective identification involved references to split-off parts, and thus, recognition of dissociation as an important aspect of projective identification is implicit, the way that the process is generally understood does not extend this thinking to its logical conclusion, which would involve dissociated parts of a multiple self.

One reason that projective identification is often so hard to understand is that it tends to be conflated with an assumption of unitary selfhood. Even though splitting or dissociation is generally assumed to be part of the meaning of the term, it seems that the person *as a unitary agent* is assumed to project, or to evacuate, affects, thoughts, or parts of the self. Or it is assumed that a unitary unconscious does these things. The projector locates the disowned aspect of self in the representation of another person, and then interacts with this dissociated aspect of self in that other person, all the while believing it to be a quality or trait inherent in the other person. How can this be? How, specifically, can the self as a unity do this?

This conundrum shares similar logical problems with that of repression, which is described in the chapter on concepts. As Stern (1997) observes, a problem with the concept of repression is that it ultimately requires an infinite series of inner homunculi to do the repressing. The repressing part of the self must repress the fact that it is repressing, and so on, in an infinite regression. But the case is even more complicated for projection and projective identification. The projecting self must somehow simultaneously both know and not know, not only that it is projecting, but what it is projecting. Who decides what is to be projected? With reference to our hypothetical unitary self, if the self did not somehow know the disavowed material, how would it know what to anticipate in terms of the recipient's feelings, thoughts, and behavior? Yet, if this unitary self knows, then the knowledge must be conscious. How do we get around this contradiction? If we assume that the projector both knows and does not know, we are necessarily already talking in the languages of dissociation and a multiple self, but we need a way to do this without an infinite series of inner homunculi.

There are two solutions to this dilemma, and both involve multiple dissociated selves. One involves implicit procedures that are functionally, although not necessarily dynamically, separated from declarative, autobiographical (episodic) experience. In that case, the question of who represses what becomes irrelevant, for these implicit procedures were never repressed. The other solution pertains to dissociated discrete states of mind, or self-states, that include aspects of declarative, autobiographic experience. Of course, in actuality, the world is not so neatly divided into declarative and procedural (Ryle, 2003). In fact, segregated parts of experience contain elements of both to varying degrees. The main point is that the problems of infinitely repressing the repressor and of how the person knows what to project no longer exist when we think in terms of multiple dissociated self-states.

Dissociated Self-States: Interpersonal and Interstate Dynamics

I would like to illustrate a way of looking at projective identification in terms of dissociated self-states. Since interpersonal trauma damages the boundaries between self and other, when a person does not know about, or is not conversant with, personal self-states, the locus of feelings may be unknown, and may then be found in another person in the current dyad. Let's say, for example, that a part of me that is inaccessible to the currently experiential, present "I," is feeling something that is unfamiliar, unbearable, or both, to the experiential, present "I." Let's say, for example, that this other part of me is experiencing anger. I, as the current thinker, don't know about this other part's affects, but I am likely, on occasion, to feel something "out of the blue," something leaked from this other part. This "out of the blue" intrusive feeling may or may not register consciously, but it is definitely "in my bonnet." If I know about it, I certainly don't know where it came from.

While I have this affect "in my bonnet," I am interacting with you. Since I don't know what other parts of me are feeling, I conclude that *you* must be the cause of these unclear feelings. I imagine you are feeling what I am feeling in another part of me because "I," as the current thinker, don't know what this other part of me is thinking and feeling. This "projective identification" is unconsciously motivated because a part of me, of which "I" am currently unaware, *wants* to live and engage with others, to have its own way, and to be understood empathically.

So far, in describing projective identification, I have been referring primarily to the intrapsychic aspect of the phenomenon. This arrangement involves relationships of parts to each other in a way that is intrapersonal or interstate. Different affects may characterize different self-states. Thus, one could say that parts of the self project affects and thoughts that are unacceptable to that particular self-state into another self-state. However, to speak of projective identification in this way runs into the same logical problems as does projection into another person. It may be simpler just to speak of dissociation.

Let us return to the hypothetical scenario of my not knowing. In accordance with what a dissociated part of me is feeling, my body may be rigid, my facial expression may be angry, or I may express some "fighting words." In short, I am acting angrily, without registering the existence of these behaviors, their meaning, or both. The currently experiencing "I" does not know this. However, you respond in kind to my angry behavior, and now I accuse you of mistreating me, *me,* who has "done nothing."

This perspective enables us to connect the intrapersonal and the interpersonal dimensions. The dissociated affect is located in another part of the self and may be found in other people, often simultaneously. In this way, projective identification may be viewed simply as an interpersonal manifestation of intrapsychic dissociation. However, the process is fundamentally an interpersonal one, which can ultimately be expected to affect the other people involved if they are at all responsive. Although one can certainly confine one's observations to the individual as a unity, these intrapersonal and interstate processes are considered to be derivative of, or internalizations of, earlier interpersonal ones, as Janet, Vygotsky, Lyons-Ruth, and Ryle, among others, suggest. Inasmuch as the intrapsychic contents are understood to be derivative of the interpersonal, projective identification can be understood as the interpersonal language of dissociated self-states.

Projective Identification as Involving Implicit, Procedural Communication

One way of thinking about dissociation involves the concept of implicit, procedural knowledge, which is not accessible to ordinary verbal consciousness. Thus, the procedural is dissociated from the declarative. Schore (2003) believes that implicit procedural processes underlie projective identification. Schore's view of projective identification as a process utilizing right-brain-to-right-brain intersubjective affective responsivity has an interesting consistency with Klein's original conceptualization involving fantasies of bodily experience. Emphasizing that it is affects rather than impulses that are projected, Schore sees projective identification as an unconscious coping strategy for the regulation of intense affect states that developed early in life.

These affects are communicated by somatic states, by the rhythmicity of bodily response, by other mind–body communications, by affect, and by facial expressions, all in a right-brain-to-right-brain way. One of the prime ways that such affects are communicated is by facial expression, which can be extremely subtle, nuanced, and split-second to normal perception. But this is not so nuanced to the right brain, which processes information holistically and "can appraise facially expressed emotional cues in less than 30 milliseconds . . . far beneath levels of awareness" (Schore, 2003, p. 71). Because this unconscious processing of affective information is so rapid, the processes are not consciously perceived. Not only is the right brain specialized in receptive processing of facial expressions, but it is also dominant in evaluating the trustworthiness of faces.

Facial affective expression has also been found to be extremely important in transference–countertransference processes. Schore (2003) states, "Thus, in the clinical context, although it appears to be an invisible, instantaneous, endogenous unidirectional phenomenon, the bidirectional process of project identification is actually a very rapid sequence of reciprocal affective transactions within the intersubjective field that is coconstructed by the patient and the therapist" (p. 73).

Schore notes that the primitive avoidant strategy of dissociation that occurs as a consequence of trauma is known to produce permanent changes in the maturing brain, such that memory of the traumata are stored in implicit procedural memory, thereby increasing the later use of dissociation. He emphasizes that the memory of the trauma is stored in implicit procedural memory in the right brain and is communicated nonverbally. Schore also observes that, in contrast to the frequently held view that projective identification is an intentional attempt to control the other, there is instead intense disorganization, insecurity, helplessness, and lack of organized coping. Schore believes that trauma-related contents are very likely to be projected in this right-brain sense rather than consciously communicated. Although Schore seems to believe that the recipient receives the message of this subliminal communication, he has less to say about how the recipient is affected.

Sands's (1997) beautifully written case description illustrates the kind of subliminal communication in projective identification of which Schore writes. Sands describes how she "became aware of a *'pull,' like something tugging on the center of my chest.* As this bodily experience became more conscious, I realized that I had in fact felt this pull from the first moment I met him. I also become more aware of a *subtle countermovement* in myself to resist this pull, to dig in my heels" (p. 651, italics added). When she put these visceral feelings into words in the therapy session, the patient was able to articulate his own experience more fully, including that he had always felt a pull to take care of his mother which he had resisted. After this, there was a shift in the treatment that included the disappearance of Sands's own bodily sense of *pull* (p. 652, italics added).

Positing a selfobject need to communicate unsymbolized affective experience through the other's (in this case, the therapist's) experience, Sands (1997) explains this kind of interaction as one in which a person needs to be understood "from the inside out." She states, "If the analyst cannot make herself available to be used in this way and cannot receive the patient's indirect, visceral communication, then those dissociated 'not-me' aspects of self that are being communicated will be unconsciously experienced as intolerable to the analyst as well" (p. 663). Her case illustrates the affective communication between dissociated self-states of which Schore writes, as well as the sensorimotor components of these experiences.

Lyons-Ruth (1999), in her attachment-derived concept of a two-person unconscious, emphasizes as do Schore and Sands, the paramount importance of enactive procedures. For Lyons-Ruth, enactments represent unconscious procedural relational knowledge of being with another person—a product of a two-person interaction, rather than a purely intrapsychic unconscious. Different procedural ways of being with another, or implicit models of relationships, may be dissociated. For example, two contradictory working models may be played out procedurally. Understood this way, interpersonal history clings to the concept of projective identification.

In this way of thinking, projective identification and enactment are two sides of the same coin. For instance, in a clinical example that I provided in the first chapter, a therapist suddenly began to feel lovingly about a patient's sweet vulnerability, and the therapist's eyes momentarily fell on the patient's breasts. Awareness of these unfamiliar thoughts caused the therapist internally to recoil with shock. After a while, the patient began to talk about her painful, shameful experiences of sexual abuse at her father's hands. Apparently, the patient had been wearing on her skin, so to speak, and exhibiting in her posture, a procedural enactive representation of a particular kind of relationship—an unconscious, nonverbal anticipation of a particular kind of engagement with an other.

Interpersonal Projective Identification and Enactment

Often projective identification and enactment are related in the following way: The projective identification "disowns" the affect, but stimulates it in the other person, and the enactment puts all of this into play (Maroda, 1998). Another way of saying this would be: The dissociated state is communicated, largely in a nonverbal way, to another person in an emotionally significant interaction. This communication engages a dissociated state in the other person's psyche. The induction part of projective identification requires a dissociative self-organization in the recipient as well as in the sender.

Once a dissociated self-state is expressed (in whatever way), it enters the interpersonal field as a way of being with another. But this way of being with another confronts another person, who has his or her ways of being with another. Understood this way, projective identification does not have to be imbued with magic, but involves various communicative modalities, including the nonverbal communication of dissociated self-states.

Interpersonal Dynamics: Countertransference and Role Relationships

In an early paper on countertransference, Sandler (1976) observes that the interaction between the patient and the analyst is in large part "determined by what I shall refer to as the intrapsychic role-relationship which each party tries to impose on the other" (p. 43). His thinking emphasizes the internalized, and therefore anticipatory, dyadic interaction. He writes,

> What I want to emphasize is that the role-relationships of the patient in analysis at any particular time consists of a role in which he casts himself, and a *complementary* role in which he casts the analyst at that particular time. The patient's transference would thus represent an attempt by him to impose an interaction, an interrelationship (in the broadest sense of the word) between himself and the analyst. Nowadays many analysts must have the conviction . . . that the conceptualization of transference as the patient's libidinal or aggressive energic cathexis of a past object being transferred to the image of the analyst in the present is woefully inadequate. The patient's unconscious wishes and mechanisms with which we are concerned in our work are expressed intrapsychically in (descriptively) unconscious images or fantasies, in which both self and object in interaction have come to be represented in particular roles [p. 43].

Sandler (1976) suggests that parallel to free-floating attention is "free-floating responsiveness." The analyst's thoughts, feelings, and overt behavior constitute a kind of "role responsiveness" that not only underlie his feelings and thoughts toward the patient, but fuel a "useful countertransference" (p. 44). Sandler gives as an example an interactive style that he developed with one particular patient, with whom he had begun to notice he was unusually loquacious. He then began to observe that the patient ended every sentence with an interrogation. When Sandler pointed out this behavior to the patient (of which he had been unaware), the patient recalled that he had acquired by this method the ability to engage his violent father in a positive fashion early in his life. The patient very much feared the disapproval of his father, who was a professional fighter, but also very much wanted his father's favor. Thus, he learned to safely engage his father by asking him questions without directly asking them.

Ryle (1994, 1997a, b) has further developed this way of understanding projective identification in terms of reciprocal role relationships; his thinking helps to elucidate the pressure felt by the recipient of projective identification. Ryle emphasizes the ongoing need for reciprocal response in all human beings; he suggests that what we call projective identification has its roots in the early mother–child relationship and continues to develop throughout childhood and adolescence. Furthermore, the procedural role sequences that children learn from their interactions with their parents form the basis of what is generally called projective identification. Children learn to anticipate the parental roles toward themselves and begin to enact these parental roles toward dolls, teddy bears, or the mother. Concurring with Ogden (1986) that the internalization of the "object" involves the internalization of the object relationship, he concludes that both reciprocal roles are present in every interaction. In time, the child acquires the ability to play both roles and begins to play the parental role toward the self. As a result, the "self can often be usefully understood as a relationship between a (parental) 'I' and a (child) 'me,' with awareness being variously distributed between the two or extending to the dialogue between them" (Ryle, 1994, p. 109).

The internalization of self–other procedures implies the corresponding ability to elicit reciprocation from others: "In the view proposed here, all role procedures, whether normal or neurotic, are maintained by the continuing elicitation from others of the expected confirmatory reciprocations. In enacting a role there is always pressure on the other to relate and reciprocate in a particular way" (Ryle, 1994, p. 110). Acknowledging that we all need confirmation and acceptance from others, Ryle (1994) comments, "The specificity of this expectation, the force with which it is communicated and the degree to which the requirement is directly, verbally, and consciously made all vary. The phenomena usually described as projective identification are characterized by narrow expectations conveyed indirectly and forcefully" (p. 112).

When the reciprocal role patterns are more limited and narrow, the projector will have a more urgent need for reciprocation in order to obtain confirmation of the self. People whose self-states are more isolated and whose repertoire is more limited tend to interact more forcefully with others and to do so in search of a specific response. Because deprivation and abuse can interfere with integrative personality organization, as Putnam has spelled out in his DBS model, there will be greater isolation of reciprocal role procedures and greater personality fragmentation. Hence, the more narrow the reciprocal role patterns, the greater will be the need for confirmation of self from others within these limited role repertoires. Consequently, the other person in interaction is more likely to feel pressured.

Ryle observes that his model is consistent with the Kleinian descriptions of the transformative developmental role of projective identification via the projection of bad parts, which are made tolerable by the recipient and fed back. His model is also quite consistent with Sands's case presentation when she articulates her experience of a "pull" to "do something," a pull accompanied by the wish to resist, the patient articulates the pull he had always felt from his mother to care for her, along with his resistance to it.

Brothers's (1995) utilization of Kohut's concept of alter-ego selfobject, a selfobject that confirms a sense of alikeness with other human beings, is also close to Sands's and Ryle's points of view. Because the part of the self seeking resonance is dissociated, the alter-ego selfobject fulfills the "need to experience the presence of essential sameness or alikeness with disavowed or hidden aspects of self" (p. 63). Racker's (1968) concepts of concordant and complementary identification in the countertransference are applicable to this model as well. In concordant identification the analyst's current self-experience matches that of the patient. In complementary identification, the analyst's identification is with the reciprocal pole of the self state (in Ryle's terms) that the patient is enacting.

Do We Need "Projection" in Projective Identification?

Sandler ends his 1974 article on countertransference with this statement:

> I do not find the terms "projection," "externalization," "projective identification" and "putting parts of oneself into the analyst" sufficient to explain and to understand the processes of dynamic interaction which occur in transference and countertransference. It seems that a complicated system of unconscious cues, both given and received, is involved [p. 46].

I agree. Projection is usually considered to be a rather specific form of externalization and displacement with a specific target. Projective identification is often conceptualized in terms of the projector trying to get rid of, to disown, or to evacuate an impulse or a part of the self. Without losing the original grounding in physical experience, it is now possible to broaden the emphasis to include the sending and the receipt of the affective message through sensory and sensorimotor modalities. Although "intestinal" and "urethral" do imply evacuation, sensorimotor does not. Conceptualized as an interactive process, projective identification does not necessarily depend on the "projector" trying to get rid of something. For me, a conception of a multiple self with dissociated procedural states, enactments, and self-states is the precondition for what we call projective identification. A person will enact procedurally the parent–child, other–self, or me–you patterns that were learned early in life. Many of these patterns are, by definition, not conscious. The person may enact the self-role because that is the way the person knows how to act procedurally in relation to significant others; or the person may enact the other, the parent role, because this is the other way the person knows how to act in a particular kind of relational configuration. Both of these are frequently rehearsed repertoires. Depending on the severity of early trauma and the extent of dissociation, the person may switch between various self–other patterns without much conscious recognition of the change in personal behavior. The social environment, along with its requirements and opportunities, may have changed, and the person has merely adjusted in the process. This reciprocal role is not necessarily being projected, disowned, or evacuated, although it is to some extent, small or large, being elicited, or even created, in the other person in the interaction. Either the so-called projector is behaving in ways that were experienced or observed and that to varying degrees, worked, or that were required, *in relation to* significant others, or the projector is enacting the behaviors or role of the significant other relevant to this particular type of situation.

This brings us to the question of why the other in the dyad reacts in accordance to the procedural script of the projector. The other person plays his part to varying degrees. When people get caught up in an enactment, it is because dissociated self-states in the projector have engaged dissociated self-states in the recipient (Bromberg, 1998). It is often because there are very common, powerful dyadic engagements to which a large number of people have been exposed. For instance, issues common to many people concern attachment, dependency, care, control, power, submission, love, and anger; these problematic issues have usually taken on their particular patterns in a person's early significant relationships (Ryle, 2003). Thus, the other person may also have certain procedural blind spots that have been "contacted" and become caught up in the enactment.

Externalization

This concept also assumes a unitary self. A standard way of conceptualizing projective identification is to say that when children experience overwhelming affects, they project these into the parents, who then take in these projected feelings, contain them, and return them in more metabolized form. Alternatively, one may say that when children have frightening experiences and strong affects that threaten to overwhelm them, they "externalize" their distress by turning to a significant "external" other for help in managing the affect. If such a person is unavailable, they may be overwhelmed and traumatized. The child's only recourse then is, in different ways, to partition the distress internally, with the result that the current self is less likely to be overwhelmed by the immediate distress, but the aggregate of self-states, the person as a whole, becomes more vulnerable to stress in the future. In particular, this aggregate "I" is more likely to construct current relationships in accordance with divisions of experience that were post-traumatic reactions or adaptations to earlier relationships.

In this way, the process known as projective identification depends on a multiple, dissociated self.

9

CONCEPTS OF PSYCHIC PROCESSES, DEFENSE, AND PERSONALITY ORGANIZATION

> The theory of repression is the cornerstone on which the whole structure of psychoanalysis rests.
>
> –Sigmund Freud

We now move on to a reconsideration of certain concepts from the standpoint of dissociation theory. Among the defenses covered in this chapter are repression, dissociation, and splitting. Among issues of personality organization and treatment are enactment, abreaction, catharsis, integration, and what I call interstate intersubjectivity.

Within the collective psyche of psychoanalysts there is a conflict regarding the hegemony of concepts of defense and personality organization. With respect to repression and dissociation, until very recently repression has reigned supreme, with little challenge. Today, dissociation is regarded in many circles as more central. However, it is not so easy to clearly identify the contenders. In both repression and dissociation some psychic contents are made inaccessible or are prevented from obtaining consciousness. Repression and dissociation are often used interchangeably to describe the same psychic phenomena; dissociation and splitting, although often differentiated (Stern, 2004), are in some circles, such as within object relations in the United Kingdom (Tarnopolsky, 2003), regarded as synonymous.

The most important difference between repression and dissociation is in the implied model of the mind and of the unconscious. Repression and dissociation have separate implications for how we construe the mind–as unitary or polypsychic, as one or many. Indeed, dissociation is both the cause and the marker of polypsychism (many minds), and dipsychism (two minds) (Ellenberger, 1970; Erdelyi, 1994). These concepts imply different versions of the unconscious. Is there one unified unconscious or are there multiple centers of dissociated and therefore unconscious activity? Repression corresponds to the first idea, with the unconscious as the container for the repressed material; dissociation corresponds to the latter. However, the question is not rightfully either/or: endorsement of the multiple-centers view does not rule out the unitary view, because repression of unitary contents may occur separately within different self-states.

In the late 1800s and early 1900s, dissociationism was the hot psychological topic on both sides of the Atlantic. Yet, by 1914, Freud's statement that the "theory of repression is the cornerstone on which the whole structure of psychoanalysis rests" (Freud, 1914, p. 16) was an accurate representation of truth in the public mind at that time. However, with the ascendancy of Freudian theory, many of the old meanings of dissociation were largely assimilated to the new term, *repression,* similar to how the architectural structures of a newly dominant civilization are often built on top of older ones.

The issues are both conceptual and semantic, but the simplest solution is on a conceptual level: Repression can properly be understood as a type of dissociation (Erdelyi, 1994; Epstein, 1997). One realm of experience is inaccessible to another.

Repression

The central idea behind repression is that it is a willful exclusion of information from consciousness. As Freud said in his essay, "On Repression, the "essence of repression lies simply in turning something away, and keeping it at a distance, from the conscious" (1915, p. 147).

At first, Freud placed all psychic defense under the rubric of repression. Soon, however, he came to regard defense as the general category, of which repression was one defense. Freud was inconsistent in what he considered to be repressed. In its first uses, repression referred to a defense against traumatic memories, primarily those of sexual abuse (Breuer and Freud, 1893–1895; Freud, 1896). In his preanalytic writings, Freud sometimes used the term *repression* to describe processes that sounded like Janetian dissociation, referring to a "second psychical group," "*conditionne seconde,*" and "incompatible ideas," and he often used the terms *repression* and *dissociation* interchangeably (Erdelyi, 1990, 2001). In these preanalytic writings, repressed contents tended to concern traumatic or shameful experiences that happened to the patient. In contrast, after his rejection of the seduction theory, repression had more to do with wishes and fantasies.

Even later, in some of Freud's more popular writing, such as *The Psychopathology of Everyday Life,* many examples of phenomena associated with repression, such as parapraxes and slips of the tongue, work just as well, if not better, as examples of dissociative intrusions (Hilgard, 1977).

Freud's two different contents of repression, painful memories and wishes, correspond with the two major uses of repression today, as either a way of trying to expel from consciousness frightening and traumatic memories or as an attempt to push impulses back down. Erdelyi (1990) puts this in terms of the economic difference. The first one has to do with the avoidance of emotional pain, and the second has to do with the counterpressure "down" against a continuous wish or impulse. In the former case, because there is no continuous endogenous pressure "upward," the goal of repressive amnesia for an isolated unpleasant event should not require continuous expenditure of energy. In contrast, when repressed material is constantly being re-presented, much effort and ingenuity is required to accomplish the repression proper.

Problems with Repression

Generally, repression is understood as an unconscious process. There is a logical problem, though, with the view of repression as unconscious defense which requires knowing and not knowing at the same time. One potential problem with the concept of repression is that it can ultimately require an infinite series of inner homunculi to do the repressing (Kihlstrom, 1984; Erdelyi, 1994; Stern, 1997). The repressing part of the ego must repress that it is repressing, and so on. How do we get around this? Freud's (1900) solution to the repression problem was to posit an internal censor. Stern (1997) observes that this paradox was part of the reason that Freud adopted the structural model. By adopting the structural model, Freud could then say that the ego and the superego both had unconscious portions. An unconscious part of the ego performed the function of what Freud had earlier described as the "censor." Thus, the decision to repress does not have to be repressed because the decision was made unconsciously. However, the problem here is that now the censor both knows and doesn't know, with the result that we have the same problem we had before, only "once removed."[1]

Solutions

One solution involves the idea that repression does not always have to be unconscious. One version of this comes from cognitive psychology. It has been suggested (Eriksen and Pierce, 1968, cited in Erdelyi, 1990; Kihlstrom, 1984) that repression begins as suppression, a conscious procedure. With adequate practice, this activity becomes a highly skilled, but unconscious, procedure. Such procedural knowledge may begin as declarative structures. Conscious defense can become automatic and, by overlearning, unconscious. Furthermore, an initially conscious defense may become unconscious if a person is uncomfortable with the awareness of having repressed some material, and the person may repress this knowledge of having repressed, and so on (Erdelyi, 1985). This solution is not tantamount to an inner homunculus because it does not require initial unconsciousness. Matthew Erdelyi (1992, 1994, 2001) observes that much of Freud's work suggests that repression includes conscious, willful forgetting and that "Freud–Sigmund, not Anna–used suppression and repression interchangeably, from his earliest writings . . . to his last" (1990, p. 12). Underscoring Freud's constructivism, Erdelyi also (1994, 2001) notes that repression can be understood as reconstruction, which makes things more "palatable." We forget, and we reconstruct. Forgetting may partially involve a conscious act. In both cases, the effect is to make part of memory and experience inaccessible.

Sternian and Janetian dissociationism are also solutions. Whereas Erdelyi has solved the problem by emphasizing that repression can be conscious, Stern's (1997) solution to the problem of how we know and not know at the same time is that we do not "know" in the first place because we avoid formulating the experience. We do not unconsciously expel preformulated knowledge or experience from consciousness. However, we do selectively inattend, as Sullivan observed; we may also have an inkling of what to avoid noticing, of what to selectively inattend. Here Stern draws on James's discussion of certain "feelings of tendency," which can function as guides in the choice as to whether to formulate an experience or avoid it. These feelings of tendency may be linked with anxiety, adding to the probability that certain issues will not be formulated.

Janetian dissociationism is another solution to this "knowing and not knowing" problem. Different parts of the self, self-states, "know" different things. When self-states are dissociated, the different parts do not all have the same access to knowledge. The right hand often really does not know what the left hand is doing. Using the dissociation paradigm, "knowing and not knowing" is no longer a dilemma at all.

The Janetian view of multiple centers of consciousness helps us to understand that, although reconstruction is understood as an activity of a constructing "I," à la Erdelyi, various reconstructing "I"s can be dissociated, kept apart. Contents reconstructed within a given self-state may not be accessible to another one. Although the dissociated material has not been constructed by the currently experiencing self, it is possible that another self-state, inaccessible to the first one, does have a construction of the dissociated event.

Repression and Dissociation

Definitions of repression and dissociation are diverse and often overlapping. Although the most parsimonious way to understand repression is that it is a type of dissociation (Erdelyi, 1994), at this point it may be useful to describe some of the usual differentiations between repression and dissociation.

1. Repression is both motivated and defensive. In contrast, dissociation often is, but does not have to be motivated or psychologically defensive. For example, dissociation can arise automatically in the moment of trauma, or nondefensively in response to hypnosis.
2. Repression refers to formulated experience, and dissociation generally refers to unformulated experience (Stern, 1997).
3. Repression usually refers to a piece of information that was accessible at one time but not at another, whereas dissociation usually refers to divisions of experience in which the parts are side by side, contrasting, and may be concurrent in time. Dissociation refers to states and systems of states, which are often mutually exclusive (Spiegel, 1994).
4. Dissociated memories are especially context-dependent.

Repression Is Motivated and Defensive. In contrast, dissociation and splitting can be understood as either active, motivated, defensive processes or as automatic, psychologically passive processes. Because repression is motivated and active, it assumes a kind of mastery that dissociation generally does not assume (Davies and Frawley, 1994). Although repression generally concerns the conflict between wishes and internalized prohibitions and serves to avoid the anxiety and troublesome consequences that would be brought on by not heeding these prohibitions (Hilgard,

1977; Ryle, 1997, 2002), it also concerns the motivated exclusion of unwanted memories from consciousness (Breuer and Freud, 1893–1895; Hilgard, 1977b). These strategies are all motivated.

Repression is always something that one *does,* but dissociation can happen *to* one. Dissociation can be understood as both psychologically motivated and as automatic and psychologically passive. Dissociation and splitting have both been described as passive and active processes (Fischer and Pipp, 1984; Fischer and Ayoub, 1994). Passive dissociation refers to the overwhelmed psyche. Some overwhelming event or series of events are simply more than the mental structure can process. Active dissociation generally refers to both Sternian and Janetian dissociationism, including both the refusal to formulate experience and the maintenance of dissociation. Generally, both active and passive dissociation are involved in dissociative phenomena.

Formulated Versus Unformulated Experience. Generally, repression has been thought to refer to experience that has been formulated and then rejected from consciousness, to declarative knowledge that was once known and then forgotten. As Davies and Frawley (1994) say, "repressed materials are experienced as once familiar, rediscovered aspects of mental life . . . [which] have been previously experienced, psychologically digested, encoded, and then forgotten. . . . They can be maintained out of awareness, distorted, and psychically elaborated, via fantasy, their derivatives finding verbal expression" (p. 66).

In contrast, dissociation refers to unformulated experience (Stern, 1997). Some integration of this concept of unformulated experience with Janetian-type dissociation is possible on the basis that dissociated experience is "kept apart" (Tarnopolsky, 2003) from the currently experiencing self or selves because it has not been formulated, either in interaction with another person or with other parts of the self, or both.

Knowing and Not Knowing at Different Times Versus Knowing and Not Knowing at the Same Time. The model of repression usually refers to a piece of information that was accessible at one time but not at another, whereas dissociation usually refers to divisions of experience in which the parts are side by side, contrasting, and may be concurrent in time. (These are basically Erdelyi's, 1994, recovery and dissociation paradigms.) Repression is often considered to refer to the "absence of small, limited units of mental life" (Tarnopolsky, 2003, p. 15), whereas dissociated material is generally organized in such a way that one set of material requires the exclusion of other material: "Dissociation, as a mode of defense . . . carries with it the implication of two or more incompatible mental contents that are structured so as to exclude one another from consciousness" (Spiegel, 1990b, p. 126). Generally, units of declarative knowledge are considered to be repressed (Erdelyi, 1990, 1994), whereas affect states and self-states, which include procedural memories (as well as declarative knowledge [Kilstrom and Hoyt, 1990]), may be dissociated. This in some ways proceeds from the distinction of formulated versus unformulated experience, because once information is formulated it becomes declarative, explicit memory which can then be repressed and is subject to various forms of reconstruction. Once in this state, units of declarative information can, by various means, disappear from consciousness—for example, be forgotten (Erdelyi, 1994). Because dissociated experience is not integrated with some other aspects of self-experience, its emergence may be in a side-by-side or one-at-a-time way.

It is not just discrete memories or affects that are dissociated, but a piece of living experience. Competing organizations of experience are kept apart in dissociation, as for instance, when the traumatized person keeps the "apparently normal" part, which functions well in daily life, separate from the more overtly traumatized "emotional personality" part (Nijenhuis, 1999), or when the daytime persona does not want to know about the persona who has been traumatized at night (Davies and Frawley, 1994). Repressed memories are often reconceptualized as dissociated memories because not only memories subject to amnesia, but also aspects of living experience, have been excluded from consciousness. These pieces are always living in the present tense, without a sense that "this will be over soon." Once they are converted into declarative memory, they can be known to be past.

Trauma impedes the processing of experience into narrative memory. "Prior to integration, traumatic memories are experienced and expressed primarily as sensorimotor experiences, i.e., they remain in somatoform organization" (Van der Hart et al., 2000, p. 44). That is why dissociated traumatic events often begin to make themselves known piecemeal, with often strange and terrifying contents. Even when an event emerges in horrifying clarity in a flashback, it is often expressed in a sensory way that requires interpretation. For example, when Laurie came into treatment, her former therapist raised with me his suspicion that she may have been sexually abused. But she had no memories of any such thing. However, she began to have dream images of a shed in the woods that had an ominous feeling about it. Then she began to remember voracious frightening squirrels that scampered about this shed. And then she began to have dream images of parts of male sexual genitalia. Finally, after she had been in treatment for several years, she began to experience terrifying flashbacks. In one, she saw herself as a little girl, "limp like a rag doll," being abused by her father. Sometimes she would hallucinate her father's presence in the consulting room, right beside me. She knew he wasn't really there, but her felt sense of terror was almost overwhelming. The hallucinations represented the intrusion of a self-state other than that of ordinary consciousness. Only when she became able to talk about these intrusive dissociated sensorimotor experiences did they gradually become a part of narrative memory.

The above example fits with the metaphor of vertical splitting, in that experience was split between two concurrent centers of awareness. Kohut (1971) and Hilgard (1977) both proposed that repression could be contrasted to dissociation on the basis that repression represents a horizontal split: Psychic contents are pushed down, repressed into the unconscious. In contrast, splitting and dissociation are thought to involve vertical splitting, involving side by side, vertical partitions of mental contents. Thus, split-off and dissociated material is not "out of sight" continuously or forever, but will reappear at different times. Because repressed material is pressed down, rather than to the side, repression is considered to be "deeper." According to another visual metaphor, repressed material has been "buried."

Affect cannot be so buried. It can be reframed and placed in different cognitive meanings, but the affect itself cannot be reformulated. Although both repression and dissociation are used to refer to the exclusion of memories, traumata, thoughts, wishes, and fantasies from consciousness, repression posits that the affect remains conscious whereas the thought connected to it is made unconscious (Valillant, 1990). According to Laplanche and Pontalis (1973), "it is only the ideational representatives of the instinct (ideas, images, etc.) that are repressed" (p. 393). In contrast, affect states may be and often are dissociated. I contend with Chefetz (1997) that isolation of affect is a form of dissociation. Dissociated self-states are often organized around affect.

Dissociated Memories Are Context-Dependent. Alice was sitting in my office with her brother telling us about how she escaped from the home of her uncle where she had been held as a sexual and household slave—having been sent by her family in good faith to protect her from a war-torn country—for almost five years, from age 10 to 15. Her uncle, who had impregnated her, had arranged for an illegal, midterm abortion, from which she nearly died. Her father, knowing none of this, made his first transcontinental trip to visit his daughter when she was 15. While her father was visiting, she noticed that her uncle would not let her father and her out of his sight. However, he did find time to talk to her father out of her sight. Suddenly, her normally mild-mannered and upstanding father, whom she had always obeyed and respected, and who had always treated her with respect and decency, was behaving toward her in a way that was completely out of character. He was furious, his face contorted, swearing at her, calling her a "whore," and waving a broom at her as if to beat her. At this moment, he was standing with her uncle and aunt on the stairs of their basement. Fearing for her life, this timid 15-year-old girl quickly slammed the basement door closed and turned the key, locking them all in. Then she ran upstairs to call her oldest brother on the telephone. Having never used the telephone because she had not been permitted to, she punched a number of buttons indiscriminately until she got an operator. Since she knew her brother's name and location, she reached him on the telephone and told him how her father was acting and that she needed him. He arrived within a few hours, in time to save the day, but in the intervening time, while they were locked in the basement, her uncle had let slip to her father that he had "made a woman" of his daughter. Now her father was outraged at the uncle, rather than at her, and he departed with his daughter.

The crucial part of this story concerns the issue of context. In her recounting of the story that day, Alice remembered something that she said she had not remembered before, a crucial memory that allowed the story to hang together. Always before, it had never made sense how she got away from her suddenly rampaging father to make that important phone call. That was a blank space in the story. In this particular session, she remembered for the first time that she had turned the key in the basement door, locking them all in. Would we say that this was a repressed memory or dissociated, unformulated experience? As Alice told the story, and described herself remembering turning the key (30 years later), it certainly sounded like she had suddenly recovered a preformulated traumatic memory. This, on first blush, sounds like repression. It is quite possible, however, that her desperation in the circumstances evoked an agentic part of herself that had long languished from disuse. I suspect that in the desperate act of locking the grown-ups in the basement, she activated a part of her psyche that had belonged to an early childhood life that she has described as being full of fun and mischief, and in which she was very agentic.

In the moment when she was telling this story for the first time to her favorite brother with whom she had been recently reunited, something enabled her to "remember" how she managed to forestall the occurrence of something unthinkably terrifying. It is meaningful *when* Alice recalled this particular piece of this dramatic chapter in her life. She recalled or constructed the memory for the first time while in the presence of her brother, who had always been her playmate and playful adversary when they were children. According to her report, she had been a child who was full of life. Perhaps telling the story to her brother, with whom she had always been able to be agentic, helped her to remember again that playful aggressive "self" that saved her. The interpersonal field influences what kinds of constructions we are able to make (Stern, 1997), which is to say the accessibility of memories varies with their context (Kihlstrom, 1984).

Does it matter in this case whether we call the operative defense causing memory loss repression or dissociation? The most important thing is that Alice recovered the memory, and that she now has a narrative of that particular piece of her life that allows it to hang together, unlike so much of that period, which feels to her more like disconnected visual shards. The only story that she has had as an adult of what her life was like from the ages of 10 to 15 has been largely composed of scenes or groups of scenes, like stills in a movie. More and more, and often with excruciating pain, these scenes are being filled out and linked. Now, at least, that particular piece of her story makes sense, and she knows that she lived through it and made part of it happen. That story has become part of her life. It is hers.

On the level of neurobiology, the issue of knowing and not knowing as a conscious act may seem irrelevant. The brain processes information on so many different intermediary levels and with so many different feedback loops that it is difficult to even locate the source of consciousness (Hopenwasser, 1998). The decision making for most of our conscious life is made outside consciousness (Bargh and Chartrand, 1999). What particular information makes its way into long-term memory is a matter that is most often decided for us, without that decision being a conscious process. One prominent traumatologist and neurobiologist has stated that once we "begin to study the brain using neuroimaging techniques and discover what is happening in the brain, it really does not make much difference whether we call something repression or dissociation" (Van der Kolk, 2003). Yet, what the phenomenon is and how we think of it are two different things. Dissociation theory is the model of mind most useful today for understanding psychological trauma and problematic patterns of human relationships, especially as they emerge in the form of enactments.

Enactments

We need psychodynamic models that bridge the interpersonal and the intrapsychic, in which each can be examined from the standpoint of the other. The concept of enactments does just this. Interpersonal enactments are dependent on intrapersonal dissociation. The reason that the intrapsychic and the interpersonal generally mirror each other is not just that people tend to repeat themselves, creating current relationships in accordance with their early significant relationships (re-enactments); it also reflects the presence of rigidified dissociation and consequent difficulties with conflict. Dissociated self-states often have incompatible goals, but the vigilant tenacity of each to a single point of view clearly decreases the capacity for creativity. There is a limited sense of reflectiveness about different options or alternative points of view. In this way, dissociation makes the experience of intrapsychic conflict less likely. In both interpersonal and interstate enactments, conflict has not been resolved.

Conflict in an Interstate Enactment

In the following vignette from an ongoing treatment with Brenda, a person with dissociative identity disorder, the initial problem was that an interstate (intrapsychic) conflict had not been articulated. When the conflict was articulated through both interpersonal and interstate communication, the immediate problem at hand was solved.

As a child, from the age of five or younger, until she was about 12, Brenda had been raped at night, night after night, by her father, while her mother was asleep in bed, knocked out on pills. Until recently, Brenda has not herself remembered most of these incidents, but other child parts of her have. They remembered horrifying things: bloody underwear, terrible pain, not being able to sit down, wetting her pants, and other strategies to try to deter her father's violations. These child parts have only been able to tell of their pain bit by bit because what they had to say would have been too destabilizing and painful to bear in large doses to Brenda herself, as well as to the adolescent and other adult parts of Brenda. Needless to say, these child parts have not finished telling their stories. And they had definitely not finished telling their stories one morning when Brenda's husband called me to cancel her session that day because she was in the hospital from a frightening drug overdose.

The odd thing about this incident was that Brenda had no memory of taking any pills and had always insisted that she was not suicidal. Later on, when we met, in the process of Brenda's and my discussion of the possible antecedents of this event, I asked to speak to "T," a very precocious child part, who at times takes a managerial role with respect to younger child parts, and who accordingly thinks of herself as "'T' the Lifesaver, who has a hole in the middle." It turned out that "T" had gotten sick and tired of hearing the constant, excruciating crying of a younger child part, Michael. "T" knew that Michael was in terrible pain, but she did not know why he was crying so much more than usual now. She just couldn't bear to hear Michael's crying anymore, and she decided to take matters into her own hands. She decided to give him pills to shut him up and knock him out. There were reasons that the younger part, Michael, was in so much grief. Brenda was about to take a trip back to the town where she grew up, and Michael thought the father, who was in reality dead, was still alive, still there, and capable of raping him again.

It was a one-sided coercion, not an overt conflict between Michael and "T," which yielded this incident. The child-part "T" who had always had to fend for herself and had had to take too much responsibility for her young age made a decision unilaterally, without consulting anyone. It was a decision that she was too young to make. When we were able to talk about Michael's and "T's" feelings and fears, Michael could talk about why he was frightened and why he was crying, and "T" could talk about hating to hear Michael's crying. After these interactions, "T" knew why Michael was crying so much. She also understands now that she is too young to give anyone pills, and she has agreed to call me rather than undertake any unilateral action if she is in severe distress. Brenda has now been able to articulate a conflict, and she knows how to get help to deal with it. (To simply speak of Brenda's parts as she experiences them is not to reify them, for she already experiences them as distinct and separate parts of herself. Furthermore, finding out in detail why different self-states feel as they do helps Brenda to articulate aspects of her conflict: All of these parts are, after all, aspects of her.)

Covert conflict characterized the events in this vignette, in the sense that Brenda did not know about the events concerning "T" and

Michael. Miller (1976) has eloquently described the frequency of covert conflict in relationships between dominant and subordinate.[2] In this power arrangement, the conflict is covert because "subordinates won't tell." Although the subordinates know a great deal about the dominants, they know less about their own feelings because their own needs and affects are irrelevant to their survival and welfare. When subordinates attempt to articulate and negotiate the conflict, the dominants often mistake covert conflict for absence of conflict and accuse subordinates of creating conflict. Subordinates may take different routes in response to covert conflict. These include open conflict or acceptance of the status quo. In the latter situation, which is far more frequent, power is exercised indirectly and covertly. In relationships between dominant and subordinate that are abusive, in which the subordinate is a child, the covert conflict may go underground, becoming part of the child's psychic structure, with the result that the family and social structure becomes mirrored in a collusive psychic structure. "T" saw no recourse but to take control without communication or negotiation with other parts, and in a way that was hidden to Brenda. Similarly, Brenda, as a child, had had little power to negotiate with her father about his abuse of her. In this way, intersubjective failure in primary interpersonal relationships is at the root of the intrapersonal dissociation.

The larger point here is the correspondence between the covert interpersonal conflicts and the intrapsychic, or what I call interstate, ones. In both cases the covert conflict had initially not been articulated, and the separate but colluding parts had not been differentiated.

Parts and Wholes

Koestler (1967) devised a term he called a *holon* to refer to a part that is also a whole. It is derived from the Greek *holos,* meaning "whole," and the suffix, *on,* signifying a part. This term is apt in describing individuals who are members of larger units, such as families, as well as parts of individuals that, in aggregate, constitute the "self." Miller described covert conflict in social systems that involve individuals. But covert conflict is just as powerfully a characteristic of systems that constitute an individual. For example, neither "T" nor Michael was able to articulate their dilemma to Brenda.

For the covert conflict to become overt, parts of the internal organization of the system needs to be in a meaningful relationship to, and influencible by, someone outside the system. Without meaningful interaction from the outside, there is a closed system of various collusions and hostile interactions among parts. These relationships among the parts, when they are dissociated, can only be seen from a point outside the system. Even then, for the pattern to be intelligible, the subjectivity of each of the constituent parts must be known. Here Chefetz's (Chefetz and Bromberg, 2004) concept of "isolated subjectivity" is invaluable: "What is not so obvious is that when we use a word like subjectivity we are thinking a level of abstraction that involves the confluence of multiple self-states . . . [in which] affect . . . is isolated, the self-state(s) has(ve) a quality of not being known. This is isolated subjectivity" (p. 431).

The organizational form of constituent "parts," taken as a whole, may not be intelligible to the outside observer. For instance, Brenda's seeming suicide attempt made no sense, because she admitted to no suicidal ideation. For the action of Brenda, a human "holon" in Koestler's sense, to be intelligible, I needed to contact "T" and Michael, among others. However, when the parts were consulted, the emergent understanding of suicidality, homicidality, silencing another's unbearable crying, and enacting the solution that she had observed in her mother was quite different. The way this emergent understanding was achieved was by my getting to know the parts and helping them to know each other. This link to the outside is what Bromberg refers to as a "relational bridge." However, the relational bridge is not in itself sufficient to heal the dissociation. What is needed to bridge the dissociation of the parts is an internalization of the relationship of the parts with the outside knower, often the therapist. For the dissociation in Brenda to begin to be healed, I had to know "T" and Michael, and each of their own fears and desires. Then Brenda had to learn to know what I knew. In Murray Bowen's family therapy terms, one could say that in the process of my engaging in relationship with "T" and Michael, they became more differentiated. Alternatively, one may say that the parts "T" and Michael became more formulated to Brenda and to each other–which means that they became less dissociated.

I am not suggesting an absolute isomorphism between dissociative identity disorder and less severe personal problems that are dissociation based. In DID, the internal dissociative barriers between parts are often much stronger, and the parts are more narcissistically invested in their own "pseudodelusional" (Kluft, 1984) sense of separateness. There is more of a sense of separate autobiographical centers, which Braude (1995) calls "apperceptive centers." Thus, working at linking the parts to the whole often takes longer and is a highly intense emotional endeavor. I believe, however, that the basic model is the same.

Interpersonal Enactments

I would now like to shift the frame of reference to interpersonal enactments. When we think of interpersonal enactments, our focal attention is on the person as a whole. However, the enactment itself results from actions and procedures of particular parts. The difference between interpersonal and interstate enactments is that in the former the conflict is located between individuals (Stern, 1997), whereas in the latter, the locus of the conflict is between self-states. In the former case, there is an experience of conflict (between the two people); in the latter case, the experience of the person is most likely one of puzzlement. In an interpersonal enactment there is no initial relational bridge because there is not enough communication between the activated dissociated self-state(s) of one person and the integrative presence of the other, a mutual nonbridging. One of the individuals must be willing to serve as a relational bridge to the other's dissociated self-states. When this happens, the new interaction can be internalized (by one or both), which allows the self-states to be differentiated (by one or both), which enables the issue to be formulated (by one or both).

Stern (2004) observes that experience that is unformulated because it has never been attended to must, of necessity, be enacted, and he views dissociated self-states as enactments. Noting that the enactment is coconstructed and dissociatively engaged in by both parties, Stern (2004) emphasizes that each of the parties in an enactment endorses one pole of the conflict. As a result, the two parties are at loggerheads until (at least) one of the parties can formulate some version of the big picture and understand and accept what the other is communicating from this new perspective. The conflict here is between two persons. In interpersonal enactment, neither party experiences this particular conflict intrapsychically. Stern differentiates such enactment from repression and splitting, which assume preformulated contents. In repression, the contents were once known and then forgotten. In splitting, according to traditional theory, the intrapsychic conflict has been disavowed.

Proceeding from Stern's premise and the one I have outlined here, however, the conflict between the separate self-states in the constellation we generally identify as splitting cannot be disavowed, because it was never known. The dissociated parts must be in a meaningful relationship with someone on the outside first before the conflict between them can be adequately articulated and made overt. Each of the split states, usually dual and affectively opposite, appears from the perspective of an outside observer or the theorist to be preformulated. As clinicians, we often think we know what is being excluded from consciousness: In splitting, it is the other half of the split experience, either the love or the aggression (Kernberg, 1975).

Even if the theorist, who postulates that one part is libidinal and the other aggressive, is right, this "knowledge" is not healing in itself. Healing requires the internalization of each part's relationship with the therapist. Splitting, of course, can be highly influential in interpersonal enactments, but strictly speaking, it is an interstate enactment, a topic that I will return to shortly.

Enactments: Internalizations of Multiple Relationships in Different Contexts

Enactments derive from relational processes of cognition, affect, and behavior that are learned implicitly as we grow up. Enactments can be dissociated, but they do not have to be. They are unconscious, but not necessarily dynamically unconscious (Lyons-Ruth, 2001b). They signify that relational processes involving aspects of relationships between the self and important others have been internalized (Lyons-Ruth, 2001b; Ryle, 2002). Rather than a static object, what is internalized and enacted is a relational process that embodies all sorts of meanings, intentions, and predictions. Because we are all continually engaged in personal and interpersonal dialogue that is based on internalization of earlier dialogues with real others, a new, post-Cartesian aphorism, "We interact, therefore I become" (Ryle and Kerr, 2002), replaces the Cartesian mind–body dualism of "I think, therefore I am" (*Cogito ergo sum,* as Descartes wrote in 1637).

We have seen that Anthony Ryle (1994, 1997a, b, 2002) conceptualizes these processes as reciprocal role procedures (RRPs), which are relational units involving generalized procedural memories. These reciprocal role procedures, which are acquired and linked in sequences in the course of development, not only incorporate but seek and predict responses from the other. For Ryle, a self state is a construct describing a partially dissociated reciprocal role relationship of which either pole may be subjectively identified with, and experienced as, a state. An advantage of thinking of self-states in this way is that some universal reciprocal patterns, for example, those concerning power, dependency, and attachment, in which the interpersonal and intrapsychic patterns reflect each other, are brought into focus. Ryle's emphasis on the dyadic processes of self-states is highly compatible with understandings of enactment in the psychoanalytic literature.

Enactments of reciprocal role procedures or "ways of being with another" (Lyons-Ruth, 1999) constitute much of our interpersonal and intrapsychic lives. The multitude of these implicit relational processes, internalized from different interpersonal contexts, is the basis of the multiple self (Slavin and Kreigman, 1992). The multiple self beneficially enables us to layer and contextualize aspects of our experience and engage in inner dialogue. The problem is when certain patterns of self-states become rigidly and chronically dissociated. The problem is not the separation of context itself, which is broadly necessary to separate foreground from background. The problem is when we cannot willfully move from one foreground–background configuration to another and hold them together in consciousness. For instance, even in "highway hypnosis," we need to be able to snap to attention, for safety's sake. Dissociated processes and self-states can span the gamut from transference–countertransference and other interpersonal enactments to automatisms and interstate enactments in the form of flashbacks and other intrusive dissociative phenomena.

Too much pathological dissociation can result in switches and intrusions. *Switch* is a term used in the dissociative disorder literature to refer to a change from one dissociated part of the self, or alter, to another; but the same thing happens on a smaller scale and less dramatically whenever there is a shift from one "way of being with another" to another "way of being with another," without much internal commentary, or much capability for internal commentary, on the shift. Encouraging and enlarging this commentary is the heart of the work with enactments, and the mutative core of treatment is often working with enactments.

Sullivan's "Not-Me"

Even though Sullivan conceptualized the self-system as a whole, his overall vision lends itself to the conception of a multiple self. The same is true of "not-me." We can usefully think of "not-me" as an unbound disaggregate of many dissociated self-states. "Not-me" contains constellations of experience that are so terrifying, so "awe-ful," that they could not be symbolized or thought about. According to Sullivan (1953), not-me is "made up of poorly grasped aspects of living which will presently be regarded as 'dreadful,' and which still later will be differentiated into incidents which are attended by awe, horror, loathing, or dread" (p. 163).

The question is, "How can the terrifying and 'dreadful' contents of 'not-me' become thinkable and symbolized?" Inevitably, this constellation of meaning must be enacted. These not-me states of mind can only be communicated by enactment because "they must first become 'thinkable' while becoming linguistically communicable through enactment in the analytic relationship" (Bromberg, 1998, p. 252).

When dissociated self-states have different affects and goals, the bridging of the conflict can be facilitated by the therapist's ability to hold different self-states in mind at the same time, functioning as a relational bridge (Bromberg, 1998). This increases the capacity for what Bromberg (1998) calls "health": the "ability to stand in the spaces between realities without losing any of them" (p. 186).

Bromberg (1998) describes how a core unresolved piece of unsymbolized, dreadful material is the affect of shame, an affect that rightfully belongs to both parties. Shame can motivate the analyst to maintain affective distance from the shame-filled parts of the patient's experience. The result is that many very painful and extremely challenging enactments ensue, enactments that would not be so difficult if shame did not impede the patient's and the analyst's vision. As a result, in enactments, the analyst's parts are resonating with, but not communicating with, the patient's.

"Interstate Enactments" and "Isolated Subjectivities"

Let us now expand the domain of the term *enactments* to include the interstate as well as the interpersonal. In the case presented, "T" could not stand to be exposed to Michael's crying, Michael was overwhelmed with pain, and Brenda often was just too exhausted to want to know about either of them. If dissociation is unformulated experience, how do we understand dissociative identity disorder, in which large aspects of experience or self-states are dissociated from each other, but appear to be consistent within themselves and to be "formulated experience" from that perspective? My answer is that this apparent formulation is only true from the perspective of an outside observer; these dissociated self-states ("not-me") are unknown by "me." They are unformulated by at least some other self-states, quite often including the host. Certain self-states or alters are more coconscious, aware of, and in communication with others; in that case they are relatively more formulated, each to the other, than those that are amnestic of the others' activities. In other words, the more dissociated such self-states are, the more unformulated they are to each other. The same argument goes for the concept of splitting.

Flashbacks can be understood as interstate enactments. Often the contents split off or dissociated during trauma are sensory or motor memories. The trauma prevented these experiences from ever becoming processed by the parts of the brain that encode them into conscious narrative experience. Thus, the reason that dissociated experience is repeated over and over again in flashbacks or in behavioral repetitions with new people is that it was never consciously registered, metabolized, and formulated. Much dissociated experience has this character—that the terrifying events could not be registered in consciousness either for psychological or for neurobiological reasons: the mind–brain is overwhelmed, and the information simply never gets to consciousness in whole form. Traumatized people suffer from many different forms of flashbacks: visual, auditory, somatic, and so on.[3] These fragments of living, but unsynthesized, experience are enacted vis-à-vis other parts of the self.

Splitting

Splitting is also a particular kind of interstate enactment. That is, the contents of the split self also involve the idea of opposite halves of experience, usually dominated by opposite affects, often, as in Fairbairnian splitting, in accordance with attachment dilemmas. Splitting often involves an alternation of these parts of the self. As Celani (2001) says, referring to Fairbairn's subegos, the "intense and undifferentiated emotionality of the subegos—one oversaturated with a desperate need for love, the other with enormous fear and anger—results in an adult with two subpersonalities that are fanatic, single-dimensional, and lack knowledge of each other" (pp. 401–402).

In this unremitting conflict lies one important difference between the more general concept of posttraumatically split-off dissociated parts and that of splitting. In splitting, as a process, there is what might be called a "splitting standoff": The parts are by definition at loggerheads—with opposing, contradictory views of reality. Although neither gives way to the other, they desperately need each other, for each represents the rescue from and antidote to what the other represents. In chapter 7, I suggested that splitting can be understood as alternating dissociated victim/masochistic, abuser/rageful self-states which develop on the axis of relational trauma. Their oscillation appears to be a continual reenactment of the traumatic violation of the relational boundary and may be heavily influenced by what we call "identification with the aggressor." Too much attachment need can sometimes be dangerous, anxiety arousing, and shameful. Vigilance, anger, or both are the antidote to this and can be self-protective. This approach to the world, however, does not accommodate attachment need. The attached, needy state is an antidote to the angry one, because it preserves, as Kernberg (1975) has noted, the sense of personal goodness and prevents this sense of self from becoming overwhelmed by rage and hatred. In splitting, there is a balance of power, but the constituents do not have a way of achieving a harmonious interaction.

In the "splitting standoff," what might appear from the outside to be a formulation of the other part's experience is really only a rebuttal, as can occur in interpersonal enactments as well. Thus, although it can be highly influential in interpersonal enactments, splitting is a form of interstate enactment. In the view of splitting proposed here, the person is of two minds, each one unformulated to the other. *We,* the clinicians, often think we know what is dissociated based on inference from our own observations and from our theories. The view that splitting represents preformulated experience then runs into one of the same problems that repression sometimes does, in that clinicians may find or feel themselves in the position of knowing something that the patient does not.

Conversion Disorder Versus Somatoform Dissociation

Conversion Disorder

Freud's early idea (1894) was that the incompatible idea is "rendered innocuous by its *sum of excitation being transformed into something somatic.* For this I would like to propose the name of *conversion*" (p. 49). Thus, conversion refers to the conversion of emotional pain into somatic innervation.

The conventional understanding of conversion hysteria is that the affected body part expresses both a wish and a punishment for the wish. The function of a body part is dedicated and "sacrificed to the expression of a hidden impulse" (Cameron and Rychlak, 1985, p. 233). An unconscious conflict is linked with, and transformed into, a bodily symptom; this symbolic expression then reduces the anxiety about its cause, functioning as self-punishment. In a textbook explicating psychopathology from a Freudian perspective, Cameron and Rychlak (1985) define somatoform dissociation in terms of the dynamics of conversion. Describing how the symptom can combine the body part, the wish, and the defense against it all in a single symbol, they suggest that a paralyzed arm might express the fact that

> it is an arm that was killed, an arm that can no longer kill and the self-punishment (superego wish) or paralysis for having killed. It is guilty, innocent, and punished at the same time. If, in addition, the paralyzed arm also expressed childhood sin, denial, and penance, as usually it does, then the paralysis is further reinforced by forgotten fantasies, which like forgotten and repressed happenings are influential without becoming conscious.... To begin using such an arm again would also be to rekindle old fires of early superego punishment [p. 233].

Somatoform Dissociation

A less circuitous way of understanding many somatoform disorders is in terms of trauma-related somatoform dissociation. That is, to understand how "hysterics suffer mainly from reminiscences" (Breuer and Freud, 1893–1895, p. 7) is to view somatoform dissociation as psychophysiological "memory" (Hopenwasser, 1998), in which experience has been split off into isolated somatosensory aspects without integration into an explanatory narrative.

In a discussion of Freud's famous Schreber case, Erdelyi (1990), cites Schatzman's (1973) conclusion that Schreber also suffered from "reminiscences." Schatzman described the *Kopfhalter,* a helmet and chin band contraption that Schreber's physician father invented to force the child to keep his head erect by pulling the child's hair if his posture slackened. While he was in the insane asylum, Schreber wrote that he suffered terrible headaches that were like a "sudden pulling inside my head . . . and may be compared with the tearing off of the bony substance of my skull—at least that is how it feels" (Schreber, 1903, p. 164, in Schatzman, 1973, pp. 49–50). For Schreber's "body embodies his past. He retains memories of what his father did to him as a child; although part of his mind knows they are memories" (Schatzman, 1973, pp. 49–50, cited in Erdelyi, 1990, p. 18). In commentary, Erdelyi (1990) offers his own more parsimonious view of conversion: "It may be incorrect that the symptoms are 'conversions' of the once-conscious memory complex; rather, the symptoms may be the procedural memory component of the original memory complex that, in contrast to the declarative memory component, repression failed to dislodge from active memory" (p. 18).

Traumatologists have noted that extremely high levels of emotional arousal cause a deficiency in the ability to create semantic constructs for body experience because the terrifying information is inadequately evaluated in the hippocampus and the cortex, where meaning is created (Van der Kolk, 1996b). Indeed, traumatic experience is processed differently in the brain than is nontraumatic experience. A study using PET (positron emission tomography) indicated less activation of Broca's area (speech) during flashbacks (Rauch et al., 1996, cited in Hopenwasser, 1998).[4]

Common symptoms of hysterical shell shock among soldiers in World War I were paralysis, mutism, anesthesia of a limb, and other somatosensory functional losses. Amnesia for the event almost always accompanied these symptoms. Somatoform symptoms have been significantly correlated with peritraumatic dissociation (Nijenhuis, 2000; Nijenhuis, Van Engen, Kusters, and Van der Hart, 2001). Nijenhuis et al. (2001) found that somatoform dissociation was best predicted by physical abuse and threat to life by another person. And certain medical conditions, such as chronic urogenital pain, were predicted by physical and sexual abuse (Nijenhuis, 1999).

Nijenhuis (1999) has observed that certain somatoform manifestations may be explained by animal defense reactions. For instance, freezing and stilling arise in response to serious threat, and threat to life can result in analgesia and numbness. Van der Hart et al. (2000) provide evidence from World War I records indicating that many somatoform conditions of soldiers involving paralysis, contractures, and tics seem to represent a freezing response at the moment of trauma.

Survivors of sexual abuse often describe constant vaginal and rectal pain; survivors of physical abuse often describe back pain, again corresponding to the location of previous injuries, even though there is no current medical explanation for such continual experiences. Thus, in many cases, the simplest explanation of somatoform dissociation would be that the trauma prevented the experience from being processed in a way that it could become narrative memory. Instead, the "memory" remained an aspect of sensorimotor memory. This is not to say that body parts and organs cannot also symbolize conflicts, that secondary gains are not important motivational factors, or that somatic means of expressing distress are not purposeful or communicative in themselves (Laria and Lewis-Fernandez, 2001).

Abreaction and Catharsis Versus Integration

The idea behind abreaction and catharsis is that emotional discharge of affects connected with traumatic memories is healing. The terms *abreaction* and *catharsis* have been used interchangeably, with the only difference being that abreaction refers to mental reliving, whereas catharsis refers to bodily physical expression (Cameron and Rychlak, 1985). Laplanche and Pontalis (1973), define abreaction as

> emotional discharge whereby the subject liberates himself from the affect attached to the memory of a traumatic event in such a way that this affect is not able to become (or to remain) pathogenic. Abreaction may be provoked in the course of psychotherapy, especially under hypnosis, and produce a cathartic effect. It may also come about spontaneously, either a short or a long interval after the original trauma [p. 1].

In some of the PTSD literature and some of the New Age therapy literature there has been much emphasis on the expected healing properties of planned abreactions. Within the last decade or so, however, observations have accumulated that planned abreactions carry a high risk for traumatization. These observations complement Van der Hart and Brown's (1992) detail of a fascinating history of the concept of abreaction. They cite the work of MacMillan (1991) and Hirshmuller (1978), the latter, Breuer's biographer, in support of the view that the "talking cure" did not require her to abreact: "Nowhere in his initial descriptive notes did Breuer stress emotional expression. Rather it seems that this dimension was later added by Breuer and Freud" (1893–1895). According to these authors, Breuer emphasized verbal, more than emotional, expression of feelings, and Freud added emotional expression in 1895 in *Studies on Hysteria*. Nonetheless (and here it is relevant that Anna O had a severe dissociative disorder),[5,6] most of the position outlined in the "Preliminary Communication" is still within the dissociation framework. The problem, according to Van der Hart and Brown, arose with the introduction of the constancy principle, according to which

> the nervous system endeavors to keep constant something in its functional condition that may be described as the "sum of excitation." It seeks to establish this necessary precondition of health by dealing with every sensible increase of excitation along associative lines or by discharging it by an appropriate motor reaction. Starting from this theorem, with its far-reaching implications, we find that the psychical experiences forming the content of hysterical attacks have a common characteristic. They are all of them impressions that have failed to find an adequate discharge [Freud, letter to Breuer, 1892, p. 32, quoted in Van der Hart and Brown, 1992, p. 130].

The cathartic treatment technique espoused in the "Preliminary Communication" followed from this "quasineurological model" based on the constancy principle. According to Van der Hart and Brown (1992), the "key problem here is to relate the latter abreaction-catharsis model based on the discharge of excitation and the principle of constancy with the association-reintegration therapeutic model based on the concept of dissociation" (p. 131).

Almost a century of research has, by and large, indicated two things: (1) the potential for retraumatization posed by exclusively abreactive techniques and (2) the lack of consistent evidence that it actually helps heal traumatization in the long run (Horowitz 1986; Van der Hart and Brown, 1992). In an evaluation of abreactive techniques used in World War II, Horowitz (1986) wrote,

> Abreaction led to more abreaction, to seemingly endless accounts. . . . abreaction may relieve anxiety, but this effect can be non-specific and transient. To obtain durable improvement, it seems necessary to understand the individual patient, the meaning of the experience . . . and to revise discrepancies in self-object representations and other organizing constructs [p. 119].

As opposed to abreaction, Van der Hart and Brown (1992) emphasize the importance of integration in the healing of trauma. This is consistent with Van der Hart's position that the presence of PTSD implies dissociation. Integration, or resynthesis, which does not require affective arousal or motor discharge, is healing of dissociation. Van der Hart and Brown are emphatic that, "since Janet, it has been repeatedly demonstrated that in most cases of posttraumatic stress, particularly chronic disorders, treating the traumatic memories alone (whether by abreaction or by any other approach) is insufficient" (p. 136).

The model of phase-oriented treatment, in which careful stabilization and ego building precede any work with traumatic memories, was initially proposed by Janet and has become increasingly accepted as an appropriate approach to the treatment of posttraumatic stress and dissociative disorders. Such a phase-oriented treatment approach is specified in the 2005 ISSD (International Society for the Study of Dissociation) guidelines for the treatment of dissociative disorders.

Integration and "Interstate Intersubjectivity"

Generally, integration, at least in the broadest sense, is the goal of treatment: It is often considered synonymous with health. The term *integration,* however, can cover much territory; there are potentially many different forms of integrations. Thus, integration might signify a collusive organizational structure of the self in which some affects are markedly subdued in the service of social adaptation and security. This is not usually what we mean by integration, but it does represent how parts can be integrated in one organic whole. I would like to suggest an appreciation of interstate intersubjectivity, according to which the affects of different parts of the person are important in their own right, and *belong,* both to themselves and to the person. Ideally, integration will allow all of the different "voices" of different self-states to retain their own tenor, even though they may be integrated and often blended. In other words, integration need not cover over multiplicity, or even the capacity for dissociation. Rather than a monolithic integration, a better ideal is harmonious interaction among the multiple self-states. In agreement with Bromberg (1993), I see in health the "ability to stand in the spaces between realities without losing any of them" (p. 186).

10

NARCISSISM
A Relational Aspect of Dissociation

The mythological Narcissus spurned the overtures of all who wanted to be close to him. Incapable of needing others, Narcissus's life became a closed intrapersonal system, an internal hall of mirrors. And he drowned in his own reflection. The legend does not tell us if Narcissus suffered disorganized attachment or trauma, but if he lived today those would be likely antecedents for his condition. Although the Greeks thought the cause of Narcissus's problem was punishment from the gods, we might see it today as the result of dissociative processes.

In this chapter we argue that pathological narcissism,[1] relationally understood, is an inevitable result of trauma-generated dissociation. The term *narcissism* is used to refer to pathological preoccupation with the self, survival, and self-esteem; lack of recognition of the other's separateness (or lack of intersubjectivity); isolation, being closed off from external influence (a closed system); unilaterality, false-self processes; excessive use of other people (or other parts of the self) as narcissistic objects or selfobjects; a sense of omnipotence; and excessive grandiosity. All of these aspects of narcissism are linked with dissociation. In point of fact, dissociation and pathological narcissism are inextricably intertwined, each reflecting aspects of the other, each implying the other. As one lessens, so does the other.

Fairbairn, who emphasized dissociative processes in the etiology of the schizoid dilemma, observed that schizoid individuals have a sense of inner superiority (1952) and that both grandiosity and idealization increase as a function of the severity and chronicity of the dissociative processes. In many ways, Fairbairn's description of schizoid patients is remarkably similar to Kohut's description of narcissistic patients (Grotstein and Rinsley, 2000; Robbins, 2000; Sutherland, 2000).

When a child must dissociate parts of the self in order to maintain attachment to a neglectful, frightening, or abusive caretaker, the self becomes more and more a self-contained system in which intense attachment to internal objects contributes to narcissistic self-sufficiency, omnipotence, and grandiosity. In this sense of narcissism, the self is all there is. Self-care is provided by parts of the self, not by the outside interpersonal world. This means that the behavior and intentions of others will be misinterpreted for the worst, overidealized, or both; that it will be hard to "get through" to or to make a real impact on such a person; and, conversely, that the person will often be unaware of the profound effect she can have on others. In this way, pathological narcissism is a relational aspect of dissociation.

By definition, a closed system precludes interpersonal intersubjectivity, the mutual recognition of separate, self-reflective, and agentic selves. Lack of awareness of one's impact on others characterizes the closed system. For instance, Terry, a patient with DID who was prone to fugues and who had recently been actively suicidal, failed to keep scheduled phone contacts while traveling on business. It did not occur to her that her therapist might be extremely concerned about what had happened to her. Such occurrences are understandable in terms of the early life history of many traumatized patients, a history in which their responses, feelings, and wishes may not have been important to their attachment figures. However, one of the tasks of therapy is to help such patients to understand how their behavior really does impact on others in the present. Therapeutic transformation involves making an attachment that breaks into the closed system, healing both chronic dissociation and narcissism.

The Self-Care System

As we have seen, the attachment system can be understood as a psychological system for combating stress and modulating stressful arousal (Lyons-Ruth, 2001a). It fails to work adequately in traumatic attachments, in which the attachment figure fails to provide a protective shield against the dangers of the environment or is herself dangerous. Since the attachment system functions as a buffer against extreme fearful arousal, the effects of such failure are profound, potentially attacking the linkage of states and creating dissociated self-states.

Kalsched (1996) posits the "self-care system" as a mechanism for defending the self against traumatic attachments and supplementing the scarce supplies available in the interpersonal environment. Substantial reliance on the self-care system is a consequence of a failure of the attachment system (Richard Chefetz, personal communication). The threat of "unthinkable" agonies and the terror of going mad

(Winnicott, 1963; Bromberg, 1998) activates the self-care system, which operates by using dissociative defenses, such as splitting, psychic numbing, trance states, self-hypnosis, and projective identification. The self-care system splits off the parts of the self that experience these unbearable traumas. It not only restores missing aspects of the needed attachment relationships as aspects of the self, but also uses such quasidelusional methods as perceptually "blanking out" threatening figures. The self-care system thus provides two important things: an imaginative use of omnipotence to purvey hope and a self-structure that provides an automatic, effective, and often lifesaving coping strategy in a frightening or abusive interpersonal environment. But it also results in the narcissism of a closed system.

The self-care system generates a sense of psychic stability by creating illusory sources of protection and comfort. Under conditions of abuse, neglect, or gross insensitivity, an inordinate degree of self-sufficiency is required of the young child. Because this is generally more than the child can genuinely muster, she may invent an omnipotent protector, helper, or inner caretaker (Beahrs, 1982; Bliss, 1986). For example, Janice, a person with DID who had been brutally sexually abused, isolated, and periodically subjected to severe neglect and terror as a young child, described how she would make friends and protectors of the rocks and bushes, convincing herself that they would care for her. This illusion of self-parenting is an important part of the self-care system.

As I see it, the grandiose self, a construct used differently by Kohut (1971) and Kernberg (1975), is a special instance of the self-care system. Bromberg (1983) defines it as a "core patterning of self–other representation designed to protect the illusion of self-sufficiency at all cost" (p. 362). A person with narcissistic personality disorder fiercely depends on this structure for a sense of identity. In my view, the grandiose self is an aspect of the self-care system as applied to interpersonal relationships. It has the function of providing the mirroring, admiration, and sense of appreciation that a narcissistic person craves but cannot rely on others to provide. In this way, it may supplement an inadequate primary attachment relationship.

The self-care system is self-protective and compensatory rather than relational. As such, it cannot gain understanding from experience (Kalsched, 1996). Because it functions protectively to prevent retraumatization, the self-care system strenuously resists transformation. The illusions of the self-care system are only temporarily helpful and must be continuously replenished. Without a benign-enough connection to the interpersonal world, hope cannot last. The child needs a real caretaker who can respond to his needs for comfort and protection. Thus, the self-care system is necessarily narcissistic and dissociative.

The construct of the self-care system can be helpful in understanding the function of internal persecutors. It is often noted in the dissociation literature that protector parts frequently end up as persecutors. The problem is that the self-care system can only seek care from the self. One reason that the protector becomes a persecutor is that there has been more persecution than protection from the outside; an imitation cannot be better than what it imitates. The protector becomes the persecutor in part because there never was enough real protection—only that in fantasy.

Hostile, Dominating, Grandiose Self-States and Helpless, Dependent Ones

Overreliance on the self-care system is a consequence of the failure of the attachment system. When the child faces the dilemma of both fearing and seeking safety from the caretaker, her attachment strategies are likely to become disorganized. Lyons-Ruth has discussed the developmental trajectory of D-attached infants. As they grew toward school age, these formerly disorganized infants reorganized their attachment behaviors such that they began to control their mothers and other people in particular ways. These controlling behaviors were grouped into a hostile, punitive style and an oversolicitous, helpless, caregiving style. In either pattern, the child's attachment system fails to regulate fear arousal, and dominance and submission are not balanced. As a consequence, their internal working models of attachment tend to involve traumatic affects, promoting the dissociation of the hostile and the helpless strategies for maintaining attachment.

How does this play out in personality structure and psychodynamics with respect to narcissistic and dissociative problems? The child had to accommodate to the omnipotent domination, grandiosity, silencing, exploitation, terrorizing, and objectification of attachment figures, because these were the caretakers on whom the child depended. The relationship dynamics are reenacted intrapsychically by parts of the self that seek to dominate, silence, and terrorize each other, as well as interpersonally (Schwartz, 2000). Yet, this process requires at least two states in interaction. Hostile and helpless internal working models, each holding affects dissociated from the other, are bound together in a dominant–submissive relationship.

Writing of narcissism from a Kleinian perspective rather than in the language of the dissociation literature, Rosenfeld (1971) articulates this interaction between dissociated hostile and dependent self-states:

> It appears that these patients have dealt with the struggle between their destructive and libidinal impulses by trying to get rid of their loving, dependent self and identifying themselves almost entirely with the destructive, narcissistic part of the self which provides them with a sense of superiority and self-admiration [p. 174].

Recognition of a meaningful interpersonal relationship would threaten the hegemony of the omnipotent part. Thus, the destructive aggression of this part is directed against recognition of such a relationship and against any part of the self that would desire as much. The success of treatment depends on gaining access to the part that can recognize dependency. Yet, this part seems to be enthralled by the hostile, omnipotent part, "as if one were dealing with a powerful gang dominated by a leader" (p. 174). When the patient begins to make progress, there is often a negative therapeutic reaction, frequently personified by dream figures such as Mafia members or delinquent adolescents. In some of these patients, the omnipotent destructive part is linked to a split-off, psychotic, delusional structure. This delusional part may seduce the more sane part, which recognizes emotional dependency, to join it in turning away from the need for connection to others. The ability of the therapist to rescue the dependent, sane part depends on the patient's gradually becoming conscious of the omnipotent destructive part. This part "can only remain all-powerful in isolation. . . . The patient becomes gradually aware that he is dominated by an omnipotent infantile part which . . . prevents him from growing up, by keeping him away from objects who could help him to achieve growth and development" (pp. 175–176). We may add to Rosenfeld's description the more current perspective that focuses on the persecutor state's self-care role to protect the patient from the abusive parent.

For both dissociative patients and narcissistic ones, the attachment of the dependent part to the grandiose, omnipotent part of the self has replaced the capability for trust of another person to a significant degree. In both cases, the omnipotent part, like the original perpetrator, is often out of control, as it attempts to control. Hostile self-states function as trauma membranes (Putnam, 1989), designed to protect the individual from memories of the trauma, and defending against the experience of helplessness. Schwartz's (2000) conceptualization of hostile self-states in DID as "personified narcissistic and sociopathic defenses" that defend against dependency, vulnerability, and guilt (p. 265) applies just as well to pathologial narcissism. However, an important distinction is that although many narcissistic patients may identify themselves almost entirely with the destructive, grandiose, narcissistic part, dissociative patients more often deal with the same dilemmas by dissociative shifts between attachment and self-protection, both of which are needed for survival (Blizard, 2001). Whereas certain narcissistic persons direct their contempt on other persons, dissociative patients just as often direct contempt on other parts of the self.

In chronic, complex PTSD including BPD and DID, rage, which cannot be contained or expressed by a helpless self-state, is often located in and/or "projected into" a persecutor state that in turn unleashes furious punishment onto the helpless state, even though its overall purpose seems to be to protect the latter. The fact that the helpless state often does not want to know about traumatic childhood experiences renders it unappreciative of the intended-to-be-helpful activity of the protector–persecutor state and perpetuates the dissociation as well as the grandiosity of the persecutor state. By allying with the omnipotence of the persecutor, the helpless state does not have to feel the terror and may be shielded from memories. The narcissistic grandiosity of a protector–persecutor part in a highly dissociative person is comparable to the grandiosity of a highly narcissistic person without DID. For example, Sally is a patient with DID who has a grandiose, dominating part, called Devil. This part persecutes the helpless, host, self-state with brutal self-injury, and will at times erupt into demonic-sounding laughter, sounding much like the original perpetrator. Devil boasts to Sally about how powerful he is. Yet, when the therapist tries to engage him and to encourage him to wield his power by defending Sally against domineering people, he disappears. He does not come forward to defend. To the contrary, the only real interpersonal defense comes from a precocious nine-year-old part within the intrapsychic system. Devil exerts tremendous power toward counterparts that are weak and helpless; it is this relational configuration that affords Devil his feeling of power. But Devil is only powerful internally. Because this self-state apparently originated from a childhood identification with the original perpetrator, this part only has the power of a child.

Now let's compare Devil with Jim, a highly narcissistic patient. Jim tends to be domineering, aggressive, humiliating to others, and intensely grandiose. His grandiosity has at times seriously compromised reality-testing. For instance, he asked to be considered for the CEO position of his company, despite being a lower level administrator. However, his bombast, like that of Devil, the malevolent self-state of Sally, was only hot air. One day, when his wife threatened to leave him, and he knew she meant it for real, this domineering man suddenly became a whimpering, terrified little boy. He repeatedly begged her not to leave him and promised to be good. Unlike Sally, he was not amnestic for the switch from a dominating to a helpless self-state. He reported that his wife had been totally surprised by the sudden emergence of this frightened, childlike self-state.

Jim's dominant, grandiose self-state, which was usually evident, appears also to have been based on an identification with an abusive, aggressive father. From infancy, Jim was chronically treated like a narcissistic object, even though his family appeared to be well-functioning. As a result of chronic, gross parental insensitivity, Jim may, as an infant, have been plunged into nameless terror, leading to irresolvable attachment dilemmas and disorganized attachment, which eventually evolved into a personality organization structured by alternating hostile and helpless states. Perhaps because there was apparently only mild, overt trauma, these alternating states were only partially dissociated. In contrast, Sally, who had experienced much more severe and continuous abuse, developed alternating hostile and helpless states with full dissociation. In both cases, the bombast worked to intimidate other parties, albeit in the intrapsychic arena with Sally and in the interpersonal arena with Jim. In both cases, the power of the aggressive part derives from the relational dynamics. However, the feeling of omnipotence is an illusion because it is based on a denial of the relational configuration in which the power of the dominant part is dependent on the weakness of other parts.

Narcissistic, Unilateral, Aggressive Parts

In accordance with the self-care system, various models of psychic structure (e.g., Freud's harsh superego and Fairbairn's antlibidinal ego) converge on the notion that a part of the self, often an internal persecutor, has become autonomous in monitoring behavior and thought. A part of the self has the "job" of cordoning off the experience and/or expression of affect and knowledge that could be overwhelming if known and dangerous if expressed. This part, often called a protector–persecutor (Kalsched, 1996; Howell, 1997a), usually starts out as a protector, but ends up as a persecutor. As we have noted, it may be modeled on, and anticipate the behavior of, the abuser, and generally contains a substantial portion of the rage of the system.

Although these dominating states are maintained according to the self-care system, how do they originate? How does it happen that an "internalized object" becomes a part of the self that can take executive control, as is often seen in DID? An answer resides in the enactive dynamics we have considered in our review of attachment theory and dissociation (chapter 5). As a result of being intensely attached to the aggressor (often much more intensely than if there had been no abuse), the child's mimicking of the aggressor's behavior is a form of enactive, procedural, dyadic learning. In contrast to nontraumatic identifications, which add to a person's already coherent identity and repertoires of behaviors and understandings, trauma-related identifications detract from a person's identity. The aggressor's goals and behaviors appear to have supplanted the child's own agency, initiative, and rage, because, as a consequence of peritraumatic dissociation, the latter have not been adequately synthesized among various self-states. However, this apparent supplanting is fueled by and actually represents the child's *own* rage.

These dominating and rageful self-states, which we generally think of as deriving from "identification with the aggressor," and which often embody rage, contempt, and omnipotence, may arise as procedural, imitative, dyadic enactments. They arise from the confluence of trauma and attachment, and may be understood as internal working models in Bowlby's sense. These working models may lie at the root of some of the narcissistic and entitled behavior that dissociative and narcissistic patients alike exhibit. If the discordant attachment paradigms are not examined, then the dissociated self-states remain like two identically magnetized poles that are contiguous, but unjoinable.

Transformation, Aggression, and Dependency

Overreliance on the self-care system necessitates dependency on dissociative solutions. This dissociative organization of self, which arises largely because of collapse of intersubjective space in relationships with early attachment figures, is relied on for self-regulation, making the experience of dependency difficult. As a result of its protective function, the self-care system resists transformation. When the person is no longer in a dangerous interpersonal environment, these self-protective functions persist. The behaviors and intentions of real others are perceived through the lens of internal experience. In order to heal both chronic dissociation and narcissism, therapy needs to provide the opportunity for transformation, especially around the pivotal issues of aggression and dependency.

Beahrs (1982) and Blizard (1997a, b) emphasize how accessing the vitality of malevolent self-states is the key to overcoming resistance. Empathic confrontation (Chu, 1998) is an invaluable way to recognize and contain dissociated aggressive states. This two-stage process first establishes empathic resonance and understanding about the subjective meaning of an aggressive behavior, followed by a containing confrontation. The empathic framing makes the message easier for the patient to hear. Containment of the patient's destructive aggressiveness also models for the patient that the original perpetrator's aggression was unacceptable.

Winnicott (1971) described how the patient's experience and expression of aggression toward the therapist, who in turn does not retaliate, can enable the therapist to become "real in the sense of being part of shared reality and not just a bundle of projections" (p. 88). This transformation involves a very important psychological shift away from a relatively primitive form of interacting "that can be described in terms of the subject as an isolate" (p. 88) in which the object is experienced primarily in terms of projection and identification. The object (the other person) becomes real by virtue of having been killed in fantasy, surviving, and not retaliating. The experience of unfettered and unpunished aggression toward a loved one has often been absent in dissociative and narcissistic patients. An important event of this kind, which undoubtedly influenced his theory, occurred in Winnicott's early childhood. In response to his father's mildly humiliating taunts, he "bashed flat" with a croquet mallet the nose of one of his sister's dolls, and his father "good-temperedly" repaired the doll's face in his presence (Winnicott, 1989, pp. 7–8). Thus, when things go well, the child (and the psychotherapy patient) learns that his aggression can be tolerated and that the attachment figure is "real." Only when the other is perceived as "real" and separate from the self can dependency be acknowledged, and only then can the closed system begin to open up. Excessive dependency and fear of dependency are ubiquitous for traumatized patients. Therapy cannot be a transformative experience without recognition of dependency.

Pathological narcissism is an inevitable result of trauma-generated dissociation. The omnipotent self-sufficiency of the closed system depends on pathological dissociation and generates various forms of pathological narcissism. Grandiose, domineering self-states often appear to arise from procedural, dyadic enactments. These working models are at the core of much of the narcissistic entitlement, grandiosity, domination, and self-sufficiency that are so often found in dissociative disorders and narcissism. As an attachment figure with expertise, the therapist has the opportunity to invite formerly hidden and omnipotent parts of the self to come out in the open. And this real connection to the outside in turn mobilizes the patient's capacity for transformation.

11

"GOOD GIRLS," "SEXY BAD GIRLS," AND WARRIORS
The Role of Trauma and Dissociation in the Creation and Reproduction of Gender

Although our theories of gender have recognized the pathology of gender prescriptions, they have failed to discriminate aspects of gendered behavior that are clearly pathological from those that are not necessarily so—for example, passivity and masochism in females and narcissism and hyperaggressivity in males. In this chapter, I argue that much of gendered behavior and experience, especially the pathological aspects, is, in interaction with other forces, trauma generated, and that it is the posttraumatic and dissociated aspects of this gendered behavior that make it so resistant to change. When one views gender stereotypes (e.g., men are independent, active, tough, unemotional, and violent; women are dependent, passive, emotional, and caring) through the prism of trauma, the bifurcation of typology along dominant and submissive lines becomes immediately evident. As a case in point, consider Freud's categorizations of male, masculine, active, aggressive, dominant, and female, feminine, passive, submissive, masochistic (Schafer, 1974). Trauma and dissociation tend to shatter subjectivity and agency, forcing the person into dominant versus submissive modalities of thinking and behavior. However, the presence of gendered characteristics in a given individual should in no way be taken as *prima facie* evidence that trauma or abuse has occurred.

The rates of child trauma in this country continue to be unacceptably high (Chu, 1998, 2001). The hypothesis presented in this chapter is that different patterns of child trauma experienced by boys and girls, along with their broader repercussions, correspond to the different patterns of gendered behavior and experience. Indeed, some of the stereotypic norms may reflect posttraumatic states and affects that have been normalized. On the whole, boys are more often victims of physical violence (Boney-McCoy and Finkelhor, 1995), whereas girls are more often subject to sexual abuse (Finkelhor and Dziuba-Leatherman, 1994). The patterns of child sexual abuse also differ for boys and girls, such that boys, more than girls, tend to be abused outside the home by extrafamilial persons (Finkelhor, 1990). The gender of the perpetrators also varies: Although males are the most frequent perpetrators for both boys and girls, the male-to-female ratio is higher for girls. In a large study involving interviews of 900 women, Russell (1986) found that the rate of contact child sexual abuse of girls before the age of 18 was 38%, and the rate of incest was 16%. Ninety percent of the abusers were male. Results of Lisak, Hopper, and Song's (1996) study of 600 college men indicated that although 34% of the men reported physical abuse as children, 18% reported contact sexual abuse before the age of 16, with 3% to 4% of that being incestuous. Sixty-one percent of the sexual abusers were male, and 28% were female; 11% of the boys had both male and female abusers. It should be borne in mind, however, that self-report measures, especially self-report measures of boys' sexual abuse, may be underestimates (Gartner, 1999). Furthermore, definitions of incest and child sexual abuse may vary with investigator. Child sexual abuse is a broad category that encompasses vast differences in type, chronicity, and severity.

Although both sexes are subject to violence and harm, some ways in which children are harmed vary by gender. Crime statistics indicate that boys are subject to much more homicide and assault, whereas girls are much more subject to rape (Finkelhor, 1990). A recent national survey, conducted by telephone, of 2000 randomly selected youths, aged 10 to 16 (Boney-McCoy and Finkelhor, 1995), found that about one half (47.4%) of the boys had been subjected to some form of violent victimization as compared to one third of the girls. About twice as many girls had been subject to attempted kidnapping. Taken together, over 40% of these children had been victimized. (Only 5.7% of these incidents had been reported to the police; about one quarter had never been disclosed to anyone before the survey.) Again, patterns were found to vary in and out of the home: A slightly higher percentage of girls than boys had been subject to parental and family assault, but the boys had been exposed to about three times as much aggravated assault and simple assault by nonfamily members than the girls. A follow-up, prospective, longitudinal study (Boney-McCoy and Finkelhor, 1995), which controlled for the quality of the parent–child relationship, found that both male and female participants who had been victimized experienced more PTSD symptoms than those who had not. In addition, perhaps in consonance with the idea that boys, even little ones, should be "tough," boys, much more than girls, tend to be subject to a potentially traumatic premature separation from their mothers (Pollack, 1998).

In order to support and clarify my thesis, I will first cover some background, including the differentiation of "gender" from "sex," and the prevailing theories and politics in academic feminist psychology. Following this, I will delineate what I see as the posttraumatic gendering of girls and boys with reference to the girls' picture, the boys' picture, Bruce Perry's contribution, and the reproduction of gender.

Gender and the Divided Feminist Agenda

Originally a word denoting "kind" (*genus, genre, generic*) and used in some languages to classify nouns and pronouns by sex (Pinker, 1994), the term *gender* has been adopted by feminists to make a needed conceptual distinction between the effects of biology and culture. Having only one word, *sex,* made it difficult to understand and talk about behavior that is sex-typed but culturally mediated. It also led to circular thinking: Even though we may know that behavior is influenced by situations, context, and history, without a word to designate this knowledge it is easy to conflate sex and gender, and especially to ascribe the effects of the latter to the former, thereby reducing gendered behaviors to a biological essence dictated by genes and hormones.

Until very, very recently, women have usually been represented in the mental health field and other disciplines as deficient in one important way or another, and therefore deserving of reduced status relative to men (Hare-Mustin and Marecek, 1990; Unger, 1990; Kemelgor and Etzowitz, 2001). In the social sciences, there has been a divided feminist response to the *homme manqué* model of the female, one that minimized gender differences in order to deemphasize the alleged deficiency, and one that maximized but valorized them (Hare-Mustin and Marecek, 1990; Bohan, 1993). Many feminist social scientists in the first group have concentrated their efforts on showing that men and women are not markedly different, and that what we see as gender is largely a cultural and social artifact. This agenda has had mixed success, depending on what particular kinds of differences are being considered, and by whom. A second group of feminist psychologists, often known as the "cultural feminists," including writers such as Jean Baker Miller and Carol Gilligan (Mednick, 1989; Hare-Mustin and Marecek, 1990; Bohan, 1993), have revalued the earlier devalued "feminine" characteristics.

Miller, author of the groundbreaking *Toward a New Psychology of Women* (1976), recategorized women's service and relational orientation as strength rather than weakness; later, she and her colleagues (Jordan et al., 1991) at the Stone Center at Wellesley College promulgated the "self-in-relation" theory of female psychology. Six years after the publication of Miller's book, Gilligan's highly acclaimed *In a Different Voice* (1982) appeared, presenting one of the more popular recent theories about the origins of gender differences. She claimed that women's and girls' often overlooked relationality is, in fact, an often unheard or misunderstood "different voice." Grounding her presentation of the genders in Chodorow's (1974, 1978) work and in Kohlberg's (1966) cognitive developmental theory, Gilligan proposed that girls and women follow a "care" orientation, a path of cognitive and moral development that differs from the "justice"-oriented moral developmental path that she considered more characteristic of males. Two important criticisms of this strand of feminist thinking have been that it may give support to the stereotypes of femininity, legitimizing the patriarchal status quo, and that it is an essentialist point of view, conceptualizing gender as an inherent, immutable, and indelible aspect of self (Mednick, 1989; Bohan, 1993). Nonetheless, the theory resonates with the experience of many people, especially women, of themselves and others.

Perhaps one reason for this resonance is that people's experience is embedded in context. An impressive array of social psychological studies has illustrated the ways in which gender is determined by context. Women and men, as roughly separate groups, tend to find themselves in differing situations that differentially elicit "feminine" and "masculine" behaviors. This can lead to the perception that gender refers to enduring and stable traits that are either learned or are linked to a biological substrate that determines feminine and masculine behavior. Much of this research indicates that a great deal of the "gender" ascribed to people may be more in the situations they inhabit than in them (Unger, 1990). From this point of view, Gilligan's (1982) thesis about the female caring orientation may be understood as a reflection of context: that women are more frequently in situations that elicit or demand caring. When men are in similar situations, they may be just as caring (Mednick, 1989; Clopton and Sorrell, 1993). Furthermore, more recent moral development research has indicated that males as a rule do not score higher than females on Kohlberg's moral development scale (Ryan, David, and Reynolds, 2004). From my point of view, the most important contribution of Gilligan's and others' uncovering of the caring orientation is in the importance of nurturing a caring orientation in both sexes.

Oppression is a powerful context as well as an ongoing source of socialization. There is a voluminous literature on the relationship between gender and oppression, an exegesis of which is beyond the scope of this chapter. The correspondence between so-called feminine behaviors and those of subordinate, oppressed groups has been variously and compellingly described by Mill (1869), Beauvoir (1953), and Allport (1954), among many others. Because gender is so endemically interwoven with daily life, gender-linked oppression is inescapable. In particular, psychological self-oppression resulting from the internalization of sexist mores and stereotypes, such as that described by Horney (1934), by Thompson (1964), and by Hacker (1981), is an important aspect of the reproduction of gender.

Although oppressive circumstances contribute to the socialization and perpetuation of gendered behavior, they also tend to be traumatogenic. As Brown (1991) and Herman (1992) observe, the frequency with which females are exposed to trauma (and the kinds of trauma) are not outside the range of the normative, and the impact of trauma on psychic life and psychopathology is considerable. Accordingly, it may often be the trauma, rather than oppression per se, that substantially mediates many gendered conditions. Oppression, especially behavioral oppression (i.e., the exercise of overt power), is not of necessity traumatic (i.e., overwhelming and exceeding the mind's capacity to register it, rendering the person helpless to understand). My thesis is that much of the behavior we think of as gendered is derivative of trauma specifically, that specifically "gendered" (typed) self-states are created by trauma. These include the "good girl," the "sexy bad girl," and the male "warrior" state, among others. Gendering is a multipart and multilayered process. Because child trauma is so ubiquitous and frequent, these behaviors become labeled and codified. Because the types of traumatic experience tend to be distributed in accordance with biological sex, these labels tend to cohere with the (usually patriarchal) social structure and become gender stereotypes.

Regardless of the degree to which stereotypes represent bias in the observer or actual behavior in the observed, they tend to be internalized in psychic life, where they can become gender role standards (Howell, 1975, 1981) serving as modulators of self-esteem (shame and guilt), thereby influencing behavior. The gender-socialized individual is now situated as a player in a social process that depends on gender-related prior learning and training, involves gender-related contextual demands, unconscious self-monitoring, and the high possibility of past and future trauma.

Trauma is by definition overwhelming, changing physiology, cognition, and emotion. The core of trauma is the experience of being rendered completely helpless (Spiegel, 1990a). Although posttraumatic states are not inherently masculine or feminine, they do tend, as a result of socialization, trauma, and sex-differentiated biological predispositions, to be disproportionately distributed among males and females. The resulting psychodynamics, taken in conjunction with traumatic circumstance, socialization patterns, and genetic predispositions, contribute to generally different types of enactments in accordance with gender.

In brief, dissociated self-states, although neither male nor female in themselves, are sometimes distinctly gender-linked. In particular, the process of identification with the abuser may replicate the abuser's gender identity, sexual orientation, or both, injecting confusion in some survivors about their own gender identity and sexual orientation. In clinical populations, for example, we may find a self-identified heterosexual man who was repeatedly abused by an uncle, and who at times compulsively seeks homosexual liaisons; a self-identified heterosexual man who was abused by his mother, and who has a seductive female part; females who were abused by males and who have male parts; females who were abused by females and who have lesbian parts (Blizard, 1997b). None of the foregoing is meant to imply that childhood abuse causes homosexuality. In cases where abusers were of both sexes, there may be an overriding general confusion about gender identity and sexual orientation, such that we can only extrapolate that the gender of some of the self-states is probably based on the gender of the perpetrator.

To a significant extent, then, the highly gendered psyche, especially in its pathological aspects, may be a fragmented, unintegrated one. Gender roles and gendered states end up "containing" trauma (Layton, 1998), keeping knowledge of, and outrage about, trauma out of awareness, and perpetuating it all at the same time. As reenactment, gender repeats itself interpersonally, socially, and transgenerationally.

Most of the foregoing speaks to the social construction of gender. Recently, Copjec (1994) has introduced a formulation of the later Lacanian concept of the real in terms of gender. This has to do with the way in which trauma is itself unknowable and unrepresentable. She depicts a view of gender in terms of the "impossibility of meaning" (Dyess and Dean, 2000; D. B. Stern, 2000) rather than the possibility of many meanings posed by social constructivism. Trauma punctures the psyche; the hole or lack is itself unknowable, unsymbolizable. We can only infer it in terms of its aftereffects. In accordance with the view that trauma has a significant shaping impact on gender, the gendered psyche may not only be a fragmented one but a punctured one, and this interrelationship between trauma and gender combinations may contribute to the special resistance of gender to change.

Finally, a last objection to the caring orientation: Caring and tenderness need to be distinguished from passivity, dependency, and masochism. The caring orientation in itself fails to explain the latter characteristics, which are not necessarily "caring" at all. The alternative presented here is that a certain part of stereotypical femininity, the pathological part, is substantially trauma-generated. Likewise, hyperaggressivity and pathological narcissism in men needs to be distinguished from healthy self-esteem and from healthy aggression that protects self and others.

The Posttraumatic Gendering of Girls and Boys

The Girls' Picture

It is my hypothesis that a portion of the gender stereotypic cultural norms for females derives from the susceptibility of girls to be sexually abused, narcissistically used as sex objects, or both—directly from the impact of trauma and indirectly from other sources, as will be described. This certainly fits with the pattern that Gilligan and Brown (1993) as well as Belenky, Clinchy, Goldberger, and Tarule (1986) observe: that girls tend to lose their voices in early adolescence. Sexually abused girls are often instructed to lose their voices—that is, "Don't tell."

Implicit in the caring orientation is emphasis on the importance of attachments. Although awareness of attachment may directly underlie certain commonly gendered characteristics such as emotionality and nurturance, attachment itself cannot account for other gendered characteristics, such as masochism, dependency, passivity, and so on. It is in the interaction between attachment and trauma/dissociation, especially in the configurations that emerge when attachment to an abusive caretaker becomes markedly more important than the abused person's own agendas and desires, that female gendering begins to take a fuller conventional form.

Among the sequelae of child sexual abuse are mental states that exemplify some of the common stereotypes: the feminine-linked passivity, dependency, masochism, helplessness, and seductive or highly sexual states as well as the masculine-linked tough-guy, violent, and rageful states (Rivera, 1989; Shusta, 1999). Trauma can fracture the person into various self-states along the lines of dominant–subordinate and predator–prey relationships. The feminine-gendered form of these may be the "good girl" and the sexualized "bad girl," corresponding to the age-old madonna–whore split. The "good girl" is socially acceptable, and is perhaps the template for many academic lists of feminine stereotypes, such as passivity, dependency, emotionality, excitability, talkativeness, indecisiveness, insecurity, suggestibility, illogicalness, intuitiveness, affectionateness, temperamentalness (Broverman et al., 1970).

The "Good Girl." In psychopathology, whether the clinical outcome is dissociative identity disorder (DID), borderline personality disorder (BPD), or what we think of as neurosis characterized by intrapsychic conflict and compromise formation, the usual presenting self-state in females (usually a version of the "good girl") tends to be drained and depleted of life, relatively helpless, depressed, masochistic, and feminine-identified. Certainly, females with DID may have male-gendered parts, and females with BPD can have self-states that are explosively angry and violent. However, the posttraumatic states that are most frequently available to conscious experience are predictably those that were most adjusted to the power dynamics of the social context of early life, and possibly the present one as well.

The other-orientation so often imputed to females may amount to a "gendered subjectivity" according to which females are always required to respond to someone else's needs (Miller, 1976; Profitt, 2000). As Gilligan (1982) states,

> here the conventional feminine voice emerges with great clarity, defining the self and proclaiming its worth on the basis of the ability to care for and protect others. The woman now constructs a world perfused with the assumptions about feminine goodness that are reflected in the stereotypes of the Broverman et al. studies (1972), where all the attributes considered desirable for women presume an other—the recipient of (such qualities as tact, gentleness, and emotional expressiveness) which allow the woman to respond sensitively while evoking in return the care (of the recipient) [p. 79].

The other-orientedness described here may be less extreme, but not different in kind from that of the abused female child, who feels herself into the mind and body of her abuser in order to stay alive (Ferenczi, 1949). Her mental and emotional activity is focused on the welfare of her abuser, because her welfare depends on his state of mind.

The "Sexy Bad Girl." Compulsive seductive sexuality, the inability to refuse sexual advances (see Freyd's, 1996, "consensual sex decision mechanism"), or both, even to the point of prostitution, are not infrequent outcomes of child sexual abuse (Davies and Frawley, 1994). This is not the kind of sexuality that is characterized by vitality and high self-esteem. As Ferenczi (1949) observed about the consequences of child sexual abuse in "Confusion of Tongues":

> When subjected to sexual attack, under the pressure of such traumatic urgency, the child can develop instantaneously all the emotions of mature adults and all the potential qualities dormant in him that normally belong to marriage, maternity and fatherhood. One is justified—in contradistinction to the familiar regression—to speak of a *traumatic progression,* of a *precocious maturity.* It is natural to compare this with the precocious maturity of the fruit that was injured by a bird or insect [p. 229].

Ferenczi goes on to describe how the sexually abused child may become a "guilty love-automaton imitating the adult anxiously, self-effacingly" (p. 230).

One manifestation of the "bad girl, fallen woman" aspect of femininity is the femme fatale. Consider the interpersonal dynamics involved. The femme fatale enslaves men, reversing her own earlier traumatic enslavement—for example, Odysseus's Circe, the "black widow," and the "vamp." We see them in movies such as *Cat People, Black Widow,* and *The Last Seduction.* The femme fatale is always reenacting trauma. Indeed, reenactment of trauma is both her modus operandi and her raison d'être. Such compulsivity is characteristic of a posttraumatic state that reenacts abuse; the femme fatale understands this reenacting state to be "female."

Rage. It is dangerous for subordinated and terrorized people to show rage, especially at the time of trauma. Lott (1990) has observed that, in contrast to an angry voice, the caring voice may be the only voice the male world will recognize. Rage, which tends to be male associated, is generally considered "unfeminine" and hence unattractive in women. For many women rage is suppressed, repressed, or dissociated. Although this may vary with subculture, women with borderline personality disorder (BPD) may frequently exhibit violent, explosive rage states, all the while disavowing these states and maintaining a view of themselves as always meek and mild. In women with dissociative identity disorders, the aggressor, protector states are frequently male-gendered. As Rivera (1988) observes, "through creating personalities who declared themselves male, [abused females] were able to identify with the aggression of their abusers and use it in the service of their own protection without consciously challenging their socialization as girls and women" (p. 44).

Vicarious Trauma and Indirect Effects of Trauma. Many girls who have not themselves been abused have likely witnessed abuse to a sibling, parent, relative, or friend. They may simply know that as girls they are vulnerable (Waites, 1993). Such vicarious trauma will probably not cause the fragmentation that may be generated within the victims, but it can create fear. Just as the trauma of the Holocaust can be transmitted intergenerationally (Danieli, 1985), the trauma of child sexual abuse may be passed on. As a case example, a mother who experienced incest as a child attempted to protect her daughter by instructing her to "watch out" for the dangers of abuse that she herself had been unable to avoid. Perhaps the warning helped her daughter, but perhaps some of the mother's paralysis was transmitted as well, for the daughter reports that when she was in fact sexually violated as an adult by an acquaintance, she felt helpless to resist and laughed nervously in response to the abuser's behavior. Remarkably, when told of the occurrence by her daughter, the mother uttered a similar nervous laugh. Although only the mother had been subjected to childhood trauma, the daughter replicated her mother's posttraumatic response despite the warning. The "warning" may have carried with it the additional messages of the futility of struggle, confrontation, and self-defense.

Thus, although direct sexual abuse is fortunately not the lot of the majority of girls, its threat is pervasive. Girls often learn about it from family members and friends. Even without direct physical contact, verbally incestuous remarks can be damaging to self-esteem and a person's sense of safety and security. Abuse-related remarks, conveyed repeatedly, with a certain intonation, and as part of a general atmosphere—particularly in combination with other trauma, with neglect, or both—may amount to a cumulative trauma.

How do these characteristics of passivity, dependency, masochism, and helplessness that may reflect trauma become gender-stereotypical? The "caring orientation" is two-sided. Miller (1976) states that what women want is to serve without being subservient. Mature caring and attachment needs are often conflated, and their respective implications need to be differentiated. Certainly autonomous, self-selected service is the most desirable way to serve, but the other side of the caring orientation, the side without autonomy, is masochism and passivity. The dark side of the caring orientation is the other-orientation of terrified subjugation and devaluation.

The Boys' Picture

The typography most often cited for stereotypical masculinity is Brannon's (1976) description of four clusters of masculine norms: the Sturdy Oak (which emphasizes physical strength and emotional fortitude), the Big Wheel (emphasizing success and achievement), Give 'em Hell (aggression), and No Sissy Stuff (avoidance of anything feminine). Various writers in men's studies focus on the problematic "gender straitjacket" in which boys are raised (Pollack, 1998), but it is at the same time generally acknowledged that deviance from gender role prescriptions and proscriptions has more severe consequences for males than for females (Pleck, 1995; Unger and Crawford, 1995). Men are often described as being unemotional in outward behavior. Indeed, Levant (1995) claims that there is a "high incidence among men of at least a mild form of alexithymia–the inability to identify and describe one's feelings in words" (p. 238). Nonetheless, measures of physiological responsivity indicate male emotionality equal to that of women (Pollack, 1998). Men are often less practiced in expressing their feelings, which may then be channeled into anger (Kilmartin, 1994; Levant, 1995; Pollack, 1998). Many authors emphasize the general unacceptability of expressing emotions other than anger. Especially forbidden are feelings of loss, vulnerability, and shame. In contrast to females, who are more often shame-sensitive, boys tend to be shame-phobic (Pollack, 1998, p. 33). As a result, narcissistic defenses may be overdeveloped (Betcher and Pollack, 1993; Krugman, 1995; Pollack, 1995). According to Krugman, narcissistic character pathology is a "caricature of the male gender role stereotype: emotionally unflappable, powerful, and in control" (p. 116).

The most often discussed cause of the above is harsh gender role socialization (Kilmartin, 1994; Levant, 1995; Pleck, 1995; Pollack, 1995).

However, harsh socialization of behavioral norms does not explain the origin of these norms. Specifically, it does not explain the violence, misogyny, and emotional dissociation so characteristic of masculinity in so many cultures (Brooks and Silverstein, 1995). I have suggested that certain aspects of what we think of as gendered behavior for girls are largely an outcome of trauma and dissociation, tantamount to a "posttraumatic style." Much of stereotypical masculinity may also be posttraumatic. Although the key ingredients are still attachment and dissociation, the trauma route is somewhat different for boys.

The sexual abuse of boys tends to be extrafamilial (79% and 83% prevalence, from Lisak et al., 1996, and Finkelhor, 1984, respectively) and out of the home. Sexually abused boys can develop dissociative symptoms, and highly dissociative boys may also have female-gendered parts resulting from identification with female aggressors, executing the female-linked tasks, or both (Grand, 1997). Although sexually abused boys can exhibit psychological patterns similar to those of girls, such as shame, depression, anxiety, suicidality, and self-mutilation, they are more likely than sexually abused girls to behave aggressively toward others (Finkelhor, 1990; Putnam, 1997; Gartner, 1999). This is a complicated matter. A homophobic society in which needy vulnerability is equated with femininity—which, in turn, is often equated with homosexuality—does not foster integration of gender-linked states in males.

Boys are subjected to very high levels of physical abuse. Perhaps because our culture teaches us that boys are supposed to be able to "take it," we fail to comprehend the seriousness of such abuse. Pollack (1998) cites a recent Navy study that found that 39% of its male recruits had been exposed to physical violence from their parents. A recent national survey of violent victimization of children and adolescents (Boney-McCoy and Finkelhor, 1995) found that about one half of the boys (47.4%) had been subjected to some form of violent victimization, including 18.4% who had been victims of aggravated assault, and 16.3% who had been victims of simple assault. In addition, 13.5% had experienced genital violence—violence directed at the genitals with the intent of physical harm. Similarly, Pollack (1998) states that 1 in 10 boys has been kicked in the groin before junior high school. At the same time that they are exposed to high levels of physical threat and violence, boys are socialized to experience and express anger (Fuchs and Thelin, 1988; Fivush, 1989; Kilmartin, 1991; Pleck, 1995; Levant, 2000) and discouraged from expressing emotional need and vulnerability (Miller, 1976; Unger and Crawford, 1995). In this way, a combination of childhood trauma, dissociation, and social pressure may push more boys in the direction of hypermasculinity and aggressivity.

In addition to physical and sexual abuse, boys are more often subjected to ruptures of attachment described as the "male wound" (Hudson and Jacot, 1991), and as a "normative developmental trauma" (Betcher and Pollack, 1993; Pollack, 1995, 1998). Such ruptures involve dissociation of affectional longings and result in fears of isolation and feelings of deprivation. Greenson (1968) coined the term *disidentification* to refer to the (assumed) need for the *male* (emphasis added) child to emotionally separate himself from his primary object of identification, his mother. Greenson felt that the boy then needed to "counteridentify" with the father in order to attain a healthy sense of masculinity. Hudson and Jacot (1991), whose notion of the "male wound" brings together these two processes, refer to a permanent psychical fissure or dissociation that generates difficulty with emotion. Stoller (1974, 1985) was even more specific, stating that the boy must erect an internal "protective shield" of "symbiosis anxiety" against his early "protofemininity": "The first order of business in being a man is don't be a woman" (1985, p. 183).

The achievement of masculine gender identity therefore comes at the cost of repudiating the identification with mother, and often of everything that is female-identified. Stoller's work, in particular, effectively turned Freud's viewpoint about the greater difficulty of the girl in attaining gender identity on its head. Chodorow (1978), incorporating Stoller's observations into her earlier work on gender (1971, 1974), maintained that because women universally mother, the differences between the sexes will follow in accordance with their necessary identifications and disidentifications. Men, fearing merger and symbiosis, have more rigid interpersonal ego boundaries and are less relational and more patriarchal; and women, experiencing themselves and being experienced by their mothers as similar and connected each with the other, are more relational. Like Stoller, Chodorow emphasized that masculinity comes to be defined as "not female."

It should be noted that Stoller's, and then Chodorow's, and Gilligan's theorizing is based on a Mahlerian (Mahler, Pine, and Bergman, 1975) concept of a symbiotic phase of development. Stern's (1985) seminal work on infant development casts much doubt on the likelihood or extent of such a phase. In addition, recent anthropological evidence and reinterpretation of older evidence (Eisler, 1987) suggests that despite near-universal mothering, not all cultures have been patriarchal.[1] These findings cast doubt on Chodorow's claim that near-universal mothering by women results in men who are less relational and more patriarchal. Perhaps the long-standing appeal of these theories has something to do with the unstated underlying femiphobic assumption that a boy's identification with mother and with femininity is to be feared, or at least is highly undesirable. Herek (1987) has offered an interesting sociological explanation for the same construct: the belief that femininity taints masculinity and must therefore be avoided by "real" (heterosexual) men.

Pollack is the gender theorist who has most explicitly linked the masculine-gendered style with trauma. He has postulated that, partly as a result of gender identity issues for the very young boy, "there may be a developmental basis for a gender-specific vulnerability to *traumatic abrogation* of the early holding environment . . . an *impingement* in boys' development—a normative life-cycle loss—that may, later in life, leave many adult men at risk for fears of intimate connection" (1995, p. 41). In later work (1998), Pollack suggested that the vulnerable period for boys is around the time they begin school and are pushed out of the nest by their mothers. His emphasis on the potentially traumatogenic nature of this premature separation is consistent with many clinical and research findings suggestive of a common or frequent blunting or dissociation of emotional longings in men. He feels that one result of these repressed yearnings in males may be the "creation of *transitional* or *self-object* relationships with mother substitutes that are meant to repair and assuage the unspeakable hurt of premature traumatic separation and simultaneously to deny the loss of the relational bond" (1995, pp. 41–42).

Pollack's point—that boys tend to be more vulnerable to premature separation from their mothers and that certain characteristics of male-gendered behavior are derivative of traumatic separations—provides the basis for a simpler alternative to the perspective on masculinity offered by Stoller, Chodorow, Greenson, Hudson, and Jacot. According to this viewpoint, the more rigid interpersonal ego boundaries, fears of merger, and less relational characteristics associated with masculinity derive from the fact that the boy is a different gender from his early caretaking figure and must therefore repudiate his identification with mother and females in general in order to achieve masculine gender identity. This alternative perspective says that the trauma of maternal emotional abandonment may itself be genderless, but because such abandonment happens more often to boys, and because masculinity becomes narcissistically invested with superiority, the privilege of being so deprived becomes cherished as part of the gender role. This hypothesis is consistent with the cognitive developmental theory of gender typing (Kohlberg, 1966), according to which gender identity precedes and organizes gendered behaviors (i.e., "I am a boy; therefore, I do boy things"; "Boys don't cry or get sad. I get mad, because I am a boy"). Compensatory narcissistic patterns, in addition to the dissociation of emotional vulnerability and attachment needs, typically become components of stereotypical masculinity (Krugman, 1995; Levant, 1995; Pollack, 1995). This male pattern is characteristic of males, but not specific to them. There are clinical and anecdotal reports of girls who have cut off their attachment longings, and who exhibit the same characteristics of blunted emotionality, ragefulness, and narcissism.

The Coriolanus Complex: The Warrior. One important variant of this masculine pattern might be called the Coriolanus complex. Coriolanus, a Roman patrician of the fifth century, B.C.E., was the tragic hero of one of Shakespeare's lesser known plays. In the play, Coriolanus personifies the warrior mentality. He was close to his mother, but was banished from her presence as a young child so that he would become the kind of man that she admired: a fierce, emotionally illiterate warrior. The tragedy is in how his banishment by a woman who used him as her narcissistic extension, her warrior, deforms his humanity. His need for attachment dissociated, he became brutally narcissistic, and his emotionality and rage redirected into war. As an adult, he became once again banished from the city that he needed and loved because he had become so characterologically damaged. Stoller and Herdt (1985) offer a description of the Sambia, a New Guinea tribe, notable for its fierce warriors and its extreme devaluation and fear of femininity. The boys in this tribe spent their early childhood in extreme, perhaps blissful physical closeness to their mothers, only to be suddenly and forcibly ripped away, sometimes from their mothers' arms, to live in an all-male community. The men in this community, who were physically close, affectionate, and dependent on their mothers and who were then traumatically separated from their mothers while still children, became fierce warriors and misogynistic, heterosexual husbands. Although Stoller and Herdt invoked this information about the Sambia in a different context, it also supports the more general point that the premature, forced cutoff of emotional longings can be traumatic, inducing a kind of blind rage that can be effectively redirected in war. And males may be genetically predisposed to respond to trauma with aggression (B. D. Perry, 2000).

In sum, boys, like girls, are exposed to very high rates of trauma, including physical, sexual, and emotional abuse; but unlike girls, boys are often routinely deprived of one important means to deal with their trauma: emotional closeness with their mothers, other attachment figures, or both. In particular, if their blunted vulnerability and emotional neediness have become part of their male gender role identity, they will be limited in their ability to grieve, and hence to resolve trauma and loss (Pleck, 1995). Perhaps it is not just socialization but also trauma that contributes to problematic masculine attributes considered normative: the "Give 'em Hell" hyperaggressivity, the "No Sissy Stuff," and the narcissistic "Big Wheel."

Bruce Perry's Contribution to Evolutionary Theory

The last decade has seen remarkable progress in the understanding of the biological aspects of gender and gender identity (Hoyenga and Hoyenga, 1993; Breedlove, 1994; Diamond and Sigmundson, 1997; Halpern, 1997; Colopinto, 1999). We know much more than before about the undeniable impact of genes and hormones on much of sex-differentiated abilities and behavior. However, along with this knowledge has come a greater degree of sophistication, such that the either/or model of nature versus nurture has generally been replaced with a psychobiosocial model in which determinism is understood to be highly interactive and in which specific, unitary causes are not always isolatable (Halpern, 1997; Schore, 1997).

Perry's (1999a, b) findings that children's physiological responses to trauma tend to be sex-differentiated are particularly exciting. These findings suggest differing biological predispositions for the form of posttraumatic physiological response. Perry describes how exposure to trauma affects neurodevelopmental processes: hyperarousal and hypoarousal responses become more pronounced with more early, severe, and chronic trauma. Perry found that both sexes employ both kinds of responses to trauma, but that boys' responses tend more toward hyperarousal than do girls', whereas girls and very young children exhibit hypoarousal and dissociative responses. The hyperarousal response involves fight or flight, which begins as a neurophysiological alarm reaction and continues with elevated heart rate, startle response, behavioral irritability, and increased locomotion. The vigilance for threat can increase the probability of aggression. Hypoarousal involves dissociative symptoms such as fugue, numbing, fantasy, analgesia, derealization, depersonalization, catatonia, and fainting. This defeat response, characterized by robotic compliance, glazed expressions, passivity, and decreased heart rates, is similar to learned helplessness. Perry postulates an evolutionary basis for his findings. In his "environment of evolutionary adaptiveness," men caught in an enemy attack were more likely to be killed, whereas the women and young children were more likely to be captured. Men's best chance of survival would be to attack or flee; women's and young children's best chance of survival would be in hypoarousal and dissociative responses, which are adaptive to immobilization or inescapable pain.

Perry's findings enlarge our understanding of the socialization process. In particular, they underscore how the posttraumatic aggressivity of boys may appear indistinguishable from stereotypical masculinity, disguising the underlying trauma and pain. Perry's findings also underscore how girls' posttraumatic responses are more often dissociative and apparently passive. Both aggressivity and passivity are considered aspects of stereotypical gender and as such are prescriptive. Today, however, there is reason to see the heightened gendered form of these responses as posttraumatic, and, as such, symptomatic of unresolved pain, trauma, and grief.

The Reproduction of Pathological Gender

Gender is reproduced in many ways. It is elicited by social context, learned, internalized, socially constructed, reenacted, and so on. In this chapter, our primary emphasis has been on the reproduction of pathological gender via the cycle of abuse. Although a number of studies have indicated that most perpetrators of violence and abuse were themselves abused (Finkelhor, 1990; Romano and de Luca, 1997), most victims do not go on to become perpetrators (Lisak et al., 1996; Gartner, 1999). Thus, the prevalence of abuse would decrease if it were not for the fact that perpetrators tend to have multiple victims and to be recidivists. One estimate is that approximately one third of those who were sexually abused, physically abused, or extremely neglected will subject their children to one of these; the remaining two thirds will not be abusive or neglecting (Kaufman and Zigler, 1987, in Johnson, 2004).

One of the problems is the misreading of posttraumatic hyperaggressivity and violence as normative—the "boys will be boys" point of view. Intertwined with this is the tendency for the descriptive to become prescriptive. In this way, observed male behavior becomes the way males *should* behave.

Another pathway is via projective identification and mutual projective identification, whereby individuals and dyads, respectively, project affects and states that are not perceived as gender-appropriate into and onto others as well as into other parts of the self. For example, if a woman projects her rage into an already hyperaggressive male, this may not only be immediately dangerous to herself but it may perpetuate the traumatogenic culture both in herself and in the others involved. Or a male may project gender-inappropriate feelings of neediness into other individuals whom he then physically punishes for what he has disavowed in himself. Such aggression may be traumatic to the others involved, reproducing gendered states in them. In *The Batterer,* Dutton and Gollant (1995) introduce another perspective on the phenomenon of near-universal mothering: "One reality that may differentiate boys from girls is that the former develop a stronger bond to an opposite gender person at an earlier developmental stage" (p. 107). In adult heterosexual relationships, the man's attachment figure is female, like his mother. If the boy was intermittently abused in his early attachment or if his security needs have otherwise been overly frustrated, his attachment needs are likely to be intensified, and the threat of separation is likely to produce very strong responses, often of terror and anger. Although the anger may be motivated by a desire for soothing, its violent expression can be devastating. This configuration is an important one in the reproduction of gender, especially since children may be witnessing such parental, male–female violence.

These problems are aided and abetted by the all too frequent collective and individual unwillingness to do what is required to ensure the cessation of child abuse. Most perpetrators are male, and one effect of a patriarchal power structure is to give covert license to perpetrators of abuse and terror within our own culture. Because this confuses victims and bystanders, it gives added cover to perpetrators (Herman, 1981).

In conclusion, trauma contributes substantially to the creation of gendered states. With increasing psychological health and ability to grieve, these gendered states tend to become better integrated. By grasping how much of pathological gendered behavior (which is so endemic in our culture) has roots in trauma, we may hope to reduce this kind of trauma in the future.

In chapter 12, we turn to another species of dissociation-based pathological behavior that is culturally prevalent and for which the possibility of growth-promoting integration is far more remote.

12

THE DISSOCIATIVE UNDERPINNINGS OF PSYCHOPATHY

When the Terrible Is True, Not Only Are We Not Safe, But, More Important, We Can No Longer Imagine

Although this chapter concerns the psychopath as a particular type of person, this focus should not obscure the existence of psychopathy and evil in all of us to varying degrees and in different forms. Psychopathic violations and atrocities leave an imprint on others, leading them to reproduce evil (Grand, 2000). Each person's personality structure and each society responds to, and registers the impact of, psychopathic actions in different ways. Psychopaths are not necessarily criminals, that is, lawbreakers who have been caught. On the contrary, they may occupy the upper echelons of our society and never even come in contact with the law. One of the most disturbing things about psychopaths is how brilliantly they can gain the complicity of others. Consider, for example, the character of Iago in Shakespeare's *Othello*. However, there are other examples, in which the complicit ones are less innocent. Psychopathy is a hidden streak in our accepted cultural mores in which "successful" exploitiveness is often condoned rather than condemned. At the same time, there is a cultural denial of the existence of human predators. In relation to psychopathy, then, we face multiple double binds.

In contrast to the fictional Walter Mitty, whose fantasy world soothed and gave balance to a menial reality, the psychopath enacts his illusion on the stage of the world shared with everyone else. Whereas Walter Mitty's approach to a painful and interpersonally empty world was autoplastic by virtue of his active fantasy life, the psychopath is alloplastic, converting personal illusion to reality by changing other people's material reality, psychic reality, or both. The soothing illusions that Walter Mitty clearly understood as his own fantasy are understood more concretely as absolute rights by the psychopath.

However, psychopathy has regressive effects in that changing interpersonal reality by deception, intimidation, and appropriation reinforces the illusion of absolute entitlement and the defense of omnipotence. The psychopath experiences his wish as a justifiably enforceable command on reality. Whereas the narcissist lives in a hall of human mirrors, or like Walter Mitty, erects those mirrors in his own mind, the psychopath bends them to their most flattering angle; and if they will not bend, he breaks them.

Who Is the Psychopath?

In his classic book on psychopathy, *The Mask of Sanity,* Cleckley (1941) describes the psychopath as appearing to be sane but actually being insane. He says that the psychopath assumes a *mask* of sanity: "His mask is that of robust mental health. Yet he has a disorder that often manifests itself in conduct far more seriously abnormal than that of the schizophrenic" (p. 383). To be sure, psychopaths may be psychotic, but rarely so (Meloy, 2001a). When he initially linked psychopathy to psychosis, Cleckley (1941) did not have available to him the current conceptual language of borderline personality organization (Kernberg, 1975). Kernberg (1975, 1989) argues that antisocial personality disorder (his term, to be distinguished from the *DSM-IV* diagnostic category) is a subdivision of narcissistic personality disorder, itself a subcategory of borderline personality organization.[1]

Today, the term closest in meaning to psychopathy in *DSM-IV* is antisocial personality disorder. But the *DSM-IV* categorization, which rests on behavior criteria, fails to focally address the salient personality characteristics that contribute to the dangerousness of these people.[2] Meloy (1997) addresses the psychodynamics of the psychopath's "evil, and his wish to destroy goodness" (p. 172) in elaborating three primary characteristics of psychopathy: aggressively narcissistic behavior often expressed in repetitive devaluation of others; chronic emotional detachment from others; and deception of others (i.e., mendacity).

Psychopaths do not wear a sign warning us of what their inner world is like and of their potential intentions toward us. In fact, they generally look very normal, often even better than normal. Hare (1993) quotes William March's words in *The Bad Seed,* on the frontispiece of his book, *Without Conscience:* "Then too, the normal are inclined to visualize the (psychopath) as one who's as monstrous in appearance as he is in mind, which is about as far from the truth as one could well get. These monsters of real life usually looked and behaved in a more normal manner than their actually normal brothers and sisters."

Allopathic Instrumentality

It is difficult to ascertain all the causes of psychopathy.[3] But its placement under borderline personality organization does imply the probability of a history of relational trauma (Howell, 2002; Howell and Blizard, accepted for publication). As in other personality disorders, one of the effects of relational trauma is concrete thinking, a shrinking of the scope of a playful imagination, and a reliance on "as-if" behavior. The offshoot of such trauma-induced shrinking of the scope of imagination, as we have repeatedly observed, is a dissociation of experience that tends to remain unsymbolized. When survival must take priority, nuances of emotional and experiential content are less likely to be attended and linked in experience. In the absence of symbolic playing with reality in which different roles and identities can be represented and linked, reality gets "re-played out" in deadly earnest.

Mimicry

Deutch (1942) long ago described as-if personalities, who substitute imitative performances for authentic relating. Constantly shifting their outward appearance in accordance with situational demands, as-if personalities mimic and mold themselves to those around them, playing one role in one interpersonal situation, only to shift to another persona in the next. Here mimicry, ordinarily a medium of play, is enacted in a way that is devoid of playfulness. And mimicry is a dominant feature of the psychopath (Cleckley, 1941; Meloy, 1988, 2001b).

Cleckley described the essence of the psychopath's dysfunction as an overdevelopment of and almost exclusive reliance on mimicry. In contrast to a person with narcissistic personality disorder, who may sometimes feel that he or she is being a fake, the "psychopathic character has no awareness of this 'false self'" or the as-if quality of his phenomenal experience. He does not merely play the role, observing the limits of his character, but lives the part, sometimes oblivious to the deceptions promulgated by his behavior (Meloy, 1988, p. 132). The psychopath uses words to mimic human emotions, rather than to express meaning and feeling of a deeply felt and complexly personally symbolized nature.

Cleckley (1941, p. 338) suggests that this "semantic disorder"[4] is the key to what makes the psychopath "mad": "His rational power enables him to mimic directly the complex play of human living" (p. 383).

In what way are psychopaths semantically insane? Within normal limits of intelligence, they can distinguish right from wrong. What is it about their use of words that could be insane? Like many traumatized people, psychopaths tend to operate concretely, on the basis of signs and signals, rather than through symbols of meaning. According to Langer (1942), signs and signals are essential elements of conditioning, shared by humans and lower forms of life, in which two things are paired. They can elicit or trigger a particular response. In contrast, symbols evoke a complexly contextual array of meaning that specifically denotes the particular person, thing, or idea that they signify. Whereas signs and signals express a command or name, symbols are metaphors for some one thing, as expressed in the language of something else. Symbols, which emanate from the potential space of play (Meares, 1995), evoke and awaken the creative network of the whole person. The symbol illuminates both the thinker and the subject of contemplation. The concreteness of reliance on signs and signals in the form of words, which lack emotional meaning, is exemplified by a remark that "dumbfounded" Hare. The criminal in question commented that the person he murdered had "learned a hard lesson in life" (Hare, 1993, p. 41).

Used instrumentally, words do not share the self or communicate with the other, but function as triggers to effect targeted behavior in another person. Even when the psychopath uses words imbued with a highly symbolic meaning, such as religious words or words evoking trust, he is not operating in the realm of symbolic thought. Thus, psychopaths "may *appear or seem* to be involved with symbols, as others are, but they are using their knowledge of others' relationships with these forms of meaning structures and manipulating through them" (Harvey Schwartz, personal communication, 2004). Unimpeded by concern for the other or considerations of conscience, the psychopath uses language in a manner that can be highly effective in achieving the desired ends (Meloy, 2001b). And to the degree that the instrumental behavior proves to be effective, it will be repeated.

Even mimicry, ordinarily a medium of play, is enacted in a way that is devoid of symbol. The person is stuck in the role play, but there is no play to the role. Meloy (1988, 2001b) describes as-if mimicking in psychopathy as simulations, emphasizing the pseudoidentificatory qualities. He emphasizes *malignant pseudoidentification* (1988, p. 139), in which the psychopath simulates certain behaviors or interests in order to achieve the victim's identification with himself, so as to create a fertile territory for exploitation.

Similarly, Cleckley (1941) had one diagnostic criterion for the psychopath that was based on his own personal susceptibility:

> A saying current among psychiatric residents, secretaries, medical associates, and others familiar with what goes on in my office may illustrate . . . that excellent evidence for the diagnosis of psychopathic personality can be found in my own response to newcomers who seek to borrow money or cash checks. It is rather generally believed that only psychopaths are successful and that in typical cases success is inevitable [p. 342].

Because psychopaths can be so charming and so good at simulation and pseudoidentification, clinicians should be wary of overestimating their capacity for, and wish to undergo the anxiety of, psychological growth (Meloy, 1988, 2001b). A fairly recent study indicates that, rather than growing, psychopaths often become more dangerous as a result of treatment, through which they have learned the appropriate buzzwords with which to con clinicians and judges (Rice, 1997). Meloy counsels us to remember that "when one gazes on the psychopath there is less than meets the eye" (2001, p. 13). Psychopaths "possess an emotional range and depth and object relatedness similar to, although not identical with, those of a young toddler prior to sustained interaction with his peers" (Meloy, 2001a, p. 16). The beholder tends to fill in the blanks to conform to the level of emotional and affectional complexity that is associated with adults who are verbally competent and emotionally mature.

The Accidental Success of Instrumental Alloplasticity

By the use of words (and behavioral cues and triggers) as manipulative instruments rather than as modes of communication, the psychopath may literally convert wish to reality or apparent reality. A successful lie, or a string of successful lies, can dramatically change the way a person is regarded and treated in the world. A successful deception also blurs the more normal distinction between grandiose, wishful fantasies and reality. Most of us face disillusionment daily at least, and we do not persist in believing that the outer world corresponds to the inner grandiosity. But the chronic liar (at least until he or she is found out) can achieve a change in other people's response to her by waving a verbal magic wand. For the psychopath, the "duping delight" (Salter, 2003) of "putting one over" is intensely rewarding, because conscience and the capacity for remorse are lacking. The more successful this behavior, the more the differentiation between self and other is blurred, and the stronger the illusion that the other exists as a possession and extension of oneself in reality.

The psychopath's ability to change reality by deception, theft, and undermining others reinforces the illusion of absolute entitlement and the defense of omnipotence. The psychopath perceives his or her wish as a justifiably enforceable command on reality on the basis that she is somehow superior and therefore entitled. (This is the theme that Raskolnikov so tortuously acted out and about which he finally achieved resolution and redemption in Dostoyevsky's *Crime and Punishment.*) When the psychopath achieves external success by these means, it may camouflage to himself, and to others, the real confusion about what feelings and thoughts exist in whom.

The psychopathic lie is an enactment of the contemptuous attitude. Indeed, psychopaths self-regulate with contempt. For most of us, contempt can be a temporarily comforting illusion. Within the privacy of our own minds we may temporarily entertain it, but we know, if pressed, that it is an illusion. However, the psychopathic lie acts out that illusion and makes the fantasy concrete, bridging fantasy and reality, making the illusion really real.

The psychopath's omnipotence and devaluation, then, are to some extent reality, not just a psychic defense, for these become self-fulfilling prophecies. Take devaluation, for example. In a controlled circumstance, such as with a person's own children or a weak spouse or dependent employees, devaluation works to make others feel and behave less adequately—an event that can, in reality, build the devaluing person up.

When the psychopathic process works, it may superficially appear to be adaptive and indicative of good reality-testing. However, when the psychopath is deprived of the ability to lie, cheat, steal, and control others with promises, threats, or force—activities that shore up omnipotence, entitlement, and devaluation—then deficits begin to appear, and they may gain expression in massive paranoia and emotional instability.

The foregoing are ways in which sagacious instrumentality make one "mad." The psychopath may assume the appearance of sanity through the alloplastic use of words and linguistic acts as instrumental tools of deception. Certain maneuvers, which are mostly verbal, including deception and intimidation, actually alter the psychic worlds of others, their behavioral responses, or both. To the extent that this behavior is successful, it reinforces the psychopath's illusions of omnipotence and absolute entitlement. The success of this behavior compromises reality testing. These maneuvers make the psychopath's underlying primitive structure and insanity look sane.

Dissociation in Psychopathy

Dissociation is "ubiquitous in psychopaths" (Meloy, 1988, p. 151). But psychopaths are not dissociative in the same way that persons with DID are (Reid Meloy, personal communication). The dissociative self-structure of those with DID involves preserving parts of the self for later developmental purposes, whereas the deeper, grosser kind of dissociation that characterizes psychopaths precludes this positive use. Like the dissociation in other personality disorders (Bromberg, 1998), the dissociation in psychopathy tends to be ego-syntonic. However, the dissociation in psychopathy goes even deeper: The sine qua non of psychopathy is a severe developmental arrest involving the dissociation of attachment need (Howell, 1996) and shame states to such an extent that it makes them "outsiders to love."

This distinction does not mean that persons with DID cannot have psychopathic parts of their personality, which are dealt with in treatment by enlisting the cooperation of the nonpsychopathic parts. Nor does it rule out dissociative amnesia and dissociative states in psychopaths. Indeed, psychopaths, often the victims of severe relational trauma, have dissociative amnesia about many events (Stein, 2001, 2003, 2004). Stein (2004) states that a "very high percentage of violent offenders have horrific histories of maltreatment at caretakers' hands, and there is clinical evidence suggesting that much of this early trauma has been dissociated" (p. 511).

For the psychopath, depersonalization and derealization are common experiences, especially during the commission of violent acts (Meloy, 1988). According to Meloy, these experiences, which tend to correlate with high affective or autonomic arousal, are not unwelcome because psychopaths tend to have autonomic hyporeactivity and therefore to be stimulus-seeking. In addition, their

> impaired capacity to form attachments and deeply internalize objects of identification renders conscious experiences of dissociation, or separateness from self or reality, unusual but quite tolerable. Dissociative states enhance and exaggerate the psychopath's normal feelings of detachment or removal from actual objects or surroundings. Dissociative states would accelerate the propensity of the psychopath to disidentify with his or her external reality [p. 154].

The Structure of Evil: The Timeless Unconscious Reenacted

Bollas (1995) positions the serial killer as the extreme exemplar of psychopathy. As opposed to a person who kills a loved one in passion, or a schizoid person who "goes postal," the serial killer's murderousness is unfathomable:

> Even though we know that the world is in part dangerous, and even though we are aware of our own destructive ideas and feelings, we seem able to delude ourselves that the world and the self are basically benign. This is one reason why the serial killer so alarms us: we cannot see where he is coming from and cannot comprehend his motivations, and whatever we know about him does not help us find him before he appears out of the blue and strikes again [p. 190].

In a powerful chapter of his book, *Cracking Up,* Bollas articulates his view of "The Structure of Evil," which he believes inhabits the unconscious minds of those of us in Western civilization. Bollas outlines six steps in the development of this structure: "presentation of good to the other," "creation of a false potential space," "malignant dependence," "shocking betrayal," "radical infantilization," and "psychic death" (p. 211). Bollas describes how severe trauma can deprive a person of fantasy, of illusion, and of personal dreams. Normally, we are able to imagine the terrible in counterpoise to the knowledge that we are safe. When the terrible is true, not only are we not safe, but, more important, we can no longer imagine. As Bollas says,

> the structure of evil exploits our primitive belief in the goodness of the other. However much the child's projective processes may invest the parent with nasty qualities, he ultimately knows the difference between his imagined constitution of the parent as a monster (e.g., in dreams, daydreams, willfully vindictive sulking) and the moment when a parent does something that is truly monstrous [p. 200].

Bollas goes on to describe how the psychopath, who, early in life experienced annihilation terrors and a death-in-life murder of his imagination, recreates that traumatic shock in others, forcing them to live the death-in-life, the never-ending hell that he, himself, at one time "lived through." Similarly Stein (2004) describes early annihilation fears that are "realized rather than simply imagined . . . [and] form the basis for a dissociative adaptation that exponentially magnifies the destructive power of ensuing elaboration . . . and the propensity for violent enactment."

On an individual level, the psychopath is "turning the tables." On a social level, the past terrorization of one person is visited on many in an endless future. Underlying this multiplication of victims is the timelessness of the dissociated memories of the unconscious. As a result, there will never be enough victims.

Attachment Gone Awry: "Do Unto Others *Before* They Do Unto You"

It appears that something has gone wrong with the attachment system of psychopaths. Meloy (1988, 2001a) points to a failure of identification, and in particular, to a "dearth of soothing internalization experiences (in psychopathy) . . . such that the child may come to anticipate hard, aggressive objects and may identify with such objects for adaptive and defensive reasons" (2001a, p. 10). He refers to Grotstein's (1982) concept of identification with a *stranger selfobject,* a fantasy that helps the infant anticipate the real presence of a predator. In the psychopathic process, Meloy (1988) says, the "stranger, or predator selfobject as a narcissistic identification is the predominant archetypal internalization of the infant" (p. 46). He says, "The experience of the mother figure as an aggressive predator, or more benignly as a passive stranger, leaves the child no choice but to disavow a primary emotional attachment to an actual object outside the child's skin boundary" (Meloy, 1988, p. 54). Meloy believes that the psychopath is characterized by a paucity of deep identifications with caregivers, by failures of internalization, and by a "deactivation of a need for attachment" (Bowlby, 1980, p. 54).

Bowlby (1980), we recall, outlined three successive stages following the disruption of early attachment: protest, despair, and detachment (see chapter 6). When it sets in, detachment precludes bonding with others, and it is often irreversible. Indeed, one of Bowlby's earliest studies (1944) focused on juvenile delinquents who were emotionally indifferent and affectionless as a result of maternal rejection and neglect. If detachment is viewed as a defense, as Bowlby viewed it, then what is excluded from consciousness? In my view, what is kept out of consciousness is the experience of the lost, abandoned, terrified, and enraged child, which is sequestered from the rest of consciousness in the phase of detachment.

Bowlby (1980) use the word *deactivation* to describe one of the psychological defenses against disorganization in the face of attachment loss. This deactivation involved the exclusion of all affect and thought that "might activate attachment behaviour and feeling" (p. 70), and resulted in a state of emotional detachment. To be sure, attachment categories of avoidant and dismissing attachment, in which Bowlby's description of detachment come to fruition, includes a very large number of people (the second largest category after securely attached). I suggest that whether the avoidant strategy is a *distraction* in which the reality is largely assimilated or a *dissociation* depends on the severity of the circumstances. What we see in the violence of the psychopath is the far end of the continuum: The violence derives from intense dissociated experiences of the self as shamed (see also H. Lewis, 1971, 1981, 1990; M. Lewis, 1992). For the serious psychopath to identify with the shame state would be tantamount to experiencing psychic annihilation all over again, as Bollas suggests.

Ann Rule, author of *The Stranger Beside Me,* an account of Ted Bundy's life and that part of her life that intersected with his, states that he was at best an unwanted illegitimate child. His mother went to a distant city from her home to deliver the baby and left him in that distant city for three months while she decided what to do. She retrieved him and brought him to live with her parents, who told him that he was their son. The grandfather was a volatile, maniacal tyrant who was sadistic with animals. Evidence of severe psychological damage was soon apparent, as indicated in the chilling tale of his aunt, who went to visit when the young Ted was three years old. She woke up from a nap to find her body surrounded with knives laid out on her bed and a smiling young Ted looking up at her (p. 469). When Ted was a young adult he was engaged to be married to a woman named Stephanie, who had long, dark hair, which she wore parted slightly in the middle. After she jilted him, his killing sprees began. He mostly picked young women who wore their hair as Stephanie did.

Meloy (1988, pp. 155–158) also describes a case in which intense feelings of humilated rage were instantaneously elicited by rejection, causing the man to "snap," resulting in a murder by electrocution and strangling. Stein (2004) describes the case of an extremely sadistic rape and murder, committed jointly by two sexual psychopaths, which she relates to a feeling of rejection even of the fact of one's birth. She indicates that like many such perpetrators, these men "attempted to fill the victim with varied detritus, having the vagina and the uterus double as a garbage can" (p. 11). Stein states that in contrast to the affirming birth narratives that many people hear from their mothers, "through traumatic imposition, the abusing or abandoning mother may actually assist in the perceived undoing of birth" (p. 11). She suggests that the perpetrators must "get back inside" to stem existential panic, but that they then pay the price of trying to enter a place where they are so unwanted. But she also suggests that, since there has been such unbearable rejection there, "only the destruction of the maternal symbol can reinstate separateness and restore homeostasis" (p. 11). These particulars illustrate in the extreme the horrifying results of the dissociation of unendurable shame. It is a great understatement to say that in such cases the perpetrators could not find reparative interaction that would activate attachment. As Stein says, the "more legitimately terrifying the actual interactions upon which the fantasies are based were, the greater the likelihood that a terror-inspiring resolution will be attempted" (p. 15).

The scorched narcissism of one of Stein's (2004) murderers is stunning in its disconnection. In recalling his response to the victim's threat to call for help by yelling "rape" (because she was clearly being threatened with rape), he stated, "The threat of someone crying rape is pretty hard on a guy" (p. 9). Stein's account of these perpetrators' narratives often sounds like pieces of experience positioned separately in disconnected space. The ultimate horror of such cases is that these reparative fantasies and actions seem to be what hold such people together as a bulwark against the dissociated shame states and consequent lack of integration.

Reciprocal Role Relationships

In the trauma literature, identification with the aggressor is often invoked as an explanation of either "character" or switches in behavior. I have suggested understanding identification with the aggressor as a dissociative defense (chapter 7). Understood this way, there are two stages in identification with the aggressor: first, a phase that is an automatic, self-protective act of the organism, including somatosensory mimicking; and, second, dissociation as an active defense maintaining the separation of self-states, each with different affects and worldviews. In borderline personality disorder, this dissociation of the psyche is reflected in predominantly two distinct self-states, one aggressive, and one attachment-oriented; alternation between these two self-states is the basis of the borderline personality's characteristically stable "instability." In contrast, in psychopathy, and in the "Kernberg type" of narcissism as well, one pole is more dominant, and switching between self-states is less frequent. The psychopath, and to a large degree the narcissist, tend to stay in the omnipotent, grandiose, devaluing aggressor-identified states, dissociating the victim-identified states of fear, shame, and neediness.

Each of these role positions (aggressor and victim) is the reciprocal of the other, and the two are bound together in a procedural, relational unit (Ryle, 1994; Ryle and Kerr, 2002; see Ryle in chapter 4). Whereas the reciprocal role relationship of bully and victim (Ryle and Kerr, 2002) is shared in BPD and in psychopathy, in BPD the particular victim and aggressor roles frequently switch. In psychopathy, although both roles are internalized as part of the inner world, only the sadistic, aggressor role is experienced. Yet it still exists in relation to its reciprocal role. Often the sadistic role is itself layered, such that the view of self as victim serves to rationalize the harm done or to be done by the sadistic self. Meloy (2001a, p. 16) notes a research study (Hazelwood and Warren, 2000) indicating that some sexual sadists are able to role-play the victim with a consensual partner, suggesting both intrapsychic oscillation and intimate knowledge of the position of victim. However, although switches to the fearful, victimized state may appear to reflect an inner reality, they may also be feigned. That is, a person may imitate a needy, victim-state on the basis of some past experience of the self, without really feeling it in the moment. Such simulation can produce a chameleonlike effect.

Conclusion

Grand (2000) describes how psychopathic predators often feel that their actions are not real. She writes that "there is no sense of personal, moral accountability for one's acts. . . . As a result the perpetrator's depravities coalesce in an internal environment in which the act is *not really real, not really evil, not really mine*" (p. 14). Even though in many ways psychopaths do not feel themselves responsible for their acts, it would be a mistake to regard them only as misunderstood victims with horrific attachment histories. Even though it speaks to their envy of the love and attachment to which they are outsiders, a birthright tragically denied them, the continuous defiling of others is intentional. The promise of destructive action looms addictively as condensed hope and revenge. As Meloy (2001) observes, "we have now entered the diagnostic and psychodynamic landscape of the evildoers, the wicked ones, in psychology: psychopaths and sadists. If we think about the psychology of wickedness, these are the men we must study and understand, yet fear" (p. 171).

Yes, we must fear them; but we must also fear our own attachment-based and trauma-based collusive dissociativity, for psychopaths do not live in a social vacuum. On one hand, we are horrified by what psychopaths do; yet as members of a group culture, we have accepted the occurrences of atrocities, ranging from genocide to child abuse. The emerging scandal in the Catholic Church (Frawley-O'Dea, 2004a, b), although fortunately coming to light, is only the tip of the iceberg with respect to many atrocities that have been widely denied. The outright psychopathic abuse of children can range from the activities of a single parent or a single priest or rabbi, to child abuse that is coordinated among adults, especially in group settings where children are housed, such as in "religious" cults or sleep-away camps. Like the Nazi doctors who "doubled" their identities in order to execute horrors (Lifton and Marcusen, 1990), most such adults do not think of themselves as psychopaths.

In his essay, "The Fascist State of Mind," Bollas (1992) notes that often the most gifted practitioners of what he calls "intellectual genocide" seem to achieve social prominence by viciously attacking others, and that their very viciousness seems to enable them to become objects of endearment to others who, one might expect, would be horrified by such viciousness. Instead, they are often viewed as "cute monsters" whose deeds are dismissively laughed away and therefore unopposed. Bollas stresses how the "act of dissociative acceptance" (p. 196) (the vicious cute monster is really a very nice and charming person) humanizes the inhuman. Earlier in this chapter we noted Bollas's (1995) view that in all of us in Western civilization there is an unconscious knowledge of the structure of evil. Juxtaposed to this knowledge is people's primitive belief in the goodness of the other, which is preyed on and exploited by the psychopath. Perhaps by denying the reality of evil, we enact a preemptive defense to keep our minds and our capacity for imagination from being taken from us. We dissociatively seek to protect ourselves from the fear of being shocked, overwhelmed, rendered speechless and unable to think. It is not only our own capacity for evil, our own streaks of, or potential for, psychopathy, that we keep out of awareness, but our fears of this kind of psychic annihilation that the psychopath embodies that prevents us from seeing more clearly. However, the defense of being ready for the potential trauma around every corner (Bromberg, 1998) makes us more vulnerable to not notice traumatizing evil when it does occur, whether to ourselves or to someone else.

ENDNOTES

Chapter 1

1. The DES is a screening instrument. Even though highway hypnosis is one item on the DES, it is so normative that, in and of itself, it should never be construed as an indication of the presence of a dissociative disorder.

2. *DSM-II* linked conversion hysteria and dissociative hysteria together, under the same broad category of hysteria. While the reorganization resulting in *DSM-III* was intended to free it from automatic subscription to Freudian theory, it added to the confusion surrounding somatoform dissociation, without addressing or solving the problems posed by the Freudian view of conversion hysteria (Cardena and Nijenhuis, 2000).

3. Hilgard (1977) observed that the fact that the demons spoke to Jesus–in the case of Gadarene asking to be sent into a herd of swine, who then rushed over a bank and drowned in the sea–is indicative of dissociative identity disorder (DID). Likewise, it seems that many descriptions of demon possession, and especially those in the *New Testament* of Jesus' casting out demons, may have been expressions of dissociative disorders.

Chapter 3

1. This may be an oversimplification. Janet's interests were broad, and he wrote on many psychological topics, including, but not limited to, hysteria, psychasthenia (a diagnostic grouping that included, among other disorders, obsessive-compulsive disorders and phobias), psychoses, psychology of conduct, and religion. Moreover, the time periods in which different interests were prominent, differed. From 1880 to 1900, hysteria was in the forefront for Janet; then he concentrated more on psychasthenia, in which the female-to-male ratio was more balanced.

From 1920 to 1930, he wrote more about psychoses (Van der Hart, personal communication).

2. The splitting of the ego (or actually the self) (Greenberg and Mitchell, 1987; Padel, 2000; Sutherland, 2000).

3. Fairbairn observes that his concepts of ego structures are in some ways comparable to Freud's concepts of ego, id, and superego. The libidinal ego is comparable to the id, the central ego to Freud ego, and the antilibidinal ego to the superego. Fairbairn emphasizes, among other differences, that the id is not a structure, but only energy, and that the superego is not a dynamic structure because it is an internalized object. Only the ego is a dynamic structure. Furthermore, in contrast to the superego, the antilibidinal ego is not moral. (Fairbairn postulates the development of a superego by a separate process.)

Chapter 4

1. Also known as species identity theorem, which stated, "Everyone and anyone is much more simply human than otherwise, more like everyone else than different" (letter, dated about 1944, photocopied on frontispiece of Sullivan, 1962, *Schizophrenia as a Human Process*).

2. Sullivan viewed the unconscious as a hypothetical construct without which psychological events are or appear to be erratic and unpredictable. It fills all the discontinuities that are present in mental life and in theory, at the least it restores orderly continuity. The hypothetical unconscious includes (1) much that has been conscious but has not been verbalized (i.e., preverbal or subverbal), (2) selectively inattended phenomena, and (3) dissociated processes, much of which has been never represented in consciousness (Mullahy, 1970, p. 296). Referring to how dissociated integrating tendencies can be "choked off," Sullivan said, "It is because there are such things that Freud was led into what I feel is the flat mistake of assuming that the unconscious is largely the habitation of the primitive, the infantile, the undeveloped, etc." (1956, p. 66).

Chapter 5

1. Vygotsky was a follower of both Janet and Piaget, who was Janet's student. In constructing his principle that individual consciousness is built from the outside through relations with others, Vygotsky

followed Janet's claim that intrapersonal processes are transformed interpersonal ones, and quotes Janet as follows: "Each function in the child's cultural development appears twice. First on the social level, and later, on the individual level; first between people (interpsychological) and then inside the child (intrapsychological)" (Janet, quoted in Kozulin, 1999, p. xxvi).

2. Somatoform: Citing the work of Levine (1997), Scaer points to the outcome for nondomesticated animals who have undergone a freeze response: They begin to shake and run, or continue doing what they were doing just before the freeze. After they shake, if the shaking and reorienting process is not interrupted, they seldom develop adverse symptoms. In contrast, some domesticated animals or zoo animals, whose discharge response is inhibited, may become symptomatic. Levine (1997) believes that posttraumatic responses are "fundamentally, incomplete physiological responses suspended in fear" (p. 34). Levine believes that humans need to feel and then to release the pent-up energy in their bodies to heal. In this regard, he works in the mold of an old tradition, extending from Reich's concepts of character armor to those of his student Lowen (1967), who also believed that tension accumulates in the body and must be released. For this, Lowen developed a form of body therapy called bioenergetics.

Chapter 8

1. Grotstein further suggests that the two-person, or interpersonal, process occurs by means of hypnotic influence, preferring to call this process projective transidentification.

2. Morrison writes of her discovery that "traditional, canonical American literature is free of, uninformed and unshaped by, the four-hundred-year-old presence of the first Africans [and] assumes that the characteristics of our national literature emanate from a particular 'Americanness' that is separate from, and unaccountable to, this presence" (pp. 4–5). She continues,

> These speculations have led me to wonder whether the major and championed characteristics of our national literature—individualism, masculinity, social engagement vs. historical isolation; acute and ambiguous moral problematics; the thematics of innocence coupled with an obsession with figurations of

> death and hell—are not in fact responses to a dark, abiding signing Africanist presence. It has occurred to me that the very manner by which American literature distinguishes itself as a coherent entity exists because of this unsettled and unsettling population [p. 6].

She notes that "because European sources of cultural hegemony were dispersed but not yet valorized in the new country—the process of organizing American coherence through a distancing Africanism became the operative mode of a new cultural hegemony" (p. 8). She adds that so many of the first Americans were, most of all, unfree. They were escaping various forms of ostracism, poverty, even imprisonment in their native countries, and the slave population offered

> itself up as surrogate selves for meditation on problems of human freedom, its lure and its elusiveness. This black population was available for mediations on terror—the terror of European outcasts, their dread of failure, powerlessness, Nature without limits, natal loneliness, internal aggression, evil, sin, greed. In other words, this slave population was understood to have offered itself up for reflections on human freedom in terms other than the abstractions of human potential and the rights of man [pp. 37-38].

Chapter 9

1. In the 1893 paper, "On the Psychical Mechanism of Hysterical Phenomena," written in collaboration with Breuer, which later became the first chapter of *Studies on Hysteria,* the authors note that the "trauma concerned something which the patient wished to forget and therefore deliberately repressed and excluded from his conscious thoughts" (1963, p. 42). I am referring here to a 1963 collection of Freud's early writings, edited by Rieff, because of a particular footnote, in which Rieff notes that this was the first time Freud used the term *repression,* and that "later it became the technical term for the *unconscious* process by which thoughts are excluded from consciousness" (p. 42). The "later" of the previous sentence suggested to me that in Rieff's opinion, Freud had at the occasion of that writing viewed repression as a conscious defense. Erdelyi who has written extensively on this subject, highlights another, better known, footnote, from

Strachey's translation (in collaboration with Anna Freud), of the same passage: "It was a question of things which the patient wished to forget, and therefore intentionally repressed from his conscious thought and inhibited and suppressed" (1893, p. 10). Here Strachey states that the "word 'intentionally' merely indicates the existence of a motive and carries no implication of conscious intention" (1893, p. 10). Erdelyi (1990) believes that this footnote is "revisionist" (p. 8) and states that Freud "was never completely unambiguous" about this matter, which did not appear to be "ever that salient for Sigmund Freud. It is Anna Freud's book *The Ego and the Mechanisms of Defense* ([1936] 1946) that established the diktat, followed ever since, inside and outside psychoanalysis, that defense mechanisms are necessarily unconscious" (p. 13).

The following are also illustrative of this view that Freud at times included consciousness in his meanings of "intentional" and "deliberate" defense. In 1894, in "The Defense Neuro-Psychoses," he writes, "Their ego was faced with an experience, an idea, or feeling which aroused such distressing affect that the person decided to forget it because he had no confidence in his power to resolve the incompatibility between that unbearable idea and his ego by the process of thought-activity" (p. 47). He then goes on to write, "The patients can recollect as precisely as could be desired their efforts at defense, their intention of pushing the thing away, of not thinking of it, of suppressing it" (p. 47).

2. I say dominant and subordinate rather than dominant and submissive deliberately. Dominant and subordinate identifies roles and positions of real power in relationships. In contrast, dominant and submissive suggests empowerment or lack of it deriving from psychological sources, which can be quite complex and convoluted. From this point of view, "submissive" may be either a misattribution on the part of a dominant or a self-attribution, accurately or inaccurately, having to do with the condition of subordination.

3. Putnam (1989) reports on the flashbacks of one DID patient whose incestuous father killed her dog on the railway tracks and then threatened her that if she ever told what he had done to her, that her dog's fate would be hers as well. Her flashback memories occurred in separate sensory modalities of the scene of her dog's murder, which only made sense when pieced together.

4. In this study, subjects were exposed to their own written trauma narratives. During flashbacks there was less activation of Broca's area (speech), simultaneous with heightened activity in the right cortex, in particular, the visual cortex. Van der Kolk (1996b), the second author of the study, states, "We believe this to reflect the

speechless terror experienced by these patients, and their tendency to experience emotions as physical states rather than verbally encoded experiences" (p. 293).

5. Today, Anna O could be understood as having a severe dissociative disorder (Breger, 2000) and probably DID (Ross, 1989). Her "absences" and her different states of mind, characterized by striking amnesia, including changes in ability to speak different languages, would certainly suggest this possibility. Breger (2000) writes,

> It seems that throughout the earlier years, she went about her duties with an entirely separate, secret self, and no one noticed. In short, she was emotionally isolated–abandoned–in this death-ridden family. Well before her breakdown, she was a divided person, with a false outward self–compliant, dutiful, but unemotional–and an inner self where her genuine feelings were kept alive in fantasy. These emerged as the "good" and "evil" selves of her illness [p. 109].

He reports that according to Breuer's biographer, Hirshmuller, a review of Pappenheim's history reveals that not sexuality, but "personal and intellectual suffocation, neglect, oppression, death, loss, and abandonment were at the core of her disturbance" (p. 124). Her later social activism, centered around helping abused girls, unwed mothers, and combating "white slavery," may also speak to possible underlying issues, the "themes that precipitated her breakdown: abused and mistreated girls and women whose rights were denied. . . . Her later life was an adaptive, productive mastery of the conflicts that were earlier apparent in her hysterical illness" (Breger, p. 109).

6. I have read in several separate sources the story that Breuer's treatment of Pappenheim was precipitously broken off around the issue of his inability to deal with her sexual feelings toward him. Breger (2000) offers a correction to this story that I consider important enough to repeat here. "The first Freud–Jones tale has it that toward the end of his treatment of Bertha Pappenheim, Breuer was called to her house and found her in the midst of a hysterical pregnancy, calling out that she was 'giving birth to Dr. Breuer's baby.' This manifestation of an erotic transference supposedly caused Breuer to flee from her and from work with neurotic patients entirely" (pp. 122–123). The story became more elaborated in one of Freud's letters, according to which "not only did Breuer stop treating Bertha when her sexual transference appeared, but his wife was jealous, causing him to feel guilt. He

fled from his patient 'in horror' and went to Venice for a second honeymoon, where his daughter, Dora, was conceived. This daughter then committed suicide in New York, years later" (p. 123). Breger states that "there is no factual support for this tale. Even in Freud's own account, he 'suspects,' 'interprets' and 'reconstructs,' implying that the events must have occurred in the way he imagined because his theories of sexuality and transference required them to" (p. 123). Breger adds that Dora was conceived before Bertha's treatment was ended, that the Breuers did not vacation in Venice at the time Jones had suggested, and finally that "Dora did not commit suicide in New York, but took poison when the Gestapo came for her in 1936 and died in a Viennese hospital" (pp. 123–124). Finally, the reason that Breuer gave up the cathartic treatments of hysterics was that he was burned out. Breger quotes one of Breuer's letters: "It is impossible for a physician . . . to treat such a case without having his practice and private life completely ruined by it. At the time, I swore never again to submit to such an ordeal" (p. 124). Breuer saw Pappenheim daily for two years, and she recovered several years after that. Breuer's statement attests to the fact that working with severely dissociative patients can be exhausting.

Chapter 10

1. The term *pathological narcissism* is not used here in Kernberg's sense.

Chapter 11

1. Eisler (1987), on the basis of archeological artifacts, documents Neolithic peaceful, nonpatriarchal, advanced civilizations that had highly developed aesthetic sensibilities and art (including indoor plumbing on Crete), worshiped nature and goddesses (as well as gods). These "partnership" civilizations were invaded and conquered by nomadic bands who brought with them worship of male gods of war, metallurgy (the sword), and a "dominator" model of social organization.

Chapter 12

1. Kernberg (1975, 1989) has argued and Meloy (2001a) presents evidence from Rorschach studies (Gacano and Meloy, 1994) to

support Kernberg's argument: Psychopathy comes under the classification of borderline personality organization (BPO), an organization of personality, neither neurotic nor psychotic, which is characterized by the borderline defenses of splitting, projective identification, omnipotence, devaluation, primitive idealization, and denial (Kernberg, 1975). In this category of BPO there are low-level character disorders and certain addictions.

2. The diagnosis is confounded by education, social class, and intelligence. In addition, it is overinclusive (Meloy, 2001, p. 196). For instance, only about one third of the inmates in maximum-security prisons are actually psychopaths, although approximately three quarters of the inmates will qualify for a diagnosis of antisocial personality disorder (Hare, Hart, and Harper, 1971, cited in Meloy, 2001b).

Furthermore, one of the prerequisites for APD is childhood conduct disorder. As Winnicott's (1956) way of understanding the "antisocial tendency," today called conduct disorder, indicates, "antisocial" behavior in children can be a cry for help, which, given understanding by parents, has a potentially positive prognosis.

3. Meloy (1988, 2001a) cites specific evidence of a "psychobiological" foundation to psychopathy. This includes hyporeactivity and underarousal, among other elements.

4. Noting that the schizophrenic fails to preserve the intact outer form and function of a complete personality, whereas the psychopath does, Cleckley (1941) presented an interesting analogy, comparing speech disorders to personality disorders (pp. 378–384). He observed a continuum in speech disorders, from disarthria, which is marked by peripheral damage in which the person has access to thoughts but cannot speak adequately, to semantic aphasia, in which a person has central damage of language function, but can disguise this damage by putting words together in intact superficial ways. Using the same peripheral-to-central-damage concept, Cleckley compared speech disorders to psychical ones. With respect to disorders of the psyche, at one end of the pole are florid delusional states that manifest glaring psychopathology, but may hide some real capabilities. At the other end of the pole is psychopathy, in which the outer picture of sanity hides an inner deficit. (Cleckley believed that in between are "masked schizophrenia" and "ambulatory schizophrenia.") Thus, in his book, disarthria is to semantic aphasia as psychotic delirium is to psychopathy. The analogy portrays Cleckley's view that psychopathy involves some kind of semantic disorder, that it is "central" in some important way, and that it is hidden. He called this "semantic dementia."

REFERENCES

Allport, G. W. (1954), *The Nature of Prejudice.* Cambridge, MA: Addison-Wesley.

Alvarado, C. S. (2002), Dissociation in Britain during the late nineteenth century: The Society for Psychical Research, 1892–1890. *J. Trauma & Dissoc.,* 3(2):9–34.

American Psychiatric Association (1980), *Diagnostic and Statistical Manual of Mental Disorders, Third Edition (DSM-III).* Washington, DC: American Psychiatric Association.

_______ (1994), *Diagnostic and Statistical Manual of Mental Disorders, Fourth Edition.* Washington, DC: American Psychiatric Association.

Armstrong-Perlman, E. M. (2000), The allure of the bad object. In: *Fairbairn and the Origin of Object Relations,* ed. J. S. Grotstein & D. B. Rinsley. New York: Other Press, pp. 222–233.

Aron, L. & Harris, A. (1993), Sándor Ferenczi: Discovery and rediscovery. In: *The Legacy of Sándor Ferenczi,* ed. L. Aron & A. Harris. Hillsdale, NJ: The Analytic Press, pp. 1–35.

Baker, S. (1997), Dancing the dance with dissociatives: Some thoughts on countertransference, projective identification and enactments in the treatment of dissociative disorders. *Dissociation,* 10:214–222.

Bakhtin, M. (1981), *The Dialogic Imagination.* Austin: University of Texas Press.

_______ (1984), *Problems of Dostoyevsky's Poetics.* Minneapolis: University of Minnesota Press.

_______ (1986), *Speech Genres and Other Late Essays.* Austin: University of Texas Press.

Bandura, A. & Huston, A. C. (1961), Identification as a process of incidental learning. *J. Abnorm. & Soc. Psychol.,* 63:311–318.

_______ Ross, D. & Ross, S. A. (1963), A comparative test of the status envy, social power, and secondary reinforcement theories of identificatory learning. *J. Abnorm. & Soc. Psychol.,* 67:527–534.

Bargh, J. A. & Chartrand, T. L. (1999), The unbearable automaticity of being. *Amer. Psychol.,* 54:462–479.

Barrett, D. L. (1994), The dream character as a prototype for the multiple personality "alter." In: *Dissociation,* ed. S. J. Lynn & J. Rhue. Washington, DC: American Psychological Association Press, pp. 123–135.

_______ (1996), Dreams in multiple personality disorder. In: *Trauma and Dreams,* ed. D. Barrett. Cambridge, MA: Harvard University Press, pp. 68–81.

Beahrs, J. O. (1982), *Unity and Multiplicity.* New York: Brunner/Mazel.

Belenky, M., Clinchy, B., Goldberger, N. & Tarule, J. (1986), *Women's Ways of Knowing.* New York: Basic Books.

Benjamin, J. (1990), Recognition and destruction: An outline of intersubjectivity. In: *Relational Psychoanalysis: The Emergence of a Tradition,* ed. S. A. Mitchell & L. Aron. Hillsdale, NJ: The Analytic Press, 1999, pp. 181–210.

Bennett, D., Pollock, P. & Ryle, A. (2005), The states description procedure: The use of guided self-reflection in the case formulation of patients with borderline personality disorder. *Clin. Psychol. Psychother.*, 12: 58–66.

Betcher W. & Pollack, W. S. (1993), *In a Time of Fallen Heroes.* New York: Guilford Press.

Bion, W. (1957), Differentiation of the psychotic from the non-psychotic personalities. In: *Melanie Klein Today: Developments in Theory and Practice, Vol. 1: Mainly Theory,* ed. E. B. Spillius. New York: Routledge, pp. 61–78.

_______ (1959), Attacks on linking: Differentiation of the psychotic from the non-psychotic personalities. In: *Melanie Klein Today: Developments in Theory and Practice, Vol. 1: Mainly Theory,* ed. E. B. Spillius. New York: Routledge, pp. 87–101.

Bliss, E. L. (1986), *Multiple Personality, Allied Disorders, and Hypnosis.* New York: Oxford University Press.

Blizard, R. A. (1997a), The origins of dissociative identity disorder from an object relations theory and attachment theory perspective. *Dissociation,* 10: 223–229.

_______ (1997b), Therapeutic alliance with abuser alters in dissociative identity disorder: The paradox of attachment to the abuser. *Dissociation,* 10:246–254.

_______ (2001), Masochistic and sadistic ego states: Dissociative solutions to the dilemma of attachment to an abusive caretaker. *J. Trauma & Dissoc.,* 2(4):37–58.

_______ (2003), Disorganized attachment, development of dissociated self-states, and a relational approach to treatment. *J. Trauma & Dissoc.,* 4(3):27–50.

Bohan, J. S. (1993), Regarding gender: Essentialism, constructionism, and feminist psychology. *Psychol. Women Quart.,* 17:5–21.

Bollas, C. (1992), *Being a Character.* New York: Hill & Wang.

_______ (1995), *Cracking Up.* New York: Hill & Wang.

Boney-McCoy, S. & Finkelhor, D. (1995), Psychosocial sequelae of violent victimization in a national youth sample. *J. Consult. & Clin. Psychol.,* 63: 726–736.

_______ & _______ (1996), Is your victimization related to trauma symptoms and depression after controlling for prior symptoms and family relationships? A longitudinal, prospective study. *J. Consult. & Clin. Psychol.,* 64: 1406–1416.

Bonomi, C. (2002), Identification with the aggressor: An interactive tactic or an intrapsychic tomb? Commentary on paper by Jay Frankel. *Psychoanal. Dial.,* 12:151–158.

Bowers, K. (1994), Dissociated control, imagination, and the phenomenology of dissociation. In: *Dissociation, Culture, Mind and Body,* ed. D. Spiegel. Washington DC: American Psychiatric Press.

Bowlby, J. (1944), Forty-four juvenile thieves: Their characters and home-life. In: *The Mark of Cain: Psychoanalytic Insight and the Psychopath,* ed. J. R. Meloy. Hillsdale, NJ: The Analytic Press, pp. 35–41.

_______ (1969), *Attachment and Loss, Vol. 1: Attachment.* New York: Basic Books.

_______ (1973), *Attachment and Loss, Vol. 2: Separation: Anxiety and Anger.* New York: Basic Books.

_______ (1980), *Attachment and Loss, Vol. 3: Loss: Sadness and Depression.* New York: Basic Books.

_______ (1984), Psychoanalysis as a natural science. *Psychoanal. Psychol.,* 1:7–22.

_______ (1988), *A Secure Base: Clinical Applications of Attachment Theory.* London: Routledge.

Brannon, R. (1976), The male sex role: Our culture's blueprint for manhood: What it's done for us lately. In: *The Forty-Nine Percent Majority: The Male Sex Role,* ed. D. David & R. Brannon. Reading, MA: Addison-Wesley, pp. 1–48.

Braude, S. E. (1995), *First Person Plural: Multiple Personality and the Philosophy of Mind.* Lanham, MD: Rowman & Littlefield.

Breedlove, M. (1994), Sexual differentiation of the human nervous system. *Annu. Rev. Psychol.,* 45:389–418.

Breger, L. (2000), *Freud: Darkness in the Midst of Vision.* New York: Wiley.

Brenner, I. (2001), *Dissociation of Trauma: Theory, Phenomenology, and Technique.* Madison, CT: International Universities Press.

Bretherton, I. (1992), The origins of attachment theory: John Bowlby and Mary Ainsworth. In: *Attachment Theory: Social, Developmental and Clinical Perspectives,* ed. S. Goldberg, R. Muir & J. Kerr. Hillsdale, NJ: The Analytic Press, 1995, pp. 45–84.

Breuer, J. & Freud, S. (1893a), On the psychical mechanism of hysterical phenomena: Preliminary communication. *Standard Edition,* 2:1–17. London: Hogarth Press, 1955.

_______ & _______ (1893b), On the psychical mechanism of hysterical phenomena. In: *Freud: Early Psychoanalytic Writings,* ed. P. Rieff. New York: Crowell-Collier, 1963, pp. 35–50.

_______ & _______ (1893–1895), Studies on hysteria. *Standard Edition,* 2. London: Hogarth Press, 1955.

Bromberg, P. (1983), The mirror and the mask: On narcissism and psychoanalytical growth. *Contemp. Psychoanal.,* 19:359–387.

_______ (1991), On knowing one's patient from the inside out: The aesthetics of unconscious communication. In: *Standing in the Spaces: Essays on Clinical Process, Trauma, and Dissociation.* Hillsdale, NJ: The Analytic Press, 1998, pp. 127–146.

_______ (1993), Shadow and substance: A relational perspective on clinical process. In: *Standing in the Spaces: Essays on Clinical Process, Trauma, and Dissociation.* Hillsdale, NJ: The Analytic Press, 1998, pp. 165–187.

_______ (1994), "Speak! That I may see you": Some reflections on dissociation, reality and psychoanalytic listening. In: *Standing in the Spaces: Essays on Clinical Process, Trauma, and Dissociation.* Hillsdale, NJ: The Analytic Press, 1998, pp. 241–266.

_______ (1995), Psychoanalysis, dissociation, and personality organization. In: *Standing in the Spaces: Essays on Clinical Process, Trauma, and Dissociation.* Hillsdale, NJ: The Analytic Press, 1998, pp. 189–204.

_______ (1996a), Hysteria, dissociation, and cure: Emmy von N revisited. In: *Standing in the Spaces: Essays on Clinical Process, Trauma, and Dissociation.* Hillsdale, NJ: The Analytic Press, 1998, pp. 223–237.

_______ (1996b), Standing in the spaces: The multiplicity of self and the psychoanalytic relationship. In: *Standing in the Spaces: Essays on Clinical Process, Trauma, and Dissociation.* Hillsdale, NJ: The Analytic Press, 1998, pp. 267–290.

_______ (1998), Staying the same while changing: Reflections on clinical judgment. In: *Standing in the Spaces: Essays on Clinical Process, Trauma, and Dissociation.* Hillsdale, NJ: The Analytic Press, pp. 291–308.

_______ (2000), Potholes on the royal road, or is it an abyss? *Contemp. Psychoanal.,* 36:5–28.

_______ (2001a), The gorilla did it: Some thoughts on dissociation, the real and the really real. *Psychoanal Dial.,* 11:385–404.

_______ (2001b), Treating patients with symptoms—and symptoms with patience: Reflections on shame, dissociation, and eating disorders. *Psychoanal. Dial.,* 11:891–912.

_______ (2003a), One need not be a house to be haunted: On enactment, dissociation, and the dread of "not-me." A case study. *Psychoanal. Dial.,* 13:689–710.

_______ (2003b), Something wicked this way comes. Trauma, dissociation, and conflict: The space where psychoanalysis, cognitive science, and neuroscience overlap. *Psychoanal. Psychol.,* 20:558–574.

_______ (2003c), Presenting statement: Dissociation and personality disorders: Configurations of self-states "on-alert" for trauma. Presented at 20th International Fall Conference of the International Society for the Study of Dissociation, Chicago, November 3.

Brooks, G. & Silverstein, L. (1995), Understanding the dark side of masculinity: An interactive systems model. In: *A New Psychology of Men,* ed. R. F. Levant & W. S. Pollack. New York: Basic Books, pp. 280–336.

Brothers, D. (1995), *Falling Backwards: An Exploration of Trust and Self Experience.* New York: Norton.

Broverman, I. K., Broverman, D. M., Clarkson, F. E., Rosenkrantz, P. S. & Vogel, S. R. (1970), Sex-role stereotypes and clinical judgments of mental health. *J. Consult. & Clin. Psychol.,* 34:1–7.

Brown, L. S. (1991), Not outside the range: One feminist perspective on psychic trauma. *Amer. Imago,* 48:119–133.

Butler, J. (1993), *Bodies That Matter: On the Discursive Limits of "Sex."* New York: Routledge.

Butler, L. D. (2004), The dissociations of everyday life. *J. Trauma & Dissoc.,* 5(2):1–12.

_______ & Palesh, O. (2004), Spellbound: Dissociation in the movies. *J. Trauma & Dissoc.,* 5(2):61–88.

Cameron, N. & Rychlak, J. F. (1985), *Personality Development and Psychopathology: A Dynamic Approach.* Boston: Houghton Mifflin.

Cardena, E. (2001), The domain of dissociation: A cross-cultural perspective. Presented at 18th International Fall Conference of the International Society for the Study of Dissociation, New Orleans, LA, December 3.

_______ & Nijenhuis, E. R. S. (2000), Embodied sorrow: A special issue on somatoform dissociation, *J. Trauma & Dissoc.,* 1(4):1–7.

Carlson, E. A. (1998), A prospective longitudinal study of attachment disorganization/disorientation. *Child Dev.,* 69:1107–1128.

Celani, D. (2001), Working with Fairbairn's ego structures. *Contemp. Psychoanal.,* 37:391–416.

Chefetz, R.A. (1997), Abreaction: Baby or bathwater? *Dissociation,* 10:203–213.

_______ & Bromberg, P. M. (2004), Talking with "me" and "not-me": A dialogue. *Contemp. Psychoanal.,* 40:409–464.

Chodorow, N. (1971), "Being and doing": A cross cultural examination of the socialization of males and females. In: *Women in Sexist Society: Studies in Power and Powerlessness,* ed. V. Gornick & B. K. Moran. New York: Basic Books, pp. 173–197.

_______ (1974), Family structure and feminine personality. In: *Woman, Culture and Society,* ed. M. Z. Rosaldo & L. Lamphere. Stanford, CA: Stanford University Press, pp. 43–66.

_______ (1978), *The Reproduction of Mothering.* Berkeley: University of California Press.

Chu, J. A. (1998), *Rebuilding Shattered Lives.* New York: Wiley.

_______ (2001), A decline in the abuse of children? *J. Trauma & Dissoc.,* 2(2):1–4.

Cleckley, H. (1941), *The Mask of Sanity.* Augusta, GA: Emily Cleckley, 1988.

Clopton, N. & Sorell, G. (1993), Gender differences in moral reasoning: Stable or situational? *Psychol. Women Quart.,* 17:85–101.

Coates, S., Friedman, R. & Wolfe, S. (1991), The etiology of boyhood gender identity disorder: A model for integration temperament, development, and psychodynamics. *Psychoanal. Dial.,* 1:481–523.

_______ & Moore, M. (1995), Boyhood gender identity: The interface of constitution and early experience. *Psychoanal. Inq.,* 15:6–38.

_______ & _______ (1997), The complexity of early trauma: Representation and transformation. *Psychoanal. Inq.,* 17:286–311.

Colapinto, J. (2000), *As Nature Made Him: The Boy Who Was Raised as a Girl.* New York: HarperCollins.

Copjec, J. (1994), *Read My Desire.* Cambridge, MA. MIT Press.

Courtois, C. (1999), The scientifically based treatment of memories of trauma. Presented at 16th Annual Conference of the International Society for the Study of Dissociation, Miami, FL, November.

Dalenberg, C. J. (2004), What is normal about normal and pathological dissociation? Presented at 21st Annual Conference of the International Society for the Study of Dissociation. New Orleans, LA, November 19.

Danieli, Y. (1985), The treatment and prevention of long-term effects and intergenerational transmission of victimization: A lesson from Holocaust survivors and their children. In: *The Study and Treatment of Post-traumatic Stress Disorder,* ed. C. R. Figley. New York: Brunner/Mazel, pp. 295–313.

Davies, J. M. (1996), Linking the "pre-analytic" with the postclassical: Integration, dissociation, and the multiplicity of unconscious process. *Contemp. Psychoanal.,* 32:553–576.

_______ (1997), Dissociation and therapeutic enactment. *Gender & Psychoanal.,* 2:241–257.

_______ (1998a), Repression and dissociation—Freud and Janet: Fairbairn's new model of unconscious process. In: *Fairbairn, Then and Now,* ed. N. J. Skolnick & D. E. Scharff. Hillsdale NJ: The Analytic Press, pp. 53–70.

_______ (1998b), The multiple aspects of multiplicity: Symposium on clinical choices. *Psychoanal. Dial.,* 8:195–206.

_______ (1999), Getting cold feet, defining "safe-enough" borders: Dissociation, multiplicity, and integration in the analysts experience. *Psychoanal. Quart.,* 68:184–208.

_______ (2004), Whose bad objects are we anyway? Repetition and our elusive love affair with evil. *Psychoanal. Dial.,* 14:711–731.

_______ & Frawley, M. G. (1991), Dissociative processes and transference–countertransference paradigms in the psychoanalytically oriented treatment of adult survivors of childhood sexual abuse. In: *Relational Psychoanalysis: The Emergence of a Tradition,* ed. S. A. Mitchell & L. Aron. Hillsdale, NJ: The Analytic Press, 1999, pp. 269–299.

_______ & _______ (1994), *Treating the Adult Survivor of Childhood Sexual Abuse.* New York: Basic Books.

de Beauvoir, S. (1953), *The Second Sex.* New York: Knopf.

de Zuletta, F. (1993), *The Traumatic Roots of Destructiveness: From Pain to Violence.* Northvale, NJ: Aronson.

Dell, P. (1998), Axis II pathology in outpatients with dissociative identity disorder. *J. Nerv. & Ment. Dis.,* 186:352–356.

_______ (2001), Why the diagnostic criteria for dissociative identity disorder should be changed. *J. Trauma & Dissoc.*, 2(1):7–37.

_______ (accepted for publication), Subjective/phenomenological model of dissociation. In: *Dissociation and the Dissociative Disorders: DSM-V and Beyond,* ed. P. F. Dell & J. A. O'Neil.

Dennett, D. C. (1991), *Consciousness Explained.* Boston: Little Brown.

Deutch, H. (1942), Some forms of emotional disturbance and their relationships to schizophrenia. *Psychoanal. Quart.,* 11:301–321.

Devereux, G. (1953), Why Oedipus killed Laius—A note on the complementary Oedipus complex in Greek drama. *Internat. J. Psycho-Anal.,* 32:132.

Diamond, M. & Sigmundson, H. K. (1997), Sex reassignment at birth: A long-term review and clinical implications. *Arch. Pediatr. & Adolesc. Med.,* 151:298–304.

Dupont, J., ed. (1988), *The Clinical Diary of Sándor Ferenczi.* Cambridge, MA: Harvard University Press.

Dutton, D. G. & Painter S. (1981), Traumatic bonding: The development of emotional attachments in battered women and other relationships of intermittent abuse. *Victimology,* 6:139–155.

_______ & Gollant, S. K. (1995), *The Batterer: A Psychological Profile.* New York: Basic Books.

Dyess, C. & Dean, T. (2000), Gender: The impossibility of meaning. *Psychoanal. Dial.,* 10:735–756.

Eagly, A. (2000), On comparing women and men. In: *The Gender and Psychology Reader,* ed. B. Clinchy & J. Norem. New York: New York University Press, pp. 159–166.

Ehling, T., Nijenhuis, E. R. S. & Krikke, A. P. (2003), Volume of discrete brain structures in florid and recovered DID, DDNOS and healthy controls. Presented at 20th Annual Conference of the International Society for the Study of Dissociation, Chicago, November 4.

Eisler, R. (1987), *The Chalice and the Blade.* New York: HarperCollins.

Ellenberger, H. (1970), *The Discovery of the Unconscious.* New York: Basic Books.

Emch, M. (1944), On the "need to know" as related to identification and acting out. *Internat. J. Psycho-Anal.,* 25:13–19.

Epstein, S. (1991), The self-concept, the traumatic neurosis, and the structure of personality. In: *Perspectives on Personality, Vol. 3, Part A,* ed. D. Ozer, J. M. Healy, Jr. & A. J. Stewart. London: Jessica Kingsley, pp. 63–98.

Erdelyi, M. H. (1985), *Psychoanalysis: Freud's Cognitive Psychology.* New York: Freeman.

_______ (1990), Repression, reconstruction, and defense: History and integration of the psychoanalytic and experimental frameworks. In: *Repression and Dissociation: Implications for Personality Theory, Psychopathology, and Health,* ed. J. L. Singer. Chicago: University of Chicago Press, pp. 1–32.

_______ (1992), Psychodynamics and the unconscious. *Amer. Psychol.,* 47: 784–787.

_______ (1994), Dissociation, defense, and the unconscious. In: *Dissociation, Culture, Mind and Body,* ed. D. Spiegel. Washington, DC: American Psychiatric Press, pp. 3–20.

_______ (2001), Defense processes can be conscious or unconscious. *Amer. Psychol.,* 56:761–762.

Fairbairn, W. R. D. (1931), Features in the analysis of a patient with a physical genital abnormality. In: *Psychoanalytic Studies of the Personality.* Boston: Routledge & Kegan Paul, pp. 197–222.

_______ (1935), Child assault. In: *From Instinct to Self: Selected Papers of W. R. D. Fairbairn, Vol. 2,* ed. E. F. Birtles & D. E. Scharff. Northvale, NJ: Aronson, 1994, pp. 165–183.

_______ (1940), Schizoid factors in the personality. In: *Psychoanalytic Studies of the Personality*. Boston: Routledge & Kegan Paul, 1952, pp. 3–27.

_______ (1943), The repression and the return of bad objects. In: *Psychoanalytic Studies of the Personality*. Boston: Routledge & Kegan Paul, 1952, pp. 59–81.

_______ (1944), Endopsychic structure considered in terms of object relationships. In: *Psychoanalytic Studies of the Personality*. Boston: Routledge & Kegan Paul, 1952, pp. 82–136.

_______ (1951), A synopsis of the author's views regarding the structure of the personality. In: *Psychoanalytic Studies of the Personality*. Boston: Routledge & Kegan Paul, 1952, pp. 162–179.

_______ (1958), On the nature and aims of psycho-analytical treatment. In: *From Instinct to Self: Selected Papers of W. R. D. Fairbairn, Vol. 1,* ed. E. F. Birtles & D. E. Scharff. Northvale, NJ: Aronson, 1994, pp. 74–92.

_______ (1963), An object-relations theory of the personality. In: *From Instinct to Self: Selected Papers of W. R. D. Fairbairn, Vol. 1,* ed. E. F. Birtles & D. E. Scharff. Northvale, NJ: Aronson, 1994, pp. 155–156.

Ferenczi, S. (1929), The principle of relaxation and neocatharsis. In: *Final Contributions to the Problems and Methods of Psycho-Analysis,* ed. M. Balint (trans. E. Mosbacher). London: Karnac Books, 1980, pp. 108–125.

_______ (1930), Notes and fragments: Thoughts on "pleasure in passivity." In: *Final Contributions to the Problems and Methods of Psycho-Analysis,* ed. M. Balint (trans. E. Mosbacher). London: Karnac Books, 1980, pp. 224–227.

_______ (1931), Notes and fragments: Relaxation and education. In: *Final Contributions to the Problems and Methods of Psycho-Analysis,* ed. M. Balint (trans. E. Mosbacher). London: Karnac Books, 1980, pp. 236–238.

_______ (1949), Confusion of tongues between the adult and the child. *Internat. J. Psycho-Anal.,* 30:225–231.

Finkelhor, D. (1984), *Child Sexual Abuse: New Theory and Research.* New York: Free Press.

_______ (1990), Early and long term effects of child sexual abuse: An update. *Profess. Psychol.: Res. & Pract.,* 21:325–330.

_______ & Dziuba-Leatherman, J. (1994), Victimization of children. *Amer. Psychol.,* 49:173–183.

Fischer, K. W. & Ayoub, C. (1994), Affective splitting and dissociation in normal and maltreated children: Developmental pathways for self in relationships. In: *Rochester Symposium on Developmental Psychopathology: Disorders and Dysfunctions of the Self,* ed. D. Cicchetti & S. L. Toth. Rochester, NY: Rochester University Press, pp. 149–222.

_______ & Pipp, S. L. (1984), Development of the structures of unconscious thought. In: *The Unconscious Reconsidered,* ed. K. S. Bowers & D. Meichenbaum. New York: Wiley, pp. 88–149.

Flax, J. (1996), Taking multiplicity seriously: Some consequences for psychoanalytic theorizing and practice. *Contemp. Psychoanal.,* 32:577–694.

Fonagy, P. (2001), *Attachment Theory and Psychoanalysis.* New York: Other Press.

_______ Gergely, G., Jurist, E. L. & Target, M. (2002), *Affect Regulation, Mentalization, and the Development of the Self.* New York: Other Press.

_______ Steele, M., Steele, H., Leigh, T. Kennedy, R., Mattoon, G. & Target. M. (1995), Attachment, the reflective self, and borderline states: The predictive specificity of the Adult Attachment Interview and pathological emotional development. In: *Attachment Theory: Social, Developmental and Clinical Perspectives,* ed. S. Goldberg, R. Muir & J. Kerr. Hillsdale, NJ: The Analytic Press, pp. 233–278.

Frankel, J. (2002), Exploring Ferenczi's concept of identification with the aggressor: Its role in everyday life and the therapeutic relationship. *Psychoanal. Dial.,* 12:101–140.

Frawley-O'Dea, M. G. (1997), Who's doing what to whom? Supervision and sexual abuse. *Contemp. Psychoanal.,* 33:5–18.

_______ (1999), Society, politics, psychotherapy and the search for "truth" in the memory debate. In*: Fragment by Fragment: Feminist Perspectives on Memory and Child Sexual Abuse,* ed. M. Rivera. Charlottetown, Canada: Gynergy Books, pp. 73–90.

_______ (2004a), The history and consequences of the sexual abuse scandal in the Catholic Church. *Stud. Gender & Sexuality,* 5:11–30.

_______ (2004b), Psychosocial anatomy of the Catholic sexual abuse scandal. *Stud. Gender & Sexuality,* 5:121–138.

Freud, A. (1966), *The Ego and the Mechanisms of Defense.* New York: International Universities Press.

Freud, S. (1894), The neuropsychoses of defense. *Standard Edition,* 3:45–61. London: Hogarth Press, 1962.

_______ (1896), The aetiology of hysteria. *Standard Edition,* 3:189–221. London: Hogarth Press, 1962.

_______ (1900), The interpretation of dreams. *Standard Edition,* 4 & 5. London: Hogarth Press, 1953.

_______ (1901), The psychopathology of everyday life. *Standard Edition,* 6. London: Hogarth Press, 1960.

_______ (1914), On the history of the psychoanalytic movement. *Standard Edition,* 14:7–66. London: Hogarth Press, 1957.

_______ (1915), Repression. *Standard Edition,* 14:146–158. London: Hogarth Press, 1957.

_______ (1917), Mourning and melancholia. *Standard Edition,* 14:237–258. London: Hogarth Press, 1957.

_______ (1921) Group psychology and the analysis of the ego. *Standard Edition,* 18:65–143. London: Hogarth Press, 1955.

_______ (1923), The ego and the id. *Standard Edition,* 19:1–16. London: Hogarth Press, 1961.

_______ (1925), Some psychical consequences of the anatomical distinction between the sexes. *Standard Edition,* 19:243–258. London: Hogarth Press, 1961.

_______ (1927), Fetishism. *Standard Edition,* 21:149–157. London: Hogarth Press, 1961.

_______ (1933), New introductory lectures. *Standard Edition,* 22:5–182. London: Hogarth Press, 1964.

_______ (1938), Splitting of the ego in the process of defense. *Standard Edition,* 23:275–278. London: Hogarth Press, 1964.

Freyd, J. (1996), *Betrayal Trauma: The Logic of Forgetting Childhood Abuse.* Cambridge, MA: Harvard University Press.

Fromm, E. (1980), *Greatness and Limitations of Freud's Thought.* New York: Signet.

Fuchs, D. & Thelen, M. (1988), Children's expected interpersonal consequences of communicating their affective state and reported likelihood of expression. *Child Dev.,* 59:1314–1322.

Gartner, R. (1999), *Betrayed as Boys.* New York: Basic Books.

Gay, P. (1988), *Freud: A Life for Our Time.* New York: Norton.

Gazzaniga, M. (1985), *The Social Brain.* New York: Basic Books.

Gergen, K. J. (1991), *The Saturated Self.* New York: Basic Books.

Gilligan, C. (1982), *In a Different Voice.* Cambridge, MA: Harvard University Press.

_______ & Brown, L. M. (1993), *Meeting at the Crossroads.* New York: Ballantine Books.

Gold, S. N. (2000), *Not Trauma Alone: Therapy for Child Abuse Survivors in Family and Social Context.* Philadelphia, PA: Brunner/Routledge.

_______ (2004a), *Fight Club:* A depiction of contemporary society as dissociogenic. *J. Trauma & Dissoc.,* 5(2):13–34.

_______ (2004b), On dissociation, mainstream psychology, and the nature of the human being. Presented at 21st International Fall Conference of the International Society for the Study of Dissociation, New Orleans, LA, November 2.

Goldberg, S. (1995), Introduction. In: *Attachment Theory: Social, Developmental and Clinical Perspectives,* ed. S. Goldberg, R. Muir & J. Kerr. Hillsdale, NJ: The Analytic Press, pp. 1–15.

Golynkina, K. & Ryle, A. (1999), The identification and characteristics of the partially dissociated states of patients with borderline personality disorder. *Brit. J. Med. Psychol.,* 72:429–445.

Goodwin, J. & Attias, R. (1999), The self assumes animal form. In: *Splintered Reflections: Images of the Body in Trauma,* ed. J. Goodwin & R. Attias. New York: Basic Books, pp. 257–280.

Grand, S. (1997), On the gendering of traumatic dissociation: A case of mother–son incest. *Gender & Psychoanal.,* 1:55–77.

_______ (2000), *The Reproduction of Evil: A Clinical and Cultural Perspective.* Hillsdale, NJ: The Analytic Press.

Greaves, G. B. (1980), Multiple personality disorder: 165 years after Mary Reynolds. *J. Nerv. & Ment. Dis.,* 168:577–596.

_______ (1993), A history of multiple personality disorder. In: *Clinical Perspectives on Multiple Personality Disorder,* ed. R. P. Kluft & C. G. Fine. Washington, DC: American Psychiatric Press, pp. 355–380.

Greenberg, J. R. & Mitchell, S. A. (1983), *Object Relations in Psychoanalytic Theory.* Cambridge, MA: Harvard University Press.

Greenson, R. (1968), Dis-identifying from mother: Its special importance for the boy. *Internat. J. Psycho-Anal.,* 49:370–374.

Grotstein, J. S. (1999a), The alter ego and déjà vu phenomena. In: *The Plural Self: Multiplicity in Everyday Life,* ed. J. Rowan & M. Cooper. Thousand Oaks, CA: Sage, pp. 28–50.

_______ (1999b), Projective identification reassessed: Commentary on papers by Stephen Seligman and by Robin C. Silverman and Alicia F. Lieberman. *Psychoanal. Dial.,* 9:187–203.

_______ (2000), Notes on Fairbairn's metapsychology. In: *Fairbairn and the Origin of Object Relations,* ed. J. S. Grotstein & D. B. Rinsley. New York: Other Press, pp. 112–148.

_______ & Rinsley, D. B. (2000), Editors' introduction. In: *Fairbairn and the Origin of Object Relations,* ed. J. S. Grotstein & D. B. Rinsley. New York: Other Press, pp. 3–16.

Hacker, H. M. (1981), Women as a minority group. In: *Female Psychology: The Emerging Self,* ed. S. Cox. New York: St. Martin's Press, pp. 164–178.

Halpern, D. (1997), Sex differences in intelligence: Implications for education. *Amer. Psychol.,* 52:1091–1102.

Hare, R. D. (1993), *Without Conscience: The Disturbing World of the Psychopaths Among Us.* New York: Simon & Schuster.

Hare-Mustin, R. & Marecek, J. (1990), Gender and the meaning of difference: Postmodernism and psychology. In: *Making a Difference: Psychology and the Construction of Gender,* ed. R. Hare-Mustin & J. Marecek. New Haven, CT: Yale University Press, pp. 22–64.

Harris, A. (1996), The conceptual power of multiplicity. *Contemp. Psychoanal.,* 32:537–552.

Herek, G. (1987), On heterosexual masculinity: Some psychical consequences of the social construction of gender and sexual orientation. In: *Changing Men,* ed. M. Kimmel. Newbury Park, CA: Sage, pp. 68–82.

Herman, J. (1990), Discussion. In: *Incest-Related Syndromes of Adult Psychopathology,* ed. R. Kluft. Washington, DC: American Psychiatric Press, pp. 289–294.

_______ (1992), *Trauma and Recovery.* New York: Basic Books.

_______ & Hirschman, L. (1981), *Father–Daughter Incest.* Cambridge, MA: Harvard University Press.

_______ & Van der Kolk, B. (1987), Traumatic antecedents of borderline personality disorder. In: *Psychological Trauma,* ed. B. van der Kolk. Washington, DC: American Psychiatric Press, pp. 111–126.

Hermans, H., Kempten, H. & van Loon, R. (1992), The dialogical self. *Amer. Psychol.,* 47:23–33.

Hesse, E. & Main, M. (1999), Second generation effects of unresolved trauma in non-maltreating parents: Dissociated, frightened and threatening parental behavior. *Psychoanal. Inq.,* 19:481–540.

Hilgard, E. R. (1977), *Divided Consciousness: Multiple Controls in Human Thought and Action.* New York: Wiley.

_______ (1994), Neodissociation theory. In: *Dissociation,* ed. S. J. Lynn & J. W. Rhue. New York: Guilford Press, pp. 32–51.

Holmes, J. (1995), Something there is that doesn't love a wall: John Bowlby, attachment theory, and psychoanalysis. In: *Attachment Theory: Social, Developmental and Clinical Perspectives,* ed. S. Goldberg, R. Muir & J. Kerr. Hillsdale, NJ: The Analytic Press, pp. 19–44.

Hopenwasser, K. (1998), Listening to the body: Somatic representations of dissociated memory. In: *Relational Perspectives on the Body,* ed. L. Aron & F. S. Anderson. Hillsdale, NJ: The Analytic Press, pp. 215–236.

Horney, K. (1934), The overvaluation of love: The study of a common present-day feminine type. In: *Feminine Psychology,* ed. H. Kelman. New York: Norton, 1967, pp. 182–213.

Horowitz, M. J. (1986), *Stress Response Syndromes,* 2nd ed. Northvale, NJ: Aronson.

Howell, E. F. (1975), Self-presentation in reference to sex role stereotypes as related to level of moral development. Unpublished doctoral dissertation, New York University, New York.

_______ (1981), Women: From Freud to the present. In: *Women and Mental Health,* ed. E. F. Howell & M. Bayes. New York: Basic Books, pp. 3–25.

_______ (1996), Dissociation in masochism and psychopathic sadism. *Contemp. Psychoanal.,* 32:427–453.

_______ (1997a), Desperately seeking attachment: A psychoanalytic reframing of harsh superego. *Dissociation,* 10:230–239.

_______ (1997b), Masochism: A bridge to the other side of abuse. *Dissociation,* 10:240–244.

_______ (2002), Back to the "states": Victim and abuser states in borderline personality disorder. *Psychoanal. Dial.,* 12:921–958.

_______ & Blizard, R. A. (accepted for publication), Chronic relational trauma: A new diagnostic scheme for borderline personality and the spectrum of dissociative disorders. In: *Dissociation and the Dissociative Disorders: DSM-V and Beyond,* ed. P. F. Dell & J. A. O'Neil.

Hoyenga, K. & Hoyenga, K. (1993), *Gender-Related Differences.* Needham Heights, MA: Allyn & Bacon.

Hudson, L. & Jacot, B. (1991), *The Way Men Think: Intellect, Intimacy, and the Erotic Imagination.* New Haven, CT: Yale University Press.

Jacobvitz, D. (2000), Disorganized mental processes in mothers, frightening caregiving, and disorganized and disoriented attachment behavior in infants. Presented at 17th International Fall Conference of the International Society for the Study of Dissociation, San Antonio, TX, November 12.

James, W. (1890), *The Principles of Psychology.* New York: Dover, 1950.

_______ (1902), *The Varieties of Religious Experience.* New York: Random House Modern Library, 1929.

Janet, P. (1907), *The Major Symptoms of Hysteria.* New York: Macmillan.

_______ (1914–1915), Psychoanalysis, trans. W. G. Bean. *J. Abnorm. Psychol.,* 9:1–35.

_______ (1919), *Les Medications Psychologiques* (3 vols.). Paris: Alcan.

_______ (1925), *Psychological Healing, Vol. 1.* New York: Macmillan.

Johnson, T. C. (2004), Some considerations about sexual abuse and children with sexual behavior problems. *J. Trauma & Dissoc.,* 3(4):83–106.

Jordan, J., Kaplan, A., Miller, J. B., Stiver, I. & Surry, J. (1991), *Women's Growth in Connection.* New York: Guilford Press.

Kalsched, D. E. (1996), *The Inner World of Trauma: Archetypal Defenses of the Personal Spirit.* New York: Routledge.

Kemelgor, C. & Etzowitz, H. (2001), Overcoming isolation: Women's dilemmas in American academic sciences. *Minerva,* 39:239–257.

Kernberg, O. (1975), *Borderline Conditions and Pathological Narcissism.* New York: Aronson.

_______ (1989), The narcissistic personality disorder and the differential diagnosis of antisocial behavior. In: *The Mark of Cain: Psychoanalytic Insight and the Psychopath,* ed. J. R. Meloy. Hillsdale, NJ: The Analytic Press, 2001, pp. 315–337.

Kihlstrom, J. F. (1984), Conscious, subconscious, unconscious: A cognitive perspective. In: *The Unconscious Reconsidered,* ed. K. S. Bowers & D. Meichenbaum. New York: Wiley, pp. 149–210.

_______ & Hoyt, I. P. (1990), Repression, dissociation, and hypnosis. In: *Repression and Dissociation: Implications for Personality Theory, Psychopathology, and Health,* ed. J. L. Singer. Chicago: University of Chicago Press, pp. 181–208.

Kilmartin, C. (1994), *The Masculine Self.* New York: Macmillan.

Kirmayer, L. (1994), Facing the void: Social and cultural dimensions of dissociation. In: *Dissociation: Culture, Mind and Body,* ed. D. Spiegel. Washington, DC: American Psychiatric Press, pp. 91–122.

Klein, M. (1946), Notes on some schizoid mechanisms. In: *The Writings of Melanie Klein, Vol. 3: Envy and Gratitude and Other Works, 1946–1963.* New York: Free Press, pp. 1–24.

Kluft, R. (1984), Treatment of multiple personality disorder. *Psychiat. Clin. North Amer.,* 7:9–29.

_______ (1987), First-rank symptoms as a diagnostic clue to multiple personality disorder. *Amer. J. Psychiat.,* 144:293–298.

Knapp, H. (1989), Projective identification: Whose projection–whose identity? *Psychoanal. Psychol.,* 6:47–58

Koestler, A. (1967), *The Ghost in the Machine.* Chicago: Henry Regnery.

Kohlberg, L. (1966), A cognitive-development anaysis of children's sex-role concepts and attitudes. In: *The Development of Sex Differences,* ed. E. E. Maccoby. Stanford, CA: Stanford University Press, pp. 82–173.

_______ (1971), From is to ought: How to commit the naturalistic fallacy and get away with it in the study of moral development. In: *Cognitive Development and Epistemology,* ed. T. Mischel. New York: Academic Press, pp. 151–235.

Kohut, H. (1971), *The Analysis of the Self.* New York: International Universities Press.

_______ (1984), *How Does Analysis Cure?* Chicago: University of Chicago Press.

Koss, M. P. & Burkhart, B. R. (1989), A conceptual analysis of rape victimization. *Psychol. Women Quart.,* 13:27–40.

Kozulin, A. (1986), Vygotsky in context. In: *Thought and Language,* ed. L. Vygotsky. Cambridge, MA: MIT Press, pp. xi–xvi.

Krippner, S. (1990), Cross-cultural treatment perspectives on dissociative disorders. In: *Dissociation: Clinical and Theoretical Perspectives,* ed. S. J. Lynn & J. W. Rhue. New York: Guilford Press, pp. 338–361.

Krugman, S. (1995), Male development and the transformation of shame. In: *A New Psychology of Men,* ed. R. F. Levant & W. S. Pollack. New York: Basic Books.

Krystal, H. (1995), Trauma and aging: A thirty-year follow-up. In: *Trauma: Explorations in Memory,* ed. C. Caruth. Baltimore, MD: Johns Hopkins University Press, pp. 76–99.

Kupersmid, J. (1993), Freud's rationale for abandoning the seduction theory. *Psychoanal. Psychol.,* 10:275–290.

Lancaster, B. (1999), The multiple brain and the unity of experience. In: *The Plural Self: Multiplicity in Everyday Life,* ed. J. Rowan & M. Cooper. Thousand Oaks, CA: Sage, pp. 132–150.

Langer, S. K. (1942), *Philosophy in a New Key.* Cambridge, MA: Harvard University Press.

Laplanche, J. & Pontalis, J. B. (1973), *The Language of Psycho-Analysis,* trans. D. Nicholson-Smith. New York: Norton.

Laria, A. L. & Lewis-Fernandez, R. (2001), The professional fragmentation of experience in the study of dissociation, somatization, and culture. *J. Trauma & Dissoc.,* 2(3):17–48.

Laub, D. & Auerhahn, N. C. (1989), Failed empathy—A central theme in the survivor's Holocaust experience. *Psychoanal. Psychol.,* 6:377–400.

_______ & _______ (1993), Knowing and not knowing massive psychic trauma: Forms of traumatic memory. *Internat. J. Psycho-Anal.,* 74:287–302.

Layton, L. (1998*), Who's That Girl? Who's That Boy? Clinical Practice Meets Postmodern Gender Theory.* Northvale, NJ: Aronson.

Le Doux (2002), *The Synaptic Self.* New York: Viking Penguin.

Levant, R. (1995), Toward a reconstruction of masculinity. In: *A New Psychology of Men,* ed. R. F. Levant & W. S. Pollack. New York: Basic Books.

Levine, P. A. (1997), *Waking the Tiger: Healing Trauma.* Berkeley, CA: North Atlantic Books.

Lewis, H. B. (1971), *Shame and Guilt in Neurosis.* New York: International Universities Press.

_______ (1981), *Freud and Modern Psychology, Vol. 1: The Emotional Basis of Mental Illness:* New York: Plenum Press.

_______ (1990), Shame, repression, field dependence and psychopathology. In: *Repression and Dissociation: Implications for Personality Theory, Psychopathology and Health,* ed. J. Singer. Chicago: University of Chicago Press, pp. 233–258.

Lewis, M. (1992), *Shame: The Exposed Self.* New York: Free Press.

Lewis-Fernandez, R. (1994), Culture and dissociation: A comparison of Ataque de Nervos among Puerto Ricans and possession syndrome in India. In: *Dissociation, Culture, Mind and Body,* ed. D. Spiegel. Washington, DC: American Psychiatric Press.

Lifton, R. J. & Markusen, E. (1990), *The Genocidal Mentality.* New York: Basic Books.

Liotti, G. (1992), Disorganized/disoriented attachment in the etiology of the dissociative disorders. *Dissociation,* 5:196–204.

_______ (1995), Disorganized/disoriented attachment in the psychotherapy of the dissociative disorders. In: *Attachment Theory: Social, Developmental and Clinical Perspectives,* ed. S. Goldberg, R. Moiré & J. Kerr. Hillsdale, NJ: The Analytic Press, pp. 343–363.

_______ (1999), Understanding the dissociative processes: The contribution of attachment theory. *Psychoanal. Inq.,* 19:757–783.

Lisak, D., Hopper, J. & Song, P. (1996), Factors in the cycle of violence: Gender rigidity and emotional constriction. *J. Traumatic Stress,* 4:721–743.

Lott, B. (1990), Dual natures or learned behaviors? In: *Making a Difference: Psychology and the Construction of Gender,* ed. R. Hare-Mustin & J. Marecek. New Haven, CT: Yale University Press, pp. 65–101.

Lowen, A. (1958), *The Language of the Body.* New York: Macmillan.

Lowenstein, R. J. (1990), Somatoform disorders in victims of incest and child abuse. In: *Incest-Related Syndromes of Adult Psychopathology,* ed. R. Kluft. Washington, DC: American Psychiatric Press, pp. 75–112.

_______ (1991), An office mental status examination for complex chronic dissociative symptoms and multiple personality disorder. *Psychiat. Clin. North Amer.,* 14:567–604.

Lyons-Ruth, K. (1999), Two-person unconscious: Intersubjective dialogue, enactive relational representation, and the emergence of new forms of relational organization. *Psychoanal. Inq.,* 19:576–617.

_______ (2001a), The two-person construction of defenses: Disorganized attachment strategies, unintegrated mental states and hostile/helpless relational processes. *Psychol. Psychoanal.,* 21(1):40–45.

_______ (2001b), The emergence of new experiences: Relational improvisation, recognition process, and non-linear change in psychoanalytic theory. *Psychol. Psychoanal.,* 21(4):13–17.

_______ (2003), Disorganized attachment and the relational context of dissociation. Presented at 19th Annual Meeting of the International Society for Traumatic Stress Studies, Chicago, November 1.

Macmillan, M. (1991), *Freud Evaluated: The Completed Arc.* Amsterdam & New York: North-Holland Biomedical Press.

Mahler, M., Pine, F. & Bergman, A. (1975), *The Psychological Birth of the Human Infant.* New York: Basic Books.

Main, M. (1995), Recent studies in attachment: Overview, with selected implications for clinical work. In: *Attachment Theory: Social, Developmental and Clin-*

ical Perspectives, ed. S. Goldberg, R. Moiré & J. Kerr. Hillsdale, NJ: The Analytic Press, pp. 407–474.

_______ & Morgan, H. (1996), Disorganization and disorientation in infant strange situation behavior: Phenotypic resemblance to dissociative states. In: *Handbook of Dissociation: Theoretical, Empirical and Clinical Perspectives,* ed. L. K. Michelson & W. J. Ray. New York: Plenum Press, pp. 107–138.

_______ & Solomon, J. (1986), Discovery of a new, insecure-disorganized/disoriented attachment pattern. In: *Affective Development in Infancy,* ed. T. B. Brazelton & M. Yogman. Norwood, NJ: Ablex, pp. 95–124.

Maldonado, J. R. & Spiegel, D. (1998), Trauma, dissociation, and hypnotizability. In: *Trauma, Memory, and Dissociation,* ed. J. D. Bremner & C. R. Marmar. Washington, DC: American Psychiatric Press, pp. 57–106.

Maroda, K. J. (1998), Enactment: When the patient's and analyst's pasts converge. *Psychoanal. Psychol.,* 15:517–535.

Masson, J. M. (1984), *The Assault on Truth.* New York: Signet.

Masterson, J. F. (1976), *Psychotherapy of the Borderline Adult: A Developmental Approach.* New York: Brunner/Mazel.

Meares, R. (1995), Episodic memory, trauma, and the narrative of self. *Comtemp. Psychoanal.,* 31:541–556.

Mednick, M. (1989), On the politics of psychological constructs: Stop the bandwagon, I want to get off. *Amer. Psychol.,* 44:1118–1123.

Meloy, J. R. (1988), *The Psychopathic Mind: Origins, Dynamics, and Treatment.* Northvale, NJ: Aronson.

_______ (1997), The psychology of wickedness: Psychopathy and sadism. In: *The Mark of Cain: Psychoanalytic Insight and the Psychopath,* ed. J. R. Meloy. Hillsdale, NJ: The Analytic Press, 2001, pp. 171–179.

_______ (2001a), Introduction to section I. In: *The Mark of Cain: Psychoanalytic Insight and the Psychopath,* ed. J. R. Meloy. Hillsdale, NJ: The Analytic Press, pp. 3–25.

_______ (2001b), Introduction to section II. In: *The Mark of Cain: Psychoanalytic Insight and the Psychopath,* ed. J. R. Meloy. Hillsdale, NJ: The Analytic Press, pp. 183–204.

Mill, J. S. (1869), The subjection of women. In: *Feminism: The Essential Historical Writings,* ed. M. Schneir. New York: Vintage, 1972, pp. 162–178.

Miller, J. B. (1976), *Toward a New Psychology of Women.* Boston: Beacon Press.

Mitchell, S. A. (1981), The origin and nature of the "object" in the theories of Klein and Fairbairn. In: *Fairbairn and the Origin of Object Relations,* ed. J. S. Grotstein & D. B. Rinsley. New York: Other Press, 2000, pp. 66–111.

_______ (1988), *Relational Concepts in Psychoanalysis.* Cambridge, MA: Harvard University Press.

_______ (1993), *Hope and Dread in Psychoanalysis.* New York: Basic Books.

_______ (2000), *Relationality: From Attachment to Intersubjectivity.* Hillsdale, NJ: The Analytic Press.

Morrison, T. (1992), *Playing in the Dark: Whiteness and the Literary Imagination.* Cambridge, MA: Harvard University Press.

Mullahy, P. (1967), The theories of Harry Stack Sullivan, In: *The Contributions of Harry Stack Sullivan,* ed. P. Mullahy. New York: Science House, pp. 13–59.

_______ (1970), *Psychoanalysis and Interpersonal Psychiatry: The Contributions of Harry Stack Sullivan.* New York: Science House.

Myers, C. S. (1940), *Shell Shock in France 1914–1918.* Cambridge, MA: Cambridge University Press.

Nijenhuis, E. R. S. (1999), *Somatoform Dissociation: Phenomena, Measurement, and Theoretical Issues.* Assen, The Netherlands: Van Gorcum Press.

_______ (2000), Somatoform dissociation: Major symptoms of dissociative disorders, *J. Trauma & Dissoc.,* 1(4):7–32.

_______ (2003), Looking into the brains of patients with dissociative disorders. *Internat. Soc. Study Dissoc. News,* 21(2):6–9.

_______ Spinhoven, P., Vanderlinden, J., Van Dyck, R. & Van der Hart, O. (1998a), Somatoform dissociative symptoms as related to animal defensive reactions to predatory imminence and injury. *J. Abnorm. Psychol.,* 107:63–73.

_______ _______ Van Dyck, R. & Van der Hart, O. (1998b), Degree of somatoform and psychological dissociation in dissociative disorder is correlated with reported trauma. *J. Traumatic Stress,* 11:711–730.

_______ & Van der Hart, O. (1999a), Forgetting and reexperiencing trauma. In: *Splintered Reflections: Images of the Body in Trauma,* ed. J. M. Goodwin & R. Attias. New York: Basic Books, pp. 39–65.

_______ & _______ (1999b), Somatoform dissociation: A Janetian perspective. In: *Splintered Reflections: Images of the Body in Trauma,* ed. J. M. Goodwin & R. Attias. New York: Basic Books, pp. 87–127.

_______ _______ Kruger, K. & Steele, K. (2004), Somatoform dissociation, trauma, and defense. *Austral. & New Zeal. J. Psychiat.,* 38:678–686.

_______ Van Engen, A., Kusters, I. & Van der Hart, O. (2001), Peritraumatic somatoform and psychological dissociation in relation to recall of childhood sexual abuse. *J. Trauma & Dissoc.,* 2(3):49–68.

_______ Vanderlinden, J. & Spinhoven, P. (1998c), Animal defensive reactions as a model for trauma-induced dissociative reaction. *J. Traumatic Stress,* 11:243–260.

Norretranders, T. (1998), *The User Illusion: Cutting Consciousness Down to Size.* New York: Viking.

Ogawa, J. R., Sroufe, L. A., Weinfeld, N. S., Carlson, E. A. & Egeland, B. (1997), Development and the fragmented self: Longitudinal study of dissociative symptomatology in a nonclinical sample. *Dev. & Psychopathol.,* 9:855–879.

Ogden, T. H. (1983), The concept of internal object relations. In: *Fairbairn and the Origin of Object Relations,* ed. J. S. Grotstein & D. B. Rinsley. New York: Other Press, 2000, pp. 88–111.

_______ (1986), *The Matrix of the Mind: Object Relations in the Psychoanalytic Dialogue.* Northvale, NJ: Aronson.

Padel, J. (2000), "Narcissism" in Fairbairn's theory of personality structure. In: *Fairbairn and the Origin of Object Relations,* ed. J. S. Grotstein & D. B. Rinsley. New York: Other Press, pp. 289–301.

Perry, B. D. (1999), The memory of states: How the brain stores and retrieves traumatic experience. In: *Splintered Reflections: Images of the Body in Treatment*, ed. J. Goodwin & R. Attias. New York: Basic Books, pp. 9–38.

_______ (2000), Neurodevelopment and dissociation: Trauma and adaptive responses to fear. Presented at 17th International Fall Conference of the International Society for the Study of Dissociation, San Antonio, TX, November 14.

Perry, H. S. (1962), Introduction. In: *Schizophrenia as a Human Process,* ed. H. S. Sullivan. New York: Norton, pp. xi–xxxi.

Pines, M. (1989), On history and psychoanalysis. *Psychoanal. Psychol.,* 6:121–136.

Pinker, S. (1994), *The Language Instinct.* New York: HarperCollins.

Pizer, S. (1998), *Building Bridges: Negotiating Paradox in Psychoanalysis.* Hillsdale, NJ: The Analytic Press.

Pleck, J. (1995), The gender role strain paradigm: An update. In: *A New Psychology of Men,* ed. R. F. Levant & W. S. Pollack. New York: Basic Books, pp. 11–32.

Pollack, W. S. (1995), No man is an island: A new psychoanalytic psychology of men. In: *A New Psychology of Men,* ed. R. F. Levant & W. S. Pollack. New York: Basic Books, pp. 33–67.

_______ (1998), *Real Boys.* New York: Random House.

Pollock, P. H. (2001), *Cognitive Analytic Therapy for Adult Survivors of Abuse.* New York: Wiley.

Profitt, N. (2000*), Women Survivors, Psychological Trauma, and the Politics of Resistance.* Binghamton, NY: Haworth Press.

Putnam, F. W. (1989), *Diagnosis and Treatment of Multiple Personality Disorder.* New York: Guilford Press.

_______ (1992), Discussion: Are alter personalities fragments or figments? *Psychoanal. Inq.,* 12:95–111.

_______ (1997), *Dissociation in Children and Adolescents.* New York: Guilford Press.

Rachman, A. W. (1993), Ferenczi and sexuality. In: *The Legacy of Sándor Ferenczi,* ed. L. Aron & A. Harris. Hillsdale, NJ: The Analytic Press, pp. 81–100.

_______ (1997), *Sándor Ferenczi: The Psychotherapist of Tenderness and Passion.* Northvale, NJ: Aronson.

Racker, H. (1968), *Transference and Countertransference.* New York: International Universities Press.

Rappoport, L., Baumgardner, S. & Boone, G. (1999), Postmodern culture and the plural self. In: *The Plural Self: Multiplicity in Everyday Life,* ed. J. Rowan & M. Cooper. Thousand Oaks, CA: Sage, pp. 93–106.

Rhodes, G. F. (2003), Culture-bound syndromes. *Internat. Soc. Study Dissoc. News,* 21(3):3–6.

Rice, M. E. (1997), Violent offender research and implications for the criminal justice system. *Amer. Psychol.,* 52:414–423.

Rieff, P. (1963), Introduction. In: *Freud: Early Psychoanalytic Writings,* ed. P. Rieff. New York: Collier Books, pp. 7–10.

Rivera, M. (1989), Linking the psychological and the social: Feminism, poststructuralism and multiple personality. *Dissociation,* 2:24–31.

_______ (1996), *More Alike Than Different: Treating Severely Dissociative Trauma Survivors.* Toronto: University of Toronto Press.

Robbins, M. (2000), A Fairbairnian object relations perspective on self-psychology. In: *Fairbairn and the Origin of Object Relations,* ed. J.S. Grotstein & D.B. Rinsley. New York: Other Press, pp. 302–318.

Romano, E. & de Luca, R. V. (1997), Exploring the relationship between childhood sexual abuse and adult sexual perpetration. *J. Fam. Violence,* 12(1): 85–98.

Rosenfeld, H. (1971), A psychoanalytic approach to the theory of the life and death instincts: An investigation into the aggressive aspects of narcissism. *Internat. J. Psycho-Anal.,* 52:169–178.

Ross, C. (1989), *Multiple Personality Disorder.* New York: Wiley.

_______ (1999), Subpersonalities and multiple personalities: A dissociative continuum? In: *The Plural Self: Multiplicity in Everyday Life,* ed. J. Rowan & M. Cooper. Thousand Oaks, CA: Sage, pp. 183–197.

Ross, J. (1982), Oedipus revisited–Laius and the "Laius complex." *The Psychoanalytic Study of the Child,* 37:169–174. New Haven, CT: Yale University Press.

Rule, A. (1980), *The Stranger Beside Me.* New York: Signet

Russell, D. (1986), *The Secret Trauma: Incest in the Lives of Girls and Women.* New York: Basic Books.

Ryan, M. K., David, B. & Reynolds, K. J. (2004), "Who cares": The effect of gender and context on the self and moral reasoning. *Psychol. Women Quart.,* 28:246–255.

Ryle, A. (1994), Projective identification: A particular form of reciprocal role procedure. *Brit. J. Med. Psychol.,* 76:107–114.

_______ (1997a), The structure and development of borderline personality disorder: A proposed model. *Brit. J. Psychiat.,* 170:82–87.

_______ (1997b), *Cognitive Analytic Therapy and Borderline Personality Disorder: The Model and the Method.* New York: Wiley.

_______ (2003), Something more than the "something more than interpretation" is needed: A comment on the paper by the Process of Change Study Group. *Internat. J. Psycho-Anal.,* 84(pt. 1):109–118.

_______ & Kerr, I. A. (2002), *Introducing Cognitive Analytic Therapy: Principles and Practice.* New York: Wiley.

Sagan, E. (1988), *Freud, Women and Morality: The Psychology of Good and Evil.* New York: Basic Books.

Salter, A. (2003), *Predators: Pedophiles, Rapists and Other Sex Offenders.* New York: Basic Books.

Salyard, A. (1988), Freud as Pegasus yoked to the plough. *Psychoanal. Psychol.,* 5:403–429.

Sander, L. (2002), Thinking differently: Principles of process in living systems and the specificity of being known. *Psychoanal. Dial.,* 12:11–42.

Sandler, J. (1976), Countertransference and role-responsiveness. *Internat. Rev. Psycho-Anal.,* 3:43–47.

Sands, S. (1997), Self psychology and projective identification: Whither shall they meet? A reply to the editors. *Psychoanal. Dial.,* 7:651–668.

Scaer, R. C. (2001), *The Body Bears the Burden: Trauma, Dissociation, and Disease.* Binghamton, NY: Haworth Medical Press.

Schafer, R. (1974), Problems in Freud's psychology of women. *J. Amer. Psychoanal. Assn.,* 22:459–485.

Scharff, D. E. & Skolnick, N. J. (1998), Introduction. In: *Fairbairn, Then and Now,* ed. N. J. Skolnick & D. E. Scharff. Hillsdale NJ: The Analytic Press, pp. ix–xxviii.

Schore, A. (1997), *Affect Regulation and the Origin of the Self.* Mahwah, NJ: Lawrence Erlbaum Associates.

_______ (2003), *Affect Regulation and Disorders of the Self.* New York: Norton.

Schwartz, H. L. (1994), From dissociation to negotiation: A relational psychoanalytic perspective on multiple personality disorder. *Psychoanal. Psychol.,* 11:189–231.

_______ (2000), *Dialogues with Forgotten Voices: Relational Perspectives on Child Abuse Trauma and Treatment of Dissociative Disorders.* New York: Basic Books.

Seligman, M. E. P. (1975), *Helplessness: On Depression, Development, and Death.* New York: Free Press.

Seligman, S. (1999), Integrating Kleinian theory and intersubjective research: Observing projective identification. *Psychoanal. Dial.,* 9:129–159.

Shengold, L. (1989), *Soul Murder.* New Haven, CT: Yale University Press.

Shotter, J. (1999), Life inside dialogically structured mentalities: Bakhtin's and Volshinov's account of our mental activities as out in the world between us. In: *The Plural Self: Multiplicity in Everyday Life,* ed. J. Rowan & M. Cooper. Thousand Oaks, CA: Sage, pp. 71–92.

Shusta, S. (1999), Successful treatment of refractory obsessive-compulsive disorder. *Amer. J. Psychother.,* 53:372–391.

Shusta-Hochberg, S. R. (2003), Impact of the World Trade Center disaster on a Manhattan psychotherapy practice. *J. Trauma Pract.,* 2(1):1–16.

Siegel, D. (1999), *The Developing Mind: Toward a Neurobiology of Interpersonal Experience.* New York: Guilford Press.

Silverman, R. C. & Lieberman, A. F. (1999), Negative maternal attributions, projective identification, and the intergenerational transmission of violent relational patterns. *Psychoanal. Dial.,* 9:161–186.

Slavin, M. O. (1996), Is one self enough? Multiplicity in self-organization and the capacity to negotiate relational conflict. *Contemp. Psychoanal.,* 32: 615–646.

_______ & Kriegman, D. (1992), *The Adaptive Design of the Human Psyche: Psychoanalysis, Evolutionary Biology, and the Therapeutic Process.* New York: Guilford Press.

Somer, E. (2003), On cross-culture assessment and study of dissociation. *Internat. Soc. Study Dissoc. News,* 21(2):3–12.

_______ (2004), Trance possession disorder in Judaism: Sixteenth-century dybbuks in the Near East. *J. Trauma & Dissoc.,* 5(2):131–146.

Spiegel, D. (1986), Dissociation, double binds, and posttraumatic stress in multiple personality disorder. In: *Treatment of Multiple Personality Disorder,* ed. B. G. Braun. Washington, DC: American Psychiatric Press, pp. 61–78.

_______ (1990a), Trauma, dissociation, and hypnosis. In: *Incest-Related Syndromes of Adult Psychopathology,* ed. R. Kluft. Washington, DC: American Psychiatric Press, pp. 247–262.

_______ (1990b), Hypnosis, dissociation, and trauma: Hidden and overt observers. In: *Repression and Dissociation: Implications for Personality Theory, Psychopathology, and Health,* ed. J. L. Singer. Chicago: University of Chicago Press, pp. 121–142.

_______ (1994), Introduction. In: *Dissociation, Culture, Mind and Body,* ed. D. Spiegel. Washington, DC: American Psychiatric Press, pp. ix–xv.

_______ & Cardena, E. (1990), Dissociative mechanisms in posttraumatic stress disorder. In: *Posttraumatic Stress Disorder,* ed. M. Wolf & A. Mosnaim. Washington, DC: American Psychiatric Press, pp. 22–35.

Spillius, E. B. (1988), Part two: Projective identification. Introduction. In: *The Writings of Melanie Klein, Vol. 3: Envy and Gratitude and Other Works 1946–1963.* New York: Free Press, pp. 81–86.

Steele, C. S., Van der Hart, O. & Nijenhuis, E. R. S. (2001), Dependency in the treatment of complex posttraumatic stress disorder and dissociative disorders. *J. Trauma & Dissoc.,* 2(4):79–116.

Stein, A. (2001), Murder and memory. *Contemp. Psychoanal.,* 37:443–451.

_______ (2003), Dreaming while awake: The use of trance to bypass threat. *Contemp. Psychoanal.,* 39:179–197.

_______ (2004), Fantasy, fusion, and sexual homicide. *Contemp. Psychoanal.,* 40:495–518.

Steinberg, M. (1994), *Interview's Guide to the Structured Interview for DSM-IV Dissociative Disorders (SCID-D) Revised.* Washington, DC: American Psychiatric Press.

Stern, D. B. (1983), Unformulated experience: From familiar chaos to creative disorder. In: *Relational Psychoanalysis: The Emergence of a Tradition,* ed. S. A. Mitchell & L. Aron. Hillsdale, NJ: The Analytic Press, 1999, pp. 77–107.

_______ (1989), The analyst's unformulated experience of the patient. *Contemp. Psychoanal.,* 25:1–33.

_______ (1990), Courting surprise: Unbidden experience in clinical practice. *Contemp. Psychoanal.,* 26:452–478.

_______ (1997), *Unformulated Experience: From Dissociation to Imagination in Psychoanalysis.* Hillsdale, NJ: The Analytic Press.

_______ (2000), The limits of social construction: Commentary on paper by Cynthia Dyess and Tim Dean. *Psychoanal. Dial.,* 10:757–759.

_______ (2003), The fusion of horizons: Dissociation, enactment, and understanding. *Psychoanal. Dial.,* 13:843–873.

_______ (2004), The eye sees itself: Dissociation, enactment, and the achievement of conflict. *Contemp. Psychoanal.,* 40:197–238.

Stern, D. N. (1985), *The Interpersonal World of the Infant.* New York: Basic Books.

_______ (2004), *The Present Moment in Psychotherapy and Everyday Life.* New York: Norton.

Stien, P. T. & Kendall, J. C. (2004), *Psychological Trauma and the Developing Brain.* New York: Haworth Maltreatment & Trauma Press.

Stoller, R. J. (1974), Symbiosis anxiety–The development of masculinity. *Arch. Gen. Psychiat.,* 30:164–172.

_______ (1985), *Presentations of Gender.* New Haven, CT: Yale University Press.

_______ & Herdt, G. (1985), The development of masculinity: A cross-cultural contribution, In: *Presentations of Gender,* ed. R. J. Stoller. New Haven, CT: Yale University Press, pp. 181–199.

Stolorow, R. D. & Atwood, G. E. (1979), *Faces in a Cloud: Subjectivity in Personality Theory.* New York: Aronson.

Strachy, A. (1962), Editorial footnote. *Standard Edition of the Complete Psychological Works of Sigmund Freud,* 3:13.

Sullivan, H. S. (1940), *Conceptions of Modern Psychiatry.* New York: Norton.

_______ (1953), *The Interpersonal Theory Of Psychiatry.* New York: Norton.

_______ (1954), *The Psychiatric Interview.* New York: Norton.

_______ (1956), *Clinical Studies in Psychiatry.* New York: Norton.

_______ (1962), *Schizophrenia as a Human Process.* New York: Norton.

Sutherland, J. D. (2000), Fairbairn's achievement. In: *Fairbairn and the Origin of Object Relations,* ed. J. S. Grotstein, & D. B. Rinsley. New York: Other Press, pp. 17–33.

Tabin, J. (1993), Freud's shift from the seduction theory: Some overlooked reality factors. *Psychoanal. Psychol.,* 10:291–298.

Tarnopolsky, A. (2003), The concept of dissociation in early psychoanalytic writers. *J. Trauma & Dissoc.,* 4(3):7–25.

Terr, L. (1990), *Too Scared to Cry: How Trauma Affects Children and Ultimately Us All.* New York: Basic Books.

_______ (1994), *Unchained Memories.* New York: Basic Books.

Thompson, C. (1942), Cultural pressures in the psychology of women. In: *Psychoanalysis and Women,* ed. J. B. Miller. New York: Penguin Books, 1973, pp. 69–84.

_______ (1967), Sullivan and psychoanalysis. In: *The Contributions of Harry Stack Sullivan,* ed. P. Mullahy. New York: Science House, pp. 101–116.

Unger, R. (1990), Imperfect reflections of reality: Psychology constructs gender. In: *Making a Difference: Psychology and the Construction of Gender,* ed. R. Hare-Mustin & J. Marecek. New Haven, CT: Yale University Press, pp. 102–149.

_______ & Crawford, M. (1995), *Women and Gender: A Feminist Psychology.* New York: McGraw-Hill.

Valillant, G. E. (1990), Repression in college men followed for half a century. In: *Repression and Dissociation: Implications for Personality Theory, Psychopathology, and Health,* ed. J. L. Singer. Chicago: University of Chicago Press, pp. 259–274.

Van der Hart, O. (2000), Dissociation: Toward a resolution of 150 years of confusion. Presented at 17th International Fall Conference of the International Society of Dissociation, San Antonio, TX, November 14.

_______ & Brown, P. (1992), Abreaction re-evaluated. *Dissociation,* 5:127–140.

_______ & Dorahy, M. J. (accepted for publication), Dissociation: History of a concept. In: *Dissociation and the Dissociative Disorders: DSM-V and Beyond,* ed. P. F. Dell & J. A. O'Neil.

_______ & Friedman, B. (1989), A readers guide to Pierre Janet on dissociation: A neglected intellectual heritage. *Dissociation,* 2:3–15.

_______ Nijenhuis, E. R. S., Steele, K. & Brown, D. (2004), Trauma-related dissociation: Conceptual clarity, lost and found. *Austral. & New Zeal. J. Psychiat.,* 38:678–686.

_______ Van Dijke, A., Van Son, M. & Steele, K. (2000), Somatoform dissociation in traumatized World War I combat soldiers: A neglected clinical heritage. *J. Trauma & Dissoc.,* 1(4):33–66.

Van der Kolk, B. (1996a), The complexity of adaptation to trauma: Self-regulation, stimulus discrimination, and characterological development. In: *Traumatic Stress: The Effects of Overwhelming Experience on Mind, Body, and Society,* ed. B. van der Kolk, A. McFarland, O. van der Hart & L. Weisaeth. New York: Guilford Press, pp. 182–214.

_______ (1996b), Trauma and memory. In: *Traumatic Stress: The Effects of Overwhelming Experience on Mind, Body, and Society,* ed. B. van der Kolk, A. McFarland, O. van der Hart & L. Weisaeth. New York: Guilford Press, pp. 279–302.

_______ (1996c), The body keeps the score: Approaches to the psychobiology of posttraumatic stress disorder. In: *Traumatic Stress: The Effects of Overwhelming Experience on Mind, Body, and Society,* ed. B. van der Kolk, A. McFarland, O. van der Hart & L. Weisaeth. New York: Guilford Press, pp. 214–241.

_______ (2003), What is dissociation? One philosopher's view. Presented at 19th Annual Meeting of the International Society for Traumatic Stress Studies, Chicago, November 1.

_______ & Van der Hart, O. (1989), Pierre Janet and the breakdown of adaptation in psychological trauma. *Amer. J. Psychiat.,* 146:1530–1540.

_______ & _______ (1991), The intrusive past: The flexibility of memory and the engraving of trauma. *Amer. Imago,* 48:425–454.

Vygotsky, L. (1986), *Thought and Language.* Cambridge, MA: MIT Press.

Waelde, L. C. (2004), Dissociation and mediation. *J. Trauma & Dissoc.,* 5: 147–162.

Waites, E. A. (1993), *Trauma and Survival: Post-Traumatic and Dissociative Disorders in Women.* New York: Norton.

Watkins, J. C. & Watkins, H. H. (1997), *Ego States: Theory and Therapy.* New York: Norton.

Winnicott, C. (1956), The antisocial tendency. In: *The Mark of Cain: Psychoanalytic Insight and the Psychopath,* ed. J. R. Meloy. Hillsdale, NJ: The Analytic Press, 2001, pp. 133–144.

Winnicott, D. W. (1960), Ego distortion in terms of true and false self. In: *The Maturational Processes and the Facilitating Environment.* New York: International Universities Press, 1965, pp. 140–152.

_______ (1963), Fear of breakdown. In: *Psychoanalytic Explorations,* ed. C. Winnicott, R. Shepherd & M. Davis. Cambridge, MA: Harvard University Press, 1989, pp. 87–95.

_______ (1971), Use of the object and relating through identifications. In: *Playing and Reality.* New York: Tavistock, pp. 86–94.

_______ (1989), D. W. W.: A reflection. In: *Psychoanalytic Explorations,* ed. C. Winnicott, R. Shepherd & M. Davis. Cambridge, MA: Harvard University Press, pp. 1–18.

Wolff, P. H (1987), *The Development of Behavioral States and the Expression of Emotions in Early Infancy.* Chicago: University of Chicago Press.

Zeddies, T. (2002), Sluggers and analysts: Batting for the average with the psychoanalytic unconscious. *Contemp. Psychoanal.,* 38:423–444.

INDEX